PERGAMON INTERNATIONAL LIBRARY
of Science, Technology, Engineering and Social Studies

*The 1000-volume original paperback library in aid of education,
industrial training and the enjoyment of leisure*

Publisher: Robert Maxwell, M.C.

Free and Ennobled

Source Readings in the Development of Victorian Feminism

THE PERGAMON TEXTBOOK
INSPECTION COPY SERVICE

An inspection copy of any book published in the Pergamon International Library will gladly be sent to academic staff without obligation for their consideration for course adoption or recommendation. Copies may be retained for a period of 60 days from receipt and returned if not suitable. When a particular title is adopted or recommended for adoption for class use and the recommendation results in a sale of 12 or more copies, the inspection copy may be retained with our compliments. The Publishers will be pleased to receive suggestions for revised editions and new titles to be published in this important International Library.

Free and Ennobled

Source Readings in the Development of Victorian Feminism

Edited, and with Introductions and Commentaries

by

CAROL BAUER
Associate Professor

and

LAWRENCE RITT
Professor Emeritus

Both of
C. W. Post Center of Long Island University

PERGAMON PRESS
Oxford · New York · Toronto · Sydney · Paris · Frankfurt

U.K.	Pergamon Press Ltd., Headington Hill Hall, Oxford OX3 0BW, England
U.S.A.	Pergamon Press Inc., Maxwell House, Fairview Park, Elmsford, New York 10523, U.S.A.
CANADA	Pergamon of Canada, Suite 104, 150 Consumers Road, Willowdale, Ontario M2J1P9, Canada
AUSTRALIA	Pergamon Press (Aust.) Pty. Ltd., P.O. Box 544, Potts Point, N.S.W. 2011, Australia
FRANCE	Pergamon Press SARL, 24 rue des Ecoles, 75240 Paris, Cedex 05, France
FEDERAL REPUBLIC OF GERMANY	Pergamon Press GmbH, 6242 Kronberg-Taunus, Pferdstrasse 1, Federal Republic of Germany

First edition 1979

British Library Cataloguing in Publication Data

Free and ennobled. - (Pergamon international library).
  1. Feminism - Great Britain - History - 19th century - Sources 2. Women - Great Britain Social conditions - Sources
  I. Bauer, Carol II. Ritt, Lawrence
  301.41'2'0941   HQ1596   78-41265

ISBN 0-08-022272-2 (Hard)
      0-08-022271-4 (Flexi)

Printed in Great Britain by A. Wheaton & Co., Ltd., Exeter

Men can be truly civilized . . . only when women
are free and ennobled

Frances Power Cobbe,
The Duties of Women

Contents

Acknowledgements

Acknowledgements of the sources of the material selected by the editors for inclusion in the text have been made on the pages where the material in question first appears in the text. While every attempt has been made to trace original copyright holders, in some cases this has not proved possible. Copyright holders are therefore requested to get in touch with the publishers concerning material the source of which has not been acknowledged.

Preface

This book is the outgrowth of a college course on the Victorian Woman. Our efforts to provide the students with appropriate readings from primary sources revealed that a vast amount of such material, particularly from nineteenth-century British journals, was either out of print or for a variety of other reasons unavailable. This volume is an attempt to rectify that deficiency. We hope that it will fill what seems to be an obvious gap in the field of Victorian feminist studies itself, and that it will also give a broader perspective to the conventional college course in nineteenth-century British history, which is usually presented from a point of view so male-oriented as almost to justify its being described in the catalogue as "Landscape Without Women".

By contrast, the landscape we present is a heterosexual one, populated not only by men, but by a large number of dedicated, capable, and occasionally brilliant women, whose names are hardly household words, but whose efforts to raise women to a level of equality with men, entitle them to our respect and a place in the history of the era.

In assembling these readings we have had to make arbitrary choices. We excluded both Annie Besant and Florence Nightingale on the grounds that they were outside the mainstream of feminism, and limited our discussion of the Pankhursts because we wished to give more attention to the earlier pioneers in the struggle for the vote. In our treatment of the "redundant woman" question, we could not devote as much space as we should have liked to certain of its peripheral aspects, such as emigration and prostitution, chiefly because the length of the book precluded it. Moreover, women were engaged in such a wide range of philanthropic activities that we had to edit very selectively, with the result that we were obliged to omit many examples of feminine dedication to social improvement, such as shelters for abandoned women, ragged schools, orphanages, and other institutions designed to help the casualties of Victorian society.

The reader may wonder why these particular selections were chosen over others that were available. It is because they passed the tests of relevance, significance, and readability, and because they seemed to reflect most accurately the main concerns of nineteenth-century feminine activists. It should be noted that we have given the opponents of the woman's movement a fair hearing. If, with every apparent advantage on their side—the Church, science, the law, custom and precedent— they did not emerge the victors in the polemic war in which they were engaged, it may be because they did not deserve to.

C. B.
L. R.

August 1978

CHAPTER I

"The Stainless Sceptre of Womanhood"

The task confronting English feminists of the nineteenth century was a formidable one — so formidable in fact that, as the current struggle in the United States and England over women's rights indicates, it has still not been fully accomplished. It was nothing less than an attempt to peel away the layers of convention surrounding women in Victorian England in order to replace the stereotype with something approaching a realistic appraisal of woman's capabilities, rights, and legitimate spheres of action. What this involved was an attack on the whole concept of the ideal Victorian woman.

That masterpiece of myth and fantasy, of sugar and spice and everything nice — the ideal Victorian woman — was a uniquely paradoxical creature. Revered as a semi-sacred mother figure, but considered incapable of sexual enjoyment; regarded as superior to man morally and spiritually, but held to be inferior to him in intellect and personality; credited with enormous influence at precisely the moment in modern history when she was probably most powerless; ostensibly idolized as the bearer of "the stainless sceptre of womanhood" in terms which seemed to suggest a measure of contempt; lauded (within limits) for her physical charms, while her normal sexual processes were labeled "pathological"; surely there are few beings who have been described in such contradictory terms.

Who was she? Who was the ideal Victorian woman? Let it be said at the outset that she was middle class or upper middle class. It was not to women of the lower middle class (shopkeepers' wives, for example) that the art critic John Ruskin delivered his lectures, or the social arbiter Mrs. Ellis addressed her books. As for women of the working classes, at least one nineteenth-century male essayist implied that such creatures were merely biological females, and hardly deserved being called women at all.[1]

Furthermore, if the woman of the lower classes had been downgraded

---

[1] T. H. Rearden, "Woman's Mission", *Westminster Review*, LII (1849-50), 357.

to the status of a mere female, the upper middle-class woman had been elevated in the social scale so that the term "woman" no longer sufficed to describe her. The self-image of the model Victorian woman now demanded that she be considered not merely a woman, but a lady, a conception that effectively placed her outside and beyond the world of her humble working-class sister.[1] The term "lady" had formerly been reserved for women of the aristocratic or gentry classes; in the nineteenth century, however, it came to signify, in addition, a woman whose economic role was confined to conspicuous consumption, and whose social role was primarily ornamental.

Although physically, the Victorian lady was a creature of flesh and blood, in the eyes of her adulators she was of the stuff as dreams are made on—unreal, untainted, unsmirched, untroubled, an everflowing fountain of tender compassion and devotion—a view that bore the same relation to her actual nature as her bell-shaped, petticoated, and bustled figure bore to the Venus de Milo. Fragile, pure, and ethereal, she glided through life like an elegant swan, presumably untroubled by the lusts of the flesh, while the professional provider of sex, the largely working-class prostitute, made it possible for the lady to lead the asexual life that society deemed proper and natural for her. It was held that the prostitute, by providing the rampant middle-class male with a sexual outlet, enabled his wife to remain unsullied, and in effect, became the sexual surrogate of the Victorian lady or, as one authority put it, "ultimately the most efficient guardian of virtue. But for her, the unchallenged purity of countless happy homes would be polluted".[2] The lady and the harlot were supposedly involved in a symbiotic relationship. Her husband's respect for the lady's chastity drew him into the arms of the harlot; the harlot's services freed him from the necessity of making sexual demands on his wife. At least, so the theory ran.

Denied sexual feelings and largely deprived of her economic usefulness, the Victorian lady was thrown a rhetorical sop by a number of propagandists who tried doggedly to demonstrate that this powerless female had enormous moral influence, not merely on those in her immediate circle, but on society as a whole. But a price was demanded of her for this theoretical power: "Victorian society, in terms of its official culture, was very demanding of its women. It expected them to be perfect ladies,

[1] See J. A. and Olive Banks, *Feminism and Family Planning* (New York: Schocken Books, 1964), pp. 58-84, for a discussion of the transformation of Perfect Victorian woman into Perfect Victorian lady; also see C. Willett Cunnington, *Feminine Attitudes in the Nineteenth Century*, 2nd ed. (New York: Haskell House Publishers Ltd., 1973), pp. 105-30 and *passim;* and Martha Vicinus, "The Perfect Victorian Lady", in *Suffer and Be Still* (Bloomington: Indiana University Press, 1972), pp. viv-xv.

[2] William Edward Hartpole Lecky, *History of European Morals*, 2 vols. (New York: George Braziller, Inc., 1955), II, 283. In a similar manner the novelist, Grant Allen, noted: "Our existing system is really a joint system of marriage and prostitution in which the second element is a necessary corollary and safeguard of the first". Cited in Peter T. Cominos, "Late-Victorian Sexual Respectability and the Social System", Part III, *International Review of Social History*, VIII (1963), 230.

perfect wives, and perfect mothers''.[1] In return, the somewhat extravagant (not to say cryptic) claim was made, for example, that "her work on earth is imaged by the sunlight and life-awakening air; her presence noiseless though felt everywhere;. . . [there] shall blossom in every busy field of human labour, in strength and beauty, seeds she has scattered to the wind''.[2]

And the reality? The lady to whom these impressive powers were attributed was, in fact, a political nullity and a legal cipher. If she was married, she had no power (at least until 1870) to dispose of her own property, little opportunity to earn her own living, and if employed, no right to her earnings. Not until 1839 had she been granted the possibility of winning custody of her children if she was divorced or separated. Since she could not vote, she lacked the power to change her situation by political action. Most middle-class Victorian women, however, took this state of affairs for granted. If they were not precisely content with their lot, they were certainly not sufficiently concerned to go to the barricades, or even attempt to go to the hustings, to improve their condition.

Although somewhere, sometime, the person idealized as the Victorian lady may have existed in the flesh, she was, in fact, a largely literary creation, brought into being and described at (sometimes appalling) length by persons of both sexes who probably believed the myths they were elaborating and who justified them by reference to the two great authorities of nineteenth-century England—God and Darwin. Theirs was a demanding task: to provide a seemingly rational justification for the obviously irrational abasement of the very sex which was held to be the well-spring of all that linked the human race with the divine.

That heavenly connection, which inspired the poet Coventry Patmore to describe the Victorian woman as "the Angel in the House",[3] required of her that she seek her pleasure and fulfill her function by serving others— her god, her sovereign, the poor, the ill, the heathen at home and abroad, her less fortunate sisters, her children, and—primarily—her husband. Self-denial and self-sacrifice were to be her lot, a lot to be cheerfully borne because, as the most sophisticated and persuasive oracles of the day repeatedly assured her, it was the role that Providence had prescribed for her. But it was not the role that feminists envisaged.

---

[1] Patricia Branca, *Silent Sisterhood: Middle Class Women in the Victorian Home* (Pittsburgh: Carnegie-Mellon University Press, 1975), p. 152. Branca, incidentally, is a revisionist who is highly critical of what she calls the "pedestal image of the idle Victorian woman".

[2] Rearden, *Woman's Mission,* p. 364.

[3] For an analysis of Patmore's poem and its cultural implications, see Carol Christ, "Victorian Masculinity and the Angel in the House", in Martha Vicinus, ed., *A Widening Sphere* (Bloomington: Indiana University Press, 1977), pp. 146-62; also see Walter E. Houghton, *The Victorian Frame of Mind* (New Haven: Yale University Press, 1957), pp. 391-92.

Sarah Stickney Ellis, *The Wives of England, Their Relative Duties, Domestic Influence, and Social Obligations* (New York: Edward Walker, 1850), pp. 10, 16-17, 19, 22-28, 47, 49-51, 55-58.

The career of Sarah Stickney Ellis, a lady of considerable fame in the nineteenth century, illustrates the extent to which it was possible for a public-spirited Victorian woman to be active outside her home. She established and supervised a school for young ladies (Rawdon House), was also concerned with the education of lower-class women, was engaged with her husband in missionary work, was active in the temperance movement, and produced a large number of books, including some on poetry, art, nature, and literature. But she was best known as the author of several books which were intended to provide social and moral guidelines for the women of Victorian England. Written in an earnest manner, these manuals (including *The Wives of England, The Daughters of England,* and *The Mothers of England*) established Mrs. Ellis as the acknowledged authority on questions of etiquette and domestic management. In addition, her books provided English women with a series of guidelines by which they might chart their progress to the state of Perfect Womanhood and assume those moral responsibilities and duties incumbent on a Victorian lady. Despite her own considerable achievements, however, Mrs. Ellis' views on the relations of the sexes were safely conventional, as the following excerpt demonstrates.

Chapter I. Thoughts Before Marriage

. . . One important truth sufficiently impressed upon your mind will materially assist in this desirable consummation [to be satisfied in marriage]—it is the superiority of your husband, simply as a man. It is quite possible you may have more talent, with higher attainments, and you may also have been generally more admired; but this has nothing whatever to do with your position as a woman, which is, and must be, inferior to his as a man. For want of a satisfactory settlement of this point before marriage, how many disputes and misunderstandings have ensued, filling, as with the elements of discord and strife, that world of existence which ought to be a smiling Eden of perpetual flowers. . . .

It is to sound judgment then, and right principle, that we must look, with the blessing of the Bestower of these good gifts, for ability to make a husband happy—sound judgment to discern what is the place designed for him and for us, in the arrangements of an all-wise Providence—and right principle to bring down every selfish desire, and every rebellious thought, to a due subserviency in the general estimate we form of individual duty. . . .

Chapter II. The First Year of Married Life

. . . Far be it from me to attempt to divest that day [of marriage] of its solemn and important character, or to lower the tone of feeling with which it ought to be regarded; but . . . I own I should like to see the preparation of a bride consist more of mental discipline than of personal adornment — more of the resources of a well-stored under-standing, already thoroughly informed on the subjects of relative position and prac-tical duty; and with these, the still higher ornament of a chastened spirit, already imbued with a lively consciousness of the deep responsibilities devolving upon a married woman. After such a preparation, there would be no unwelcome truth to reveal, no unexpected reproof to endure. . . .

But let us turn the page, and after welcoming home the happy couple from the wed-ding tour, let us venture to whisper into the ear of the bride a few sage words, from which, whether properly prepared or not, she may possibly, from the simple fact of her inexperience be able to gather something for her future good.

If ever, in the course of human life, indecision may be accounted a merit rather than a defect, it is so in the conduct of a young and newly married woman. While every circumstance around her is new and untried, the voice of prudence dictates caution before any important step is taken, either with regard to the formation of inti-macies or the general style and order of living. A warm-hearted, dependent, and affec-tionate young woman, ardently attached to her husband, will be predisposed to lean upon the kindness of his relatives and even to enter rashly into the most intimate and familiar intercourse with them. . . .

Nothing, however, can be more injudicious than for her to take part in . . . family matters. If possible, she ought to wait and see for herself, before her opinion is formed upon any of the subjects in question. And this, by great care, may be done without any violation of that respectful behavior which she ought to lay down for herself as a rule, in associating with her husband's relatives, and from which she ought never to deviate, let her opinion of their merits and attractions be what it may. . . .

It is sometimes supposed that the maintenance of personal dignity is incompatible with this exercise of respect towards others. But on no subject do young people make greater mistakes, than on that of dignity. True dignity must always be founded upon a right understanding of our own position in society; . . . As a wife, then, a woman may be always dignified, though, simply as a woman, she may at the same time be humble, and as a Christian self-abased. As a wife — as the chosen companion of an honorable and upright man, it is her duty so to regulate her whole conduct, that she shall neither offend others, nor bring offence upon herself; and this is never more effec-tually done, than by standing aloof from family disputes, and taking no part either in the partialities or the prejudices of those with whom she is associated. . . .

It is unquestionably the best policy then for a bride to be in all things the opposite of eccentric. Her character, if she have any, will develop itself in time; and nothing can be gained, though much may be lost, by exhibiting its peculiarities before they are likely to be candidly judged or rightly understood. In being unobtrusive, quiet, impar-tially polite to all, and willing to bend to circumstances, consists the great virtue of a bride; and though to sink, even for a short time, into an apparent nonentity, may be a little humbling to one who has occupied a distinguished place amongst her former friends, the prudent woman will be abundantly repaid, by being thus enabled to make her own observations upon the society and the circumstances around her, to see what pleasant paths she may with safety pursue, or what opportunities are likely to open for a fuller development of her powers, either natural or acquired. . . .

Nothing shows more plainly the mistake under which people in general labor, with regard to the degree of mental and moral capability requisite in a really good wife, than the common expression used to describe a merely well-disposed and ignorant female, when it is said of her, that she is "a good sort of body, and will make an excellent wife." The generality of men, and even some of the most intelligent amongst them, appear peculiarly disposed to make the experiment of marrying such women, as if the very fact of their deficiency in moral discipline, and intellectual power, was of itself a recommendation rather than otherwise, in the mistress of a family; and until women shall really find themselves neglected by the loftier sex, and actually consigned to oblivion, because they are indolent, selfish, or silly, it is to be feared that books may be multiplied on this subject, and even sermons preached, with little or no effect.

Still there is surely something in the deep heart of woman capable of a nobler ambition than that of merely securing as a husband the man she most admires. To make that husband happy, to raise his character, to give dignity to his house, and to train up his children in the path of wisdom—these are the objects which a true wife will not rest satisfied without endeavoring to attain. And how is all this to be done without reflection, system, and self-government? Simply to mean well, may be the mere impulse of a child or an idiot; but to know how to act well, so as that each successive kind impulse shall make to tell upon the welfare and the happiness of others, is the highest lesson which the school of moral discipline can teach. . . .

Chapter III. Characteristics of Men

In approaching this part of my subject, I cannot but feel that it is one which I have neither the understanding nor the skill to treat with ample justice. All I will venture upon, therefore, is to point out a few of those peculiarities, which women who have been but little accustomed to the society of men, might otherwise be surprised to find in a husband. If, in pursuance of this task, what I am compelled to say, should appear in any way disparaging to the dignity of men in general, my apology must be this—that it is the very peculiarities I am about to point out, which constitute the chief difficulties a married woman has to contend with, and which, therefore, claim the sympathy of such as are anxious to assist her in the right performance of her duties as a wife. . . .

All women should . . . be prepared for discovering faults in men, as they are for beholding spots in the sun, or clouds in the summer sky. Nor is it consistent with the disinterested nature of women's purest, deepest affection, that they should love them less, because they cannot admire them more.

Much allowance should be made in all such calculations, for the peculiar mode of education by which men are trained for the world. From their early childhood, girls are accustomed to fill an inferior place, to give up, to fall back, and to be as nothing in comparison with their brothers; while boys, on the other hand, have to suffer all the disadvantages in after life, of having had their precocious selfishness encouraged, from the time when they first began to feel the dignity of superior power, and the triumph of occupying a superior place.

Men who have been thus educated by foolish and indulgent mothers; who have been placed at public schools, where the influence, the character, and the very name of woman was a by-word for contempt; who have been afterwards associated with sisters who were capricious, ignorant, and vain—such men are very unjustly blamed for being selfish, domineering, and tyrannical to the other sex. In fact, how should they be otherwise? It is a common thing to complain of the selfishness of men, but I have often thought, on looking candidly at their early lives, and reflecting how little cultivation of the heart is blended with what is popularly called the best education, the wonder should be that men are not more selfish still.

With all these allowances, then, we may grant them to be selfish, and pity, rather than blame them that they are so; for no happy being ever yet was found, whose hopes and wishes centred in its own bosom.

The young and inexperienced woman, who has but recently been made the subject of man's attentions, and the object of his choice, will probably be disposed to dispute this point with me, and to argue that one man at least is free from selfishness; because she sees, or rather *hears* her lover willing to give up everything for her. But let no woman trust to such obsequiousness, for generally speaking, those who are the most extravagant in their professions, and the most servile in their adulation before marriage, are the most unreasonable and requiring afterwards. Let her settle it then in her own mind . . . that men in general are more apt than women, to act and think as if they were created to exist of, and by, themselves; and this self-sustained existence a wife can only share, in proportion as she is identified in every thing with her husband. Men have no idea, generally speaking, of having themselves and their affairs made subservient to an end, even though it may be a good one. They are, in fact, their own alpha and omega — beginning and end. But all this, I repeat, is the consequence of a want of that moral training which ought ever to be made the prominent part of education.

Beyond this, however, it may be said to be a necessary part of man's nature, and conducive to his support in the position he has to maintain, that he should, in a greater degree than woman, be sufficient unto himself. The nature of his occupations, and the character of his peculiar duties, require this. The contending interests of the community at large, the strife of public affairs, and the competition of business, with the paramount importance of establishing himself as the master of a family, and the head of a household, all require a degree of concentrated effort in favor of self, and a powerful repulsion against others, which woman, happily for her, is seldom or never called upon to maintain.

The same degree of difference in the education of men and women, leads on the one hand, to a more expansive range of intellect and thought; and on the other, to the exercise of the same faculties upon what is particular and minute. Men consequently are accustomed to generalize. They look with far-stretching views to the general bearing of every question submitted to their consideration. Even when planning for the good of their fellow-creatures, it is on a large scale, and most frequently upon the principle of the greatest good to the greatest number. By following out this system, injustice is often unconsciously done to individuals, and even a species of cruelty exercised, which it should be woman's peculiar object to study to avert; but at the same time, to effect her purpose in such a way, as neither to thwart nor interfere with the greater and more important good.

We see here, as in a thousand other instances, the beautiful adaptation of the natural constitution of the two sexes, so as to effect a greater amount of good by their joint efforts, than either could effect alone. Were an island peopled only by men, the strictness of its judicial regulations, and the cold formality of its public institutions, would render it an ungenial soil for the growth of those finer feelings, and those subtler impulses of nature, which not only beautify the whole aspect of human life, but are often proved to have been blossoms of the richest fruit, and seeds of the most abundant harvest. And were a neighboring island peopled by women only, the discord of Babel, or the heated elements of a volcano, could scarcely equal the confusion, the ebullition, and the universal tumult, that would follow the partial attention given to every separate complaint, the ready credence accorded to every separate story, and the prompt and unhesitating application of means to effect at all times the most incompatible ends.

Those who argue for the perfect equality—the oneness of women in their intellectual nature with men, appear to know little of that higher philosophy, by which both, from the very distinctness of their characters, have been made subservient to the purposes of wisdom and of goodness; and after having observed with deep thought, and profound reverence, the operation of mind on mind, the powerful and instinctive sympathies which rule our very being; and the associated influence of different natures, all working together, yet too separate and distinct to create confusion; to those who have thus regarded the perfect adjustment of the plans of an all-wise Providence, I own it does appear an ignorant and vulgar contest, to strive to establish the equality of that, which would lose not only its utility, but its perfection, by being assimilated with a different nature. . . .

The love of woman appears to have been created solely to minister; that of man, to be ministered unto. It is true, his avocations lead him daily to some labor, or some effort for the maintenance of his family; and he often conscientiously believes that this labor is for his wife. But the probability is, that he would be just as attentive to his business, and as eager about making money, had he no wife at all—witness the number of single men who provide with as great care, and as plentifully, according to their wants, for the maintenance of a house without either wife or child.

As it is the natural characteristic of woman's love . . . to be perpetually doing something for the good or the happiness of the object of her affection, it is but reasonable that man's personal comfort should be studiously attended to; and in this, the complacence and satisfaction which most men evince on finding themselves placed at table before a favorite dish, situated beside a clean hearth, or accommodated with an empty sofa, is of itself a sufficient reward for any sacrifice such indulgence may have cost. In proofs of affection like these, there is something tangible which speaks home to the senses—something which man can understand without an effort, and he will sit down to eat, or compose himself to rest, with more hearty goodwill towards the wife who has been thoughtful about these things, than if she had been all day busily employed in writing a treatise on morals for his especial benefit.

Again, man's dignity, as well as his comfort, must be ministered unto. I propose to treat this subject more fully in another chapter, but in speaking of man's peculiarities it must never be forgotten that he ought not to be required to bear the least infringement upon his dignity as a man, and a husband. The woman who has the bad taste, and worse feeling, to venture upon this experiment, effectually lowers herself; for in proportion as her husband sinks, she must sink with him, and ever, as wife, be lower still. Many, however, from ignorance, and with the very best intention, err in this way. . . .

It is unquestionably the inalienable right of all men, whether ill or well, rich or poor, wise or foolish, to be treated with deference, and made much of in their own houses. It is true that in the last mentioned case, this duty may be attended with some difficulty in the performance; but as no man becomes a fool, or loses his senses by marriage, the woman who has selected such a companion must abide by the consequences; and even he, whatever may be his degree of folly, is entitled to respect from her, because she has voluntarily placed herself in such a position that she must necessarily be his inferior. . . .

. . . It is perhaps when ill, more than at any other time, that men are impressed with a sense of their own importance. It is, therefore, an act of kindness, as well as of justice, and a concession easily made, to endeavor to keep up this idea, by all those little acts of delicate attention which at once do good to the body, and sustain the mind. Illness is to men a sufficient trial and humiliation of itself, as it deprives them of their free agency, cuts them off from their accustomed manly avocations, and shuts them up to a kind of imprisonment, which from their previous habits they are little calculated to bear. A sensible and kindhearted woman, therefore, will never inflict upon the man she loves, when thus circumstanced, the additional punishment of feeling that it is possible for him to be forgotten or neglected.

But chiefly in poverty, or when laboring under depressed circumstances, it is the part of a true wife to exhibit by the most delicate, but most profound respect, how highly she is capable of valuing her husband, independently of all those adventitious circumstances according to which he has been valued by the world. It is here that the dignity of man is most apt to give way—here that his stout heart fails him—and here then it must be woman's part to build him up. Not, as many are too apt to suppose, merely to comfort him by her endearments, but actually to raise him in his own esteem, to restore to him his estimate of his moral worth, and to convince him that it is beyond the power of circumstances to degrade an upright and an honest man.

And, alas! how much of this is needed in the present day! Could the gay and thoughtless Daughters of England know for what situations they are training—could they know how often it will become their duty to assume the character of the strong, in order to support the weak, they would surely begin betimes to think of these things; and to study the different workings of the human heart, so as to be able to manage even its masterchords, without striking them too rudely, or with a hand too little skilled. . . .

Chapter IV. The Love of Married Life

. . . If there be one principle in woman's nature stronger than all others, it is that which prompts her to seek sympathy and protection from some being whom she may love, and by whom she may be loved in return. . . .

It is only in the married state that the boundless capabilities of woman's love can be fully known or appreciated. There may, in other situations, be occasional instances of heroic self-sacrifice, and devotion to an earthly object; but it is only here that the lapse of time, and the familiar occasions of every day, can afford opportunities of exhibiting the same spirit, operating through all those minor channels, which flow like fertilizing rills through the bosom of every family where the influence of woman is alike happy in its exercise, and enlightened in its character. . . .

And now, having thus loved your husband, and cast in your lot with his—having chosen his portion, his people, and his God for yours, it is meet that you should love him to the last. It is true, there are cases where a gradual deterioration of character, or a sudden fall from moral rectitude, renders affection the last offering a stranger would think it possible to make at such a shrine; but if others turn away repelled, there is the more need for such a man, that his wife should love him still—there is the more need that one friend should remain to be near him in his moments of penitence, if such should ever come; or to watch the lingering light of better days, so as if possible to kindle it once more into a cheerful and invigorating flame.

Of all the states of suffering which have ever swelled the ocean of human tears, there is none in the smallest degree comparable to the situation of such a wife; yet, as if by some law of nature, which raises the sweetest flowers from out the least apparently congenial soil, it is here that we so often see the character of woman developed in all its loveliest and noblest attributes. It is here that we see to what an almost superhuman height that character can rise, when stripped of its vanity, and divested of its selfishness. . . .

Happily for our sex, however, there are means of securing this treasure, more efficacious than the marriage vow; and among these, I shall mention first, the desirableness of not being too requiring. It must ever be borne in mind, that man's love, even in its happiest exercise, is not like woman's; for while she employs herself through every hour, in fondly weaving one beloved image into all her thoughts; he gives to her comparatively few of his, and of these perhaps neither the loftiest nor the best. His highest hopes and brightest energies must ever be expected to expend themselves upon the promotion of some favorite scheme, or the advancement of some public measure; and if with untiring satisfaction he turns to her after the efforts of the day have been completed; and weary, and perhaps dispirited, comes back to pour into her faithful bosom the history of those trials which the world can never know, and would not pity if it could; if she can thus supply to the extent of his utmost wishes, the sympathy and the advice, the confidence and the repose, of which he is in need, she will have little cause to think herself neglected.

It is a wise beginning, then, for every married woman to make up her mind to be forgotten through the greater part of every day; to make up her mind to many rivals too in her husband's attentions, though not in his love; and among these, I would mention one, whose claims it is folly to dispute; since no remonstrances or representations on her part will ever be able to render less attractive the charms of this competitor. I mean the newspaper, of whose absorbing interest some wives are weak enough to evince a sort of childish jealousy, when they ought rather to congratulate themselves that their most formidable rival is one of paper.

The same observations apply perhaps in a more serious manner to those occupations which lead men into public life. If the object be to do good, either by correcting abuses, or forwarding benevolent designs, and not merely to make himself the head of a party, a judicious and right-principled woman will be too happy for her husband to be instrumental in a noble cause, to put in competition with his public efforts any loss she may sustain in personal attention or domestic comfort.

A system of persecution carried on against such manly propensities as reading a newspaper, or even against the household derangements necessarily accompanying attention to public business, has the worst possible effect upon a husband's temper, and general state of feeling. So much so, that I am inclined to think a greater amount of real love has been actually teased away, than ever was destroyed by more direct, or more powerfully operating means.

The same system of teasing is sometimes most unwisely kept up, for the purpose of calling forth a succession of those little personal attentions, which, if not gratuitously rendered, are utterly destitute of value, and ought never to be required.

To all married women, it must be gratifying to receive from a husband just so much attention as indicates a consciousness of her presence; but with this acknowledgement, expressed in any manner which may be most congenial to her husband's tastes and habits, a woman of true delicacy would surely be satisfied without wishing to stipulate for more. . . .

Chapter VII. The Trials of Married Life

. . . Married life has its peculiar trials, . . . and while we gladly admit the fact, that it is possible to be happier in this state, than any human being can be alone; we must also bear in mind, that it is possible to be more miserable too—perhaps for this very reason, that the greatest trials connected with this state of existence, are such as cannot be told, and therefore such as necessarily set the sufferer apart from all human sympathy and consolation. Many of these, however, may be greatly ameliorated by a willingness to meet them in a proper way; but more especially, by an habitual subjection of self to the interests and the happiness of others.

Among the trials peculiar to married life, we will first speak of those of temper. . . .

I have always been accustomed to consider it as the severest trial to the temper of a married woman, to have an idle husband; and if in addition to neglecting his business, or such manly occupations as an exemption from the necessities of business would leave him at liberty to pursue, he is personally idle, sitting slipshod at noontime, with his feet upon the fender, occasionally jarring together the whole army of fire irons with one stroke of his foot, agitated at intervals by the mere muscular irritation of having nothing to do, or not choosing to do anything; and if he should happen to have chosen for his wife a woman of active bustling character, as such men not unfrequently do, I believe I must . . . leave it to the reader to suggest some possible means by which such a woman may at all times control her temper, and keep the peace at her own fireside.

One thing, however, is certain in such a case—it is not by ebullitions of momentary indignation that an idle man can be stimulated into action. So far from it, he will rather be made worse, and rendered more obstinately idle by any direct opposition to the indulgence of his personal inclination. Whatever good is to be done in such a case, can only be effected from the convictions of his own mind, brought about by the quiet operation of affectionate and judicious reasoning; for if the wife should be unguarded enough to throw out reproaches against him, representing the disgusting nature of idleness in its true colors; or if she should seek to establish her own claims to his exertions, so as to convey an idea of her arguments tending to a selfish end, she might as well "go kindle fire with snow," as attempt to rouse her husband into healthy and consistent habits of activity by such means.

Here, too, we might mention as pre-eminent among the trials of married life. . . the ruinous propensity inherent in the nature of some men, to spend their own money, and sometimes the money of their friends, in vague speculations and visionary schemes.

The man who is possessed with this mania, for in certain cases it deserves no other name, is neither to be convinced by argument nor experience, that after ninety-nine failures, he is not very likely to succeed the hundredth time; and the wife who knows that the maintenance of herself and her family is entirely dependent upon him, has abundant need for supplies of strength and patience beyond what any earthly source can afford. . . .

It is a well-known fact, that men in general appear to consider themselves justly entitled to the privilege of being out of humor about their food. Thus the whole pleasure of a social meal is sometimes destroyed by some trifling error in the culinary department, or the non-appearance of some expected indulgence. But here again, our forbearance is called into exercise, by remembering the probability there is, that such men have had silly mothers who made the pleasures of their childhood to consist chiefly of such as belong to the palate; and here too, if the wife cannot remedy this evil, and in all probability it will be beyond her power to do so, she may by her judicious efforts to promote the welfare of the rising generation, impart to the youthful minds committed to her care, or subject to her influence, a juster estimate of what belongs to the true enjoyment of intellectual and immortal beings. . . .

A causeless and habitual neglect of punctuality on the part of the master of a house, is certainly a grievance very difficult to bear; because as he is the principal person in the household, and the first to be considered, the whole machinery of domestic management must necessarily be dependent upon his movements; and more especially, since it so happens, that persons who are the most accustomed to keep others waiting, have the least patience to wait for others. Thus it not unfrequently occurs, that a wife is all day urging on her servants to a punctual attention to the dinner-hour appointed by her husband, and when that hour arrives, he has either forgotten it himself, or he allows some trifling hindrance to prevent his returning home until one, or perhaps two, hours later. Yet the same man, though in the habit of doing this day after day, will be excessively annoyed, if for once in his life he should be punctual to the appointed time, and not find all things ready on his return.

Perhaps too the master of a family, on days of household bustle, when extra business has to be done, will not choose to rise so early as usual; or he will sit reading the newspaper while his breakfast waits, and thus keep every member of his family standing about unoccupied, with all the business of the day before them. Or, he may be one of those who like that women should be always ready long before the necessary time, and thus habitually name an hour for meeting, or setting out from home, at which he has not the remotest intention of being ready himself.

Now, as the time of women, if properly employed, is too precious to be wasted, something surely may be done, not by endeavoring to overrule the movements of such a man so as to make him true to his own appointment, but by convincing him, that common honesty requires him simply to state the actual time at which he does intend to be ready. And here we see at once, one of those numerous instances in which a reasonable man will listen, and endeavor to amend; while an unreasonable man will either not listen, or not take the slightest pains to improve.

Again, there are men who like the importance, and the feeling of power and decision which it gives them, to set out on a journey as if upon the spur of the moment, without having communicated their intentions even to the wife, who is most interested in making preparations for such a movement. And there are others, who when consulted about anything, cannot be brought to give either their attention or their advice, so as to assist the judgment of a wife, who would gladly give satisfaction if she could; yet when the time to act upon their advice is past, will bestow their attention a little too severely upon the unfortunate being, who, consulting her own judgment as the only guide she had, will most probably have done exactly what they did not wish.

But it would be an endless task, to go on enumerating instances of this description. I have merely mentioned these as specimens of the kind of daily and hourly trials which most women have to expect in the married state; and which, as I have before stated, may be greatly softened down, if not entirely reconciled, by the consideration already alluded to. Besides which, it is but candid to allow, that the greater proportion of these offences against temper and patience, originate in one of those peculiarities in the character of man which I have omitted to mention in its proper place. I mean the incapability under which he labors, of placing himself in idea in the situation of another person, so as to identify his feelings with theirs, and thus to enter into what they suffer and enjoy, as if the feeling were his own.

This capability appears to be peculiarly a feminine one, and it exists among women in so high a degree, as to leave them little excuse if they irritate or give offence to others; because this innate power which they possess of identifying themselves for the moment with another nature, might, if they would use it for such a purpose, enable them not so much to know, as to feel, when they were giving pain, or awakening displeasure. Men, as I have just stated, are comparatively destitute of this power, as well as that of sympathy, to which it is so nearly allied. When, therefore, they appear to women so perverse, and are consequently so difficult to bear with, it is often from their being wholly unconscious of the actual state of the case; of the long entanglement of inconveniences which their thoughtless ways are weaving; and consequently of the wounded feeling, disappointment, and vexation, which such thoughtlessness not unfrequently inflicts upon the weaker mind of woman, when the whole framework of her daily existence must be regulated by the movements of a husband who thinks of "none of these things". . . .

From *The Daughters of England* (New York: Edward Walker, 1850), pp. 7-8.

Chapter I. Important Inquiries

If it were possible for a human being to be suddenly, and for the first time, awakened to consciousness, with the full possession of all its reasoning faculties, the natural inquiry of such a being would be, "What am I?—how am I to act?—and, what are my capabilities for action?" . . .

As women, the first thing of importance is to be content to be inferior to men— inferior in mental power, in the same proportion that you are inferior in bodily strength. Facility of movement, aptitude, and grace, the bodily frame of woman may possess in a higher degree than that of man; just as in the softer touches of mental and spiritual beauty, her character may present a lovelier page than his. Yet, as the great attribute of power must still be wanting there, it becomes more immediately her business to inquire how this want may be supplied. . . .

I have already stated, that women, in their position in life, must be content to be inferior to men; but as their inferiority consists chiefly in their want of power, this deficiency is abundantly made up to them by their capability of exercising influence; it is made up to them also in other ways, incalculable in their number and extent, but in none so effectually as by that order of Divine Providence which places them, in a moral and religious point of view, on the same level with man; nor can it be a subject of regret to any right-minded woman, that they are not only exempt from the most laborious occupations both of mind and body, but also from the necessity of engaging in those eager pecuniary speculations, and in that fierce conflict of worldly interests, by which men are so deeply occupied as to be in a manner compelled to stifle their best feelings, until they become in reality the characters they at first only assumed. Can it be a subject of regret to any kind and feeling woman, that her sphere of action is one adapted to the exercise of the affections, where she may love, and trust, and hope, and serve, to the utmost of her wishes? Can it be a subject of regret that she is not called upon, so much as man, to calculate, to compete, to struggle, but rather to occupy a sphere in which the elements of discord cannot with propriety be admitted—in which

beauty and order are expected to denote her presence, and where the exercise of benevolence is the duty she is most frequently called upon to perform?

Women almost universally consider themselves, and wish to be considered by others,
as extremely affectionate; scarcely can a more severe libel be pronounced upon a
woman than to say that she is not so. Now the whole law of woman's life is a law of
love. I propose, therefore, to treat the subject in this light — to try whether the neglect
of their peculiar duties does not imply an absence of love, and whether the principle
of love, thoroughly carried out, would not so influence their conduct and feelings as to
render them all which their best friends could desire.

Let us, however, clearly understand each other at the outset. To love, is a very different thing from a desire to be beloved. To love, is woman's nature — to be beloved is
the consequence of her having properly exercised and controlled that nature. To love,
is woman's duty — to be beloved, is her reward. . . .

John Ruskin, "Of Queens' Gardens", in *Sesame and Lilies* (1865), reprinted in *The Complete Works of John Ruskin,* Illustrated Cabinet
Edition, 26 vols. (Boston: Dana Estes & Co. [1897]), XXI, 77-78, 84-88,
98-105.

In 1864 John Ruskin, the renowned author and critic, delivered at the
Manchester Town Hall a series of lectures on education. Having
addressed his first lecture, "Of Kings' Treasures", to men (who, he maintained, might come to possess kingly power through the proper education), Ruskin turned his attention to the ladies in order to disclose to
them the extent to which they, too, might come to acquire a type of
royal power that would enable them to reign over their own territories,
the Queens' Gardens.

"Of Queens' Gardens" might stand as the quintessential Ruskin. His
concern with social questions, his nostalgic yearning — which he shared
with his friend Carlyle — for the middle ages, his search for beauty at
every level of human experience, his conviction that Christian love and
charity could abate the misery and degradation he saw around him — all
this was presented in passionate language that apparently had a great
effect on the ladies in his audience.

It is easy to see why. Unlike Mrs. Ellis, who advised women meekly to
submit, Ruskin envisioned a more glamorous and dynamic role for
them — a role which transformed woman into an angelic creature, a
guardian of morality and virtue, who, having renounced her claims to
worldly success, would serve to purify and ennoble humanity. Along
with this idealized picture of the Victorian woman, Ruskin presented an
equally idealized description of the theatre in which she would perform
her purifying and ennobling works: the home — a sanctuary, a refuge
from the sordid world, a fortress enclosing holy ground, a shelter, and a
nest.

Ruskin's ideas evidently met with approval, for this series of lectures
was published the following year in *Sesame and Lilies,* a book which be-

came one of his most widely read works. Its popularity testifies to the willing acceptance by women of the role in which Ruskin had cast them.

. . . We cannot determine what the queenly power of women should be, until we are agreed what their ordinary power should be. We cannot consider how education may fit them for any widely extending duty, until we are agreed what is their true constant duty. And there never was a time when wilder words were spoken, or more vain imagination permitted, respecting this question — quite vital to all social happiness. The relations of the womanly to the manly nature, their different capacities of intellect or of virtue, seem never to have been yet measured with entire consent. We hear of the mission and of the rights of Woman, as if these could ever be separate from the mission and of the rights of Man; — as if she and her lord were creatures of independent kind and of irreconcileable claim. This, at least, is wrong. And not less wrong . . . is the idea that woman is only the shadow and attendant image of her lord, owing him a thoughtless and servile obedience, and supported altogether in her weakness by the pre-eminence of his fortitude.

This, I say, is the most foolish of all errors respecting her who was made to be the helpmate of man. As if he could be helped effectively by a shadow, or worthily by a slave!

Let us try, then, whether we cannot at some clear and harmonious idea (it must be harmonious if it is true) of what womanly mind and virtue are in power and office, with respect to man's; and how their relations, rightly accepted, aid, and increase, the vigour, and honour, and authority of both. . . .

Let us see whether the greatest, the wisest, the purest-hearted of all ages are agreed in any wise on this point: let us hear the testimony they have left respecting what they held to be the true dignity of woman, and her mode of help to man. . . .

[*Editors' note: Ruskin now cites the greatest works of literature in all times and cultures to demonstrate that they portray woman as the "highest heroic type of humanity", incontestably superior to foolish and feckless man. Shakespeare, for example, "has no heroes; — he has only heroines. . . . The catastrophe of every play is always caused by the folly or fault of a man; the redemption, if there be any, is by the wisdom and virtue of a woman. . . ." One can imagine the delighted looks that were exchanged by the good ladies in Mr. Ruskin's audience whose self-esteem was tickled by these flattering pronouncements.*]

. . . I will ask you whether it can be supposed that these men, in the main work of their lives, are amusing themselves with a fictitious and idle view of the relations between man and woman; . . . but this, their ideal of women, is, according to our common idea of the marriage relation, wholly undesirable. The woman, we say, is not to guide, nor even to think, for herself. The man is always to be the wiser; he is to be the thinker, the ruler, the superior in knowledge and discretion, as in power. Is it not somewhat important to make up our minds on this matter? Are all these great men mistaken, or are we? Are Shakespeare and Aeschylus, Dante and Homer, merely dressing dolls for us; or, worse than dolls, unnatural visions, the realization of which, were it possible, would bring anarchy into all households and ruin into all affection? Nay, if you could suppose this, take lastly the evidence of facts, given by the human heart itself. In all Christian ages which have been remarkable for their purity or progress, there has been absolute yielding of obedient devotion, by the lover, to his mistress. I say obedient—not merely enthusiastic and worshipping in imagination, but entirely subject, receiving from the beloved woman, however young, not only the encouragement, the praise, and the reward of all toil, but so far as any choice is open, or any question difficult of decision, the direction of all toil. Chivalry . . . in its very first conception of honourable life, assumes the subjection of the young knight to the command . . . of his lady. It assumes this, because its masters knew that the first and necessary impulse of every truly taught and knightly heart is this of blind service to its lady; that where that true faith and captivity are not, all wayward and wicked passions must be; and that in this rapturous obedience to the single love of his youth, is the sanctification of all man's strength, and the continuance of all his purposes. . . .

I do not insist by any farther argument on this, for I think it should commend itself at once to your knowledge of what has been and to your feelings of what should be. You cannot think that the buckling on of the knight's armour by his lady's hand was a mere caprice of romantic fashion. It is the type of an eternal truth—that the soul's armour is never well set to the heart unless a woman's hand has braced it; and it is only when she braces it loosely that the honour of manhood fails. . . .

This much, then, respecting the relations of lovers I believe you will accept. But what we too often doubt is the fitness of the continuance of such a relation throughout the whole of human life. We think it right in the lover and mistress, not in the husband and wife. . . . Do you not see how ignoble this is, as well as how unreasonable? Do you not feel that marriage . . . is only the seal which marks the vowed transition of temporary into untiring service, and of fitful into eternal love?

But how, you will ask, is the idea of this guiding function of the woman reconcileable with a true wifely subjection? Simply in that it is a *guiding*, not a determining, function. Let me try to show you briefly how these powers seem to be rightly distinguishable.

We are foolish . . . in speaking of the "superiority" of one sex to the other, as if they could be compared in similar things. Each has what the other has not: each completes the other, and is completed by the other: they are in nothing alike, and the happiness and perfection of both depends on each asking and receiving from the other what the other only can give.

Now their separate characters are briefly these. The man's power is active, progressive, defensive. He is eminently the doer, the creator, the discoverer, the defender. His intellect is for speculation and invention; his energy for adventure, for war, and for conquest, wherever war is just, wherever conquest necessary. But the woman's power is for rule, not for battle,—and her intellect is not for invention or creation, but for sweet ordering, arrangement and decision. She sees the qualities of things, their claims and their places. Her great function is Praise: she enters into no contest, but infalliby judges the crown of contest. By her office, and place, she is protected from all danger and temptation. The man, in his rough work in open world, must encounter all peril and trial:—to him, therefore, the failure, the offence, the inevitable error: often he must be wounded, or subdued, often misled, and always hardened. But he guards the woman from all this; within his house, as ruled by her, unless she herself has sought it, need enter no danger, no temptation, no cause of error or offence. This is the true nature of home—it is the place of Peace; the shelter, not only from all injury, but from all terror, doubt, and division. In so far as it is not this, it is not home: so far as the anxieties of the outer life penetrate into it, and the inconsistently-minded, unknown, unloved, or hostile society of the outer world is allowed by either husband or wife to cross the threshold, it ceases to be home; it is then only a part of that outer world which you have roofed over, and lighted fire in. But so far as it is a sacred place, a vestal temple, a temple of the hearth watched over by Household Gods, before whose faces none may come but those whom they can receive with love, — so far as it is this, and roof and fire are types only of a nobler shade and light, — shade as of the rock in a weary land, and light as of the Pharos in the stormy sea; — so far it vindicates the name, and fulfils the praise, of home.

And wherever a true wife comes, this home is always round her. The stars only may be over her head; the glow-worm in the night-cold grass may be the only fire at her foot: but home is yet wherever she is; and for a noble woman it stretches far round her, better than ceiled with cedar, or painted with vermilion, shedding its quiet light far, for those who else were homeless.

This, then, I believe to be . . . the woman's true place and power. But do not you see that to fulfil this, she must — as far as one can use such terms of a human creature — be incapable of error? So far as she rules, all must be right, or nothing is. She must be enduringly, incorruptibly good; instinctively, infallibly wise — wise, not for self-development, but for self-renunciation: wise, not that she may set herself above her husband, but that she may never fail from his side: wise, not with the narrowness of insolent and loveless pride, but with the passionate gentleness of an infinitely variable, because infinitely applicable, modesty of service — the true changefulness of woman. . . .

. . . We come now to our last, our widest question, — What is her queenly office with respect to the state?

Generally we are under an impression that a man's duties are public, and a woman's private. But this is not altogether so. A man has a personal work or duty relating to his own home, and a public work or duty, which is the expansion of the other, relating to the state. So a woman has a personal work and duty, relating to her own home, and a public work and duty, which is also the expansion of that.

Now the man's work for his own home is, as has been said, to secure its maintenance, progress, and defence; the woman's to secure its order, comfort and loveliness.

Expand both these functions. The man's duty, as a member of a commonwealth, is to assist in the maintenance, in the advance, in the defence of the state. The woman's duty, as a member of the commonwealth, is to assist in the ordering, in the comforting, and in the beautiful adornment of the state.

What the man is at his own gate, defending it, if need be, against insult and spoil, that also, not in a less, but in a more devoted measure, he is to be at the gate of his country, leaving his home, if need be, even to the spoiler, to do his more incumbent work there.

And, in like manner, what the woman is to be within her gates, as the centre of order, the balm of distress, and the mirror of beauty; that she is also to be without her gates, where order is more difficult, distress more imminent, loveliness more rare.

And as within the human heart there is always set an instinct for all its real duties, — an instinct which you cannot quench, but only warp and corrupt if you withdraw it from its true purpose; — as there is the intense instinct of love, which, rightly disciplined, maintains all the sanctities of life and, misdirected, undermines them; and *must* do either the one or the other; so there is in the human heart an inextinguishable instinct, the love of power, which, rightly directed, maintains all the majesty of law and life, and misdirected, wrecks them.

Deep rooted in the innermost life of the heart of man, and of the heart of woman,

God set it there, and God keeps it there. Vainly, as falsely, you blame or rebuke the desire of power!—For Heaven's sake, and for Man's sake, desire it all you can. But *what* power? That is all the question. Power to destroy? . . . Not so. Power to heal, to redeem, to guide and to guard. Power of the sceptre and shield; the power of the royal hand that heals in touching,—that binds the fiend and looses the captive; the throne that is founded on the rock of Justice, and descended from only by steps of mercy. Will you not covet such power as this, and seek such a throne as this, and be no more housewives, but queens?

It is now long since the women of England arrogated, universally, a title which once belonged to nobility only, and having once been in the habit of accepting the simple title of gentlewoman, as correspondent to that of gentleman, insisted on the privilege of assuming the title of "Lady," which properly corresponds only to the title of "Lord."

I do not blame them for this; but only for their narrow motive in this. I would have them desire and claim the title of Lady, provided they claim, not merely the title, but the office and duty signified by it. Lady means "bread-giver" or "loaf-giver," and Lord means "maintainer of laws," and both titles have reference, not to the law which is maintained in the house, nor to the bread which is given to the household; but to law maintained for the multitude, and to bread broken among the multitude. So that a Lord has legal claim only to his title in so far as he is the maintainer of the justice of the Lord of Lords; and a Lady has legal claim to her title, only so far as she communicates that help to the poor representatives of her Master, which women once, ministering to Him of their substance, were permitted to extend to that Master Himself; and when she is known, as He Himself once was, in breaking of bread.

And this beneficent and legal dominion, this power of the Dominus, or House Lord, and of the Domina, or House-Lady, is great and venerable, not in the number of those through whom it has lineally descended, but in the number of those whom it grasps within its sway; it is always regarded with reverent worship wherever its dynasty is founded on its duty, and its ambition corelative with its beneficence. Your fancy is pleased with the thought of being noble ladies, with a train of vassals. Be it so: you cannot be too noble, and your train cannot be too great; but see to it that your train is of vassals whom you serve and feed, not merely of slaves who serve and feed you; and that the multitude which obeys you is of those whom you have comforted, not oppressed,—whom you have redeemed, not led into captivity.

And this, which is true of the lower or household dominion, is equally true of the queenly dominion;—that highest dignity is open to you, if you will also accept that highest duty. Rex et Regina—Roi et Reine—"*Right*-doers;" they differ but from the Lady and Lord, in that their power is supreme over the mind as over the person— that they not only feed and clothe, but direct and teach. And whether consciously or not, you must be, in many a heart, enthroned: there is no putting by that crown; queens you must always be; queens to your lovers; queens to your husbands and your sons; queens of higher mystery to the world beyond, which bows itself, and will for ever bow, before the myrtle crown, and the stainless sceptre, of womanhood. But alas! you are too often idle and careless queens, grasping at majesty in the least things, while you abdicate it in the greatest; and leaving misrule and violence to work their will among men, in defiance of the power, which, holding straight in gift from the Prince of all Peace, the wicked among you betray, and the good forget.

"Prince of Peace." Note that name. When kings rule in that name, and nobles, and the judges of the earth, they also, in their narrow place, and mortal measure, receive the power of it. There are no other rulers than they: Other rule than theirs is but *mis*rule; they who govern verily "Dei gratia" are all princes, yes, or princesses, of peace. There is not a war in the world, no, nor an injustice, but you women are answerable for it; not in that you have provoked, but in that you have not hindered. Men, by their nature, are prone to fight; they will fight for any cause, or for none. It is for you to choose their cause for them, and to forbid them when there is no cause. There is no suffering, no injustice, no misery in the earth, but the guilt of it lies lastly with you. Men can bear the sight of it, but you should not be able to bear it. Men may tread it down without sympathy in their own struggle; but men are feeble in sympathy, and contracted in hope; it is you only who can feel the depths of pain; and conceive the way of its healing. Instead of trying to do this, you turn away from it; you shut yourselves within your park walls and garden gates; and you are content to know that there is beyond them a whole world in wilderness — a world of secrets which you dare not penetrate; and of suffering which you dare not conceive.

I tell you that this is to me quite the most amazing among the phenomena of humanity. I am surprised at no depths to which, when once warped from its honor, that humanity can be degraded. I do not wonder at the miser's death, with his hands, as they relax, dropping gold. I do not wonder at the sensualist's life, with the shroud wrapped about his feet. I do not wonder at the single-handed murder of a single victim, done by the assassin in the darkness of the railway, or reedshadow of the marsh. I do not even wonder at myriad-handed murder of multitudes, done boastfully in the daylight, by the frenzy of nations, and the immeasurable, unimaginable guilt, heaped up from hell to heaven, of their priests, and kings. But this is wonderful to me — oh, how wonderful! — to see the tender and delicate woman among you, with her child at her breast, and a power, if she would wield it, over it, and over its father, purer than the air of heaven, and stronger than the seas of earth — nay, a magnitude of blessing which her husband would not part with for all that earth itself, though it were made of one entire and perfect chrysolite: — to see her abdicate this majesty to play at precedence with her next-door neighbor! This is wonderful — oh, wonderful! — to see her, with every innocent feeling fresh within her, go out in the morning into her garden to play with the fringes of its guarded flowers, and lift their heads when they are drooping, with her happy smile upon her face, and no cloud upon her brow, because there is a little wall around her place of peace: and yet she knows, in her heart, if she would only look for its knowledge, that, outside of that little rose-covered wall, the wild grass, to the horizon, is torn up by the agony of men, and beat level by the drift of their lifeblood.

Have you ever considered what a deep under meaning there lies, or at least may be read, if we choose, in our custom of strewing flowers before those whom we think most happy? Do you suppose it is merely to deceive them into the hope that happiness is always to fall thus in showers at their feet? — that wherever they pass they will tread on herbs of sweet scent, and that the rough ground will be made smooth for them by depth of roses? So surely as they believe that, they will have, instead, to walk on bitter herbs and thorns; and the only softness to their feet will be of snow. But it is not thus intended they should believe; there is a better meaning in that old custom. The path of a good woman is indeed strewn with flowers: but they rise behind her steps, not before them. "Her feet have touched the meadows, and left the daisies rosy." You think that only a lover's fancy; — false and vain! How if it could be true? You think this also, perhaps, only a poet's fancy —

> "Even the light harebell raised its head
> Elastic from her airy tread."

But it is little to say of a woman, that she only does not destroy where she passes. She should revive; the harebells should bloom, not stoop, as she passes. You think I am going into wild hyperbole? Pardon me, not a whit—I mean what I say in calm English, spoken in resolute truth. You have heard it said . . . that flowers only flourish rightly in the garden of some one who loves them. I know you would like that to be true; you would think it a pleasant magic if you could flush your flowers into brighter bloom by a kind look upon them: nay, more, if your look had the power, not only to cheer, but to guard them—if you could bid the black blight turn away, and the knotted caterpillar spare—if you could bid the dew fall upon them in the drought, and say to the south wind, in frost—"Come, thou south, and breathe upon my garden, that the spices of it may flow out." This you would think a great thing? And do you think it not a greater thing, that all this (and how much more than this!) you can do, for fairer flowers than these—flowers that could bless you for having blessed them, and will love you for having loved them?—flowers that have eyes like yours, and thoughts like yours, and lives like yours; which, once saved, you save for ever? Is this only a little power? Far among the moorlands and the rocks,—far in the darkness of the terrible streets,—these feeble florets are lying,[1] with all their fresh leaves torn, and their stems broken—will you never go down to them, nor set them in order in their little fragrant beds, nor fence them in their shuddering from the fierce wind? Shall morning follow morning, for you, but not for them; and the dawn rise to watch, far away, those frantic Dances of Death; but no dawn rise to breathe upon these living banks of wild violet, and woodbine, and rose; nor call to you, through your casement,—call . . . saying:—

> "Come into the garden, Maud,
> For the black bat, night, has flown,
> And the woodbine spices are wafted abroad
> And the musk of the roses blown?"

Will you not go down among them?—among those sweet living things, whose new courage, sprung from the earth with the deep colour of heaven upon it, is starting up in strength of goodly spire; and whose purity, washing from the dust, is opening, bud by bud, into the flower of promise;—and still they turn to you, and for you, "The Larkspur listens—I hear, I hear! And the Lily whispers—I wait".

Did you notice that I missed two lines when I read you that first stanza; and think that I had forgotten them? Hear them now:—

> "Come into the garden, Maud,
> For the black bat, night, has flown:
> Come into the garden, Maud,
> I am here at the gate, alone."

Who is it, think you, who stands at the gate of this sweeter garden, alone, waiting for you? Did you ever hear, not of a Maude, but a Madeleine, who went down to her garden in the dawn, and found one waiting at the gate, whom she supposed to be the gardener? Have you not sought Him often;—sought Him in vain, all through the night;—sought Him in vain at the gate of that old garden where the fiery sword is set?

---

[1] What Ruskin meant by this passage has become a matter of dispute. To Kate Millett (*Sexual Politics*, New York: Avon Books [1971], p. 149), the "florets" are prostitutes; to David Sonstroem ("Millett versus Ruskin", *Victorian Studies*, XX [1977], 295), "florets" are flowers that "represent all living things now torn or broken and much in need of a true queen's loving passage".

He is never there: but at the gate of *this* garden He is waiting always—waiting to take your hand—ready to go down to see the fruits of the valley, to see whether the vine has flourished, and the pomegranate budded. There you shall see with Him the little tendrils of the vines that His hand is guiding—there you shall see the pomegranate springing where His hand cast the sanguine seed;—more: you shall see the troops of the angel keepers, that, with their wings, wave away the hungry birds from the path-sides where He has sown, and call to each other between the vineyard rows, "Take us the foxes, the little foxes, that spoil the vines, for our vines have tender grapes." Oh— you queens—you queens! among the hills and happy greenwood of this land of yours, shall the foxes have holes, and the birds of the air have nests; and in your cities, shall the stones cry out against you, that they are the only pillows where the Son of Man can lay His head?

J. G. Phillimore, "Women's Rights and Duties", *Blackwood's Magazine,* LIV (1843), 373-97.

During the course of the nineteenth century the nature of woman— her character, her mission, her responsibilities, her rights, and her powers—was vigorously debated. The following document is an excerpt from only one of the many articles devoted to the question of woman's rights and duties. At the time this article was published, J. G. Phillimore was a noted jurist, an acknowledged authority on constitutional law, and author of several works on law and legal history. He later became a member of Parliament (1852—57) where he championed free trade and law reform.

The following selection is particularly interesting as an example of the literary extravagance which the question of woman's duties seemed to evoke:

. . . Great, indeed, is the task assigned to woman. Who can elevate its dignity? who can exaggerate its importance? Not to make laws, not to lead armies, not to govern empires, but to form those by whom laws are made, and armies led, and empires governed; to guard from the slightest taint of possible infirmity the frail, and as yet spotless creature whose moral, no less than his physical, being must be derived from her; to inspire those principles, to inculcate those doctrines, to animate those senti-ments, which generations yet unborn, and nations yet uncivilized, shall learn to bless; to soften firmness into mercy, to chasten honour into refinement, to exalt generosity into virtue; by her soothing cares to allay the anguish of the body, and the far worse anguish of the mind; by her tenderness to disarm passion; by her purity to triumph over sense; to cheer the scholar sinking under his toil; to console the statesman for the ingratitude of a mistaken people; to be the compensation for hopes that are blighted, for friends that are perfidious, for happiness that has passed away. Such is her voca-tion—the couch of the tortured sufferer, the prison of the deserted friend, the scaf-fold of the god-like patriot, the cross of a rejected Saviour; these are the scenes of woman's excellence, these are the theatres on which her greatest triumphs have been achieved. Such is her destiny—to visit the forsaken, to attend to the neglected; amid the forgetfulness of myriads to remember—amid the execrations of multitudes to bless; when monarchs abandon, when counsellors betray, when justice persecutes, when brethren and disciples fly, to remain unshaken and unchanged; and to exhibit, on this lower world, a type of that love—pure, constant, and ineffable—which in another world we are taught to believe the best reward of virtue.

T. H. Rearden, ''Woman's Mission'', *Westminster Review,* LII (1849—50), 352-67.

The idealization of the Victorian woman took many forms. One of them was to emphasize, as T. H. Rearden does in the following selection, woman's unique power to influence, not merely man, but the whole universe. Rhapsodic effusions of this kind were the verbal sugar-coating on a nugget of bitter fact—that in the real world, women practically had no influence at all.

The true woman speaks to every true man who sees her, refining and exalting his intellect and feeling, making him indeed know his true manhood to consist in the noble action of his soul. She sends him from her with all the subtle threads of his being in firmer tension, and remembering only that he too ''is a little lower than the angels.'' She can make him work, and dare even death for his work, and his heart ever beating with the love of the highest love. She can do this without knowing it, and because her *genius is influence.* Yes; to warm, to cherish into purer life the motive that shall lead to the heroic act—this is her genius, her madness, her song flowing out, she knows not how, going she knows not whither, but returning never again. The woman evenly developed, unfolded after her own type, the one God struck approvingly when she was created, differs from man then in this—in possessing a greater capacity—a greater genius to influence. She influences through no direct exercise of power, but because she must. Influence breathes from her, and informs every thing and creature around, and we are only conscious of it by its results.

The true woman informs everything, influences all people, men and women; . . . but with man she is an un-read book, the whole pages of which he can never turn, nor really know her unless she wills it. We find from the biographies of all great novelists and dramatists, . . . that they have sought to win her to be communicative, to reveal the subtle threads in her intellect and affections that are distinctive—are her own; aye, *more* her own than her different and more delicate physique, for this, as a garment, she will one day throw aside. She gives to and receives more good from man than woman . . . if she be truly woman, for we do not study the book the whole contents of which we know . . . ; like is not hungry for like, but for difference—difference, however, that shall create harmony. . . .

Men and women cannot . . . be what they may without each other; cannot develop fairly the love and knowledge that shall lead to wisdom. . . . In their difference they are strong, and while the one cannot do without the other, each is a distinctness, and individual, working *not* from the other, but from a law of his or her own being, and finding, as that law is better obeyed, the varied relationships with each other, from that of marriage to the most passing communion, become more subtle, intimate, and enduring. We think this could hardly be if there did not exist a great spiritual differ-ence. . . . It is the high-natured creature in man or woman who alone understands the depth and beauty of the fullest love. . . . And the woman will be the first teacher here. The faculty for a noble love is in man, but as yet very partially awake, and with much pain and privation will she have to draw it into vigorous life, to make him feel its worth, its *distinctiveness* — not merely entire personal distinctiveness, but that the true marriage requires from both a virgin *spirit* of love for it to be blessed in itself or its results. It is with her children she will begin, and must win the victory, though the monster be Hydra, and the whole way of the world be against her. For this and other kindred work was her gift of influence given, and for these is it even now exerted.

We need not say, alas! that we are speaking of women that are to be met anywhere — at the ball, the conversazione, the theatre, or at the less-pretending evening party, and still less will we allow that we are unravelling a fair vision. We speak of what is to be traced in woman as God made her, and not as the world and herself have fashioned her. The unsightly and meaningless edifice we sweep away, and find the foundations are capable of supporting a building of more strength and beauty. What *seems* may not *be*: what has seemed for ages may not be. Man and woman are no mistake, and God has never repented of having made them, though falsehood, hatred, and unclean-ness have been with us, and though these latter seem, indeed, most positive facts — have the practice of all ages as a guarantee for their existence — nevertheless they are not; they are a disease, ungraceful parasites that have checked the expansion of the tree, even hid its proportions while feeding their unbeauteousness with its vital stream, but which shall be torn off ere life be endangered, to be forgotten, to die unnourished. . . .

Much then, that seems proper to woman, and some of her so-called weaknesses and attractions, may be considered dependent on circumstance, and that circumstance a want of development. Nor is it *work* alone that can develop a nature, — for if so, the peasant-labourer's wife has work enough, — nor the absence of the necessity for labour with the leisure it involves, — for how many *ennuyé* spirits do we trace in assemblies where rank and fortune have gathered their pet children together! The work must be true to the movement of the soul, must be woman's work. We cannot realize as woman the one who goes round in the mill of merely mechanical daily work; and the kindness, industry, and constancy evinced in her labour for others that may occasionally loom out, only make us feel more strongly that she may and should be other than she is. With intellect hardly opened, . . . her eye and ear unknowing of the beauty spread around her, . . . using many things that through their suggestiveness could speak to her, but do not — for no channel has been opened through which may flow any such knowledge to her soul — *she* is not the type of her species, though earning a right to live, and winning an instinctive respect therefore. But not with her does the poet in his dreams of love hold converse, and no mistress of his soul is she. And even still less so, though on the first glance it may seem the contrary, does the woman of rank, as we often find her, afford us a type. Possessing a mind highly cultivated, a thing of most exquisite nerves, which often coexist with heartlessness of nature while they seem to guarantee the deepest sensibility, intensely selfish, brilliant, radiant with smiles, beau-tiful in all perfect grace of movement and attire, and all this through love of self; one who translates her high gift of influence, her power of intuitive perception into the characters of others, realizing all their subtleties, into the word *tact*; turning wiser and more loving natures than her own [away]; . . . having found out what gifts heaven has bestowed on her, in what she is different from those whom she seeks to influence; — her objects men, — and the women in her path, those lesser useless cards that she sacri-fices anyhow, because being in her hand they must all be played — she uses these gifts to do any but God's service. We can only wish she had a conscience, for *influence* she must. . . .

The truth is, that many women, especially among those beyond the necessity of labour for subsistence, . . . live a life most frivolous, with minds untrained to high virtue, caring only to wear, as an armour from the world's attack, the uniform of virtue. . . . But the influence they exercise is often for evil, inducing belief for awhile where no belief should be, inducing prejudice, mis-conception of persons and events, particularly in the minds of the men within the sphere of their influence, for of necessity they influence, and often healthier hearts and sounder minds than their own. These things are but evidence of a power stirring within them necessitating some expression of itself, undirected as yet by Christian law! . . .

Many mistakes will be made, many kinds of work attempted unsuited to her woman's nature as the years pass by, but always with nearer and nearer approaches to the true. Writing, speaking, governing, the warehouse and the mart, with art and science, may be each taken up to be laid down again, and a life of *Being,* be found the finest result of her nature, for her own and the world's joy, an atmosphere of light and love, from which her sons shall go forth into the world to act, as from the temple of the living God. . . . She is . . . the true and wise; her movement erect and graceful, the dark shadow of ignorance, untruth, or unkindness cannot stay before her, cannot even dwell as a hidden spot, for her genius pierces to the elementary power of which they are composed; and right enough that is, and for the time being, at least, she constrains it to perform its legitimate work. She asks for no obedience, she seeks to win none; she herself is free, and the free must be around her. She passes her subtle fingers over the thousand-stringed harp, and a hymn rises to the Most High, not music as harmonious as there may be yet utterance from a free man's soul. Not only in the closet, but in their social home, *her* people win a faith in human nature, and in the possibility of all grand things, that comes to them they know not how. They have fed on nectar, and their spirit has become that of Gods. The sinews of the soul are strengthened to conceive and do through *love* all that it achieves. Thought, word, and act are marshalled by this love, a holy fear has been around them, and it has led from holiness to a love that casteth out fear. The intellect gains depth and breadth, becomes winged, and descends again upon us with knowledge from on high. The germs of the thousand-and-one sweetnesses that could so enrich the busy day, be so real a murmur of far-off music in the dusty noisy street, have blossomed, and man asks what may not be possible on earth! . . .

Education comes then, at last, to a question of being. What the mother *is* will emanate from her, be most likely *in* her child; in the same degree in which her mind is high-toned and delicate in its moral perceptions, in other words, her own spiritual standard will be the average one of those around her. We may be allowed to lay great stress on the position of the woman as mother, because the good or evil that the discharge of its duties involves is no mooted question. Whatever other work she may consider legitimate for herself as the seasons revolve, how widely soever she may extend the sphere of her work, she will through all time love and marry, and we may be quite sure that the result of awakened conscience, and intellect in healthy activity, will *not* be to blind her to the fact that if she accepts of love in its fullest sense, she accepts also and will discharge the duties consequent on it. We certainly do incline to believe, while ever ready to accept the contrary as solemn truth, should her nature decree it so, that her work on earth is imaged by the sunlight and life-awakening air; her presence noiseless though felt everywhere; that "as flowers are the animate spring-tide," so shall blossom in every busy field of human labour, in strength and beauty, seeds she has scattered to the wind. She may not realize that they are hers, but the Lord of the Harvest shall know them for *his* own. . . .

Truly she is to be *loved*—she *is* loved whether worthy or not. She can do little good, and we may add little positive evil, unless she be loved. She wins love and an entirety of faith in many instances before grounds for a real admiration have been established. Miranda's words, "Nothing ill can dwell in such a temple," are spoken again and again. She draws you, she wills you to love her; to feel her through that genius of influence she possesses; and the defence set up by logical man, who seems to be of a far more logical nature than she, and very sound and excellent and all-sufficing is his logic save here, where, like to the card-houses of the children, it soon tumbles in ruins. And this influence we do not find exerted only on *one*, but in a greater or less degree on all, and not because she wills it, but through a native movement of the soul which may not be gainsaid. Aimé Martin [author of a book entitled *Woman's Mission*] says, "Whatever may be the customs and laws of a country, women always give the tone to morals". . . .

We would impress as distinctly as we may the fact that women do "give the tone to morals," that nothing which they really dislike,—from their souls disapprove,—can live. Man, save here and there one, has no standard of his own by which to regulate his conduct to woman, but uses hers, ever bringing it a few degrees lower; and let her scale sink, his will follow, and with it respect and therefore love for her, and she becomes a plaything—she may be something *worse*. If she have stringent rules that she wills her acts should obey, these do not form her recognized standard of action. Her Being alone erects that, what she feels, thinks, loves, is, what her conscience tolerates in idea. . . . The sooner she blames only herself for whatever displeases her in the ways of men to women, the sooner will come the remedy, and very likely not till then. . . .

That in social life, woman much oftener than man becomes the judge of appeal, is so self-evident as to need no proof. The subtle sweetnesses of her nature, when united to moderate intellect and fancy, are so powerful in winning and leading man, if he be at all more than the animal, becoming more powerful as the subtleties in his mind and affections develop themselves, — and he so surely thinks and acts in reference to her, that it may be well, perhaps, we could have arranged it no better, —that the ideal of the true and beautiful in life should be *par excellence* in woman's hands. We remember the sage who pleasantly said he wished Providence had consulted him when the world was created, that he might have suggested it should be all "down hill;" but we, far from possessing the power of thought, wonderful invention, and faculty of solving seemingly impossible problems that in such a case must have fallen to his share, are inclined to feel that all is well, is best as it is; are quite contented with the raw material of man and woman as it fell on earth shaken from the hands of the Creator, feel both to be equally worthy of love and respect, and that a noble fabric shall yet be wrought from each. Possessing much in common, we trace powers in each, not of the same kind; but equally intense in both, and a balance is preserved; thus, as we said before, they are strong in their difference. . . .

"Woman did not invent the steam-engine, nor write Macbeth," and, it may be, will never do such kind of work, but as great of a different kind; but she shall have a thorough equality here, and not by making man a standard on this point, —for so she would belie the truth in herself, —but by building up his life of thought and act by her ideal of the right. Marriage shall not be possible for the one more than for the other, when personal distinctiveness has been questioned. Reputation shall be as necessary for man as for woman, and he shall be obliged to bring to his marriage-feast a life that, in the face of day, shall run parallel in all holy reservedness to hers. It shall be a trick, a dishonour, that shall tear his right of manhood from him, that shall stain his name and house, to deceive on this point. And we know that every Christian man through the land has already received this truth into his heart and life. Work, indeed, equal to the writing of Macbeth, aye, even Hamlet, has woman yet to do, —for till her soul, not her words written or spoken, neither her acts, but her soul, lives erect and true, breathes the essence of pure high loving feeling around, making choice of the noble, determining to unfold herself after no stereotyped fashion, but daring to love or otherwise, to do or leave undone, what shall seem healthy, just, and beautiful to herself, after her soul has required of her an obedience to its high behests more perfect than the world dreams of, —will the heart in the world's social system beat even honestly. . . .

CHAPTER II

The Perpetuation of the Stereotype: Science, Law, and the Church

A strong-minded, middle-class woman who rejected the limited role that nineteenth-century society had prescribed for her might shrug off the literary extravagances of a John Ruskin, but she could not easily challenge the "scientific" dicta of a George Romanes. Science, represented by nineteenth-century physicians, biologists, anthropologists, and sociologists, gave its official sanction to the notion that woman was an inferior being, shaped by an ineluctable evolutionary process into a form which could not be altered by wishful thinking, education, or changes in the law: "What was decided among the prehistoric Protozoa can not be annulled by Act of Parliament".[1] Differences in metabolism, in function, in psychology set the sexes apart, and consequently, woman must passively accept the role which nature had riveted upon her. Fortunately, one of the attributes which evolution had produced in her — a kind of acquired characteristic — was patience.

The Victorian conception of woman's sexuality was ambivalent. From one point of view she was superior to man; from another, inferior. Women — at least, respectable ones — were assumed to be asexual. It was taken for granted that they did not enjoy sexual intercourse, which they submitted to only from a feeling of wifely obligation. In this sense, free from the taint of the flesh, they were morally superior to the other sex.

But woman was burdened with a reproductive function which made such physical and psychological demands on her that, her resources periodically depleted by child-bearing, she could not be expected to compete with the more energetic male. Woman was physically weak and debilitated by menstruation.[2] Because of these impediments, she had

---

[1] Patrick Geddes and J. Arthur Thomson, *The Evolution of Sex*, rev. ed. (London: The Walter Scott Publishing Co., Ltd., 1914), p. 286.

[2] A highly exaggerated view of the extent to which menstruation might be considered responsible for woman's physical weakness and her frequent invalidism is illustrated in the following statement: "Woman is forever suffering from the cicatrisation of an interior wound which is the cause of a whole drama. So that in reality for 15 or 20 days out of 28—one may almost say always—woman is not only invalided but wounded. She

been unable to travel as far on the evolutionary road as man. It was understandable, then, that she could not match his accomplishments; that her physical resources and mentality were inferior to his; and that she was destined for a merely complementary role.

This view of her function was not confined to her purely sexual activity; it extended to every area of her life. Since woman was weak and man was strong, she should accept a supportive role and free him to be active in the world of affairs; but she must never aspire to an active part in that world. Since she was emotional and he was intellectual, her education should not tax her mental powers; his should be sufficiently demanding to equip him for a successful career. Since she was presumed to be asexual, and he was lustful, the pleasures of sex were denied her; but he could indulge his sexual nature outside the home. All this was so, of course, because it had been preordained by Nature.

Nineteenth-century legal authorities, taking their cue from the Olympian Blackstone, came to a conclusion different from that of the scientists but, for women, no more encouraging. It was simply this: a woman upon her marriage ceased to have any legal individual identity; she and her husband were merged into a single entity. As Blackstone put it, "By marriage, the husband and wife are one person in law: that is, the very being or legal existence of the woman is suspended during the marriage, or at least is incorporated and consolidated into that of the husband".[1] This would seem to put the wife at a serious disadvantage, but Blackstone maintained "that even the disabilities which the wife lies under, are for the most part intended for her protection and benefit".[2]

Whereas married women in Anglo-Saxon England had had some control over their property, married women, at the midpoint of the nineteenth century, had none. The doctrine that the husband and wife were but one person in law, had the practical effect of depriving wives of any voice in the disposition or management of their property, rents, dividends, and gifts. Laws pertaining to property in a number of continental countries recognized the possibility that the husband might treat his wife's property in a manner inimical to her interests. But the English law ignored that possibility; it was "unique in making the act of marriage a gift of all a woman's personal property to her husband".[3]

Prior to 1870, a woman dissatisfied with the use her husband was making of her property was powerless (even if he was gambling it away or spending it on a mistress) to obtain satisfaction under a law which

suffers incessantly the eternal wound of love." Jules Michelet, *L'Amour* (1859), cited in Havelock Ellis, *Man and Woman*, 4th ed. (London and New York: The Walter Scott Publishing Co., Ltd., and Charles Scribner's Sons, 1904), p. 283.

[1] J. W. Ehrlich, *Erlich's Blackstone* (San Carlos, Ca.: Nourse Publishing Co., 1959), p. 83.

[2] *Ibid.*, p. 86.

[3] See T. E. Perry, "Rights and Liabilities of Husband and Wife", *Edinburgh Review*, CV (1851), 191, for a comparison of the legal position of women in England with that of women in continental countries.

held her legal existence had been suspended. Her husband, on the other hand, had no reason to fear that she, who had no power over her own property, might claim a right to share in his. Moreover, if a wife (even if she was separated from her husband) carried on a business, legally the profits were his. The law provided that she could earn money for him, not for herself. Nor could she save money and leave it to her children on her death; her savings belonged solely to her husband.[1]

The husband, of course, had certain obligations. Not only was he required to support his wife, but in addition, he was responsible for her debts and was held accountable for her actions. Since she was the weaker vessel, it was his obligation to protect her. In practice, however, the right of protection could be legally interpreted to permit a man to imprison his wife in the sense that he "had a right to confine her in her own dwelling house, and restrain her from liberty for an indefinite time".[2] Women, in fact, were subject, until 1891, to physical confinement by their husbands.[3] Even if a woman was not deprived of her liberty, so far as acting effectively outside the constraints of her marriage was concerned, she was what we should call a non-person.

This negative status was not the result of a mere historical accident. The findings of science, the judgments of the courts, and the dogmas of religion were deliberately and consciously arrayed against the wife. The molders of public opinion in Victorian England might disagree on various subjects, but they were as one in depicting woman as a creature clearly inferior to man in natural endowments, legal position, and the power to shape her own destiny. The voices from the laboratory and the bench were echoed in the pulpit. Science, jurisprudence, and theology were joined in a chorus whose many variations were derived from a single theme: the alleged inferiority of womankind.

Patrick Geddes and J. Arthur Thomson, *The Evolution of Sex*, rev. ed. (London and New York: The Walter Scott Publishing Co., Ltd., and Charles Scribner's Sons, 1914), pp. 17-19, 27-28, 286-91.

Patrick Geddes, Scottish biologist, sociologist, and town planner, collaborated in 1889 with J. Arthur Thomson on an influential and widely-reprinted treatise, *The Evolution of Sex*. In this work Geddes and Thomson attempted to explain the processes of reproduction for the whole animal kingdom. Using an evolutionary approach, they

---

[1] It is true that the well-to-do father of a prospective bride could establish a trust for his daughter that would place her property outside the purview of the Common Law and beyond the reach of her husband, but this protection was not available to the vast majority of English women. According to Lord Lyndhurst, who in the House of Lords discussed the extent to which women's property rights were protected, nine-tenths of marriages were entered into without benefit of marriage settlement. *Ibid.*, p. 197. See also F. P. Cobbe's statement that, in general, only women of the aristocratic classes were protected by marriage settlements; "Criminals, Idiots, Women, and Minors", *Fraser's Magazine*, LXXVIII (1868), 779-80.

[2] In *Re Cochrane* [1840], 8 Dowling's P.C. 630.

[3] *R. v. Jackson* [1891], 1 Q.B. 671.

posited a biological theory which, it was maintained, was applicable to all living creatures, and furthermore, was the key to understanding the fundamental differences between the sexes. According to the authors, primary and secondary sexual characteristics were a function of cell metabolism, the ratio of anabolic (constructive) to katabolic (destructive) changes.

Geddes' work was particularly significant, for he elaborated on the social, psychological, and moral implications of his biological theory to "prove" that social and intellectual distinctions were the result of natural laws, and were therefore immutable. This approach — the application of scientific "laws" to social questions — was typical of nineteenth-century scientists.

. . . Without multiplying instances, a review of the animal kingdom, or a perusal of Darwin's pages, will amply confirm the conclusion that on an average the females incline to passivity, the males to activity. In higher animals, it is true that the contrast shows rather in many little ways than in any one striking difference of habit, but even in the human species the contrast is recognised. Every one will admit that strenuous spasmodic bursts of activity characterise men, especially in youth, and among the less civilised races; while patient continuance, with less violent expenditure of energy, is as generally associated with the work of women.

To the above contrast of general habit, two other items may be added, on which accurate observation is still unfortunately very restricted. In some cases the body temperature, which is an index to the pitch of the life, is distinctly lower in the females, as has been noted in cases so widely separate as the human species, insects, and plants. In many cases, furthermore, the longevity of the females is much greater. Such a fact as that women pay lower insurance premiums than do men, is often popularly accounted for by their greater immunity from accident; but the greater normal longevity on which the actuary calculates, has, as we begin to see, a far deeper and constitutional explanation. . . .

. . . We are now in a better position to criticize Mr. Darwin's theory. On his view, males are stronger, handsomer, or more emotional, because ancestral forms happened to become so in a slight degree. In other words, the reward of breeding-success gradually perpetuated and perfected a casual advantage. According to the present [i.e., Geddes'] view, males are stronger, handsomer, or more emotional, simply because they are males, — i.e., of more active physiological habit than their mates. In phraseology which will presently become more intelligible and concrete, the males tend to live at a loss, are relatively more katabolic. The females, on the other hand, tend to live at a profit, are relatively more anabolic, — constructive processes predominating. in their life, whence indeed the capacity of bearing offspring.

No one can dispute that the nutritive, vegetative, or self-regarding processes within the plant or animal are opposed to the reproductive, multiplying, or species-regarding processes, as income to expenditure, or as building up to breaking down. But within the ordinary nutritive or vegetative functions of the body, there is necessarily a continuous antithesis between two sets of processes, — constructive and destructive metabolism. The contrast between these two processes is seen throughout nature, whether in the alternating phases of cell life, or of activity and repose, or in the great antithesis between growth and reproduction; and it is this same contrast which we recognise as the fundamental difference between male and female. The proof of this will run through the work, but our fundamental thesis may at once be roughly enunciated in a diagrammatic expression. . . .

Here the sum-total of the functions are divided into nutritive and reproductive, the former into anabolic and katabolic processes, the latter into male and female activities,—so far with all physiologists, without exception or dispute. Our special theory lies, however, in suggesting the parallelism of the two sets of processes. Thus maleness is associated with a life ratio in which katabolism has a relatively greater predominance than in the female. In terms of this thesis, therefore, both primary and secondary sexual characters express the fundamental physiological bias characteristic of either sex. . . .

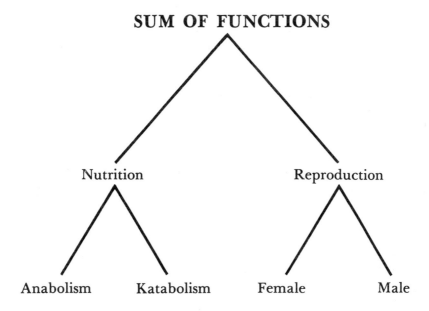

SUM OF FUNCTIONS

Nutrition   Reproduction

Anabolism   Katabolism   Female   Male

. . . We have seen that a deep difference in constitution expresses itself in the distinctions between male and female, whether these be physical or mental. The differences may be exaggerated or lessened, but to obliterate them it would be necessary to have all the evolution over again on a new basis. What was decided among the prehistoric Protozoa cannot be annulled by Act of Parliament. In this mere outline we cannot of course do more than indicate the relation of the biological differences between the sexes to the resulting psychological and social differentiations; for more than this neither space nor powers suffice. We must insist upon the biological considerations underlying the relation of the sexes, which have been too much discussed by contemporary writers of all schools as if the known facts of sex did not exist at all, or almost if these were a matter of muscular strength or weight of brain. . . .

All disputants have tolerably agreed in neglecting the historic, and still more the biological factors; while, so far as the past evolution of the present state of things is taken into account at all, the position of women is regarded as having simply been that in which the stronger muscle and brain of man was able to place her. The past of the race is thus depicted in the most sinister colours, and the whole view is supposed to be confirmed by appeal to the practice of the most degenerate races, and this again as described with the scanty sympathy or impartiality of the average white traveller, missionary, or settler.

As we have already said, we cannot attempt a full discussion of the question, but our book would be left without point, and its essential thesis useless, if we did not, in conclusion, seek to call attention to the fundamental facts of organic difference, say rather divergent lines of differentiation, underlying the whole problem of the sexes. We shall only suggest, as the best argument for the adoption of our standpoint, the way in which it becomes possible relatively to harmonise the very diverse outlooks. We shall not so readily abuse the poor savage, who lies idle in the sun for days after his return from the hunting, while his heavy-laden wife toils and moils without complaint or cease; but bearing in view the extreme bursts of exertion which such a life of incessant struggle with nature and his fellows for food and for life involves upon him, and the consequent necessity of correspondingly utilising every opportunity of repose to recruit and eke out the short and precarious life so indispensable to wife and weans, we shall see that this crude domestic economy is the best, the most moral, and the most kindly attainable under the circumstances. Again, the traveller from town, who thinks the agricultural labourer a greedy brute for eating the morsel of bacon and leaving his wife and children only the bread, does not see that by acting otherwise the total ration would soon be still further lowered, by diminished earnings, loss of employment, or loss of health. . . .

The old view of the subjection of women was not, in fact, so much of tyranny as it seemed, but roughly tended to express the average division of labour; of course hardships were frequent, but these have been exaggerated. The absolute ratification of this by law and religion was merely of a piece with the whole order of belief and practice, in which men crushed themselves still more than their mates. Being absolute, however, such theories had to be overthrown, and the application of the idea of equality, which had done such good service in demolishing the established castes, was a natural and serviceable one. We have above traced the development of this, however, and it is now full time to re-emphasise, this time of course with all scientific relativity instead of a dogmatic authority, the biological factors of the case, and to suggest their possible service in destroying the economic fallacies at present so prevalent, and still more towards reconstituting that complex and sympathetic co-operation between the differentiated sexes in and around which all progress past or future must depend. Instead of men and women merely labouring to produce things as the past economic theories insisted, or competing over the distribution of them, as we at present think so important, a further swing of economic theory will lead us round upon a higher spiral to the direct organic facts. So it is not for the sake of production or distribution, of self-interest or mechanism, or any other idol of the economists, that the male organism organises the climax of his life's struggle and labour, but for his mate; as she, and then he, also for their little ones. Production is for consumption; the species is its own highest, its sole essential product. The social order will clear itself, as it comes more in touch with biology.

It is equally certain that the two sexes are complementary and mutually dependent. Virtually asexual organisms, like Bacteria, occupy no high place in Nature's roll of honour; virtually unisexual organisms, like many rotifers, are great rarities. Parthenogenesis may be an organic ideal, but it is one which has been rarely realised. Males and females, like the sex-elements, are mutually dependent, and that not merely because they are males and females, but also in functions not directly associated with those of sex. To dispute whether males or females are the higher, is like disputing the relative superiority of animals and plants. Each is higher in its own way, and the two are complementary.

While there are broad general distinctions between the intellectual, and especially the emotional, characteristics of males and females among the higher animals, these not unfrequently tend to become mingled. . . . There is, however, no evidence that they might be gradually obliterated. The males of the seahorse, the obstetric frog, and many birds discharge maternal functions, and there are females who fight for the males, and are stronger, or more passionate than their mates. But these are rarities. It is generally true that the males are more active, energetic, eager, passionate, and variable; the females more passive, conservative, sluggish, and stable. The males, or, to return to the terms of our thesis, the more katabolic organisms, often seem more variable, and therefore, . . . may have frequently been the leaders in evolutionary progress, while the more anabolic females tend rather to preserve the constancy and integrity of the species. . . .

Along paths where the reproductive sacrifice was one of the determinants of progress, the females must have the credit of leading the way. The more active males, with a consequently wider range of experience, may have bigger brains and more intelligence; but the females, especially as mothers, have indubitably a larger and more habitual share of the altruistic emotions. The males being usually stronger, have greater independence and courage; the females excel in constancy of affection and in sympathy. The spasmodic bursts of activity characteristic of males contrast with the continuous patience of the females, which we take to be an expression of constitutional contrast, and by no means, as some would have us believe, a mere product of masculine bullying. The stronger lust and passion of males is likewise the obverse of predominant katabolism.

That men should have greater cerebral variability and therefore more originality, while women have greater stability and therefore more "common sense," are facts both consistent with the general theory of sex and verifiable in common experience. The woman, conserving the effects of past variations, has what may be called the greater integrating intelligence; the man, introducing new variations, is stronger in differentiation. The feminine passivity is expressed in greater patience, more open-mindedness, greater appreciation of subtle details, and consequently what we call more rapid intuition. The masculine activity lends a greater power of maximum effort, of scientific insight, or cerebral experiment with impressions, and is associated with an unobservant or impatient disregard of minute details, but with a stronger grasp of generalities. Man thinks more, woman feels more. . . .

George J. Romanes, "Mental Differences Between Men and Women", *Nineteenth Century*, XXI (1887), 654-72.

George J. Romanes, a well-known nineteenth-century scientist, was encouraged by his friend, Charles Darwin, to explore the relationship between mental evolution and the theory of natural selection. His work, *Mental Evolution in Animals,* which appeared in 1883, included a posthumous essay by Darwin on instinct.

In 1888 Romanes published *Mental Evolution in Man: Origin of Human Faculty,* the first installment of a planned multi-volume work which was never completed. Citing Darwin, Romanes argued that man through natural and sexual selection had become superior to woman, not merely physically but intellectually. As proof of this theory Romanes adduced the fact that women's brains weighed less than those of men, from which it followed that women were mentally inferior. The subject of brain weight was avidly discussed by nineteenth-century anthropologists, to whom the demonstration of man's heavier brain provided scientific "proof" that man had traveled farther on the evolutionary path than had woman. As one anthropologist put it, "Man has advanced somewhat alone in the intellectual evolution of the race".[1] The conclusion to which this inevitably led was that women could never be the intellectual equals of men.

The following excerpt indicates how Romanes and persons with a similar point of view could employ biological and physiological assumptions to justify woman's restriction to her traditional role.

In his *Descent of Man* Mr. Darwin has shown at length that what Hunter termed secondary sexual characters occur throughout the whole animal series, at least as far down in the zoological scale as the Articulata. The secondary sexual characters with which he is chiefly concerned are of a bodily kind, such as plumage of birds, horns of mammals, &c. But I think it is evident that secondary sexual characters of a mental kind are of no less general occurrence. Moreover, if we take a broad view of these psychological differences, it becomes instructively apparent that a general uniformity pervades them — that while within the limits of each species the male differs psychologically from the female, in the animal kingdom as a whole the males admit of being classified, as it were, in one psychological species and the females in another. . . .

It is probably due to a recognition of this fact that from the very earliest stages of culture mankind has been accustomed to read into all nature — inanimate as well as animate — differences of the same kind. Whether it be in the person of Maya, of the pagan goddesses, of the Virgin Mary, or in the personifications of sundry natural objects and processes, we uniformly encounter the conception of a feminine principle coexisting with a masculine in the general frame of the cosmos. . . .

I will now briefly enumerate what appear to me the leading features of this distinction in the case of mankind, adopting the ordinary classification of mental faculties as those of intellect, emotion, and will.

Seeing that the average brain-weight of women is about five ounces less than that of men, on merely anatomical grounds we should be prepared to expect a marked inferiority of intellectual power in the former. [*Editors' note: At this point Romanes refers to the work of Sir J. Crichton Browne, who "as a result of many observations," alleged "that not only is the grey matter, or cortex, of the female brain shallower than that of the male, but it also receives less than a proportional supply of blood". Such disparity, Browne concluded, is evidence of "a fundamental sexual distinction" between the sexes which can not be explained by differences in social or cultural training.*] Moreover, as the general physique of women is less robust than that of men — and therefore less able to sustain the fatigue of serious or prolonged brain action — we should also on

---

[1] W. L. Distant, "On the Mental Differences Between the Sexes", *Royal Anthropological Institute of Great Britain and Ireland, Journal*, IV (1874), 80.

physiological grounds be prepared to entertain a similar anticipation. In actual fact we find that the inferiority displays itself most conspicuously in a comparative absence of originality, and this more especially in the higher levels of intellectual work. In her powers of acquisition [of knowledge] the woman certainly stands nearer to the man than she does in her powers of creative thought, although even as regards the former there is a marked difference. The difference, however, is one which does not assert itself till the period of adolescence. . . . But as soon as the brain, and with it the organism as a whole, reaches the stage of full development, it becomes apparent that there is a greater power of amassing knowledge on the part of the male. Whether we look to the general average or to the intellectual giants of both sexes, we are similarly met with the general fact that a woman's information is less wide and deep and thorough than that of a man. What we regard as a highly cultured woman is usually one who has read largely but superficially; and even in the few instances that can be quoted of extraordinary female industry—which on account of their rarity stand out as exceptions to prove the rule—we find a long distance between them and the much more numerous instances of profound erudition among men. . . .

But it is in original work . . . that the disparity is most conspicuous. . . . In no one department of creative thought can women be said to have at all approached men, save in fiction. Yet in poetry, music, and painting, if not also in history, philosophy, and science, the field has always been open to both. For, as I will presently show, the disabilities under which women have laboured with regard to education, social opinion, and so forth, have certainly not been sufficient to explain this general dearth among them of the products of creative genius.

Lastly, with regard to judgment, I think there can be no real question that the female mind stands considerably below the male. It is much more apt to take superficial views of circumstances calling for decision, and also to be guided by less impartiality. Undue influence is more frequently exercised from the side of the emotions; and, in general, all the elements which go to constitute what is understood by a characteristically judicial mind are of comparatively feeble development. Of course here, as elsewhere, I am speaking of average standards. It would be easy to find multitudes of instances where women display better judgment than men, just as in the analogous cases of learning and creative work. But that as a general rule the judgment of women is inferior to that of men has been a matter of universal recognition from the earliest times. [*Editors' note: This view contrasts strongly with Ruskin's opinion, cited earlier, that Shakespeare's heroines are superior in every respect, including judgment, to his male characters, who are so foolish and ineffectual that they do not deserve to be referred to as "heroes".*] The man has always been regarded as the rightful lord of the woman, to whom she is by nature subject, as both mentally and physically the weaker vessel; and when in individual cases these relations happen to be inverted, the accident becomes a favourite theme for humorists—thus showing that in the general estimation such a state of matters is regarded as incongruous.

But if woman has been a loser in the intellectual race as regards acquisition, origination, and judgment, she has gained, even on the intellectual side, certain very conspicuous advantages. First among these we must place refinement of the senses, or higher evolution of sense-organs. Next we must place rapidity of perception, which no doubt in part arises from this higher evolution of the sense-organs—or, rather, both arise from a greater refinement of nervous organisation. . . . Reading implies enormously intricate processes of perception, both of the sensuous and intellectual order;

and I have tried a series of experiments, wherein reading was chosen as a test of the rapidity of perception in different persons. . . .   Now, in these experiments, where every one read the same paragraph as rapidly as possible, I found that the palm was usually carried off by the ladies. Moreover, besides being able to read quicker, they were better able to remember what they had just read—that is, to give a better account even of the paragraph as a whole. One lady, for example, could read exactly four times as fast as her husband, and could then give a better account even of that portion of the paragraph which alone he had time to get through. For the consolation of such husbands, however, I may add that rapidity of perception as thus tested is no evidence of what may be termed the deeper qualities of mind—some of my slowest readers being highly distinguished men. . . .

Turning now to the emotions, we find that in woman, as contrasted with man, these are almost always less under control of the will—more apt to break away, as it were, from the restraint of reason, and to overwhelm the mental chariot in disaster. Whether this tendency displays itself in the overmastering form of hysteria, or in the more ordinary form of comparative childishness, ready annoyance, and a generally unreasonable temper—in whatever form this supremacy of emotion displays itself, we recognise it as more of a feminine than a masculine characteristic. The crying of a woman is not held to betray the same depth of feeling as the sobs of a man; and the petty forms of resentment which belong to what is known as a "shrew," or a "scold," are only to be met with among those daughters of Eve who prove themselves least agreeable to the sons of Adam. Coyness and caprice are very general peculiarities, and we may add, as kindred traits, personal vanity, fondness of display, and delight in the sunshine of admiration. There is also, as compared with the masculine mind, a greater desire for emotional excitement of all kinds, and hence a greater liking for society, pageants, and even for what are called "scenes," provided these are not of a kind to alarm her no less characteristic timidity. Again, in the opinion of Mr. Lecky, with which I partly concur:

"In the courage of endurance they are commonly superior; but their passive courage is not so much fortitude which bears and defies, as resignation which bears and bends. In the ethics of intellect they are decidedly inferior. They very rarely love truth, though they love passionately what they call 'the truth,' or opinions which they have derived from others, and hate vehemently those who differ from them. They are little capable of impartiality or doubt, their thinking is chiefly a mode of feeling; though very generous in their acts, they are rarely generous in their opinions or in their judgments. They persuade rather than convince, and value belief as a source of consolation rather than as a faithful expression of the reality of things."

. . . But now, the meritorious qualities wherein the female mind stands pre-eminent are, affection, sympathy, devotion, self-denial and modesty; long-suffering, or patience under pain, disappointment, and adversity; reverence, veneration, religious feeling, and general morality. In these virtues . . . it will be noticed that the gentler predominate over the heroic; and it is observable in this connection that when heroism of any kind is displayed by a woman, the prompting emotions are almost certain to be of an unselfish kind.

All the aesthetic emotions are, as a rule, more strongly marked in women than in men—or, perhaps, I should rather say, they are much more generally present in women. This remark applies especially to the aesthetic emotions which depend upon refinement of perception. Hence feminine "taste" is proverbially good in regard to the smaller matters of everyday life, although it becomes, as a rule, untrustworthy in proportion to the necessity for intellectual judgment. In the arrangement of flowers, the furnishing of rooms, the choice of combinations in apparel, and so forth, we generally find that we may be most safely guided by the taste of women; while in matters of artistic or literary criticism we turn instinctively to the judgment of men.

If we now look in somewhat more detail at the habitual display of these various feelings and virtues on the part of women, we may notice, with regard to affection, that, in a much larger measure than men, they derive pleasure from receiving as well as from bestowing: in both cases affection is felt by them to be, as it were, of more emotional value. The same remark applies to sympathy. It is very rare to find a woman who does not derive consolation from a display of sympathy, whether her sorrow be great or small; while it is by no means an unusual thing to find a man who rejects all offers of the kind with a feeling of active aversion.

Touching devotion, we may note that it is directed by women pretty equally towards inferiors and superiors—spending and being spent in the tending of children; ministering to the poor, the afflicted, and the weak; clinging to husbands, parents, brothers, often without and even against reason.

Again, purity and religion are, as it were, the natural heritage of women in all but the lowest grades of culture. But it is within the limit of Christendom that both these characters are most strongly pronounced; as, indeed, may equally well be said of nearly all the other virtues which we have just been considering. And the reason is that Christianity, while crowning the virtue of chastity with an aureole of mysticism more awful than was ever conceived even by pagan Rome, likewise threw the vesture of sanctity over all the other virtues which belong by nature to the female mind. . . .

So much, then, for the intellect and emotions. Coming lastly to the will, I have already observed that this exercises less control over the emotions in women than in men. We rarely find in women that firm tenacity of purpose and determination to overcome obstacles which is characteristic of what we call a manly mind. When a woman is urged to any prolonged or powerful exercise of volition, the prompting cause is usually to be found in the emotional side of her nature, whereas in man we may generally observe that the intellectual is alone sufficient to supply the needed motive. . . . This comparative weakness of will is further manifested by the frequency among women of what is popularly termed indecision of character. The proverbial fickleness of *la donna mobile* is due quite as much to vacillation of will as to other unstable qualities of mental constitution. The ready firmness of decision which belongs by nature to the truly masculine mind is very rarely to be met with in the feminine; while it is not an unusual thing to find among women indecision of character so habitual and pronounced as to become highly painful to themselves—leading to timidity and diffidence in adopting almost any line of conduct where issues of importance are concerned, and therefore leaving them in the condition, as they graphically express it, of not knowing their own minds.

If, now, we take a general survey of all these mental differences, it becomes apparent that in the feminine type the characteristic virtues, like the characteristic failings, are those which are born of weakness; while in the masculine type the characteristic failings, like the characteristic virtues, are those which are born of strength. Which we are to consider the higher type will therefore depend on the value which we assign to mere force. Under one point of view, the magnificent spider of South America, which is large enough and strong enough to devour a humming-bird, deserves to be

regarded as the superior creature. But under another point of view, there is no spectacle in nature more shockingly repulsive than the slow agonies of the most beautiful
of created beings in the hairy limbs of a monster so far beneath it in the sentient as in
the zoological scale. And although the contrast between man and woman is happily
not so pronounced in degree, it is nevertheless a contrast the same in kind. The whole
organisation of woman is formed on a plan of greater delicacy, and her mental structure is correspondingly more refined: it is further removed from the struggling instincts
of the lower animals, and thus more nearly approaches our conception of the spiritual.
For even the failings of weakness are less obnoxious than the vices of strength, and I
think it is unquestionable that these vices are of quite as frequent occurrence on the
part of men as are those failings on the part of women. The hobnailed boots may
have given place to patent-pumps, and yet but small improvement may have been
made upon the overbearing temper of a navvy; the beer-shop may have been super-
seded by the whist-club, and yet the selfishness of pleasure-seeking may still habitually
leave the solitary wife to brood over her lot through the small hours of the morning.
Moreover, even when the mental hobnails have been removed, we generally find that
there still remains what a member of the fairer sex has recently and aptly designated
mental heavy-handedness. By this I understand the clumsy inability of a coarser nature
to appreciate the feelings of a finer; and how often such is the case we must leave the
sufferers to testify. In short, the vices of strength to which I allude are those which
have been born of rivalry: the mental hide has been hardened and the man carries
into his home those qualities of insensibility, self-assertion, and self-seeking which
have elsewhere led to success in his struggle for supremacy. Or, as Mr. Darwin says,
"Man is the rival of other men; he delights in competition, and this leads to ambition
which passes too readily into selfishness. These latter qualities seem to be his natural
and unfortunate birthright."

Of course the greatest type of manhood, or the type wherein our ideal of manliness
reaches its highest expression, is where the virtues of strength are purged from its vices.
To be strong and yet tender, brave and yet kind, to combine in the same breast the
temper of a hero with the sympathy of a maiden—this is to transform the ape and the
tiger into what we know ought to constitute the man. And if in actual life we find that
such an ideal is but seldom realised, this should make us more lenient in judging the
frailties of the opposite sex. These frailties are for the most part the natural consequences of our own, and even where such is not the case, we do well to remember, as
already observed, that they are less obnoxious than our own, and also that it is the privilege of strength to be tolerant. Now, it is a practical recognition of these things that
leads to chivalry; and even those artifical courtesies which wear the mark of chivalry
are of value, as showing what may be termed a conventional acquiescence in the truth
that underlies them. This truth is, that the highest type of manhood can only then be
reached when the heart and mind have been so far purified from the dross of a brutal
ancestry as genuinely to appreciate, to admire, and to reverence the greatness, the
beauty, and the strength which have been made perfect in the weakness of womanhood. . . .

T. S. Clouston, M.D., "Female Education from a Medical Point of View",
Popular Science Monthly, XXIV (1883), 214-28.

In November 1882 Dr. T. S. Clouston delivered two lectures at the
Philosophical Institution of Edinburgh in which he explained why the

higher education of women must lead to disastrous consequences for the women themselves, their children, and society at large. If a substantial share of a woman's limited amount of life force were diverted to her brain, her reproductive organs would be inadequately supplied with the energy required for the production of healthy offspring. The choice was clear: books or babies and, preferably, babies.

Clouston, who was later knighted for his medical research, was no ordinary physician. He was the first man to establish the connection between congenital syphilis and general paresis; his books were translated into foreign languages; his *Clinical Lectures on Mental Disease* and *The Hygiene of Mind* went through six and seven editions respectively; he was the author of a marriage manual, *Before I Wed: or Young Men and Marriage;* and the publication of his obituary notice in the *New York Times* is indicative of the fact that he had an international reputation. It is easy to imagine the extent to which he must have contributed to the creation of a climate of opinion hostile to the cause of education for women.

And Clouston was not alone. Other men of eminence—Herbert Spencer, Robert Lawson Tait, sometime president of the British Gynecological Society, Henry Maudsley, Professor of Medical Jurisprudence, University College, London, and Edward H. Clarke of Harvard University, author of *Sex in Education* (see p. 268), shared Clouston's opinion that women, because of their physical limitations, were incapable of competing effectively with men. In the excerpt that follows, Clouston presents a view of woman that was probably accepted by the overwhelming majority of his medical colleagues, particularly since, like Geddes, he made use of "scientific facts" to assure the preservation of traditional female roles.

. . . There is a law of Nature . . . that lies at the very root of the principles I am going to advocate to-night. It is this, that every living being has from its birth a limit of growth and development in all directions beyond which it can not possibly go by any amount of forcing. Man can not add one cubit to his stature. The blacksmith's arm can not grow beyond a certain limit. The cricketer's quickness can not be increased beyond this inexorable point. The thinker's effort can not extend further than this fixed limit of brain-power in each man. This limit is fixed at different points in each man in regard to his various powers, but there is a limit beyond which you can not go in any direction in each faculty and organ.

The capacity for being educated or developed in youth, the receptive capacity of each brain, is definitely fixed as to each brain of each young man and woman.

Then the important laws of hereditary transmission of weaknesses and peculiarities and strong points must be studied and kept in mind, so far as we know them, by the educator of youth. . . . Nothing is more certain than that every man and woman is like their progenitors in the main. It takes generations for new conditions of life to eradicate hereditary peculiarities, and then they are always tending to come back. . . . Many nervous diseases and conditions are the most hereditary of all, and we have good reason to think that, in those subject to them, the conditions of life, and the treatment to which the brain and the rest of the nervous system are subjected during the period of the building of the constitution—that is, during adolescence from thirteen to twenty-five—are of the highest importance in hastening and accentuating, or retarding and lessening, those nervous peculiarities. . . . In our present state of physiological knowledge, it is . . . a quite inconceivable thing that takes place when we have two generations of perfectly healthy persons intervening between an insane great-grandmother and an insane great-grandchild. The grandparent and the parent carried something in their constitutions which was never appreciable to us at all. Yet it was there just as certainly as if it had broken out as a disease. . . .

Another law of living beings to be kept in mind is this: There is a certain general energy in the organism which may be used in many directions, and may take different forms, such as for growth, nutrition, muscular force, thinking, feeling, or acquiring knowledge, according as it is called out or needed. But its total amount is strictly limited, and if it is used to do one thing, then it is not available for another. If you use the force of your steam-engine for generating electricity, you can not have it for sawing your wood. If you have the vital energy doing the work of building the bones and muscles and brain during the year that a girl grows two inches in height, and gains a stone in weight, you can not have it that year for the acquisition of knowledge and for study. If by undue pressure you do call up and use for education the energy that ought to go toward growth and strengthening the body, you produce a small and unhealthy specimen of humanity, just like those plants which have had their flowers unduly forced, and are deficient in bulk and hardiness, and will not produce seed. Nature disposes of her energies in a human being in due proportion to the wants of each organ and faculty. There is a natural and harmonious relation which each bears to the other. This relation is different in different persons, and at different periods of life. The plowman takes up most of his energy in muscular effort and in the repair of waste muscle, and he has little left for thinking. The student uses his up in the mental effort of his brain, and has little left for heavy muscular work. No doubt Nature is sometimes prodigal of energy, and provides enough for the high-pressure working of both the brain and the muscles in some cases. But this is not the rule, and should not be assumed as applicable to many persons. At the different periods of life Nature uses up her available energy in different ways. She allocates it in babyhood chiefly to body-growth, in early girlhood partly to growth and partly to brain development; in adolescence, the period of which I am to speak chiefly to-night, her effort is evidently to complete the building up of the structures everywhere, to bring to full development the various functions, to strengthen and harmonize the whole body and the brain, so that they shall be able to produce, and do in the succeeding years of full maturity all that they are capable of. It is certainly not a period of production, but of acquisition. If the original constitution derived from ancestry has been good, if the conditions of life in childhood have been favorable, if the education has been of the right kind, developing the whole being in all her faculties equally and harmoniously after Nature's plan, and if the period of adolescence has crowned and completed every organ and every faculty, no faculty being unduly called on to the impoverishment of the others, then we expect, and indeed must have, a woman in health, which means happiness with the full capacity for work, for production, and for resisting hurtful influences, and for living her allotted time. But this can only result from a harmonious and healthy development, which we may take as the physician's word to denote education in his sense. It can only result from regarding the woman as a unit, body and mind insepar-able; it can only result from the educator's efforts being on the lines of Nature's facts, and Nature's harmonies, and Nature's laws. . . .

There is another vital fact in the constitution of human nature that needs to be taken into account. . . . It is this, that one generation may, by living at high pressure, or under specially unfavorable conditions, exhaust and use up more than its share of energy. That is, it may draw a bill on posterity, and transmit to the next generation not enough to pay it. I believe many of us are now having the benefit of the calm, unexciting, lazy lives of our forefathers of the last generation. They stored up energy for us; now we are using it. The question is, Can we begin at adolescence, work at high pressure, keep this up during our lives (which in that case will be on an average rather short), and yet transmit to our posterity enough vital energy for their needs? How often it has happened, in the history of the world, that people who for generations have exhibited no special energy, blaze out in tremendous bursts of national greatness for a time, and then almost die out! The Tartars under Genghis Khan, the Turks when they overawed Europe, the Arabs when they conquered Spain, are examples. We must take care that this does not happen to us. How often we see a quiet country family, that has for generations led quiet, humdrum lives, suddenly produce one or two great men, and then relapse into greater obscurity than before, or become degen-erate and die out altogether!

Another fact in the body and mind history of human beings is this, that there are certain physiological eras or periods in life, each of which has a certain meaning. The chief of such eras are childhood, puberty, adolescence, maturity, the climacteric, and senility. We have to ascertain, What does Nature mean by these eras? What does it strive to attain to in each period? What are the ideal conditions of each? No one of these periods can be studied from a bodily point of view alone, or from a mental point of view alone. They must be regarded from the point of view of the whole living being, with all its powers and faculties, bodily and mental. Not only so, but in most cases the inherited weaknesses must be taken into account too. Those eras of life can not be fully understood looked at with reference to the individual. Their meaning is only seen when the social life, the ancestral life, and the life of the future race, are all taken into account. And this is what makes some proper attention to those eras so very impor-tant from the social as well as the physician's point of view. If they are not understood, and so are mismanaged, not only the individual suffers, but society and the race of the future. Particularly the era of adolescence is important, for it is the summer ripening time in the vital history. If the grain is poorly matured, it is not good for either eating or sowing.

Such is the physician's, or perhaps I should rather say the physiologist's, way of regarding a woman, her development, and her education. It is because we do not think the average parent and the professional educator in the technical sense always take this wide view, but that the professional enthusiasm of the latter takes account of, and tries to cultivate, one set of faculties only, *viz.*, the mental; because we think the public mind is getting to regard as all-important in female education what we think is not so important, and so to take little account of what we regard as of supreme impor-tance to the individual and to the race — *viz.*, the constitution and the health — that I think that the physiological view of female education should be brought forward and presented to the public mind more frequently than is the case; while the bad results in after-life of disregarding Nature's laws, as these results come under the notice of the physician, should be strongly and clearly brought before the general mass of parents and educators. It is not a matter that concerns the physician and his immediate patient only. It concerns the whole of the people. . . .

The era of adolescence is one of the greatest importance from a bodily and mental point of view in young men and women, but especially in the latter. . . . Then bodily energies of a new kind begin to arise, vast tracts of brain quite unused before are brought into active exercise. The growth assumes a different direction and type, awkwardness of movement becomes possible, and on the other hand a grace never before attainable can be acquired. The bones begin to cohere and solidify at their ends, and the soft cartilage joinings to get firmer. The tastes for food and drink often change. Bread and butter and sweets no longer satisfy entirely. Stronger and more stimulating foods are craved. The carriage and walk change. The lines of beauty begin to develop. But the mental changes are even more striking. All that is specially characteristic of woman begins to appear; childish things are put away; dolls no longer give pleasure. For the first time distinct individual mental peculiarities show themselves. The effective portion of the mental nature begins to assume altogether new forms, and to acquire a new power. Literature and poetry begin to be understood in a vague way, and the latter often becomes a passion. The imagination becomes strengthened, and is directed into different channels from before. The sense of right and wrong and of duty becomes then more active. Morality in a real sense is possible. A sense of the seriousness and responsibility of life may be said then to awaken for the first time. The knowledge of good and evil is acquired. The religious instinct arises then for the first time in any power. Modesty and diffidence in certain circumstances are for the first time seen. The emotional nature acquires depth, and tenderness appears. The real events and possibilities of the future are reflected in vague and dream-like emotions and longings that have much bliss in them, but not a little too of seriousness and difficulty. The adolescent feels instinctively that she has now entered a new country, the face of which she does not know, but which may be full of good and happiness to her. The reasoning faculty acquires more backbone, but is as yet the slave of the instincts and the emotions. A conception of an ideal in anything is then attainable and the ideal is very apt to take the place of the real. The relations and feelings toward the other sex utterly change, and the change makes its subject liable to tremendous emotional cataclysms, that may utterly overmaster the rest of the mental life. There is a subject egoism, and often selfishness, tending toward objective dualism. There is resolute action from instinct and there is a tendency to set at defiance calculation and reason. All those changes go hand in hand with bodily changes and bodily development. There is a direct action and interaction between body and mind, all through. Accompanying all these there are, when health is present, a constant ebullition of animal spirits, a joyous feeling, a pleasure in life for its own sake, and there is a craving for light and beauty in something. There should not only be enough energy in the body and mind to do work, but there should be some to spare for fun and frolic, which is just Nature's pleasant way of expending vital force that is not needed at the time for anything else.

For the origination, for the gradual evolution of all these mental changes into perfect womanhood, there are needed corresponding bodily developments. Without these we should have none of those marvelous mental and emotional phenomena properly evolved and developed. If the health is weak, the nutrition poor, the bodily functions disordered and imperfect, and the nervous force impaired, we are liable to have the whole feminine mental development arrested or distorted. If undue calls are made on the nervous force, or the mental power, or the bodily energies, the perfection of nature can not be attained, and womanhood is reached without the characteristic womanly qualities of mind or body. The fair ideal is distorted. The girl student who has concentrated all her force on cramming book knowledge, neglecting her bodily requirements; the girl betrothed who has been allowed to fall in love before her emotional nature was largely enough developed; and the girl drudge who has been exhausted with physical labor—all alike are apt to suffer the effects of an inharmonious, and therefore unhealthy, mental and bodily constitution. The body and the mind go in absolute unison, just as the blush on the maiden's cheek comes and goes with emotion, as the brightness and mobility of her features go with mental vivacity and happiness.

All those mental and bodily changes are not sudden, nor fully completed and brought to perfection at once; it takes on an average from ten to twelve years before they are fully completed. All that time they are going on, and during that time there is an immense strain on the constitution. All that time the whole organic nature is in a state of what we call instability: that is, it is liable to be upset in its working by slight causes. The calls on the inherent vital energy to carry on and to bring to the harmonious perfection of full womanhood all of these combined bodily and mental qualities I have referred to, during these ten or twelve years, are very great indeed.

We physicians maintain that this period is one of momentous importance, and we have good reason to know this, for we are often called on to treat diseases that arise then, and, having originated then, have been fully matured afterward. The risks and the dangers to body and mind are then very great indeed. We count it a fearful risk to run, not merely that actual disease should be brought on, but that a girl capable of being developed into a healthy and happy woman, with a rounded feminine constitution after Nature's type—the only type that secures happiness and satisfaction to a woman—should by bad management, misdirected education, or bad conditions of life, grow into a distorted, unnatural, and therefore unhappy woman, who can not get out of the life that she has only to live once all that it is capable of yielding her. Like all the other physiological eras of life, that of adolescence only comes once. If the developing process, which is its chief characteristic, is not completed, then it is missed for life. Whatever is done then is final; whatever is left undone is also final. If a woman is not formed at twenty-five, the chances are she will never be so; if she is not healthy then, she probably will not be so. Who in his senses can deny that it is far better for nineteen women out of twenty to be healthy than to be intellectually well educated? No acquirements of knowledge can possibly make up for health in after-life. There is an organic happiness that goes only with good health and a harmoniously constituted body and mind. Without that organic happiness life is not worth having. Cheerfulness is one of the best outward signs of this perfect health, and what woman has not missed her vocation in the world who is not cheerful? A general sense of well-being is the best conscious proof of perfect health. It underlies all enduring happiness. . . .

If in adolescence, before the bones are knit, and the growth completed, and the feminine nature far advanced toward perfection, if the brain that is in the process of doing all these things is year by year called on to exert its yet imperfect forces chiefly in acquiring book-knowledge by long hours of study, and in consequence the growth is stopped, the blood is thinned, the cheeks are pallid, the fat destroyed, the wondrous forces and faculties that I have spoken of are arrested before they attain completion, then, when the period of growth and development ceases, the damage is irreparable.

There is no time or place of organic repentance provided by Nature for the sins of the schoolmaster. . . . This is a poor lookout for the individual, but when motherhood comes, and sound minds in sound bodies have to be transmitted to posterity, how is it to be then with the future race? This aspect of the question of female education during the period of adolescence is of absolutely primary importance to the world. Yet it is wholly ignored in many systems of education. What is the use of culture, if it is all to end with the present generation? What a responsibility to transmit to future generations weak bodies and over-sensitive brains, liable to all sorts of nervous disease! Nothing can be more certain than that the qualities, good and bad, acquired in one generation are sent on to the next. The world may be all the better of a generation of healthy, ignorant and happy mothers, who can produce stalwart, forceful sons and daughters (not that I wish this lecture to be an apology for health and ignorance), but the world must be worse for a system of stopping full and harmonious development in the mothers of the next generation. My plea is, that as Nature is harmonious in mental and bodily development, we should follow on her lines, and not set up an educational standard for ourselves that is one-sided, because it takes no proper account of the constitution of the body and brain at all, only considering one brain-function—the mental.

Along with these developments of mind and emotion during adolescence there are, unfortunately, too apt to develop hereditary weaknesses, especially of the nervous kind. Physicians then meet with hysteria, neuralgia, nervous exhaustion, insanity, etc., for the first time. As normal individualities of bodily form and mental character then arise, so abnormal developments arise too where they are inherited or brought on by unfavorable treatment. . . . Unfortunately, there are very few families indeed, nowadays, free from tendencies to some hereditary disease or other. Our modern life tends to develop the brain and nervous system, and undue development means risk of disease always. What the profession of medicine specially desires to guard our population now against, is our becoming a nervous race. We want to have body as well as mind; otherwise we think that degeneration of the race is inevitable. And, therefore, we rather would err on the safe side and keep the mental part of the human machine back a little, while we would encourage bulk, and fat, and bone, and muscular strength. We think this gives a greater chance of health and happiness to the individual, and infinitely more chance of permanence and improvement to the race. This applies to the female sex, we think, more than to the male. Man's chief work is more related to the present (from a physiological point of view), woman's chief work to the future of the world. Why should we spoil a good mother by making an ordinary grammarian?

It will be said, as an hereditary fact, that most great men have had mothers of strong minds. I believe this to be true, but it is not a fact that many great men have had what would now be called "highly-educated" mothers. There were usually an innate force and a good development of mind and body in the mothers of such men, who usually had led quiet, uneventful, unexciting lives. I am inclined to believe that if the mothers of such men had been in adolescence worked in learning book-knowledge for eight or ten hours a day in a sitting posture; if they had been stimulated by competition all that time, and had ended at twenty-one by being first-prize women (as probably most of them had the power of being)—if this had befallen them, then, I think, their sons would have been small and distorted men, instead of being the lights of the world.

W. R. Greg, "Prostitution", *Westminster Review,* LIII (1850), 448-506.

William R. Greg, a very popular and prolific essayist in the 1850's, was concerned not only with political and economic problems but with moral and religious questions as well. He was a frequent contributor of articles to the leading journals of the day, and he became a well-known social commentator. In a review essay occasioned by a number of books that had recently been published on prostitution, Greg put forward what was probably the conventional attitude toward woman's sexual nature.

. . . Women's *desires* scarcely ever lead to their fall; for (save in a class of whom we shall speak presently) the desire scarcely exists in a definite and conscious form, till they *have* fallen. In this point there is a radical and essential difference between the sexes: the arrangements of nature and the customs of society would be even more un-equal than they are, were it not so. In men, in general, the sexual desire is inherent and spontaneous, and belongs to the condition of puberty. In the other sex, the desire is dormant, if not non-existent, till excited; always till excited by undue familiarities; almost always till excited by actual intercourse. Those feelings which coarse and licen-tious minds are so ready to attribute to girls, are almost invariably *consequences.* Women whose position and education have protected them from exciting causes, con-stantly pass through life without ever being cognizant of the promptings of the senses. Happy for them that it is so! We do not mean to say that uneasiness may not be felt — that health may not sometimes suffer; but there is no consciousness of the cause. Among all the higher and middle classes, and, to a greater extent than would com-monly be believed, among the lower classes also, where they either come of virtuous parents, or have been carefully brought up, this may be affirmed as a general fact. Were it not for this kind decision of nature, which, in England, has been assisted by that correctness of feeling which pervades our education, the consequences would, we believe, be frightful. If the passions of women were ready, strong, and spontaneous, in a degree even remotely approaching the form they assume in the coarser sex, there can be little doubt that sexual irregularities would reach a height, of which, at present, we have happily no conception. Imagine for a moment, the sufferings and struggles the virtuous among them would, on that supposition, have to undergo, in a country where, to hundreds of thousands marriage is impossible, and to hundreds of thousands more, is postponed till the period of youth is passed; and where modesty, decency, and honour, alike preclude them from that indulgence which men practise without re-straint or shame. No! Nature has laid many heavy burdens on the delicate shoulders of the weaker sex: let us rejoice that this at least is spared them.

William Acton, M.R.C.S., *The Functions and Disorders of the Repro-ductive Organs,* 3rd ed. (London: John Churchill, 1862), pp. 75, 88-89, 101-3.

The Victorian lady, despite the adulation lavished on her by men like Ruskin, Rearden, Patmore, and Phillimore, was in truth a pitiable creature. Not only was she physically and intellectually inferior to man, as Clouston had plausibly explained, but even in the area of sexual en-

joyment she ran a poor second. Dr. William Acton, a prominent London
physician, in the 1862 edition of his celebrated work, *The Functions
and Disorders of the Reproductive Organs,* presented an analysis of
woman's sexual nature which in effect confirmed the idea, expressed
earlier by Greg, that women—that is, "good" women—neither sought
nor enjoyed sexual activity.

This was apparently not an eighteenth-century view; ". . . it seems to
have been reserved for the nineteenth century to state that women are
apt to be congenitally incapable of experiencing complete sexual satisfaction, and peculiarly liable to sexual anesthesia".[1] There were, it is
true, dissenting voices, but the views that were most authoritative, most
representative, most widely accepted, and most firmly grounded in clinical experience were those which were most consistent with the Victorian
stereotype. There is no doubt where the medical establishment stood.
As late as 1891, Dr. Robert Lawson Tait, a noted gynecologist and the
author of several outstanding texts in the field, maintained that the
sexual life of women did not bear comparison with that of men.[2] The
extent to which such views actually reflected contemporary sexual
practices is, of course, conjectural.

> . . . In the majority of cases the modest English female, who has just gone through
> all the anxieties and fatigues of the marriage ceremony and its attendant leave takings,
> and finds herself in a position so new, so anxious, and so apparently isolated, as that
> of a newly married woman, would be generally only too happy for the first few days to
> dispense with what in most instances is to her, at least, a most painful and distressing
> climax to her other agitations. Again, it is a delusion under which many a previously
> incontinent man suffers, to suppose that in newly married life he will be required to
> treat his wife as he used to treat his mistresses. It is not so in the case of any modest
> English girl. He need not fear that his wife will require the excitement, or in any res-
> pect imitate the ways of a courtezan. . . .
>
>   If the married female conceives every second year, during the nine months that
> follow conception she experiences no great sexual excitement. The consequence is
> that sexual desire in the male is somewhat diminished, and the act of coition takes
> place but rarely. And, again, while women are suckling there is usually such a call on
> the vital force made by the organs secreting milk that sexual desire is almost anni-
> hilated. Now, as all that we have read and heard tends to prove that a reciprocity of
> desire is, to a great extent, necessary to excite the male, we must not be surprised if we
> learn that excesses in fertile married life are comparatively rare, and that the passion
> in the man becomes gradually sobered down. . . .
>
>   . . . I should say that the majority of women (happily for them) are not very much
> troubled with sexual feeling of any kind. What men are habitually, women are only
> exceptionally. It is too true, I admit, as the divorce courts show, that there are some
> few women who have sexual desires so strong that they surpass those of men, and shock

---

[1] Havelock Ellis, *Studies in the Psychology of Sex,* 6 vols., 2nd ed. rev. (Philadelphia: F. A. Davis
Company, Publishers, 1928), III, 193-94.
[2] *Ibid.,* pp. 194-95.

public feeling by their exhibition. I admit, of course, the existence of sexual excitement terminating in nymphomania, a form of insanity that those accustomed to visit lunatic asylums must be fully conversant with; but, with these sad'exceptions, there can be no doubt that sexual feeling in the female is in abeyance, and that it requires positive and considerable excitement to be roused at all; and even if roused (which in many instances it can never be) is very moderate compared with that of the male. Men, and particularly young men, form their ideas of women's feelings from what they notice early in life among loose or, at least, low and vulgar women. There is always a certain number of females who, though not ostensibly in the rank of prostitutes, make a kind of trade of a pretty face. They are fond of admiration, they like to attract the attention of those immediately above them. Any susceptible boy is easily led to believe, whether he is altogether overcome by the syren or not, that she, and therefore all women, must have at least as strong passions as himself. Such women, however, will give a very false idea of the condition of female sexual feeling in general.

Association with the loose women of London streets, in casinos, and other immoral haunts (who, if they have not sexual feeling, counterfeit it so well that the novice does not suspect but that it is genuine), all seem to corroborate an early impression such as this, and . . . it is from these erroneous notions that so many young men think that the marital duties they will have to undertake are beyond their exhausted strength, and from this reason dread and avoid marriage.

Married men — medical men — or married women themselves, would tell a very different tale, and vindicate female nature from the vile aspersions cast on it by the abandoned conduct and ungoverned lusts of a few of its worst examples.

There are many females who never feel any sexual excitement whatever. Others, again, immediately after each period, do become, to a limited degree, capable of experiencing it; but this capacity is often temporary, and may cease entirely till the next menstrual period. The best mothers, wives, and managers of households, know little or nothing of sexual indulgences. Love of home, children, and domestic duties, are the only passions they feel.

As a general rule, a modest woman seldom desires any sexual gratification for herself. She submits to her husband, but only to please him; and, but for the desire of maternity, would far rather be relieved from his attentions. No nervous or feeble young man need, therefore, be deterred from marriage by any exaggerated notion of the duties required from him. The married woman has no wish to be treated on the footing of a mistress. . . .

Jeremy Bentham, *Principles of the Civil Code,* Part III, Chapter V: Of Marriage, in *The Works of Jeremy Bentham,* published under the superintendance of his executor John Bowring, 11 Vols. (Edinburgh: W. Tait; and London: Simpkin, Marshall & Co., 1843), I, 355-56.

There were some general principles — revealed truths, one might say — on which Englishmen of the upper classes could agree, regardless of how they might have differed on other matters. One such universally accepted constant during the early part of the nineteenth century was that of the legal position of married women. Jeremy Bentham, the father of utilitarianism and the opponent of special privilege, was, for example, bit-

terly critical of Blackstone's *Commentaries,* but in his own observations
on marriage, he echoed and amplified Blackstone's pronouncement of
the necessity for the submission of wives to husbands. Whereas Blackstone, in the eighteenth century, took the wife's inferiority for granted,
Bentham, in the nineteenth, attempted to justify it; the practical results
were the same. Whether the continued subordination of wives to husbands contributed to the greatest happiness of the greatest number
seems somewhat debatable.

. . . "The wife should submit to the laws of the husband, saving recourse to justice."
Master of the wife as to what regards his own interests, he ought to be guardian of the
wife as to what regards her interests. Between the wishes of two persons who pass their
life together, there may at every moment be a contradiction. The benefit of peace
renders it desirable that a pre-eminence should be established, which should prevent
or terminate these contests. But why is the man to be the governor? Because he is
the stronger. In his hands power sustains itself. Place the authority in the hands of the
wife, every moment will be marked by revolt on the part of the husband. This is not
the only reason: it is also probable that the husband, by the course of his life, possesses
more experience, greater aptitude for business, greater powers of application. In
these respects there are exceptions, but the question is, what ought to be the general
law?

I have said, "*saving recourse to justice;*" for it is not proper to make the man a tyrant, and to reduce to a state of passive slavery the sex which, by its weakness and its
gentleness, has the greatest need of protection. The interests of females have too often
been neglected. At Rome the laws of marriage were only the code of the strongest,
and the shares were divided by the lion. But those who, from some vague notion of
justice and of generosity, would bestow upon females an absolute equality, would only
spread a dangerous snare for them. To set them free, as much as it is possible for the
laws to do so, from the necessity of pleasing their husbands, would be, in a moral point
of view, to weaken instead of strengthen their empire. The man, secure from his prerogative, has no uneasiness arising from his self-love, and derives enjoyment even from
sacrificing it. Substitute to this relation a rivalry of powers, the pride of the strongest
would be continually wounded, and would prove a dangerous antagonist for the more
feeble; and placing a greater value upon what was taken, than upon what was still
possessed, it would direct all its efforts to the re-establishment of its pre-eminence. . . .

John William Burgon, B.D., *A Sermon Preached Before the University
of Oxford, June 8, 1884* (Oxford and London: Parker and Co., 1884),
pp. 7, 9, 11-12, 14-17.

In 1884 John William Burgon, the Dean of Chichester, preached a
sermon in the chapel of New College, Oxford, in which he warned
women that, in aspiring to be equal to men, they were flouting God's
will and manifest intention. (Burgon's views, incidentally, in both religion and politics, were so notoriously reactionary that both houses of
Parliament had forced the government to withdraw his nomination to a
university commission.) In the course of explaining why higher educa-

tion for women was not consistent with Christianity, Burgon passionately defended the traditional view of woman's creation, and argued that since her inferiority was a deliberate part of the Divine Plan, it was almost an act of rebellion against the Deity to treat woman as though she were equal to man. Burgon's sermon demonstrates the extent to which the dogmas of religion could be used to perpetuate the notion of woman's innate inferiority.

GENESIS 1:27
"So GOD created Man in His own image.
In the image of GOD created He him.
Male and female created He them."

. . . Do men consider that the Creator has based the law of Marriage on the concluding clause of this His own primaeval utterance, — *"Male and female* created He them?" Attend to the matter for a moment and you will see that it is so indeed. For (as all remember) when questioned by the Pharisees whether it is "lawful for a man to put away his wife for every cause?" — our SAVIOUR'S words were, "Have ye not read that He which made them at the beginning, made them *male and female?"* Neither in the Law is it written, nor yet in the Gospel is it said, *"Man and Woman* created He them." And why? Clearly because as yet Woman had not received her being. The male and female were as yet implicitly shut up in one. The race was included in the unit. The two sexes were represented by the one sex. And the subsequent marvellous history fully justifies the expression; for, since it was determined in the Divine counsels that Woman should derive her being from and out of Man, it was competent for the HOLY SPIRIT, by Moses, to declare on the occasion of Man's Creation, "Male *and female* created He them."

. . . But the essential matter is behind. It is this original unity of the primaeval pair in the one person of Adam,—the previous unity of "male and female,"—which is made the foundation of the Divine argument respecting Marriage. . . .

Men of piety are sometimes heard to speak somewhat to the following effect: — That it would not shake their faith in Revelation even if Evolution should come to be accepted as the true account of the Origin of the Human race: and that for their own parts though they are willing to accept the Mosaic record, they are yet by no means sure that it is wrong to regard the narrative in Genesis of Man and Woman's first beginning as partaking of the nature of sacred allegory.

I find it difficult to express the offence which such language occasions me. An unbeliever's unbelief in the sacred record, I can understand: but I neither can nor will understand this playing at fast and loose with Divine Truth, — this endeavour to give one hand to Moses and the other hand to Darwin. "If the Lord be God, follow Him: but if Baal, then follow him." You absolutely must make your election. Both accounts of the matter cannot possibly be true. The two systems cannot possibly co-exist. One of them *must* be fabulous. And, since by the hypothesis I am addressing a believer, I hasten to shew that the Mosaic account of the Creation of the first Man and the first Woman must needs be taken literally. . . .

Beyond all things, pray note what is recorded concerning Woman's original Creation. On this head the SPIRIT hath been singularly full and particular. Not only the manner of Woman's beginning, but the reason of it is expressly set down. The Man having been formed of the dust of the ground, inspired with the breath of life and made a living soul, is transferred to the Garden which "the LORD GOD had planted eastward in Eden" "to dress it and keep it." *There* he is taken into solemn covenant with God. But he is a unit in Creation. Whereupon it is declared that "it is not good that he shall be alone," and so the Creator announces His intention to "*make him a help meet for him.*" The announcement is presently repeated, as if in token that "the thing is established by GOD." And lo, from Adam's side, while he sleeps—"bone of his bone and flesh of his flesh,"—a Woman is "builded" and "brought unto the Man."

Behold then, at the very outset, the reason of Woman's creation distinctly assigned. She is intended to be Man's "help."—Man's *helper*. The expression "meet for him" implies that she is to be something corresponding to him, —a second self. Yet not a rival self: for, as the SPIRIT pointed out some 4000 years later, "the Man was not created for the Woman, *but the Woman for the Man:*" and from this very consideration the SPIRIT deduces Woman's inferiority.

But the disparity of the sexes is inferred by S[t]. Paul from every part of the record of Woman's Creation. "The Man," (says he) "is the image and glory of GOD: but the Woman is the glory of the Man. For the Man is not of the Woman, but the Woman of the Man." And in another place, —"Let the Woman learn in silence with all subjection. But I suffer not a Woman to teach, nor to usurp authority over the Man, but to be in silence. For Adam was first formed, then Eve. And" (glancing on to a subsequent incident which however still belongs to the history of Woman's earliest being)— "Adam was not deceived; but the Woman being deceived was in the transgression."

. . . Now I submit that the purport of all this is unmistakeable, and that the primaeval decree concerning Woman, so reproduced and enforced by fresh sanctions in the day of the Gospel, may never more be set aside without peril—peril to the best interests of either sex. I am not overlooking the solemn fact that to Woman under the Gospel is restored *that* honour, dignity and consideration by Eve's transgression Woman had forfeited under the Law. But it is much to be noted that S. Paul's teaching concerning Woman is built entirely on the narrative in Genesis: thus proving that the primaeval decree concerning her is a thing for all time. There has been no after thought, no reversal of the original relation of the sexes. Woman's relation to Man is still what it was in the beginning. . . .

. . . My ground for saying this is because I observe that S. Paul is obliged once and again, with something like sharpness, to rebuke the overeager self-assertion (as one is apt to regard it) of the other sex, waking up to a proud consciousness of their newly-recovered privilege; giddy (so to speak) at finding themselves set on such a pinnacle of honour. Hence those sayings of S. Paul of which I reminded you just now. "Let the woman learn in silence with all subjection." "I suffer not a woman to teach, nor to usurp authority over the man, but to be in silence." "Let your women keep silence in the Churches: for it is not permitted unto them to speak: but they are commanded to be under obedience, as also saith the Law. And if they will learn anything, let them ask their husbands at home: for it is a shame for a woman to speak in the Church." You will also remember S. Paul's . . . reason why women should wear a token of subjection on their heads in the congregation. His persistent requirement of subordination, submission, obedience, no one can forget.

. . . Thus then it appears that in the very dawn of Christianity it was found needful to repress forwardness of self-assertion in the other sex: while at the same time Woman's peculiar duties, her appointed sphere, her legitimate channel of influence and method of occupation were carefully prescribed. *Home* is clearly Woman's intended place;

and the duties which belong to Home are Woman's peculiar province. The primaeval decree will never lose its force while sun and moon endure, that Woman is designed to be Man's "help." And it is in the sweet sanctities of domestic life, in home duties, in whatever belongs to and makes the happiness of *Home,* that Woman is taught by the SPIRIT to find scope for her activity, to recognize her sphere of most appropriate service. "To guide the house;" and so to guide it as "to give none occasion to the adversary to speak reproachfully;" *this* is her province! *"To be a keeper at home;"* and so to keep *at* home as to be the Keeper *of* home, the Watcher *for* the home, as well: *this* is her duty! . . .

CHAPTER III

The Emergence of Feminism

The outbreak of the French Revolution in 1789, and the events which followed, provided the ideological foundations of the feminist movement. So far as the catchwords, Liberty, Equality, and Fraternity went, the last, it is true, with its uncompromisingly masculine gender, offered little encouragement to believers in women's rights, but the call to Liberty, and particularly to Equality, struck a chord in the militant bosom of Mary Wollstonecraft. If all men were equal, why not all women, and why not all men *and* women? Wollstonecraft's book, *A Vindication of the Rights of Woman,* published in 1792, had only limited circulation, but it marked the start of the agitation for equal rights which is still going on today.

Subsequently, socialists in France and England, such as Count Henri de Saint Simon and Robert Owen, in their attempts to form a society free of social injustice, explicitly charged that women were the chief victims of the economic exploitation and sexual degradation that were characteristic of the capitalist system. Socialists, therefore, at least in theory, were committed to a demand for the liberation of women from the bonds that oppressed them.

Although the abstract ideals of the French Revolution, and later, of socialist theorists, may have provided the ideological framework of feminism, its development in England was stimulated in particular by the change in the role of middle-class women brought about by the Industrial Revolution. Prior to the nineteenth century, practically all married women had made a significant economic contribution to their marriage — so much so, in fact, that a farmer or tradesman could literally not have successfully conducted his affairs had it not been for the efforts of his hard-working wife. Spinning and weaving, making candles, taking care of the farm animals, making butter and cheese, working beside him in the field, helping to conduct his business — these were some of the activities by which the wife materially aided her husband. But with the coming of the Industrial Revolution, many of the activities which had been performed within the household were now taken over by factories or entrepreneurs willing to provide these services. Consequently, the upper middle-class woman's economic significance diminished. It shrank still further with her increasingly greater reliance on domestic help, and with her husband's growing prosperity which reinforced his desire to demonstrate that he alone was the breadwinner.[1] Finally, with the emergence of an ethos which demanded that the lady of the house perform no useful function, and that she be merely an ornamental object testifying to her husband's wealth, this formerly useful member of society was reduced to the status of a parasite. An idle wife became, at least for those sufficiently affluent, a status symbol; work — particularly outside the home — came to be considered degrading and inconsistent with the role of the Victorian lady. As Mrs. Ellis noted, "if a lady does but touch any article no matter how delicate, in the way of trade, she loses caste, and ceases to be a lady".[2]

At the same time that the economic and social position of middle-class women was changing, momentous demographic changes were taking place in England. There had always been slightly more women than men; by the middle of the nineteenth century, because of emigration and the disinclination of men to marry at an early age, the discrepancy had grown.[3] In the decades that followed, the problem seemed to be getting worse. The census of 1851, for example, noted that for the age group 40—45, one-quarter of the women were unmarried. The *Westminster Review* in 1850 claimed that there were 500,000 "surplus women"; by 1882 an essayist alleged that there were a million more women than men.[4]

Disproportionately high numbers of these surplus women were middle-class,[5] and for that reason doomed, because in order to realize Victorian society's highest ideal, a middle-class woman first had to satisfy an all-important prerequisite: she had to find a husband. The Angel in the House had to be a married angel; preferably one with children. Conse-

---

[1] Patricia Branca in *Silent Sisterhood* points out that the woman of the lower middle class, aided normally by no more than a single servant, remained an active and contributing member of the household.

[2] Sarah Stickney Ellis, *The Women of England, their Social Duties and Domestic Habits* (New York: Edward Walker, 1850), p. 104.

[3] The disinclination of middle-class men to marry derived in part from the fact that after the Industrial Revolution, marriage no longer joined a husband and wife in an economic partnership; instead, a wife became a thing "to be afforded". A man might thus defer marriage, while the "girl who should be his mate withers unwanted in the 'upholstered cage' of her parents' home". M. A., *The Economic Foundations of the Women's Movement* (London: Fabian Society, 1914), p. 11. Also see "Excess of Widows over Widowers", *Westminster Review*, CXXXI (1889), 501-05.

[4] J. R. and Olive Banks, *Feminism and Family Planning*, p. 27; "Social Reform in England", *Westminster Review*, LXXXVII (1866), 161; Adelaide Ross, "Emigration for Women", *Macmillan's Magazine*, VL (1882), 314. Even if one concedes that these figures are imprecise (and probably exaggerated), there is no doubt that there was a statistically significant, hard core of unmarried women in the nineteenth century. Although some modern writers may question the fact, to contemporaries the problem was real enough.

[5] W. R. Greg, "Why are Women Redundant?" reprinted in *Literary and Social Judgments* (Boston: James R. Osgood & Co., 1873), p. 276; J. B. Mayor, "The Cry of the Women", *Contemporary Review*, XI (1869), 197. It was "a rare thing", noted Mayor, "to meet with an old maid" in the rural lower classes, due not only to the demand for domestic servants and sempstresses but, in addition, to the fact that "all the lower-class men marry, and marry early". Neither of these conditions, of course, existed for the upper classes.

quently, many women of impeccable middle-class status were relegated
to a kind of first circle on the periphery of society simply because they
had failed to acquire husbands and produce children. They were the
rejects, almost the outcasts, of Victorian society: the old maids who
were barely tolerated by prosperous relations and were stock figures in
Victorian literature. A society which decreed that matrimony and
motherhood were the criteria for acceptance had little room for females
who had failed to pass that test. It was a brutal fact of Victorian life
that these "surplus" or "redundant" women "who in place of completing,
sweetening, and embellishing the existence of others [were] compelled
to lead an independent and incomplete existence of their own"[1] had no
raison d'être.

The problem of the surplus middle-class woman could be stated simply: pairing off the available men and women would, since there were
more of the latter, leave an unassimilable balance of single females,
who could not expect to find mates in England. What was to be done
with them? Among the Swiftian solutions offered were polygamy and
infanticide. But, the *Westminster Review* noted, emigration was the
only practical remedy, since "we cannot put our 500,000 surplus women
to death".[2] The greater number of emigration societies, however, were
concerned with women of the working class. True, a few such societies
were formed to take care of the needs of redundant middle-class females,[3]
but in general they were ineffectual, largely because the objects of their
philanthrophy did not wish to leave home for the colonies. Genteel
poverty and a single existence in England seemed preferable to the unknown fate which awaited them in Australia, Canada, or New Zealand.

As a result of their rejection of emigration as a remedy, there were
large numbers of gentlewomen whose precarious economic existence
forced them to earn their own livings in a society which provided no real
economic opportunity for them. Even those whose material needs were
taken care of were sometimes driven by a sense of frustration and futility

[1] Greg, "Why are Women Redundant?" in *Literary and Social Judgments*, p. 276. In 1870 at a meeting
of the Victoria Discussion Society, the following statement attributed to a contemporary writer was cited
approvingly: "A woman is positively and distinctly created that she may become a wife and mother. If
she misses this destiny, there is something wrong somewhere. . . . You may make an old maid, or a nun, or
a nurse all her life of her; but if you do, she is *quâ* woman, a failure, whatever great and noble things she
may do". See the remarks of J. McGrigor Allan, "A Protest Against Woman's Demand for the Privileges of
Both Sexes", *Victoria Magazine*, XV (1870), 321.

[2] "Social Reform in England", p. 161.

[3] The efforts of Maria Rye and Jane Lewin are particularly noteworthy. Miss Rye, one of the original
founders of the Society for Promoting the Employment of Women (see p. 144) came to believe that emigration rather than employment would be a more effective cure for the problem of the "redundant woman".
Miss Rye founded in 1862 the Female Middle Class Emigration Society whose specific aim was to encourage
the emigration of educated women. After 1869 Miss Lewin, who from the first had been active in this
cause, continued the work of the Society. In addition, other emigration societies were founded; one of
them, the Women's Emigration Society, also made efforts to assist educated women, but the problems
associated with such an endeavor were, of course, numerous. See, for example, "On Female Emigration",
National Association for the Promotion of Social Science, Transactions, 1862, pp. 811-13; Adelaide Ross,
"Emigration for Women", *Macmillan's Magazine*, VL (1882), 312-17.

to demand some constructive outlet for their energy and talents. "Why, oh, my God", wrote young Florence Nightingale, "cannot I be satisfied with the life that satisfies so many people? . . . Why am I starving, desperate, diseased on it? . . . My God what am I to do?"[1]

Such frustration drove some middle-class single women to embark on a campaign of education and pressure designed to force their male-dominated society to permit the participation of unmarried women — and married women who no longer had family responsibilities — in activities which had become virtually a masculine monopoly. Thus, it was not a coincidence that the feminist movement arose in the late 1850's and 60's, precisely the time both when demographic changes prevented thousands of women from filling the role of wife and mother, and when new social ideals had robbed many middle-class women of the satisfaction of being economically useful.[2]

There were, of course, comparatively few who could be classified as feminists.[3] Most women, either out of resignation, passivity, or contentment, did not aspire to an active and independent life. Bessie Rayner Parkes, Jessie Boucherett, Frances Power Cobbe, and Emily Davies, were exceptions — single, middle-class activists who shared a common concern for ameliorating the condition of women. Not surprisingly, in view of the large numbers of unmarriageable females, the efforts of these feminists were directed, in particular, toward alleviating the plight of single women. Furthermore, the unmarried woman, rather than the married one, was usually the target of feminist concern because a majority of these reformers accepted the conventional view that a married woman's first priority must be her husband and children.

To a traditionalist like W. R. Greg, author of a widely-read article, "Why are Women Redundant?" spinsterhood was an abomination, celibacy was an unnatural state, and the life of the unmarried (both men and women) was "essentially unsound, unstable, and the source of immeasureable wretchedness and mischief".[4] Consequently, attempts to invest the life of the single female with purpose and dignity, to prepare her for a useful role in society, and to create for her a meaningful and satisfactory existence, were bound to fail because they were hopelessly wrong-

[1] Cited in Cecil Woodham-Smith, *Florence Nightingale* (New York: McGraw-Hill Book Company, Inc., 1951), p. 59. Miss Nightingale, however, later became satisfied with her personal achievement of a meaningful existence, and did not become an active feminist. On the contrary, she once described herself as being "brutally indifferent to the wrongs or the rights of my sex". *Ibid.,* p. 217.

[2] The comments of Bessie Rayner Parkes on the emergence of feminism are instructive. While acknowledging the theoretical foundations of the woman's movement, Miss Parkes emphasized that "except for the material need which exerted a constant pressure over a large and educated class, the 'woman's movement' could never have become in England a subject of popular comment, and to a certain extent of popular sympathy". *Essays on Woman's Work,* 2nd ed. (London: Alexander Strahan Publisher, 1865), p. 55.

[3] According to the *Oxford Universal English Dictionary*, the term feminism, in the sense of "advocacy of the claims and rights of women", was not in use until 1895. Ellis Ethelmer in 1898 attributed the word to the French who, "in their facile tongue have assigned the fitting and comprehensive title of 'Feminisme' " to the movement for establishing the equality of the sexes. "Feminism", *Westminster Review,* CIL (1898), 59.

[4] Greg, "Why are Women Redundant?" in *Literary and Social Judgments,* p. 299.

headed and were founded on a grotesque misconception of woman's nature, abilities, and needs. The only acceptable career for women, in short, was marriage—if not at home, then in the colonies.[1]

But feminists spurned the assumption that woman's significance could be understood solely in relation to man, and that her only fulfillment could come through family life. In short, they rejected the notion that "man and woman are two halves of a perfect whole which cannot be divided without injury—that neither he nor she, standing apart from each other, have any integral completeness in his or her nature."[2] Not at all, said the rebels; married life was not the sole life worth living; an independent existence *was* compatible with womanhood.[3] Fortified with this conviction, they proceeded to demonstrate it by working to improve education, public health, reformatories, housing, and workhouses, giving a dramatic demonstration of woman's capacity to take her place beside men and, in some cases, actually to excel them in these fields. Some of the more ardent spirits went beyond this to advocate the employment of women in the private sector and actually to open some occupations to them. Others were drawn inevitably into regarding the vote as the *sine qua non* for the emancipation of women.

It should be pointed out, however, that these middle-class ladies were not the only women who could be described as feminists. Certainly, despite the limited nature of their objectives, the anonymous working-class women who formed Female Reform Societies in 1818 and 1819, or Female Political Unions and Female Charter Unions in the late 1830's, are entitled to be regarded as early feminists. There were, in addition, feminists whose advocacy of women's rights cut across sex and class lines. Early nineteenth-century socialists, for example, whether Owenites or Saint-Simonians, agitated for the political equality of women and their economic liberation. Their desire to transform society demanded not only the establishment of a new economic system but also the destruction of institutions such as marriage which, they believed, served only to perpetuate the subjection of wives to their husbands. Later nineteenth-century English socialists, both Marxist and Fabian, continued to advance feminist ideas.

In the light of the wide doctrinal spectrum of those engaged in the battle for women's rights, it is obviously simplistic to speak of a feminist "movement", with the implication that those who sought a change in woman's role were attempting to achieve a coherent and consistent program. Although they all championed women's emancipation, their

---

[1] *Ibid.*, pp. 274-308.

[2] "Social Reform in England", p. 163.

[3] A strong supporter of this view was the Christian Socialist, Charles Kingsley, who pointed out (in "Women and Politics", *Macmillan's Magazine*, XX [1869], 561), that a lady might choose to remain unmarried for a variety of reasons, including the possibility that "she will not degrade herself by marrying for marrying's sake".

ideologies and objectives were not identical.[1] Staunch middle-class advocates of women's rights such as Bessie Rayner Parkes or Barbara Leigh Smith Bodichon, who sought to expand educational and employment opportunities for women, would have been as shocked as was the rest of conventional society at the radical feminism of an Eleanor Marx Aveling, who, true to the beliefs of her famous father, insisted that woman's emancipation could never be achieved within the framework of the existing social and economic system. Even among those individuals who shared a common goal — to provide an alternative to the sterile ideal of Victorian womanhood — there was a difference of opinion regarding the extent to which women should be admitted to equal status with men. Thus, an Octavia Hill, passionately committed to raising the economic and moral standards of the lower classes, remained unconvinced that women needed the vote. On the other hand, Lydia Becker, coming from the same background and equally dedicated, not only felt that women had to have the vote but, in fact, claimed that the future of society depended upon it.

The tendency of all these women, regardless of their various outlooks and their differing stands on such questions as female suffrage, was to move out of the narrow sphere usually reserved to the female sex and into the theatre of social action. Anyone observing them might be influenced, if not compelled, to accept the claims for female equality which John Stuart Mill was shortly to express in the most persuasive feminist argument of the nineteenth century, *The Subjection of Women* (1869). In this work Mill stated his fervent conviction that the principle of "subordination of one sex to the other" was "wrong in itself, . . . and that it ought to be replaced by a principle of perfect equality. . . ."[2]

"With the Emancipation of Women Will Come the Emancipation of the Useful Class", *The Crisis*, June 15, 1833.

Anna Wheeler, an ardent champion of female emancipation in the early nineteenth century, was a beautiful and brilliant woman, the god-child of the Irish nationalist Henry Grattan, the mother-in-law of the novelist Bulwer Lytton, a close friend of Bentham and the socialists Robert Owen — whom she introduced to Fourier — and Saint Simon. She was particularly close to William Thompson, a fierce defender of feminist principles, who in the course of a debate with James Mill in 1825, published what may be regarded as the earliest explicit statement in favor of the extension of political rights to English women. His daring

[1] Bessie Rayner Parkes, among others, noted the divisions. "We must not be surprised to find that a marked diversity of practical aims has existed among the supporters of what has been generally known as the woman's movement, or that it should be quite impossible to draw up any definite programme of what they wanted or strove to attain". *Essays on Woman's Work*, p. 8.

[2] John Stuart Mill, *The Subjection of Women*, in *Essays on Sex Equality*, edited by Alice S. Rossi (Chicago and London: The University of Chicago Press, 1970), p. 125.

proposal stemmed from both his socialist and utilitarian views, and was strengthened by his friendship with Mrs. Wheeler, to whom he freely acknowledged his intellectual indebtedness. Indeed, Thompson wrote, his ideas were their "joint property", he was her "interpreter and the scribe of [her] sentiments", and the *Appeal* thus represented "the protest of at least one man and one woman".[1] With Mrs. Wheeler, Thompson believed that the highest type of society—one that would assure to women "an equality of happiness with men"—would be established on the principle of mutual cooperation, not on individual competition; it would be a society founded on benevolence, not on fear. Even within the framework of the existing imperfect social and economic order, Thompson maintained, removal of civil and political disabilities ("the rubbish of ignorant restrictions . . . which restrain women")[2] would be easy to rectify—all that was needed was for men to be willing to confer on women equal rights.

In lectures to socialist and cooperative groups, Mrs. Wheeler called for the provision of equal access to education, the abolition of the double sexual standard, and the granting to women of civil and political rights equal to those of men, including the vote. In addition, she opposed traditional religion and rejected the institution of marriage.

The following selection from a French woman's periodical, *La Femme Libre*, was translated by Mrs. Wheeler and published in *The Crisis*, Robert Owen's weekly, one of the few publications that would give the subject of emancipation a hearing. It presents the Saint-Simonian indictment of the exploitation of women and calls for their emancipation.

When the whole of the people are roused in the name of Liberty, and . . . the labouring class demand their freedom, shall we women remain passive and inert spectators of this great movement of social emancipation, which takes place under our eyes?

Is our condition as women so happy that there is nothing left for us to *desire* or to *demand?* Up to the present hour, have not women through all past ages been degraded, oppressed, and made the *property* of men? *This property in women,* and the consequent tyranny it engenders, ought now to cease. We are born as free as men—their infancy is as helpless as ours, and ours as theirs. Without our tenderness, our sympathy and care, they could never grow up to be our oppressors, and, but through the most blind and barbarous injustice; one-half the human race cannot be made THE SERVANTS *of the other.* Let us then understand our rights—let us also understand our powers—and let us learn how to employ *usefully* the intelligence and the attractions that nature has bestowed upon us. *Let us reject as a husband any man* who is not sufficiently generous to consent to share with us all the rights he himself enjoys. We will no longer accept this *form* of marraige, "Wives submit *yourselves* to your husbands." We *demand equal marriage laws*—preferring infinitely a state of celibacy *to one of slavery.* We feel and know that *nature* has made us the equals of men, and that an

[1] William Thompson, *Appeal of One Half the Human Race, Women, Against the Pretensions of the Other Half, Men* (1825), pp. vii, ix. Burt Franklin Reprint, 1970.
[2] *Ibid.*, p. xiv.

ignorantly contrived social system, *vicious in principle and practice,* has cunningly restricted the development of our intellectual, moral, and physical faculties, in order to deprive us of our social rights. . . .

Honour to those generous men [who have proclaimed the equality of women]—a halo of glory awaits them in the new world! Let us unite our voice with theirs and demand our rights as citizens. . . . Universal association has already commenced; from henceforth all nations shall be united by ties of brotherly love, by industry, science, and morals. The future will be eminently pacific—no more war, no more national antipathies; love, and sympathy, and kindness will be the all-pervading sentiment. The reign of harmony and peace will establish itself throughout the earth, and the time is arrived when woman shall find *her place,* her acknowledged, her useful, and *dignified* place upon it. *Liberty* and *equality;* that is to say, the free and equal chance of developing *all our faculties.*

This is the glorious conquest we have to make, and this we cannot effect, but on condition of forming ourselves into *one solid union.* Let us no longer form two camps — that of the women of the people, and that of the women of the privileged class. Let our *common interest* unite us to obtain this *great* end. Let all jealousy disappear from amongst us. Let us *honour worth,* and give place to superior talent and capacity, at whatever side it may appear.

Women of the privileged class—those amongst you who are young, beautiful, and rich, and who think yourselves happy, when in your splendid *salons* you breathe the incense of flattery, which all around are interested lavishly to bestow upon you—you fancy yourselves queens, but your reign is of short duration; it ends with the ball! When you return home you are slaves, you find there a *master* who makes *you feel his power,* and you soon forget all the evanescent pleasures of the feast. Women of every class, you have a noble part to perform—you are called upon to spread the principles of order and harmony everywhere. Then turn to the advantage of *society at large* the fascination of your talents and the influence of your beauty—the sweetness of your words will carry conviction with them and induce men themselves to follow you in the attainment of your glorious object.

Come and inspire the people with a holy enthusiasm for the great work which is in preparation—come and regulate and calm the warlike ardor of our young men. The elements of grandeur and true glory are in their hearts, but they have a false notion of their principles, they conceive glory and honour to consist in having a helmet on their head, and a sword in their hand. It is for *us* to tell them that the distinctive system must terminate, that the social edifice must be re-built, and that everything must become new. The Roman ladies awarded crowns of laurel to their warriors; we will weave wreaths of flowers to bind the brows of those *moral* and *pacific men* who shall *lead* on *humanity* in its *social* progress, and who shall enrich our globe by science and industry.

"An Outline of the Grievances of Women", *Metropolitan Magazine,* XXII (1838), 16-27.

The following article, an early and eloquent demand for equality, was given a great deal of advance publicity and aroused a bitter debate. The writer identifies herself as a woman, but nothing beyond that basic fact is known of her. It was widely attributed to the notorious Caroline Norton, whose marital misadventures had only recently scandalized respectable opinion, but she vigorously denied she was its author. (See pp. 180 and 239-40).

It is easy to see why sensitive and intelligent women, in a decade which had witnessed such remarkable concessions to the demands of various groups as the Catholic Emancipation Act, the Reform Act of 1832, the abolition of slavery in the colonies, and the Factory Acts, should be moved to demand that something be done for them.

"Equal rights, equal privileges, and equal laws."

At a period when the divine right of kings is a doctrine no longer tenable; when the power of a dominant aristocracy totters to its foundation; when an imperious presthood is on the eve of losing its usurped temporal power; and when the right of the people to civil and religious liberty is generally recognised; in the nineteenth century, and in one of the most civilized countries of Europe, half the population is still enslaved! the women of England—the mothers, wives, and daughters of "free-born Britons," are still forced to bend under a yoke more galling than that of the negro—a yoke which enthrals the mind! Degraded, despised, and scorned, —scorned even by those to whom they have given existence, whom they have tended with unwearied care during the helpless hours of infancy—for whom they have suffered so much and endured so many privations, —for whom they have laboured, nay, sacrificed themselves: the career of women is, with very few exceptions, marked by disappointment and sorrow, and too frequently closed in hapless despair. Denied the privileges granted to the meanest citizen, trampled upon in every relation of life, retained in profound ignorance of all, excepting religion, *that* can ennoble human nature, and only instructed in that so far as it may render them obedient slaves—they have rarely dared to think themselves the equals of those who now lord it over them, and all the exalted sentiments of their nature are subdued, and all their high and holy enthusiasm is quenched by a blind submission to those whose only title to power is a superiority in mere physical strength, and who make that superiority a plea for excluding the weaker portion of the human species from all employments, and condemning them to inactivity and servitude. . . .

. . . Have we never heard that "who would be free, himself must break the chain", and shall we any longer hesitate to wrench asunder one of the links of ours? Do we expect from others—from our masters— that justice which we refuse to struggle for ourselves? and can we hope that they whose interest it is to keep us slaves, will ever voluntarily concede to us the prerogatives of free citizens—will acknowledge our equality with themselves, or recognise our rights as human beings?

It will not be much longer possible, in a highly cultivated state of society, to prevent some gleams of knowledge from penetrating the thick darkness of female ignorance; and when that darkness is dispelled, women will learn to reflect on the position they occupy. They know that one prejudice after another has been abandoned; that one proscribed race after another has been made free, and they will at length inquire why they alone are to remain enslaved?—and when they remember that the barriers are now thrown down which excluded from a participation in social and political privileges, all who differed with their rulers in religion, colour, or nation; and rejoice that the Catholic and the Dissenter are placed, as citizens, on a footing of equality with the dominant religious sect—that the Hindoo and the Mulatto are entrusted with important and responsible offices, and that even the negro is legally entitled (if he be competent) to hold them; and when they see the last and strongest prejudice— the prejudice in favour of rank destroyed, and men of the humblest birth and meanest fortune the successful competitors of the richest and the noblest—they will ask why they should any longer submit to be deprived of a voice in the public affairs of their country?

I fearlessly ask if the women of this country are inferior to the men either in patriotism, in honour, or in honesty? Are they inferior in moral courage, in fidelity, or in political consistency? "Perhaps not; but they are inferior in ability and in knowledge." With sorrow I confess that at present they are deficient in knowledge, but that they are so in ability I deny. Have they ever been tried? On the contrary, have they not been systematically kept in ignorance—and has not every imaginable means been resorted to, in order to perpetuate that ignorance? I say it, and I say it boldly, that there is no post of trust, no important office, for which women are not naturally as well qualified as men. Every employment should therefore be open to them—no favour should be shown, and if they fail, let them incur the penalty of their incompetence. . . .

. . . Surely it requires no great genius to fulfil the duties of an overseer, of a member of the vestry, of a parish clerk, of a guardian of the poor, of a burgess, or of a parliamentary elector? When we see the hands into which these offices and trusts are thrown, we cannot suppose it is from incapacity, but from jealousy, that women are excluded from them. . . .

It is sometimes suggested, that women are adequately represented by their fathers, brothers, and husbands; and—passing by the cases in which a woman has no relation who can represent her interest—the suggestion has a slight show of plausibility, until we recollect that points are frequently discussed by the legislature, which affect women not only in their quality as citizens, but also in their distinctive character as females.

Did women constitute a portion of the senate, would not the unjust laws respecting property be abolished? would they continue after marriage in a state of perpetual tutelage? Still less, would acts have been allowed to pass which exonerate one sex from burdens which are heaped tenfold on the other?

When we reflect on these things, it will *not* require any extraordinary sagacity to discover that women are not represented by men. But another objection yet remains to be answered.

It is contended that the *influence* women are supposed to possess, both at home and in society, is so great, that it is unnecessary to grant them political privileges, since they already enjoy a power equally strong. . . . This view of the subject appears to me to be totally false. Not only is *influence* no compensation for being retained in a state of bondage, but female influence, as it is generally exercised, is positively and extensively hurtful.

Who are the influential amongst women? Not the sensible, the modest, and the discreet; but the woman of fashion, the youthful beauty, and the irreclaimably vicious, either in temper or morals. By all of these, an influence is exercised, pernicious in every way—pernicious from its leading away the young from the severe paths of duty to the pleasanter scenes of gaiety and amusement—pernicious from its allowing passion too frequently to take the place of reason—pernicious also, because it is an influence which is subject to no responsibility, to no control, which is often exercised capriciously, and dictated merely by the whim of the moment. . . .

Are any of my fair readers displeased with this view of their boasted influence? If they are, let them unite in repudiating it. Let them endeavour to exchange an irresponsible and pernicious influence for the free and legitimate exercise of constitutional rights, and let them use every available means to accomplish that object — the first and most important step towards their complete social regeneration.

"But what are the means to be employed to bring about this change?" They are simple — for they are comprised in two words, education and agitation.

(1.) To the momentous subject of education, the attention of all those is directed who are looking forward with hope to the emancipation of their countrywomen. . . . [*Editors' note: At this point the author discusses in some detail the frivolous curriculum typical of a fashionable girls' boarding school, pointing out that it is the lack of education which has reduced women to a position of inferiority. Women, the author notes, do not suffer from mental incapacity; rather, their mental powers simply die from disuse.*]

(2.) The second instrument to be employed to effect our social regeneration is agitation. It comprises active and passive resistance.

The active means of agitation we possess are chiefly derived from the press. Through the medium of that noble assistant to liberty, we ought to accomplish great things. Discussion, in this country, thank God! is free. . . .

Why do [women] not use the means that are open to them? Why do they not profit by the facility of publication, to send forth works devoted to the cause of female improvement and emancipation? Let them follow the example of political and religious partisans, and take advantage of every occurrence which can be brought to bear on their present condition. Let them conduct journals and other periodical publications expressly devoted to that object. Let not a circumstance escape them. The ordinary events of the world afford abundant materials. Facts are daily made public, which render sufficiently evident the injustice that women sustain at the hands of men in every relation of their lives. But no single person can effect this. It requires a combined and a strenuous effort — a general devotion to the cause — of the cultivated minds and the splendid fortunes, which are now dissipated in all manner of frivolous vanities.

It is not difficult to combine the energies of a nation. . . . And what a force have we in our immense numbers! No other party consists, as ours does, of half the population of the country! If we are individually weak, we are collectively strong. Union and association are therefore pre-eminently necessary for us. The very appearance of combination in a sex deemed incapable of moral energy would produce an extraordinary effect. Those who now laugh at the idea of female emancipation, would find their mirth suddenly checked, when they saw associations of enlightened and determined women springing up in every town and village, and numbering thousands and tens of thousands amongst their numbers. Even those most opposed to our views would be unable to close their eyes to the fact, that when women systematically begin to investigate their grievances, a great social revolution is at hand, and the tyranny of sex is nearly over. The instant we resolve to be free, our emancipation is half accomplished. The right to petition the legislature is, I believe, not denied us. Why do we not exercise that right to lay our complaints before Parliament? Let us not be abashed at the thought of the sneers that would follow the presentation of such petition — if indeed members could be found honest enough to present them. Better endure a sneer for doing too much than for doing too little. . . .

I now come to speak of the passive resistance, which is a principal means of agitation. The principle has been laid down, that "those who are not represented in the state are not bound to contribute to its burthens." I think I have shown that women are not

represented, and why should they not use the same means that have proved so successful in the case of the oppressed, both in England and in Ireland? What has passive
resistance not done for the Catholics and the Dissenters? Would they have obtained
the remission of even a fraction of their grievances, if their refusal to pay tithes, church-
rates, and other equally obnoxious imposts, had not made our *just* and *wise* hereditary
legislators fear for themselves?

In conclusion, then, let me call on my dear countrywomen no longer to remain voluntary slaves. I have endeavoured in this brief sketch to present an outline of the enormity
of their grievances—I have shown that the means of redress are easy, that it remains
with themselves to use those means, and that they cannot fail of success if they only are
united. Let them not allow opportunities to pass unheeded—let them commence this
great work without delay; and though hope may be so long deferred that "the heart is
sick," let them never forget that it was one of their own sex who took for her motto the
words—"*Nil desperandum.*"

"Female Politicians", *English Chartist Circular,* no. 90 (1842).

The Chartists' pleas for political reforms in the 1830's and 1840's were
indicative of the grievances of a large part of the urban working classes,
both men and women. William Lovett, the author of "The People's
Charter," favored getting the vote for both sexes, but his view was not
typical. Consequently, despite the fact that the suggestion was made—
at least initially—to include women in the demand for the franchise,
that recommendation was not incorporated into the formal Chartist
program; the first of the "six points" of the Charter became an explicit
demand for universal *male* suffrage. Although the Chartists had become formally committed to votes for men, they were supported by hundreds of women who were enrolled in the National Charter Association.
In 1848, with the presentation to the House of Commons of the third
and last Chartist petition, it was said that "in every 100,000 names there
were 8,200 women".[1] Articles in Chartist newspapers frequently reminded wives of their responsibility to encourage their husbands to
become active members of their local Chartist associations, and to co-
operate and assist them in their task.[2] Some Chartists felt that women
ought to play a more active role since they had grievances peculiarly
their own, such as wages lower than those paid men for the same work.[3]
On the other hand, some male Chartists felt compelled to warn women
that the political arena was hardly a suitable place for female activities;
women should rather continue to be "the pride and ornament of the
domestic hearth".[4] Nevertheless, Chartist women organized themselves

---

[1] Preston William Slossom, *The Decline of the Chartist Movement* (New York: Columbia University
Press, 1916), p. 207.

[2] See, for example, "To the Females of the Metropolis and its Vicinity", *English Chartist Circular,* no. 86
(1842).

[3] "Female Slaves of England", *English Chartist Circular,* no. 94 (1842).

[4] The remarks of a Mr. Cohen, paraphrased in "Meeting of Female Chartists", *The Times,* October 20,
1842, demonstrate the fact that there were people among the lower classes who were influenced by the
Angel-in-the-House stereotype.

into a number of Female Chartist Associations which passed resolutions
favoring suffrage for women.   The following selection, taken from a
Chartist newspaper, is a revealing example of working-class feminism
in the 1840's.

The *Times* of Saturday, in a lame attempt to ridicule a meeting of female Chartists,
has a coarse exordium upon the absurdity of women taking a part in politics. Every
filthy suggestion which the writer dare make (for there are some limits of decency
within which the *Times* must confine itself) he has made . . . "A meeting of hen-
Chartists," is the sentence in which the *Times* has put forth its power as a delicate
satirist . . . and ere long we shall not be surprised to read from the same hand a description of our gracious Queen as a "hen monarch.". . .

We do not design to discuss the question insinuated by the *Times,* as to the propriety of clothing women with political rights; although we confess not to perceive the
absurdity of such a question in a country where a woman, by law and constitution,
fills the highest political office in the realm — the office of chief magistrate. But of the
right of woman to exercise her volition as to how, when, and where she shall employ
her faculties . . . to promote what she believes to be the interests of her fellow-creatures,
we . . . have [not] the slightest doubt. . . .   Of the exact mode in which this right
should be exercised, we believe woman herself to be the best judge. To the promptings
of her own heart and intellect we would leave the decision; and, whether it be in private or public, through the press or on the platform, by works of charity or of zeal,
that she seeks to vindicate her claim to aid in the moral, social, or political advancement of mankind, she is entitled, not merely to the most respectful and considerate
treatment, but to the encouragement of sincere and active sympathy. If it could be
shown, by argument or testimony, that woman never suffered from bad legislation, or
the partial arrangements of society; if it could be shown that the law which deprives
man of food, brings no such penalty to woman — that of the thousands whose intellects
have been stunted, limbs crippled, or lives shortened, in the mine, the factory, and the
prison, woman formed no portion, then we might be inclined to listen with more com-
placency to those who challenge her right to meddle with political and social institutions. But it is too manifest that no such exception awaits the lot of women here. By
the laws of man and nature she is subjected to the common perils of humanity, and we
know of no mortal law which forbids her to assume the commonest of her rights. . . .

As far as the political movement is concerned to which we are attached, we have not
thought fit to act in the spirit of the *Times,* and repudiate the assistance of women.
On the contrary, we have sought their cooperation, and hundreds of women are enrolled as members of the National Charter Association. And if that association were originated, as we know it was for the holy purposes of redeeming the millions of this country from the want and degradation into which wicked rulers have plunged them, we
did right in thus enlisting the cooperation of woman; for no great benevolent or religious movement has taken place in this country for the last fifty years which has not
been sustained and cheered and promoted by her. Every mission to evangelise the
heathen; to carry the glad tidings of salvation to him that was in darkness and the
shadow of death; to educate, elevate, and civilise the barbarian; she has assisted with
purse and in person. Not an effort has been made to shake off the fetters of the negro
to which she did not largely contribute; and now in America, as formerly here, she is
the steady champion of negro emancipation. . . .   The motives which urged woman

on these great occasions to pass the threshold of her home and mingle in the arena of a more public life, cannot be wanting now, when the slavery of her own country is to be redeemed, and the ignorance of her own land to be enlightened. Such wretched and servile tools as the editors of the *Times* are ever ready to caluminate [sic] and ridicule every wise and virtuous and benevolent enterprise. But the shafts of calumny and ridicule are impotent against a strong conviction of well-doing, and no human being can be more deeply imbued with this conviction than the woman who participates according to the impulses of her nature and the circumstances of her position, in the truly christian, albeit political, movement which is now going on.

We remember a former exhibition in the *Times* of the truculent humour which we have just exposed. Several thousand women, headed by Mrs. Cobden and Mrs. Massie, met in Manchester, to petition for a repeal of the Corn Laws. The *Times* denounced them as "monsters;" told them to read their prayer-books and keep to their nurseries; and, if they presumed to close the one or step out of the other, to uphold the Corn Law Agitation, they should be annihilated by the thunder of Printing-house Square. To make puddings and dust chimney ornaments is the whole duty of woman in the opinion of this public instructor, this oracle of the press; to whom, however, we commend the reply of a witty Frenchwoman to the Emperor Napoleon, "What have women to do with politics?" exclaimed he. "Sire," replied the lady, "in a country where women are guillotined for political offences, it is but natural that they should inquire the reason." And we take the liberty of adding, that in a country where women are taxed by the state, fined by the state, imprisoned by the state, starved by the state, and liable to be hung, drawn and quarted by the state, it is not altogether unreasonable that they should ask why. — And if once they ask that question, the answer will lead them far beyond the narrow region of exclusive politics, and conventional morality.

Frances Power Cobbe, "The Final Cause of Woman", in *Woman's Work and Woman's Culture,* edited by Josephine E. Butler (London: Macmillan & Co., 1869), pp. 1-26.

Frances Power Cobbe, whose family were prominent members of the Anglo-Irish establishment (there were five archbishops and a bishop among her relations), was interested in a wide range of social, ethical, political, and humanitarian causes. In addition to publishing a number of her own works on religious subjects, she edited the fourteen-volume works of the celebrated American divine, Theodore Parker. For a while she worked with the well-known philanthropist, Mary Carpenter, in the reformatory and ragged school movements, and subsequently ministered to sick and neglected girls. Her concern for the helpless was not confined to humans; she was a founder of the National Anti-Vivisection Society and, later, the British Union for the Abolition of Vivisection. Her activities on behalf of women included speaking before the London Woman's Suffrage Committee, publishing pamphlets on various aspects of the "Woman Question" (including one, "The Fitness of Women for the Ministry of Religion", which has a very modern sound), and initiating efforts in support of the admission of women to university degrees. Miss Cobbe was an outspoken critic of Victorian male supremacy and an ardent defender of women's rights. Blessed with a trenchant style and a biting wit, she exposed with merciless clarity the fallacies of those who asserted that woman was an inferior being who should aspire to no higher destiny than that of wife and mother. Regarding the notion that man alone was made for God's service (with its inevitable corollary that woman was made merely to serve man) as "a great moral heresy" and an "abominable and ridiculous doctrine", Miss Cobbe continually urged women to remember that they were not *"first, women,* and then, perhaps, rational creatures, but first of all *human beings,* and then, secondly, women".[1] In this selection, she indicates precisely what she considers a meaningful goal for women.

Of all the theories current concerning women, none is more curious than the theory that it is needful to make a theory about them. That a woman is a Domestic, a Social, or a Political creature; that she is a Goddess, or a Doll; the "Angel in the House," or a Drudge, with the suckling of fools and chronicling of small beer for her sole privileges; that she has, at all events, a "Mission," or a "Sphere," or a "Kingdom," of some sort or other, if we could but agree on what it is, — all this is taken for granted. But as nobody ever yet sat down and constructed analogous hypotheses about the other half of the human race, we are driven to conclude, both that a woman is a more mysterious creature than a man, and also that it is the general impression that she is made of some more plastic material, which can be advantageously manipulated to fit our theory about her nature and office, whenever we have come to a conclusion as to what that nature and office may be. "Let us fix our own Ideal in the first place," seems to be the popular notion, "and then the real Woman in accordance thereto will appear in due course of time. We have nothing to do but to make round holes, and women will grow round to fill them; or square holes, and they will become square. Men grow like trees, and the most we can do is to lop or clip them. But women run in moulds, like candles, and we can make them long-threes or short-sixes, whichever we please."

Now, with some exaggeration, there must be admitted to be a good deal of truth in this view. The ideal of each successive age, as Mr. Lecky has so admirably shown, has an immense influence in forming the character of the people by whom it is adopted. . . .

In a certain modified sense, then, the "mould" theory has its justification. It would undoubtedly be beneficial to have some generally recognised types of female excellence. But, on the other hand, we must not fall into the absurdity of supposing that all women can be adapted to one single type, or that we can talk about "Woman" (always to be written with a capital W) as if the same characteristics were to be found in every individual species, like "the Lioness" and "the Pea-hen." They would have been very stiff *corsets* indeed which could have compressed Catharine of Russia into Hannah More, or George Sand into the authoress of the "Heir of Redclyffe;" or which would have turned out Mary Carpenter as a "Girl of the Period". . . .

The first Order of types or conceptions of female character are those which are based on the theory that the final cause of the existence of Woman is the service she can render to Man. They may be described as "The types of Woman, considered as an Adjective."

The second Order comprehends those conceptions which are based on the theory

[1] Frances Power Cobbe, *The Duties of Women* (London and Edinburgh: Williams & Norgate, 1888), p. 50.

FRANCES POWER COBBE, 1894
Reproduced by Courtesy of the Fawcett Collection, London

ANNA D. WHEELER   Drawn on Stone by M. Gauci
Reproduced by Courtesy of the Fawcett Collection, London

APPEAL

OF

ONE HALF THE HUMAN RACE,

WOMEN,

AGAINST

THE PRETENSIONS OF THE OTHER HALF,

MEN,

TO RETAIN THEM IN POLITICAL, AND THENCE
IN CIVIL AND DOMESTIC, SLAVERY;

IN REPLY TO A PARAGRAPH OF MR. MILL'S CELE-
BRATED "ARTICLE ON GOVERNMENT."

———

By WILLIAM THOMPSON,

AUTHOR OF "AN INQUIRY INTO THE DISTRIBUTION OF WEALTH."

———

" One thing is pretty clear, that all those individuals whose interests
" are indisputably included in those of other individuals may be struck
" off from political rights without inconvenience. In this light may be
" viewed all children up to a certain age, whose interests are involved in
" those of their parents. In this light also women may be regarded, the
" interest of almost all of whom is involved either in that of their fathers,
" or in that of their husbands."—*Encyclopædia Britannica : Supplement :
Article on 'Government,'* page 500.

" 'Tis all stern duty on the female side ;
On man's, mere sensual gust and surly pride."

LONDON:

PRINTED FOR LONGMAN, HURST, REES, ORME, BROWN, AND
GREEN, PATERNOSTER-ROW ; AND WHEATLEY AND ADLARD,
108, STRAND : AND SOLD AT THE LONDON CO-OPERATIVE
SOCIETY'S OFFICE, 18, PICKETT-STREET, TEMPLE-BAR.

———

1825.

TITLE PAGE FOR THE BOOK
Reproduced by courtesy of the Fawcett Collection, London

(BESSIE RAYNER PARKES) MADAM BELLOC   After a daguerreotype
Reproduced by courtesy of the Fawcett Collection, London

that Woman was created for some end proper to herself. They may be called "The types of Woman, considered as a Noun."

In the first Order we find Woman in her Physical, her Domestic, and her Social capacity: or Woman as Man's Wife and Mother; Woman as Man's Housewife; and Woman as Man's Companion, Plaything or Idol. . . .

The theory about woman which we have called the Physical, is simply this: That the whole meaning and reason of her existence is, that she may form a link in the chain of generations, and fulfil the functions of wife to one man and mother to another. Her moral nature is a sort of superfluity according to this view, and her intellectual powers a positive hindrance. How such things came to be given her is unexplained. Her affections alone are useful, but the simpler ones of the mother-beast and bird would probably be more convenient. In a word, everything which enables a woman to attract conjugal love, and to become the parent of a numerous and healthful progeny, must be reckoned as constituting her proper endowment. Everything which distracts her attention or turns her faculties in other directions than these, must be treated as mischievous, and as detracting from her merits. The woman who has given birth to a son has fulfilled her "mission." The celibate woman,—be she holy as St. Theresa, useful as Miss Nightingale . . .—has entirely missed it. . . .

We may happily dismiss this disagreeable subject with a short remark. . . . To admit that Woman has affections, a moral nature, a religious sentiment, an immortal soul, and yet to treat her for a moment as a mere animal link in the chain of life, is monstrous; I had almost said, blasphemous. If her existence be of no value in itself, then no man's existence is of value; for a moral nature, a religious sentiment, and an immortal soul are the highest things a man can have, and the woman has them as well as he. If the links be valueless, then the chain is valueless too; and the history of Humanity is but a long procession of spectres for whose existence no reason can be assigned. . . .

The second theory we have to consider is the Domestic, or that of Woman as a Housewife. Very beautiful and true, but also very ugly and dull, are the ideas all confounded under this same head, and current side by side amongst us. That the Home is woman's proper kingdom; that all that pertains to its order, comfort, and grace falls under her natural charge, and can by no means be transferred to a man; that a woman's life without such a domestic side must always be looked on as incomplete, or at best exceptional: all this is very true. On the other hand, that, in the lower ranks, the cooking of dinners and mending of clothes; and in the wealthier class, amateur music and drawing, the art of ordering dinner, and the still sublimer art of receiving company, form the be-all and end-all of woman, is, assuredly, stupidly false. . . .

. . . No woman can be truly domestic who is only domestic. . . . The habits of reason, the habits of mental order, the chastened and refined love of beauty, above all, that dignified kind of loving care which is never intrusive, never fussy, but yet ever present, calm, bright, and sweet; all this does not come without a culture which mere domesticity can never attain. The right punishment for those men who denounce schemes for the "Higher Education of Women," and ordain that women should only learn to cook and sew and nurse babies, should be to spend the whole term of their natural lives in such homes as are made by the female incapables formed on such principles. . . .

Domesticity then as a theory of woman's life fails in this: that by placing the secondary end of existence (namely, the making of those around us happy) before the first end (namely, the living to God, and goodness), even the object sought for is lost. The husband and father and sons who are to be made happy at home, are not made happy there. The woman, by being *nothing but* a domestic being, has failed to be truly domestic. She has lost the power of ministering to the higher wants of those nearest to her, by over-devotion to the ministry of their lower necessities. To be truly the "Angel in the House," she must have kept, and ofttimes used, the wings which should lift her *above* the house, and all things in it.

Thirdly, the theory of Woman as a Social being is . . . capable of many variations. The gifted woman who knows how to make her home a centre of intellectual and kindly intercourse; the artist, the woman of letters, the female philanthropist; all these have their place, and at one time or another, and in different coteries, stand forward as the admired types of woman in her Social capacity. In all of them there is right and reason, viewing the salon-keeping, or art, or literature, or philanthropy, as phases of life in its human aspect: the secondary purpose of existence wrought out as best may suit the woman's circumstances and abilities. In all there is wrong and error, if regarded as the ultimate ends of the existence of a human soul. . . .

Turn we now from these theories of "Woman as an Adjective," to those which proceed on the ground that she is a Noun, and that the first end of her being must be an end proper to herself. Is that basis a truer one? Shall we be told it is much more beautiful, more elevated, more Christian, to contemplate life as only a service for others, and not a trust for ourselves? There is abundance of sentimental talk of this kind always to be heard where women are concerned, but is there reason or religion in it? . . .

. . . The old hypothesis that the beasts were made chiefly for the use of man is as completely exploded as the parallel notion that the stars exist to add to our winter nights' illumination, and to afford guidance to our ships. Even the animals most completely appropriated by us would hardly be described by any one now as "made" for our use alone. . . .

But, if it be admitted as regards horses and cats that they were made, first, for their own enjoyment, and only secondly to serve their masters, it is, to say the least, illogical to suppose that the most stupid of human females has been called into being by the Almighty principally to the end that John or James should have the comfort of a wife; nay, even that Robert or Richard should owe their birth to her as their mother. Believing that the same woman, a million ages hence, will be a glorious spirit before the throne of God, filled with unutterable love, and light, and joy, we cannot satisfactorily trace the beginning of that eternal and seraphic existence to Mr. Smith's want of a wife for a score of years here upon earth; or to the necessity Mr. Jones was under to find somebody to cook his food and repair his clothes. If these ideas be absurd, then it follows that we are not arrogating too much in seeking elsewhere than in the interests of Man the ultimate *raison d'être* of Woman.

From the standpoint of independent life, having some end proper to itself, two views . . . are open: the Selfish theory of a woman's life, and the Divine.

Of course the Selfish theory, absolutely worked out, would be the conscious recognition by a woman that she took her own private Happiness for her "being's end and aim," and meant to live for it before all other objects. Actually, I presume it is very rare for any one consciously to adopt such a principle. But, without doing so to their own knowledge, many, nay, alas! perhaps a majority, do so in fact. And among those who, while repudiating Selfishness, are most profoundly selfish, are the women who loudly profess their allegiance to the Physical, or Domestic, or Social theories of woman's life. Those who are content to speak of themselves as only created to minister to the wants of their husband and children, are those oftenest to be seen sacrificing the welfare of both husband and children to their own pleasure, vanity, or ill-temper. The more basely they think of their own purpose of existence, the more meanly they are disposed to work it out.

. . . As the woman who lives only to be a Wife and Mother makes a bad wife and mother; as the woman who lives only to be Domestic, is never truly domestic; as the woman who is made a Social Idol becomes unworthy to be idolized; so the woman who seeks only her own Happiness, inevitably fails to attain Happiness. Whatever else may be uncertain concerning that mysterious thing, — felicity, — this at least is sure: to live for ourselves is to live for our own misery. Absolute Selfishness would create a hell in the midst of Paradise. . . .

Finally, for the Divine theory of Woman's life; the theory that she, like man, is created first and before all things to "love God and enjoy Him for ever;" to learn the rudiments of virtue in this first stage of being, and so rise upward through all the shining ranks of moral life to a holiness and joy undreamed of now: what shall we say to this theory? Shall Milton tell us that Man alone may live directly for God, and Woman only "for God in Him"? I answer, that true religion can admit of no such marital priesthood; no such second-hand prayer. The founders of the Quakers, in affirming that both man and woman stand in direct and immediate relationship to the Father of Spirits, and warning us that no mortal should presume to come between them, struck for the first time a note of truth and spiritual liberty which has called forth half the life of their own sect, and which must sound through all Christendom before the right theory of woman's life be universally recognised. Let it not be said that this Divine theory will take Woman from her human duties. Precisely the contrary must be its effects; for it alone can teach those duties aright in their proper order of obligation. Just as the false theories always defeat their own ends, so the true one fulfils every good end together. The woman who lives to God in the first place, can, better than any one else, serve man in the second; or rather, live to God in the service of His creatures. It is she who may best rejoice to be a wife and a mother, she who may best make her home a little heaven of love and peace; she who may most nobly exert her social powers through philanthropy, politics, literature, and art. In a word, it is not till man gives up his monstrous claim to be the reason of an immortal creature's existence; and not till woman recognises the full scope of her moral rank and spiritual destiny, that the problem of "Woman's Mission" can be solved. . . .

Frances Power Cobbe, "Celibacy v. Marriage", and "What Shall We Do with Our Old Maids?" *Fraser's Magazine,* LXV (Feb. 1862), 228-35; LXVI (Nov. 1862), 594-610. (A two-part article).

Practically all of the middle-class Victorian feminists — unlike those whose feminism was the product of a socialist commitment — agreed that wifehood and motherhood constituted the most appropriate role for women. Some unconventional spirits, however, despite their middle-class background, rebelled at the notion, which to Miss Cobbe was "disgraceful and abominable", that marriage should be the chief aim of a woman's life. In part one of her essay ("Celibacy v. Marriage"), Miss Cobbe, in fact, goes so far in the opposite direction as to suggest that—

in view of the present conjugal arrangements—celibacy for women might, in fact, be preferable to marriage and male domination. In part two ("What Shall We Do with Our Old Maids?"), she addresses the problem of the Redundant Woman, but, in contrast to W. R. Greg (see p. 55), she casts a skeptical eye on such solutions as emigration; rather she advocates what, in the feminist view, appears to be a superior solution.

[*Editors' note: Miss Cobbe has been discussing a recent article whose author suggested that the expenses of maintaining a wife and children forced professional men to make decisions from a pecuniary, rather than an ethical, standpoint. To avoid such actions, it was suggested that "all the most gifted and devoted men who do not happen to inherit £1000 a year, or to fall in love with an heiress, are bound in honour never to marry". In short "all our best men must be celibates".*]

. . . Discussions on the moral aspects of marriage assume a special significance at this moment, since from many other quarters obstacles are arising which must all tend towards rendering (for a long time, at least) celibacy more and more common and desirable. We have heard perhaps more than enough of these obstacles on the *man's* side. Let us, therefore, turn for a moment to consider those which must render women less willing than formerly to enter into such relation.

In the first place, till lately the condition of an unmarried woman of the upper classes was so shackled by social prejudices that it was inevitably a dreary and monotonous one. Mostly, the "old maid" lived in a small house or lodging, out of which she rarely dared to sally on any journey, and where, with a few female friends as closely limited as herself, she divided her life, as the Frenchman has it, between *"la médisance, le jeu, et la dévotion"*. . . . It is half piteous, half ridiculous, to hear of the trifles which occupy these poor shrivelled hearts and minds. . . .

I think, however, this sort of existence will probably end with the present generation. The "old maid" of 1861 is an exceedingly cheery personage, running about untrammelled by husband or children; now visiting at her relatives' country houses, now taking her month in town, now off to a favourite *pension* on Lake Geneva, now scaling Vesuvius or the Pyramids. And what is better, she has found, not only freedom of locomotion, but a sphere of action peculiarly congenial to her nature. "My life, and what shall I do with it?" is a problem to which she finds the happiest solution ready to her hand in schools and hospitals without number. No longer does the Church of Rome monopolize the truth, that on a woman who has no husband, parent, or child, *every* sick and suffering man, every aged childless woman, every desolate orphan, has a claim. She has not fewer duties than other women, only more diffused ones. The "old maid's" life may be as rich, as blessed, as that of the proudest of mothers with her crown of clustering babes. Nay, she feels that in the power of devoting her *whole* time and energies to some benevolent task, she is enabled to effect perhaps some greater good than would otherwise have been possible. . . .

And further, if a woman have but strength to make up her mind to a single life, she is enabled by nature to be far more independently happy therein than a man in the same position. A man, be he rich or poor, who returns at night to a home adorned by no woman's presence and domestic cares, is at best dreary and uncomfortable. But a woman makes her home for herself, and surrounds herself with the atmosphere of taste and the little details of housewifely comforts. If she have no sister, she has yet inherited the blessed power of a woman to make true and tender friendships, such as not one man's heart in a hundred can even imagine; and while he smiles scornfully at the idea of friendship meaning anything beyond acquaintance at a club or the intimacy of a barrack, she enjoys one of the purest of pleasures and the most unselfish of all affections. . . .

And on the other hand, while the utility, freedom, and happiness of a single woman's life have become greater, the *knowledge* of the risks of an unhappy marriage (if not the risks themselves) has become more public. The Divorce Court, in righting the most appalling wrongs to which the members of a civilized community could be subjected, has revealed secrets which must tend to modify immensely our ideas of English domestic felicity. . . . It has always been vaguely known, indeed, that both husbands and wives sometimes broke their most solemn vows and fell into sin; but it was reserved for the new law to show how many hundreds of such tragedies underlie the outwardly decorous lives—not only of the long-blamed aristocracy, but of the middle ranks in England. . . .

Now these things *are* so. The Divorce Court has brought dozens of them to light; and we all know well that for one wife who will seek public redress for her wrongs, there are always ten who for their children's sakes will bear their martyrdoms in silence. True martyrs they are—the sorest tried, perhaps, of any in the world—God help and comfort them! But single women can surely hardly forget these things, or fail to hesitate to try a lottery in which there may be one chance in a thousand of such a destiny. Thus, then, on the man's side, we have got arrayed against marriage all the arguments we have heard so often—economy, independence, freedom of risk of an uncongenial, a bad-tempered, a sickly, or an unfaithful wife; and, lastly, this new principle, that to pursue his calling disinterestedly, he must be untrammelled by the ties of a dependent family. And on the woman's side, we have got a no less formidable range of objections; the certainty now offered to her of being able to make for herself a free, useful, and happy life alone; and the demonstrated danger of being inexpressibly miserable should she choose either an unfaithful or a cruel husband.

The conclusion seems inevitable, that marriage will become more and more rare. . . . Instead of all young men intending at some time or other to marry, and all young women looking forward to be wives, we shall find many of them both resolving on a celibate life.

But the tide must turn at last. Marriage was manifestly the Creator's plan for humanity, and therefore we cannot doubt that it will eventually become the rule of all men and women's lives. When that time arrives both sexes will have learned weighty lessons. The Englishman of the twentieth century will abandon those claims of marital authority whose residue he still inherits from days of Western barbarism when might made right, and from lands of Eastern sensuality, where woman is first the slave of her own weakness, and then inevitably the slave of man. When the theory of the "Divine Right of Husbands" has followed to limbo that of the "Divine Right of Kings," and a precedency in selfishness is no longer assumed to be the sacred privilege of masculine strength and wisdom, then will become possible a conjugal love and union nobler and more tender by far than can ever exist while such claims are even tacitly supposed. . . .

From "What Shall We Do with Our Old Maids?"

. . .There is . . . an actual ratio of thirty per cent. of women now in England who never marry. . . . The old assumption that marriage was the sole destiny of woman, and that it was the business of her husband to afford her support, is brought up short by the statement that one woman in four is certain not to marry, and that three millions of women earn their own living at this moment in England. . . .

In an article in a contemporary quarterly, entitled, "Why are Women Redundant?" . . . it is plainly set forth that all efforts to make celibacy easy for women are labours in a wrong direction, and are to be likened to the noxious exertions of quacks to mitigate the symptoms of disease, and allow the patient to persist in his evil courses. The root of the malady should be struck at, and marriage, the only true vocation for women, promoted at any cost, even by the most enormous schemes for the deportation of 440,000 females. Thus alone (and by the enforcing of a stricter morality on men) should the evil be touched. As to making the labours of single women remunerative, and their lives free and happy, all such mistaken philanthropy will but tend to place them in a position more and more false and unnatural. Marriage will then become to them a matter of "cold philosophic choice," and accordingly may be expected to be more and more frequently declined.

There is a great deal in this view of the case which, on the first blush approves itself to our minds, and we have not been surprised to find the article in question quoted as of the soundest common-sense. . . .

A little deeper reflection, however, discloses a very important point which has been dropped out of the argument. Marriage is, indeed, the happiest and best condition for mankind. But does any one think that all marriages are so? . . . There is only one kind of marriage which makes good the assertion that it is the right and happy condition for mankind, and that is a marriage founded on free choice, esteem, and affection—in one word, on love. If, then, we seek to promote the happiness and virtue of the community, our efforts must be directed to encouraging *only* marriages which are of the sort to produce them—namely, marriages founded on love. . . . A *loving* marriage can never become a matter of "cold philosophic choice." And if *not* a loving one, then, for Heaven's sake, let us give no motive for choice at all.

Let the employments of women be raised and multipled as much as possible, let their labour be as fairly remunerated, let their education be pushed as high, let their whole position be made as healthy and happy as possible, and there will come out once more, here as in every other department of life, the triumph of the Divine laws of our nature. Loving marriages are (we cannot doubt) what God has designed, not marriages of interest. When we have made it *less* women's interest to marry, we shall indeed have less and fewer interested marriages, with all their train of miseries and evils. But we shall also have more *loving* ones, more marriages founded on free choice and free affection. Thus we arrive at the conclusion that for the very end of promoting marriage—that is, such marriage as it is alone desirable to promote—we should pursue a precisely opposite course to that suggested by the Reviewer [Greg] or his party. Instead of leaving single women as helpless as possible, and their labour as ill-rewarded—instead of dinning into their ears from childhood that marriage is their one vocation and concern in life, and securing afterwards if they miss it that they shall find no other vocation or concern;—instead of all this, we shall act exactly on the reverse principle. We shall make single life so free and happy that they shall have not one temptation to change it save the only temptation which *ought* to determine them—namely, love. . . .

. . .In another way the same principle holds good, and marriage will be found to be best promoted by aiding and not by thwarting the efforts of single women to improve their condition. . . . The reviewer alludes with painful truth to a class of the community [prostitutes] whose lot is far more grievous than either celibacy or marriage. Justly he traces the unwillingness of hundreds of men to marry to the existence of these unhappy women in their present condition. He would remedy the evil by preaching marriage to such men. But does not all the world know that thousands of these poor souls, of all degrees, would never have fallen into their miserable vocation had any *other* course been open to them, and they had been enabled to acquire a competence by honest labour' Let such honest courses be opened to them, and then we shall see, as in America, the recruiting of that wretched army becoming less and less possible every year in the country. The self-supporting, and therefore self-respecting woman may indeed become a wife, and a good and happy one, but she will no longer afford any man a reason for declining to marry. . . .

. . .If it be admitted on all hands that marriage is the best condition, and that only one-fourth of the female sex do not marry, how can we expect provision to be made for this contingency of one chance in four by a girl's parents and by herself in going through an education (perhaps costly and laborious) for a trade or profession which there are three chances in four she will not long continue to exercise?

It must be admitted here is the great knot and difficulty of the higher branches of woman's employment. It does require far-seeing care on the part of the parent, perseverance and resolution of no mean order on that of the daughter, to go through in youth the training which will fit her to earn her livelihood hereafter in any of the more elevated, occupations. Nay, it demands that she devote to such training the precise years of life wherein the chances of marriage are commonly offered. . . . If she wait till the years when such chances fail, and take up a pursuit at thirty merely as a *pis aller*, she must inevitably remain for ever behindhand and in an inferior position.

The trial is undoubtedly considerable, but there are symptoms that both young women and their parents will not be always unwilling to meet it, and to invest both time and money in lines of education which *may* indeed prove superfluous, but which likewise may afford the mainstay of a life which, without them, would be helpless, aimless, and miserable. The magnitude of the risk ought surely to weigh somewhat in the balance. At the lowest point of view, a woman is no worse off if she marry eventually, for having first gone through an education for some good pursuit; while if she remain single, she is wretchedly off for not having had such education. But this is in fact only a half view of the case. As we have insisted before, it is only on the standing-ground of a happy and independent celibacy that a woman can really make a free choice in marriage. To secure this standing-ground, a pursuit is more needful than a pecuniary competence, for a life without aim or object is one which, more than all others, goads a woman into accepting any chance of a change. . . . Only a woman who has something else than making love to do and to think of will love really and deeply. It is in *real lives*—lives devoted to actual service of father or mother, or to work of some kind for God or man—that alone spring up *real feelings*. Lives of idleness and pleasure have no depth to nourish such plants. . . .

It may be a pleasantly romantic idea to some minds, that of woman growing up solely with the hope of becoming some man's devoted wife, marrying the first that offers, and when he dies, becoming a sort of moral Suttee whose heart is supposed to be henceforth dead and in ashes. But it is quite clear that Providence can never have designed any such order of things. . . .

. . . It appears that from every point of view in which we regard the subject, it is desirable that women should have other aims, pursuits, and interests in life beside matrimony, and that by possessing them they are guaranteed against being driven into unloving marriages, and rendered more fitted for loving ones; while their single life, whether in maidenhood or widowhood, is made useful and happy.

Before closing this part of the subject, we cannot but add a few words to express our amused surprise at the way in which the writers on this subject constantly concern themselves with the question of *female* celibacy, deplore it, abuse it, propose amazing remedies for it, but take little or no notice of the twenty-five per cent. old bachelors (or thereabouts) who needs must exist to match the thirty per cent. old maids. *Their* moral condition seems to excite no alarm, their lonely old age no foreboding compassion, their action on the community no reprobation. Nobody scolds them very seriously, unless some stray Belgravian grandmother. All the alarm, compassion, reprobation, and scoldings are reserved for the poor old maids. . . .

. . . However far the emigration of women of the working classes may be carried, that of educated women must at all times remain very limited, inasmuch as the demand for them in the colonies is comparatively trifling. Now, it is of educated women that the great body of "old maids" consists; in the lower orders celibacy is rare. Thus, it should be borne in mind that emigration schemes do not essentially bear on the main point, "How shall we improve the condition of the thirty per cent. of single women in England?" The reviewer to whom we have so often alluded, does indeed dispose of the matter by observing that the transportation he fondly hopes to see effected, of 440,000 women to the colonies, will at least *relieve the market* for those who remain. We cannot but fear, however, that the governesses and other ladies so accommodated will not much profit by the large selection thus afforded them among the blacksmiths and ploughmen, deprived of their proper companions. At the least we shall have a quarter of a million of old maids . . . left on [our] hands. What can we do for them? . . .

[*Editors' note: Miss Cobbe's answer, in effect, was the quintessential feminist one: Open the arts and professions to qualified women on exactly the same terms that careers in these fields were available to men, and raise the level of female education, particularly through the admission of women to the examinations and honors of London University, and the opening of colleges for ladies.*]

Jessie Boucherett, "How to Provide for Superfluous Women", in *Woman's Work and Woman's Culture,* edited by Josephine E. Butler (London: Macmillan and Co., 1869), pp. 27-47.

Frances Power Cobbe, as we have seen, had serious doubts as to the practicability of Greg's solution — large-scale female emigration — for the problem of redundant women, particularly the educated ones. But she did not reject it completely, although she observed, a bit acidly, that she did not expect to live long enough to witness the "deportation" of thousands of women a year. Jessie Boucherett, however, had other ideas, including a back-to-the land movement and poultry and pig farming as an occupation for women. She personally supervised a middle-class school where young women were trained to be bookkeepers, cashiers, and clerks, and was a founder in 1860, with Adelaide Procter and

Barbara Leigh Smith Bodichon, of the Society for the Employment of Women (see page 144). In the following excerpt, she explains why the compulsory emigration of *men* would be the only efficacious approach to the question.

. . . If Mr. Greg's plan for draughting off half a million of English women to the United States and our own colonies could be put into execution, it would be of no advantage to the women exported, as they would merely add to the numbers of superfluous women already existing there. Their departure would be an immense relief to the women remaining at home, but unfortunately there is nowhere to send them, for nobody wants them, either in the Old world or the New. It comes to this, that unless Heaven should send a new planet alongside for us to export our superfluous women to, we must make up our minds to keep them at home. Let us, then, proceed to consider by what means we can provide for the superfluous women in England, since it is evident we cannot hope to get rid of them. . . .

. . . Let us see what would happen if . . . every young man was compelled to emigrate as soon as he reached the age of twenty-one. The wages of the men who remained behind would immediately rise, there would no longer be any necessity for married women to go to work, and of those who are now in the habit of working many would be withdrawn from the labour-market.

. . . The reason of the distress among women is, that men have not emigrated as much as they ought to do. In consequence, the wages in almost all trades which are not protected by trades unions, and especially in agricultural labour, have been driven down so low by competition, that in several counties men cannot maintain their wives and families, and the wives are forced to go out to work to add to the men's earnings; numbers of men have also engaged in women's trades, and taken possession of them; thus the women's labour-market has been invaded from two sides, and crowds of women have been rendered superfluous. . . .

If twice the number of men emigrated that emigrate now, the best consequences would ensue. Men's wages would rise, and consequently some wives would be withdrawn from the labour-market; a good many men would be withdrawn from the easier trades, and women would take their places. Thus many of our superfluous women would be enabled to find work.

It must not be supposed, moreover, that all emigrants remain single. Many of the emigrants settle in civilized parts of the country, and either marry one of the superfluous women of the country, or else some English girl who had gone out as a servant; and even the remote settlers often end by marrying: so the more men emigrate the faster the servant-girls who are sent out will marry off, and leave room for a fresh supply of maid-servants from England.

. . . It is now sufficiently clear that the emigration of men will enable our superfluous women to be provided for. . . .

My belief is that it would be for the ultimate advantage of men to emigrate more, and so leave enough easy work to the women to enable them to live; but if I am mistaken in this opinion, and if it really is the fact that men are happier following easy trades in England than doing hard work in the Colonies, I still hold that they ought to go; for it cannot be denied that a man is less unhappy cutting down trees in Canada or tending sheep in Australia, than a woman is who has no means of earning an honest livelihood. If, then, it is recognised that the happiness of women is of as much importance as the happiness of men, it follows that men ought to encounter the minor evil of hard work rather than expose women to the greater evil of having no work at all.

The national plan at present adopted in England for providing for superfluous females, is that of shutting them up in workhouses. . . .

The plan . . . which I advocate for providing for superfluous women is that of allowing them to engage freely in all occupations suited to their strength. The great merit of this plan is, that it would put an end to superfluous women altogether, by converting them into useful members of society. This is without doubt the plan intended by nature all along, and it is from failing to fulfil it that we have fallen into such difficulties. . . .

We have all laughed at the story of the New Zealand chief who, when asked how he had provided for his second wife, from whom he had parted at the recommendation of the Missionary, replied, ''Me eat her.'' It was but his way of providing for superfluous women, and, if it had the disadvantage of being disagreeable to the woman herself, the same may be said of other plans proposed by much better instructed men than the chief.

If he would have allowed his discarded wife a house and some land, as no doubt the Missionary expected, she might have provided for herself; but then, he wanted all the land for himself, and besides, he probably thought that to give women land and let them support themselves might raise up in them a dangerous spirit of independence, and quite destroy all their feminine charms and characteristics; so it seemed to him better to eat her, according to the ancient and venerable custom of the country. Is not the same principle acted on in England? Do not many people think it better that women should suffer than that professions and trades should be opened to them, on the ground that they would be "unsexed" by engaging in them?

It appears to me that our continuance in the present system can only be justified on the principle of the lady who said, "It is natural that *women* should suffer, but it is sad indeed when *men* have to endure privations.''

Eleanor Marx Aveling and Edward Aveling, "The Woman Question: From a Socialist Point of View", *Westminster Review*, CXXV (1886), 207-22.

The "vituperative" reception given in England to *Woman in the Past, Present, and Future,* by the German socialist August Bebel, prompted Karl Marx's youngest daughter Eleanor and her husband Edward Aveling to spring to Bebel's defense. Eleanor Marx had helped found the Socialist League in 1884, and she led a number of strikes of unskilled workers, including the London dockers and the gasworkers. To the Avelings the basic fact, not "understood even by those men and women. . . who have made the struggle for the greater freedom of women the very business of their lives" (p. 209), [1] was that the exploitation of women was a concomitant of capitalist economics. Although middle-class feminists like Frances Power Cobbe, Bessie Rayner Parkes, or Emily Davies were passionately committed to freeing woman from the narrow stereotype of

---

[1] Here and on following pages, direct quotations that have been taken from the source reading itself will be indicated by page references enclosed in parentheses.

Perfect Womanhood, they did not consider the class structure of Victorian society an impediment to the realization of their program. To more radical thinkers like the Avelings, however, the efforts of such feminists to extend opportunities for women through education and employment, or to rectify particular abuses such as the withholding of the franchise, were mere palliatives which failed to solve the fundamental problem of the relationship of the sexes in a capitalist society. The following selection is a good example of the late nineteenth-century socialist view of the Woman Question.

. . . The position of women rests, as everything in our complex modern society rests, on an economic basis. . . . The woman question is one of the organization of society as a whole. . . . Those who attack the present treatment of women without seeking for the cause of this in the economics of our latter-day society are like doctors who treat a local affection without inquiring into the general bodily health.

This criticism applies not alone to the commonplace person who makes a jest of any discussion into which the element of sex enters. It applies to those higher natures, in many cases earnest and thoughtful, who see that women are in a parlous state, and are anxious that something should be done to better their condition. These are the excellent and hard-working folk who agitate for that perfectly just aim, woman suffrage; for the repeal of the Contagious Diseases Act [which theoretically was intended to halt the spread of venereal disease but which, in practice, exposed large numbers of women, chiefly working-class, to arbitrary and humiliating physical examinations], a monstrosity begotten of male cowardice and brutality; for the higher education of women; for the opening to them of universities, the learned professions, and all callings, from that of teacher to that of bag-man. In all this work—good as far as it goes—three things are especially notable. First, those concerned in it are of the well-to-do classes, as a rule. . . . Scarcely any of the women taking a prominent part in these various movements belong to the working class. . . .

The second point is that all these ideas of our "advanced" women are based either on property, or on sentimental or professional questions. Not one of them gets down through these to the bed-rock of the economic basis, not only of each of these three, but of society itself. This fact is not astonishing to those who note the ignorance of economics characteristic of most of those that labour for the enfranchisement of women. Judging from the writings and speeches of the majority of women's advocates, no attention has been given by them to the study of the evolution of society. Even the orthodox political economy, which is, as we think, misleading in its statements and inaccurate in its conclusions, does not appear to have been mastered generally.

The third point grows out of the second. The school of whom we speak make no suggestion that is outside the limits of the society of today. Hence their work is, always from our point of view, of little value. We will suppose all women, not only those having property, enabled to vote; the Contagious Diseases Act repealed; every calling thrown open to both sexes. The actual position of women in respect to men would not be very vitally touched. . . . For not one of these things, save indirectly the Contagious Diseases Act, touches them in their sex relations. Nor should we deny that, with the gain of each or all of these points, the tremendous change that is to come would be more easy of attainment. But it is essential to keep in mind that ultimate change, only to come about when the yet more tremendous social change whose corollary it will be has taken place. Without that larger social change women will never be free.

The truth, not fully recognized even by those anxious to do good to woman, is that she, like the labour-classes, is in an oppressed condition; that her position, like theirs, is one of unjust and merciless degradation. Women are the creatures of an organized tyranny of men, as the workers are the creatures of an organized tyranny of idlers. Even where thus much is grasped, we must never be weary of insisting . . . that for women, as for the labouring classes, no solution of the difficulties and problems that present themselves is really possible in the present condition of society. All that is done, heralded with no matter what flourish of trumpets, is palliative, not remedial. Both the oppressed classes, women and the immediate producers, must understand that their emancipation will come from themselves. Women will find allies in the better sort of men, as the labourers are finding allies among the philosophers, artists, and poets. But the one has nothing to hope from man as a whole, and the other has nothing to hope from the middle class as a whole.

. . . To cultured people, public opinion is still that of man alone. . . . The majority still lays stress upon the occasional sex-helplessness of woman as a bar to her even consideration with man. It still descants upon the "natural calling" of the female. As to the former, people forget that sex-helplessness at certain times is largely exaggerated by the unhealthy conditions of our modern life, if, indeed, it is not wholly due to these. Given rational conditions, it would largely, if not completely, disappear. They forget also that all this about which the talk is so glib when woman's freedom is under discussion is conveniently ignored when the question is one of woman's enslavement. They forget that by capitalist employers this very sex-helplessness of woman is only taken into account with the view of lowering the general rate of wages. Again, there is no more a "natural calling" of woman than there is a "natural" law of capitalistic production, or a "natural" limit to the amount of the labourer's product that goes to him for means of subsistence. That, in the first case, woman's "calling" is supposed to be only the tending of children, the maintenance of household conditions, and a general obedience to her lord; that, in the second, the production of surplus-value is a necessary preliminary to the production of capital; that, in the third, the amount the labourer receives for his means of subsistence is so much as will keep him only just above starvation point: these are not natural laws in the same sense as are the laws of motion. They are only certain temporary conventions of society, like the convention that French is the language of diplomacy. . . .

Whether we consider women as a whole, or only that sad sisterhood wearing upon its melancholy brows the stamp of eternal virginity, we find alike a want of ideas and of ideals. The reason of this is again the economic position of dependency upon man. Women, once more like the labourers, have been expropriated as to their rights as human beings, just as the labourers were expropriated as to their rights as producers. The method in each case is the only one that makes expropriation at any time and under any circumstances possible — and that method is force. . . .

When marriage has taken place all is in favour of the one and is adverse to the other. Some wonder that John Stuart Mill wrote, "Marriage is at the present day the only actual form of serfdom recognised by law". The wonder to us is that he never saw this serfdom as a question, not of sentiment but of economics, the result of our capitalistic system. . . . Marriages thus arranged, thus carried out, with such an attendant train of circumstances and of consequence, seem to us — let us say it with all deliberation —

worse than prostitution. To call them sacred or moral is a desecration. . . .

. . . What is it that we as Socialists desire? . . . To us it seems clear that as in England the Germanic society, whose basis was the free landholder, gave way to the feudal system, and this to the capitalistic, so this last, no more eternal than its predecessors, will give way to the Socialistic system; that as slavery passed into serfdom, and serfdom into the wage-slavery of today, so this last will pass into the condition where all the means of production will belong, neither to slaveowner, nor to serf's lord, nor to the wage-slave's master, the capitalist, but to the community as a whole. . . .

And now comes the question as to how the future position of woman, and therefore of the race, will be affected by all this. . . . Clearly there will be equality for all, without distinction of sex. Thus, woman will be independent: her education and all other opportunities as those of man. Like him, she, if sound in mind and body (and how the number of women thus will grow!) will have to give her one, two, or three hours of social labour to supply the wants of the community, and therefore of herself. Thereafter she will be free for art or science, or teaching or writing, or amusement in any form. Prostitution will have vanished with the economic conditions that made it, and make it at this hour, a necessity. . . .

The . . . contract between man and woman will be of a purely private nature without the intervention of any public functionary. The woman will no longer be the man's slave, but his equal. . . .

CHAPTER IV

Feminists and the Victorian Social Conscience

The nineteenth century was a painful period of social adjustment. The industrialization of England had not created working-class misery, but had certainly made it more visible. The living conditions of the rural laborer might be partly concealed by the holly and the ivy; those of the mill-hand were exposed in all their naked hideousness. The age-old problems of crime, pauperism, and disease had been aggravated by the drift to the cities, and government agencies adequate to deal with evils of such magnitude had not yet emerged. Methods and institutions which had been appropriate to the problems of a rural society were unequal to the challenge of an increasingly urban civilization. Furthermore, the prevailing belief that the state should do as little as possible to ameliorate the plight of the poor (even if that attitude was being eroded by piece-meal concessions to the principle of state "interference"), meant that private individuals and agencies would have to carry the burden which the government declined to assume. Fortunately, it was the great age of voluntarism. Societies dealing with almost every possible aspect of every possible social problem proliferated.

Some philanthropists, convinced that there was a science of society, attempted to discover its laws by applying Comte's positivist methodology to an examination of social phenomena. Striking evidence of the belief that a scientific basis for social legislation could be derived by studying social conditions was the formation of the National Association for the Promotion of Social Science in 1857. This organization, whose annual meetings were for some years widely attended, attracted the leading re-formers of the period and provided feminists with their most effective forum.[1] As one of them, Frances Power Cobbe, defined Social Science, "it aims to embrace every department of the vast field wherein must be waged the warfare of . . . virtue against vice, innocence against crime, health against disease, knowledge against ignorance, peace against war,

---

[1] Lawrence Ritt, *The Victorian Conscience in Action: The National Association for the Promotion of Social Science, 1857-1886*, Unpublished Ph.D. Dissertation (Columbia University, 1959).

industry against pauperism, and woman against the degradation of her sex".[1]

That was an ambitious program, but the reformers—both men and women—who subscribed to it were convinced that they could indeed build a new Jerusalem in England's not so green and no longer quite so pleasant land. Their labors in the fields of public health, education, penology, and poor relief would, they felt, have the effect of so many jacks irresistibly raising the level of the whole society to something more consonant with the Christian ideal. The realization of that ideal—a society based on the principle of loving one's neighbor—was the goal of most of the men and women who dedicated themselves to a program of social action. In addition, a sense of duty, compassion for the downtrodden, horror at the spectacle of human beings living in conditions fit only for animals, concern with the contaminating effects of epidemics spawned in the slums, fear that "the perishing and dangerous classes" might become riotous and revolutionary masses, and opposition to the financial waste caused by the primitive and unresponsive social arrangements of the day—these too were motives responsible for the large scale participation by public-spirited women and men in activities designed to improve the quality of life in nineteenth-century England.

The field of social action was a particularly appropriate area for the activities of reform-minded women. Their involvement with philanthropic works was consistent with what were believed to be uniquely feminine characteristics—tenderness, sympathy, and warm-heartedness, qualities that made women appear to be congenitally equipped to undertake compassionate works. Furthermore, as feminists frequently pointed out, numerous women, denied the responsibilities of wifehood and motherhood, suffered "indescribable ennui" and a sense of having been "wrongly placed on God's earth". Such women, it was believed, might not only find purpose and meaning in their lives through selfless devotion to a higher cause but, in addition, they might fulfill their ethical duty to mankind by advancing God's kingdom beyond the borders of their homes.

In their desire to see social reform accepted as a natural outlet for woman's energy, feminists frequently pointed out that Sisters of Charity in Catholic countries undertook the care of orphan and destitute children, distributed medicines to the sick, and managed relief funds. Moreover, because of their training and experience, they performed such services effectively. The lesson to be drawn was obvious: the women of England should do the same. Anna Jameson, a British author and a forerunner of Victorian feminism, had pleaded for women to take up

---

[1] Frances Power Cobbe, "Social Science Congresses and Women's Part in Them", *Macmillan's Magazine*, V (1861), 84.

"housekeeping on a larger scale" — in prisons, hospitals, and workhouses. [1] Adopting that program of social reform required women to emerge into the outside world. By that very act, they opened the door to other more daring feminist activities. As one authority has phrased it, "Social Services and Women's Emancipation were twin sisters, born of the same reforming spirit". [2]

Although some embattled males insisted that even social uplift was not a proper sphere for the employment of female energies, woman's involvement in good works was nevertheless tolerated (if somewhat grudgingly) because it was safe, in the sense that it did not infringe on the prerogatives of the male. Social reform, therefore, unlike political activity or efforts to secure a foothold in the world of commerce, became an acceptable outlet for a Victorian woman. Thus it was possible for a Mary Carpenter and a Louisa Twining to take their stand beside an Edwin Chadwick and a Lord Shaftesbury.

It must be conceded that not all women who ventured into the netherworld of Victorian society made a significant contribution to solving the problems of the denizens of those depths. Some of them — like the self-satisfied ladies who considered it chic to go "slumming" — were mere dilettantes who merited the jibes of Charles Dickens. But the committed reformers, such as Josephine Butler, Octavia Hill, and Frances Power Cobbe pursued their efforts on behalf of the outcasts and rejects with what can only be described as a sense of mission. Despite the sneers of their critics, their labors in the vineyard furnished incontrovertible evidence that in this sphere certainly, and in others probably, they were the equals of the lords of creation.

Bessie Rayner Parkes, "Charity as a Portion of the Public Vocation of Woman", *English Woman's Journal,* III (1859), 193-96.

Bessie Rayner Parkes was the great-granddaughter of Joseph Priestley, the scientist and radical; the daughter of Joseph Parkes, a politician and reformer; and the mother of the historian, Hilaire Belloc and the novelist, Mrs. Belloc Lowndes. She was the founder and editor of the *English Woman's Journal,* for some years the only periodical devoted to the Woman Question. She and her colleague Barbara Leigh Smith Bodichon (who had been her childhood friend) could serve as prototypes of the nineteenth-century female reformer — the woman who responded to

---

[1] Mrs. Jameson expressed her ideas on woman's social role in two drawing-room lectures that were subsequently printed: *Sisters of Charity* and *The Communion of Labour. Two lectures. . . .* A new edition, enlarged and approved with a prefatory letter to Lord John Russell on the present condition and requirements of the Women of England (London: n.p., 1859). Bessie Rayner Parkes dedicated her collection of essays (*Essays on Woman's Work*) to "the dear and honoured memory of Anna Jameson", and acknowledged the debt of gratitude to her "for the influence she exerted, not only in her writings, but in her own person" (pp. 56-59).

[2] Viola Klein, "The Emancipation of Women: Its Motives and Achievements", in *Ideas and Beliefs of the Victorians* (New York: E. P. Dutton & Co., Inc., 1966), p. 266.

the challenge of a society in flux, and who attempted to deal with the glaring inequities of the day according to the doctrines of enlightened individualism and middle-class humanitarianism. Miss Parkes and Madame Bodichon were the lodestones who attracted many other women of similar views to join groups concerned with such causes as law reform, education, employment, and charity. In the following selection, Miss Parkes advances her view that women have an obligation to themselves and to society to use their special talents in the cause of social reform.

. . . We are aware that to advocate the entry of women into paths of enterprise hitherto monopolised by men, is to assail the very citadel of prejudice. But to confine them to merely subterranean channels of action without the hope of acknowledgment or distinction, is it not to degrade them into a condition little better than servile?

Moreover, women possess a moral necessity for action which cannot surely be disregarded with impunity. It is not alone in those classes incited by pecuniary need that work is called for, but among the comparitively affluent ranks women lament a monotony of existence resulting from the narrow sphere of action assigned them. This becomes the source of an indescribable *ennui* by which they reproach society, and almost Providence, for the misery of inaction and obscurity. It is the prerogative only of a few rare natures to find sufficient incitement to exertion in the pursuit of abstract ends, without the presence of exterior incentive and palpable aim. Numberless temptations beset this life-torpor, from which refuge is sought in excitements either frivolous or culpable. Impulses capable of the highest attainments, undirected to better ends, become the busy agents of a career of levity or vice. This is the more to be regretted, since it is to the finest capacities that inactivity proves most detrimental. In such cases there is a consciousness of aspiration for which no available medium of realisation appears; and nothing is so deteriorating to moral force of character as the conviction of the possession of powers perpetually debarred by adverse circumstances from the accomplishment of their legitimate aims. Surely, it should not be the stigma of an age of civilization that it permits, in any human creature, stagnation of those energies of the soul which are the pledges of our origin and destiny, as members of a glorious humanity.

. . . [Of] the various means adapted for the employment of our leisure, our resources, and our faculties, . . . there is one path of exertion open, which, immeasurable in its capacity for good, is susceptible of a peculiar degree of improvement by women. . . . This is the exercise of charity—charity in the best and highest phase, which ministers to the wants of the minds and souls of our species as well as to their bodies. The poor we have always with us, and the requirement for the exercise of this virtue is ever before us. Much is to be done in the vineyard, though too many stand all the day idle; and never was the great work of charity more appropriate, and the neglect of it more inexcusable, than in the present age. . . .

. . . It is in the power of women to become invincible agents in the work of charity. The very attributes of the feminine nature are of essential value in such a cause. Funds, programmes, and committees, indispensable though they are, form but a slender part, and can only partially effect the good which results from the comprehensive sway of charity. Kindly and sympathetic contact, the expression of benevolence ardent and sincere, is needful and irresistible to its power to console and benefit the unfortunate and distressed.

Many, sincerely compassionate, are deterred from the practice of benevolence by false and exaggerated conceptions of its requirements. Position, influence, wealth, are deemed indispensable to success, whereas the most unpretending efforts, judiciously restricted to a particular locality and a limited arena of operation, might easily achieve what is sometimes despaired of, and, directed to a single end, would prove successful. . . . If the alms bestowed in a single month capriciously, were at the expiration of that time collected and distributed with order and intelligence, how immeasurably more beneficial would the result prove! Women have it in their power to give that which is invaluable in the cause—leisure, thought, and sympathy. In charity there will ever be found a congenial sphere for the fruition of the unemployed energies of women. Let them not neglect then this crowning virtue which should "never fail," but let the energy and diligence brought to its pursuance prove them entitled to share in the inalienable rights of humanity to a free use of every faculty. To deny this prerogative to any human creature is to bring discord into the moral government of the universe. To assent, is indirectly to admit the injustice of those obstacles which render ineligible to women the varied paths of mental progress and employment, indispensable to the realisation of her human rights to life, liberty and happiness—rights which the spirit of charity itself cannot but advocate and commend.

Frances Power Cobbe, "Social Science Congresses, and Women's Part in Them", *Macmillan's Magazine*, V (1861), 81-94.

Almost from the moment the National Association for the Promotion of Social Science was founded in 1857, it met with ridicule. Its scientific pretentions were mocked, the participants in its annual congresses were referred to as cranks, and its proceedings were judged to be boring. (Said *The Times:* "Almost any one of these subjects . . . would tend to empty a drawing-room".[1]) A possible reason for its bad press was the conspicuous role played in its meetings by women. Among them were Isa Craig, who was one of the original group of women who made their headquarters the London office of the *English Woman's Journal* and who was appointed assistant to G. W. Hastings, the secretary, founder, and real head of the Association. The intellectual climate of the Social Science Association encouraged the participation of women reformers, two of whom, Louisa Twining and Mary Carpenter, presented papers at its very first meeting. In the selection that follows, another lady who was active in the society, the redoubtable Frances Power Cobbe, defends the Association and the right of women to play a significant role in it.

    . . . The most successful of all the attacks of our witty contemporaries on the Social Science Association, are those which refer to the very considerable part taken therein by ladies; and to this, therefore, we shall devote the residue of our space.
    There is a whole mine of jokes to be found at all times by the [intellectually] destitute in the subject of women. . . . A silly old woman in a mob cap, or a silly young one in a crinoline, a Belgravian mother, or a "pretty horsebreaker," women who know Greek,

[1] *The Times,* October 11, 1859, p. 6.

and women who cannot spell English, ladies who do nothing but crochet, and ladies who write two hundred letters a day for Borrioboola Gha — it is pretty much the same; who can resist the fun of the thing, even if it be repeated rather frequently? Frankly we confess, for our own parts, that, while reason tells us the joke is rather superannuated, habit still induces us to enjoy it as ever fresh and new.

We do, indeed, sometimes figure to ourselves, the employer (we cannot say originator) of such a jest as a person not naturally of a lively disposition, but rather as one whom the requirements of a despotic editor compel sometimes to become jovial — one who has a *"concern"* to be diverting; who is witty, not so much by Nature as by Grace. We hear him crying in his extreme distress, "What shall I do to be funny? Who will show me any joke? . . ." At last a blessed thought occurs to him, "We will stand on the old paths and see which were the ancient jests." And there, of course, in the first page of the first book he opens, from Aristophanes to Joe Miller, he finds a jibe at women. "Eureka!" exclaims the fortunate man; "why, of course, the women! That is always sure to succeed with the galleries." With a skip and a bound, and a sommersault [sic], amazing to beholders, the solemn critic comes out a first-rate clown. "All right!" "Here we are!" "At them again!"

Of course it is a double piece of good fortune when (as on the occasion of the holding of the late [Social Science] congress in Dublin) Penseroso in Search of a Joke lights upon it in Ireland. . . . The very dullest of Englishmen can always find a laugh for stories of Irish beggars, Irish bulls, and Irish cars. [*Editors' note: One suspects that Miss Cobbe's scorn derives from the fact of her Irish origins. She was born in Dublin.*] Possibly it may chance to be because he *is* dull that the quickness and brightness of the Irish mind strikes him as so amazing. He feels much like one of the hard-fisted *habitués* of an alehouse gazing at the rapid fingering of the fiddler. "Do look at un's hands how fast they go! Could'ee do the likes of that, man? Haw, haw, haw!" No other nation that we know of considers it so strange to be able to answer a simple question with vivacity, and to elaborate a joke in less than half an hour.

But to return to the women. A peculiar merit of the Protean joke against them is that it accommodates itself immediately to every new line of action which they may adopt. And, as in our day women are continually adopting new lines of action, the supply for the jest market seems really inexhaustible. . . .

We would not on any account be discourteous to the [female] sex; but yet we cannot help sometimes comparing them in our minds to a large flock of sheep, round which some little worrying terriers, with ears erect and outstretched tails, are barking and jumping, and (occasionally) biting. . . . The foolish sheep run hither and thither; but, whichever way they go, the terriers hunt them out of *that* corner immediately. Now they rush into this thicket — now down into that ditch — now out again into the open field. Here are two sheep running away on one side, there is another going off in the opposite direction. "Bow, wow, wow!" cry the little dogs. "Bow, wow, wow! Don't go here — don't go there — don't separate yourselves — don't run together. Bow, wow, wow, wow!" At last the idiotic sheep (any one of whom might have knocked over the little terrier quite easily if it only had the pluck) go rushing . . . down into the very worst hole they can possibly find; and then the little dogs give a solemn growl, and drop their tails, and return home in great moral indignation.

We were for ever hearing of women's proper work being this, that, or the other. But, whatever they actually undertake, it is always clear that *that* is not the "mission" in question; they must run off and try some other corner directly. In the days of our grandmothers it was . . . a subject of scorn, that "most women have no character at all," and that, while

> "*Men*, some to business, some to pleasure take,
> Yet every *woman* is at heart a rake."

The "Tea-cup age" passed away, and the sheep rushed in an opposite direction. Women would be frivolous no more. They became "Blues!" [intellectuals]—and the barking went on worse than ever! It was thought the wittiest thing in the world for Byron to sneer at his noble wife (who has so lately closed her life of honour, silent to the last regarding all *his* offences!) because she was

> "A learned lady, famed
> For every branch of every science known,
> In every Christian language ever named,
> With virtues equalled by her wit alone."

Efforts were made at the time to give young ladies, generally, an education which should transcend the wretched *curriculum* of the then fashionable schools—"French, the guitar, the Poonah painting," with "history, geography, and the use of the globes," thrown into the bargain as unimportant items. Then it was the acquirement of knowledge which was *not* "woman's mission," and which would infallibly distract her from it. . . . Those phrases which Sydney Smith called the "delight of Noodledom" were in continual circulation. "The true theatre for a woman is the sick chamber." "The only thing a woman need know is how to take care of children; that is what she was *made for,* and there is no use attempting to overstep the intentions of nature."

But of late a most singular transition has taken place. The sheep are running, it would seem, precisely where the terriers were driving them. The care of the sick and of children occupies the minds and lives of great numbers of women who have few or no domestic duties. Let us see how they are treated by the little dogs. Alas! we fear that we catch the sound of the bark again. "Ladies must not meddle with this school. Ladies must not interfere with that hospital. Ladies ought not to give evidence before committees of Parliament. Ladies cannot be admitted into workhouses. Ladies ought not to make a stir about the grievances they discover. Ladies ought not to write papers about paupers, and women's employment, and children's education. And oh! above all earthly things, ladies ought not to read such papers, even if they write them. Bow, wow, wow, wow!" They must (we are driven to conclude) nurse the sick without going into hospitals, and look after children without meddling in schools, and see evils but never publish them, and write (if they *must* write) papers, about babies and girls, and then get some man to read the same (of course losing the entire pith and point thereof) while they sit by, dumb and "diffident," rejoicing in the possession of tongues and voices which, of course, it cannot have been "the intention of nature" should ever be heard appealing in their feminine softness for pity and help for the ignorant and the suffering.

Now, we confess, in all seriousness, to be rather tired of this kind of thing. It seems to us that the world does grievously need the aid of one-half the human race to mitigate the evils which oppress it; and if, in their early and feeble endeavours to fulfil their share of the work, women should make endless blunders, the error in our eyes is a venial one, compared to the inactivity and uselessness in which (in Protestant countries) so many of them habitually vegetate. Let us not be mistaken. The private and home duties of *such women as have them* are, beyond all doubt, their first concern, and one which, when fully met, must often engross all their time and energies. But it is an absurdity, peculiar to the treatment of women, to go on assuming that all of them *have* home duties, and tacitly treating those who have none as if they were wrongly placed on God's earth, and had nothing whatever to do in it. There must needs be a purpose for the lives of single women in the social order of Providence—a definite share in the general system which they are intended to carry on. The Church of Rome found out this truth long ago. The Catholic woman who does not marry takes it almost as a matter of course that she is bound to devote herself to works of general charity and piety. While the Protestant "old maid" has been for centuries among the most wretched and useless of human beings—all her nature dwindled by restraint, and the affections, which might have cheered many a sufferer, centred on a cat or a parrot— the Romanist has understood that she has *not* fewer duties than others, but more extended and perhaps laborious ones. Not selfishness. . . . but self-sacrifice more entire than belongs to the double life of marriage, is the true law of celibacy. Doubtless it is not an easy law. It will take some time to learn the lesson; for it is far harder to preserve a loving spirit in solitude than under the fostering warmth of sweet household affections. If the single woman allow herself to drift down the stream of circumstances, making no effort for better things, then the shoals of selfishness lie inevitably beneath the prow. To row against the tide of inclination more vigorously than others, to seek resolutely for distant duties when no near ones present themselves, to give more love while receiving less—such are the stern claims of duty on a lonely woman.

But, now that she is beginning to feel somewhat of these solemn obligations, that hundreds and even thousands of women of the upper classes are saying, "What shall I do with my life? for neither balls, nor crochet, nor novels, nor *dilettante* copying of drawings and playing of music, satisfy my soul, and I would fain do some little fraction of good before I die"—shall we *now* spend our wit in trying to warn them off such fields as they may try to work, instead of helping them with all manly sense and tenderness? "Women are invading the province of men. They are not our equals, and they have no business to do it." If the inferiority be so definite, the alarm is at least very groundless. . . . Let a woman's powers be set down to the lowest figure imaginable; let it be assumed (a tolerably large assumption!) that the most clear-headed and warm-hearted woman is the inferior in all respects of the most consummate masculine "muff" of her acquaintance, and that she ought to listen in humility and prostration of mind whenever he opens his lips (for the unanswerable reason that a moustache may grow upon them), still, with Herbert Spencer, we must ask, "Is it any reason, because a woman's powers are inferior, that she should be prevented from using such powers as she *has*?" . . .

We want, in the first place, the Religious and Moral intuitions of women to be brought out so as to complete those of men, to give us all the *stereoscopic view* by which we shall see such truths as we can never see them by single vision, however clear and strong. . . . In all ages the piety of females has been noted. Any why? Doubtless because their gentler natures and more retired lives peculiarly fitted them to receive in their unruffled hearts the breath of the Divine love, and listen to that inner voice too often unheard amid the clamour of the world. We come nearer to God through the affections, wherein lie woman's great power, than through the intellect wherein man excels. . . . We have had enough of *man's* thoughts of God—of God first as the King, the "Man of War," the Demiurge, the Mover of all things, and then, at last, since Christian times, of God as the Father of the World. Not always have men been very competent to teach even this side of the truth alone; for during more than a thousand years the religious teachers of Christendom were men who knew not a father's feelings, who thought them less holy than their own loveless celibacy. But the woman's thought of God as the ''Parent of Good, Almighty,'' who unites in one the father's care and the mother's tenderness, *that* we have never yet heard. Even a woman hardly dares to trust her own heart, and believe that as she "would have compassion on the son of her womb,'' so the Lord hath pity on us all. Surely, surely, it is time we gain something from woman of her Religious nature! And we want her Moral intuition also. We want her sense of the law of love to complete man's sense of the law of justice. We want her influence, inspiring virtue by gentle promptings from within to complete man's external legislation of morality. And, then, we want woman's practical service. We want her genius for detail, her tenderness for age and suffering, her comprehension of the wants of childhood to complete man's gigantic charities and nobly planned hospitals and orphanages. How shall we get at all these things?

There are, of course, endless ways in which this may be done. . . . Each woman helps it who takes her part in the labours of poor schools and asylums, of hospitals and visiting the sick, and in the beautiful duties of a country gentleman's wife or daughter among her natural dependents. . . .

Bessie Rayner Parkes, "Ladies' Sanitary Association", *English Woman's Journal,* III (1859), 73-85.

The Ladies' Sanitary Association was formed as a sister organization of the National Association for the Promotion of Social Science in the very year, 1857, that that society began its existence under the nominal leadership of the venerable reformer, Lord Brougham.[1] Led by women like Bessie Rayner Parkes, the ladies attempted to correct conditions which, in some respects, had not improved greatly since the 1840's, when "the people of England appeared for the first time to acquire a sense of sight and smell and realize that they were living on a dung heap".[2] The Ladies' Sanitary Association was particularly concerned with the health of the working classes, to whom it distributed hundreds of thousands of tracts on such subjects as "The Worth of Fresh Air", "The Use of Pure Water", "How to Save Infant Life", and "Power of Soap and Water". In addition to reading papers at the annual meetings of the Social Science Association, the members of the Sanitary Association gave lectures on the spread of communicable diseases and warned against the dangers of overflowing cesspools, open drains, contaminated wells, poor ventilation, and the lack of adequate sanitary facilities in general. The following selection describes the conditions of public health in nineteenth-century England and illustrates the work of the members of the LSA.

[1] Brougham, then 79, was simply a figurehead. The real founder and guiding spirit of the Social Science Association was an energetic young barrister, G. W. Hastings, who devoted his life to public causes and ended it under a cloud.
[2] S. E. Finer, *The Life and Times of Sir Edwin Chadwick* (London: Methuen & Co. Ltd., 1951), pp. 212-13.

. . . A very active and promising young idea, born some time in the early part of this century, is at this moment militant in all parts of the United Kingdom. . . . We mean the Sanitary idea. The notion of cultivating health according to what we now call the laws of life is very modern indeed, . . . and has as yet hardly penetrated the official or the rustic intellect; but mid-way between these two extremes, it occupies a large portion of the English citizens' time and mind. We should like to know the increase in the manufacture and sale of tin baths alone in the last twenty years; how many sponges have been disturbed in their zoophytic meditations, and what profit has been secured upon flesh-brushes. The drains of London present a longer mileage than her streets, and the marshy places of the land are literally sown with pipes. Almost every town, large or small, has its particular type of sanitary medical man, a man who is always blinding himself over his microscope, and poisoning himself over his gases; whose acute nose is the despair of the parish authorities, and a curse to the ratepayers among whom he dwells. This man is always drawing up papers for associations, and he predicts all the fevers that come to pass. He sweeps and whitewashes with furious energy after the cholera, when for a little space the frightened authorities permit him to have his own way, and then, in spite of this extraordinary complaisance, he is cruel enough to persecute them with dreadful statistics of the ravages of death, and odious comparisons of what was, and what might have been, had he been minded at any earlier date.

. . . Until comparatively lately the virtues of medical science lay buried in the minds of the few; even physicians themselves drugged and smothered their patients as if they knew nothing of the accurate and beautiful laws under which . . . we live and move and have our being; and as a branch of popular knowledge, . . . the sanitary idea had absolutely no existence. It is of our times, and an integral part of our intensely self-conscious civilization. We no longer find health in our daily pursuits as a matter of course; the enormous growth of our towns, and the new set of evils contingent upon that growth have obliged us to set to work to find counteracting agencies, and the result is a great increase in the average longevity of our population, even over those times when the habits of life were certainly of a more healthful cast. Our ancestors went to bed earlier, and lived much more in the open air; on the other hand, we have wonderfully improved in building, drainage, and ventilation, and in the knowledge and application of the healing art. . . .

The first agency in the extension of public interest on the subject of health, must of course be attributed to the labors and the writings of scientific men, medical or non-medical. The great discoveries of the last century, as to the constitution of air and of water, of course afforded a standard of purity for those two prime elements in human health or disease hitherto unattainable. Little by little, as the writings of the scientific class filtered into public and private libraries, the attention of thinking men became more and more drawn towards the inevitable consequent deductions. Vaccination had proved that the ravages of at least one fatal disease had been arrested, and the practice of excessive bleeding as a remedy for every trifling ailment had mostly passed away.

Then came that strange and fearful foreign visitant, the Cholera. Germinated early in this century in the marshy delta of Indian Ganges, it gradually diffused itself over the length and breadth of the peninsula. . . . It reached China in 1820, . . . and in 1822 the dread fiend stood on the frontier of Europe, looking out, like Alexander, for fresh worlds to conquer. In 1823 it overleaped the boundary, and strange to relate, lingered for nearly ten years in Russia, but in 1831 it summoned Warsaw, Berlin, Hamburg, and Sunderland, and in 1832 London and Paris bent to the blow. England lost nearly 15,000 people. . . . The visitation of 1849 was even . . . more severe, London alone furnishing 14,497 deaths. . . .

It may be easily imagined what an impetus must have been given by the cholera to sanitary efforts; with what fear and trembling men must have looked round for some potent exorcism. Whether contagious or not, it was abundantly provable that hot damp weather was propitious to the disease, and that those who lived in bad air, amidst defective drainage, or who were given to intemperance or other ordinary unhealthy habits, fell soonest victims to the disease. After 1832 we may be sure that the nation thought more of washing and setting its house in order than ever it had done before.

The next great movement [for sanitary reform] was connected with the Poor Laws. In . . . 1832, Lord Grey's government issued a Commission of inquiry into the condition of the laboring class in every parish throughout England and Wales, and Mr. Edwin Chadwick was appointed Assistant Commissioner. In the course of these investigations his mind seems to have been much impressed with the importance of ill health as a cause of poverty, for in 1838 we find him obtaining the consent of the Poor Law Commissioners to a special inquiry into the physical causes of fever in the metropolis, which might be removed by proper sanitary measures. This inquiry was also extended to the whole kingdom. From this time a broad stream of interest upon sanitary matters set steadily in. . . .

That a vast reduction in our annual mortality can be ensured by the wise application of sanitary laws in the hands of men is an admitted fact; and the reasons for such united application do not appeal to the moral nature alone. . . . There is also here a direct appeal to public economy; to the pocket even of the rate-payer. Ill health is very dear. It is unequivocally dear to the individual; it is equally dear to the nation, since it is not the death alone of able-bodied citizens which is to be apprehended, but the wasting sickness or frequent illness which casts the lowest class upon the parish, and renders the bedridden cripple often a helpless burden to the workhouse for many long years. Mr. Kingsley [the noted author and Christian Socialist] speaking of unhealthy cottages, asks, "Who shall estimate the value of life destroyed, the cost of wives made widows, children orphans, parents childless, of domestic morality destroyed, or not fostered, for want of domestic decency and comfort; of a population at once weakened, diminished, and degraded." And poverty and sickness act and re-act on each other with a constant and complicated influence. A population whose savings have been absorbed by sickness has no reserved fund to meet the rainy day; little by little the furniture finds its way to the pawn-broker, and if the mill stops, or the bad harvest ruins the farmers, the clothes of the mill hand or of the farm laborer are sold for bread. And "poverty, when it attains to a certain pitch, seems to reduce all other predisposing causes of disease to insignificance in comparison with its direful influence. Scanty, uncertain and in-nutritious food, insufficient clothing, squalor of person, incessant labor, sinking of the heart, cold lodgings, filthy beds, or harsh substitutes for beds, the atmosphere of their dwellings confined for the sake of warmth, and poisoned by too many breaths or polluted by noxious exhalations. . . ." And be it ever remembered, oh! anxious mother, that the track of an epidemic does not break off upon the level on which it first arose. Contagious fever, when once it has fairly started on its rounds among the poor, visits also with unerring footstep the mansions of the neighbouring rich; and the burning heat which has consumed the little child in the cottage kitchen, will not fail to strike blank dismay into your curtained nursery. The small beds will soon be empty nests; the cradle will be put mournfully away, and the pattering sound of little feet, and the warbling trill of little voices be still for ever. . . .

. . . To say that the average rate of mortality is high in any given district, means that when a mother looks round upon her populous nursery she must expect to lose one or more of those little children before they have grown up. It means that if a child is seized with hooping cough or scarlet fever, that child has a bad chance of recovery. It means that the young mother is in more than ordinary danger of dying in childbed, and that the soldiers and sailors who are born and bred in that particular district are physically ill fitted to sustain the glory of their native land. It means that many coffins will be bought of the undertaker, and that the milliner will often sit up at night to finish mourning clothes. The doctor's charge will be heavy, and he will not be able to save the precious life, though the scanty means of the unhappy family be taxed to their utmost to meet the fruitless bill. These are the common every-day miseries which afflict a district suffering from bad drains and ill constructed houses. By some means or other the grand political agencies of Parliament with their Acts and their Boards must be narrowed down to a minute domestic application. . . .

To descend yet more to particulars, the best framed Acts of Parliament most efficiently carried out, will only result in partial reforms, until the habits of the people, engendered amidst bad conditions, and rendered careless by hopelessness, be also changed. When the house-wife has got a good supply of water, we must by hook or by crook infuse into her unaccustomed intellect the notion that it is good to wash the house and to give refractory pinafores a chance of being clean. The baby must no longer be fed upon cold sausage, and Tommy with an intermittent fever must not be laid in a four-poster with shut windows and a roaring fire. It is not good to whip [a child] till he is red hot with screaming, and then "set him on the stones to cool." A broken pane of glass is more likely to give the rheumatism than no window at all, and the dunghill by the cottage door will probably poison the household before the more distant parish officer has smelt it out. In fact we want just that a minute domestic instruction in matters sanitary for which Boards of Health may pave the way, but which they can never complete in detail. We want the action of *women* in every parish; we want the clergyman's wife and the doctor's daughter to know the laws of health, and to enforce them in the perpetual intercourse which we hope and believe they maintain with their poorer neighbours. The squire's lady, and the peeress whose husband owns half the county, the district visitor who cares for the soul, and the parish nurse who attends upon the sick — if all these women could be made to work with a will, and "a woman with a will," as the "Household Words" observes, "is a fine thing," what a difference might be wrought in the average mortality of England.

Many of our readers may be already aware that an association, [the Ladies' Sanitary Association], yet in its infancy, has been formed for supplying this very want; for inducing ladies all over the country to take a lively interest in sanitary reform, and for supplying them with domestic tracts upon the laws of health and the management of the household, to be distributed wherever the cottager or the artizan can be induced to read them. Various other plans for the diffusion of sanitary knowledge will gradually be worked into the scheme, and we shall take a few extracts from the published prospectus of the association for the sake of making these as widely known as possible. The ladies [of the Association] . . . truly consider that by far the greater part of the debility, disease, and premature mortality, is the result of *preventible causes,* but that very few

preventive measures bearing on the *personal habits* of the people have yet been adopted.
Believing that the principal cause of the low physical condition of so large a portion of
our population results from their ignorance of the laws of health, they have combined
to propagate this important branch of knowledge in various ways. They desire to establish institutions in which schoolmistresses and pupil-teachers, belonging to any schools
for the working-classes, can attend gratuitously a course of theoretical and practical
instruction in all subjects relating to health, so that they may be able to teach their
pupils. By these means schoolgirls, the future wives and mothers of the working-classes
will obtain information which, though necessary to all, is now possessed by very few.
Classes should also be formed for educated women. Special attention will be paid to
instruction in the management of infants and children, as being one of the most important duties of women. The formation of a training home for orphan infants is in con-
templation, nay, has been already begun on a very small scale at Brighton. Our readers
will see that this part of the plan ought to be carried out locally in every district, and
that it rests with themselves to appropriate and carry out the idea of a hygienic school.
If nursery-maids could be got to attend any classes formed in different towns, so much
the better; and an appeal is made to all clergymen and doctors to use their immense
influence in founding and supporting branch associations. The publication of tracts
has already been begun, the titles of several of which will be found in our advertising
columns. The establishment of loan libraries, and the delivery of popular lectures on
the preservation of health, are also desired. Finally, all inquiries or communications
may be addressed to the Secretary, at 16A, Old Cavendish Street, Cavendish Square,
London; or 17, Egremont Place, Brighton. . . .

   During February, March, and June of 1858, the [association was] enabled, through
the kindness of a medical gentleman, to provide two courses of eight free popular lectures to ladies on "Physical Education and the Laws of Health." Several papers upon
sanitary subjects have been also contributed by members . . . to some of the leading
periodicals. It is in supporting, by its moral influence, all such local activity in every
town throughout the country, that this association will chiefly do its work. We do not
want one immense centre of activity in London, Brighton, or any other place; we want
a multitude of little centres in agricultural villages and manufacturing towns, little
centres which shall be supplied with tracts by the association, and shall be connected
with it in every way which may prove to be beneficial. . . .

   The chief value of an association for the accomplishment of any reform, lies far
less in the particular items of practical reform it is able to accomplish in itself, than in
the thorough discussion of the *idea* on which it is based. Once let this idea be worked
into the public mind, once let it be condensed in domestic conversation and expanded
in penny periodicals, and taught as a common-place in schools; once let it come in as
salt to the soup, and as fuel to the fire, and the mission of an association is complete.
Look at the great religious organizations which have sown Bibles and tracts broadcast
over the country, and how they have resulted in Sunday classes and ragged schools, in
new churches, city missions, mothers' meetings, and many other active working schemes.
A great victory has been won over the religious indifference of the last century, a great
victory remains to be won over the physical indifference which degrades the human
frame. Here is a small beginning in the Ladies' Sanitary Association which may become a great work if all who read this paper with any degree of interest will endeavor,
each in their separate locality, whether it be in the murky atmosphere of the town, or
in the pleasant green places of the country, to carry out its plans, to communicate with

those who have laid its foundation, and to link themselves to it through some practical and successful effort towards the enforcement of the laws of health by our English people.

Louisa Twining, "On the Training and Supervision of Workhouse Girls", *National Association for the Promotion of Social Science, Transactions,* 1859, pp. 696-702.

Louisa Twining, the product of a middle-class family, devoted practically her entire life to the cause of workhouse reform. First visiting a workhouse in 1853 to call on an old and destitute acquaintance, Miss Twining worked for more than forty years to improve the deplorable conditions that prevailed in the domain of Mr. and Mrs. Bumble. What those conditions were can be deduced from the "lesser eligibility" criterion established by the Poor Law of 1834, which required that the living standard of the workhouse population be deliberately made inferior to that of the lowest segment of the working class. In addition, the workhouse inmates were subjected to a discipline which was almost as severe as that of a prison (there was good reason for calling them "jails without guilt"). When the Poor Law Guardians initially rejected Miss Twining's request that they extend visiting privileges to other ladies, it was on the grounds that their presence would be a threat to discipline and might, in fact, precipitate a revolution.[1] Miss Twining was able to break down the Guardians' opposition and, in 1857, at the first meeting of the Social Science Association, her proposal to form the Workhouse Visiting Society was adopted. Thereafter, the members of the Society devoted themselves to ministering to the needs of the deprived and degraded population of the workhouses. The following excerpt, written in the early years of the Workhouse Visiting Society's existence, illustrates one aspect of workhouse reform, that of training young girls for a useful occupation.

The subject of "Workhouse Relief and Management" is . . . not losing, but rather gaining ground in the estimation of the Association and of the public. . . . Efforts . . . are being made in various ways to improve the condition of the lowest classes. . . . Experience is every day showing us more clearly that all the care and teaching is in vain, if some protection is not extended to the children when they are first sent out into the world. The idea is certainly also gaining ground that, by careful teaching and training, the poor children of these schools may be made useful and valuable members of society. Suggestions have recently been made to train many of them expressly for the army and navy, a proposal which it is to be hoped will receive serious attention, as we have already far more tailors and shoemakers than can find employment. The added experience of a year has convinced the members of the Workhouse Visiting Society of the necessity of carrying out, by increased efforts, this, one of their chief

[1] Louisa Twining, "The History of Workhouse Reform", in The Baroness [Angela] Burdett-Coutts, *Woman's Mission* (London: Sampson Low, Marston & Company, Limited, 1893), p. 266.

aims, viz., "to befriend the destitute and orphan children in the schools, and after they are placed in situations."

In one of our large cities it is now proposed to organize on a small scale a plan of encouragement and protection for the girls on leaving the schools, and the proposal has met with the approbation of more than one board of guardians. It involves no expense, and would be applicable to every . . . workhouse school where ladies could be found to carry it out. It is in fact merely an extension of the present system of inspection by the chaplains of our large district schools. If the names of ladies who would undertake this work were known to the chaplain or guardians, notice would be given to them when any girl went out into service, and a friendly protection might thus be extended over her during the most perilous time of her life. . . .

The following is an outline of the plan sent to me by the lady who has established it: —

"PROPOSED PLAN FOR PROTECTING WORKHOUSE GIRLS

"1. To obtain from the matron the addresses of all girls lately sent out to service. . . . To obtain from the schoolmistress information respecting the girl's character and requirements, and take from her some message of inquiry. To call on the mistresses of these girls, explaining our wish to befriend them; offering, if needful, some small additional articles of clothing to those provided by the workhouse, and engaging the mistress to careful guardianship, and to the promise not to discharge the girl without giving us due notice. To ask to see the servant, and endeavour to make friends with her. To arrange, if possible, that she be allowed to attend a Sunday class at the house of one of the ladies, and, at all events, be visited at stated intervals.

"2. To obtain from the matron the names, and from the mistress the characters, of such girls as are fit to be sent out to service, but for whom no one has made application. Among these, to attend first to such as have reached the age at which they are threatened with removal to the women's ward; to find safe and suitable services for these girls; to visit them and bring them to classes in the same manner as the other girls, having the advantage of a previous acquaintance with them at the workhouse."

It is hoped that by these means such supervision may . . . preserve a most helpless class of girls from obvious dangers attendant on sudden discharge from service, and that they may be afforded some measure of that individual attachment of which they stand in so much need; for however well taught they may be when they leave the schools, it is a well-known fact that they later fall into ruin, from their friendless and unprotected condition. [A workhouse] . . . chaplain . . . has expressed his opinion that, had such a plan as this been in operation, scores would have been saved in that [parish] alone, who are at this moment returned to the workhouse in vice and despair. The offers of help that are frequently being received, lead us to hope that persons may not be wanting to carry out these suggestions in various localities.

In one large industrial school I found 213 children, of whom the master supposed 200 were orphans. I asked what care was taken of the girls after they leave at 14, and was told none; if they like they may come to the school to visit their teachers, and the best-disposed do so, but the others are left to their fate, being just those who require the most care; those who leave their places from no fault may return to the school within a year — the others go to the workhouse or elsewhere. The teaching, both intellectual and industrial, no doubt was excellent, but here as elsewhere there appeared to me a total want of all effort to supply that which a voluntary interest alone could give. I was told a touching instance of one poor little girl who had lately died without having had one relation since she was in the school. . . .

I would now pass on to another plan which is suggested by the Workhouse Visiting Society, and which it is hoped may be carried out in the course of a few months. . . . Many (I believe I may say nearly all) of those most hardened and difficult to deal with of all workhouse inmates—the young women—have been brought up in pauper schools. . . . [*Editors' note: Here Miss Twining noted that some pauper schools seemed to train the girls "expressly for the adult wards of the workhouse, so surely do they find their way there after a few years". How is it, she asked, "that guardians and teachers rest contented with such a state of things, without ever endeavouring to find out the cause of it?"*] . . . Let us consider for a moment what is the position of one of these girls, who leaving her place is homeless, and has therefore no refuge but the workhouse, where, above the age of sixteen, she is placed in the able-bodied women's ward. Whatever she may have been on entering it, there is scarcely a possibility of her leaving it otherwise than contaminated and ruined. In one London workhouse there were lately fifty of this class of women, the comparatively, or even entirely innocent being associated with the very worst and most hardened. What a hopeless mass did they present to the authorities! to the one over-worked matron at the head of this large establishment, and to the women whose duty it was to superintend them! . . . They were not even entirely separated from the rest of the house, but communicated with the other inmates in their hours of work as well as of idleness. Discipline was impossible, and the scene was, as may be imagined, most sad and perplexing. To such persons the workhouse ceases to be a test, for with the licence that prevails there, and the liberty of indulging in evil gossip and companionship, it is preferred by the badly-disposed and idle girls to the hard work which is required of them in service. Such work as they have to do in the workhouse is hardly any preparation for that which is expected of them as servants, and many of them are only employed in oakum-picking, which, whether it is intended as a punishment or not, certainly does not answer the purpose of deterring them from entering the workhouse.

Now, what I would suggest is, that we should endeavour to reverse this degrading process into one that would raise the character, and fit it for something better than the able-bodied women's ward. . . . All experience shows that the same persons are continually returning to the workhouse, and not only they, but their children after them will probably be life-long burdens upon the parish. . . . It is proposed by the Workhouse Visiting Society to open a home for girls of the ages when they must necessarily be admitted into the adult wards, the guardians undertaking to pay to the home the cost of their maintenance in the workhouse. In this home they would be trained, under the care of a matron, for all the duties of household work and service, and the principal aim would be to fit them for emigration to the Colonies. This is no vague and indefinite idea, for we have the positive assurance that such is the want of women, especially in Western Australia, that they would be eagerly welcomed there; and were the plan successfully carried out, we might even expect their passages to be paid by the colonists, which would thus leave only the outfits to be provided at home. Such a plan would necessarily involve careful arrangements for superintendence during the voyage as well as on arrival, but they could be easily made; and the advantages offered by a life in a new sphere, removed from all former associations and temptations, would be far greater than could be looked for at home. . . . The length of time for remaining in the home, and many other details, would be easily arranged, and also the principle of selecting the inmates, on which obviously much would depend; the visiting of this class of inmates in the workhouses by ladies would of course be a necessary part of the plan. As it is well to foresee, and as far as possible meet, all objections and difficulties before beginning a new work, I may mention that the only one that has been yet made to this proposal is that it might prove an encouragement to girls to come to the home for the sake of the advantages it would offer.

To this I can only answer that, as discipline and hard work would be the order of the house in a greater degree than in the workhouse, I do not think it would be likely to prove so very attractive to this class of persons. . . .

In one London workhouse there are now 17 women in the adult ward. Of these since 1850, one has been admited 18 times; one 15 times (age 21); one 12 times (age 20); one 11 times; one 9 times (age 22); and one 7 times, whose age is now only 17.

From what has been said, I think it must be clear to all, first, that something like reformatory discipline is the one only hope and chance for this class of persons, and secondly, that such is impossible at present in our workhouses, both from want of space (more particularly in those of large towns), as well as from the total want of persons to carry it out. As a class these women are not admissible into any of our existing institutions, even if they could be received into them; but they are neither all fit subjects for penitentiaries, refuges, or reformatories; and besides these reasons, some separate home is required which can be recognised by the guardians. . . . We are anxious to gain the sympathy and approval of those who are here met together, and who are occupied in somewhat similar plans for the benefit of their fellow-creatures, and who are capable of judging not only of the need of such a scheme, but also of the probability of its success. If the experiment can once be made and fairly carried out in London, there is no reason why it should not be tried in the country as well, so that every county should in time have its homes and penitentiaries (for the two might well be united), where every effort might be made to rescue and restore those unhappy ones who are now, whilst supported at our expense, thrust down into the lowest depths of despair and degradation in the able-bodied wards of our [workhouses].

Mary Carpenter, "Reformatories for Convicted Girls", *National Association for the Promotion of Social Science, Transactions*, 1857, pp. 338-46.

Mary Carpenter, one of the most influential reformers of the nineteenth century, became interested in philanthropy as the result of the influence of her Unitarian clergyman father. While still in her teens, after some experience as a teacher and governess, she opened a "ragged school" in Bristol with the aid of John Bishop Estlin and Matthew Davenport Hill. This was the beginning of the work—the rehabilitation of young criminals and children on the verge of criminality—that was to absorb most of her energies for the rest of her life. She was indefatigable in the pursuit of this objective, writing a book on the subject and acting as the moving spirit behind a conference of similarly motivated reformers of both sexes.

Miss Carpenter radiated good humor, good will, enormous energy, and an indomitable resolve in her untiring efforts to salvage and rehabilitate destitute and criminal children. In addition to the ragged schools, she was also active in the reformatory and industrial school movements. Frances Power Cobbe was for a while associated with her at a reforma-

tory school for girls which Miss Carpenter established at the Red Lodge
in Bristol. (Miss Carpenter, whose altruism was so all-consuming that
it made her indifferent to the creature comforts, set a bare table, much
to the dismay of Miss Cobbe, who was something of a trencherwoman,
and who described Miss Carpenter as doing "the work of three people on
the food of half a one". This was not Miss Cobbe's style, and it may
have led her to leave the Red Lodge and subsequently to engage in workhouse reform elsewhere.)[1]

Despite the demands of her various philanthropic projects, Miss
Carpenter found time to make several trips to India, where she advised
the government on education and prison discipline, and supervised a
female normal school in Bombay. She also lectured on prison reform in
the United States and Canada.

The following selection is taken from the paper which she presented
at the first meeting of the Social Science Association, in which she advanced a plan for the rehabilitation of juvenile female criminals. It will
be noted that she did not share Louisa Twining's enthusiasm for emigration as a solution to the problem of wayward girls.

It is but recently that the position of convicted girls, of young female children who
by their misdeeds or vicious tendencies have separated themselves from society, has
engaged public attention.

Until lately some have supposed, on the one hand, that little creatures of the "softer
sex" cannot have arrived at such a pitch of wickedness as to require the intervention
of the strong hand of the law, or the agency of a public institution to curb and correct
vicious propensities; while on the other hand, those whose avocations have brought
them into personal contact . . . with neglected and depraved girls, have with horror
beheld in them such an amount of desperate wickedness . . . that they have despaired
of doing anything effectual to reform them. . . . The Rev. T. Carter . . . in his speech
at the conference at Birmingham, six years ago, . . . made this statement, "Out of
twenty-six females in the Liverpool Gaol, all of whom commenced as juveniles, I found
that twenty-five had been in gaol on an average seven times each; the other I do not
think it fair or proper to bring forward as an average example, because she has been
fifty-seven times in gaol. The average time each is known to spend in gaol is five years". . . .

All persons who have come much into actual intercourse with both boys and girls of
the "perishing and dangerous classes" have fully agreed with my own experience, that
the girls are by far the most hardened and difficult to manage. . . .

. . . Many of the boys brought before magistrates and sent to prison . . . have been
guilty of nothing more than would have called forth only a reprimand or school
punishment in lads of a higher class; . . . whereas girls are seldom . . . handed into
the custody of the gaoler, until all more lenient means of correction have been previously tried unavailingly. . . . Hence we may anticipate that the girls in a reformatory will be of the very lowest class, and that the crimes with which they are charged
will frequently imply a very high degree of moral depravity, such as a trained habit of

---

[1] Frances Power Cobbe, *The Life of Frances Power Cobbe,* 2 vols. (Boston and New York: Houghton,
Mifflin & Company, 1894), I, 250-75.

picking pockets, arson, house-breaking, horse-stealing, even poisoning; young girls guilty of such crimes as these are to be found in our reformatories; while of those who have not actually committed such crimes, are the unfortunate daughters of receivers of stolen goods, of drunken and dissolute parents, young orphans of a father whose cruel usage had bereft them of a mother, and the child of one who boasted to have trained at least fifty young girls to a life of theft; these cannot be expected to have imbibed other than the most injurious influences throughout their short lives. The physical condition of young girls whose susceptible natures have grown up under such circumstances will very frequently be found to be already diseased. The experience of but three years among eighty girls has brought melancholy proofs of this; in one reformatory alone death has carried off two young girls of thirteen of organic disease, the seeds of which had been for some time latent in the constitution, and which, in the case of one, had probably been much aggravated by long previous imprisonment; two others came so worn by long neglect that they were pronounced incurable, but were happily restored to health by unremitting care; and numbers have been received with painful symptoms of scrofulous and other bad tendencies, which have gradually disappeared only by the most assiduous attention to the general health both of body and mind. . . .

The aim we must set before us in the reformation of the girls is very different from that proposed for boys. . . . Girls must be prepared for domestic life, either at service in the homes of persons in the respectable portion of society, or eventually in their own families. Emigration I believe to be usually undesirable in the case of girls; they are then removed from such salutary influences as may have guided them. . . . A factory, or any place of work where many are congregated, would be always dangerous. . . . We must aim at preparing our girls for domestic service in England. This must be kept in view in all our arrangements, and we must endeavour to make our reformatories such that Christian women may fearlessly seek for girls from them as young servants in their own families. . . .

The problem is a difficult one, and involves apparent contrarieties. We are to bring under restraint and control those who dislike any infringement of their liberty, to reform by steady discipline those who do not yet hate their evil ways and desire to leave them to work, against their will; and at the same time to bring children and teachers into a loving harmony, to diffuse as much as possible through the establishment the influences of a home, gradually inspiring a confidence in the child that all the restraint and discipline to which she is subjected are for her real good. The legal element is absolutely necessary to bring the child to the school, and to keep her there, until such time as she is fit to leave it, when she will have begun to love it as a home. But the promptings of His love must guide the working of the school, and so develope [*sic*] itself that the child may be soon conscious that those around have a sympathy with her as well as for her, and that she is no longer regarded as an outcast from society. . . .

We now proceed to consider the preliminaries for the establishment of the school. . . .

With respect to the general principles of internal management, I cannot better express my views than in the statement of them made at the meeting of the National Reformatory Union last year: —

"1st. The physical condition of these girls will generally be found very unsatisfactory; and it is well known that the moral state is much influenced by the physical. All sanitary regulations for ventilation, regular and sufficient personal ablutions, suitable temperature, &c., should be strictly attended to. The advantage of agricultural labour not being procurable, walks beyond the premises, as well as out-door play, should be regularly taken by the girls, and as much bodily exercise as possible should be devised for them in their daily industrial work, as an exercise of their physical energies. The food should be sufficient, and of a more nourishing description than is allowed in most pauper schools. . . .

"2nd. The young girl is to be placed, as far as possible, in the same kind of position as children in a well-ordered family in the working classes. She has been accustomed to be independent of authority, and to do only what is right in her *own* eyes. She must now feel under steady, regular restraint, administered with a firm, equal, but loving hand. Her irregular impulses must be curbed. She must insensibly, but steadily, be made to feel that it is necessary for her to submit to the will of *others,* and especially to be obedient to duty. . . .

"3rd. Children in this class have hitherto felt themselves in a state of antagonism with society, and totally unconnected with the virtuous portion of it. . . . They must, as far as possible, be brought to feel themselves a part of society, regarded by it with no unkind feeling, but rather, having been outcasts, welcomed into it with Christian love. . . . Nothing in their dress or appearance should mark them out as a separate caste; as far as it is found safe and expedient, they should be enabled to associate with others. . . .

"4th. The affections must be cultivated as much as possible in a healthy direction. The love of their families must not be repressed, and the natural ties must be cherished as far as can be done without evil influence being exerted over them. The school must be made a home, and a happy one; but the children must be led to feel that the possibility of this depends on their own forbearance and kindness towards each other. Mutual dependence must be cultivated. . . . They will then learn to feel it a duty and a pleasure to help each other in difficulty, and to be watchful over each other's conduct, from no censorious feeling, but from a simple regard to each other's benefit, and to do what is right. . . .

"5th. The activity and love of amusement natural to childhoold should be cultivated in an innocent and healthy manner. . . . The children should be allowed to possess little toys and articles treasured by childhood, which they may be permitted to purchase with earnings awarded them for work done. The valuable exhibitions now open to ordinary schools may be allowed to them occasionally, especially as a reward for good conduct. The Dioramas and Zoological Gardens may open their minds, and give a stimulus to the advancement of knowledge more than any other lessons.

"6th. All rewards and punishments should be, as much as possible, the natural consequences of actions. Deceit or dishonesty will occasion an amount of distrust and watchfulness, which a judicious teacher may render a very severe punishment to a child. The employment of bad language, and the indulgence of a quarrelsome disposition, will require separation from the society of others as a necessary consequence. All punishments should be administered with the greatest caution and impartiality, and should be evidently prompted by a desire to do good to the offender; the sympathy of the school, and even of the culprit, will thus be enlisted with the teacher. There should be no bribery to do right, nor deterring by fear only from doing wrong; a desire of improvement and love of duty should be cherished for themselves. . . .

"7th. As much freedom should be given as is compatible with the good order of the establishment. Those who prove themselves deserving of confidence may have situations of trust given them, and may be sent on errands beyond the premises. It is only

in proportion as there is liberty, that security can be felt in the child's real improvement.

"8th. The intellectual powers should be steadily trained, though not superficially
excited. It is only by giving the mind wholesome nourishment, that it can be prevented
from preying on garbage. . . .

"9th. . . . Every effort must be made to infuse a good moral tone into the school.
It will certainly exist if the preceding principles are well carried out. When a new
comer or a badly disposed child finds the feeling of the school in harmony with obedience, order, and duty, . . . the work of the teacher will be incalculably lightened.

"10th. The will of each individual child must be enlisted in her own reformation,
and she must be made to feel that without this, the efforts of her teachers will be useless. Such confidence must be awakened in the minds of the children towards their
teachers as to lead them willingly to submit to all the regulations for order, neatness,
and regularity, which are an important part of their training, and to yield themselves
implicitly to their guidance. From this the child must be taught to feel obedience to
the Divine Will to be the highest happiness, and to desire to obey that will."

The disposal of the girls after leaving the school is a subject which will increasingly
require attention. . . . Domestic service has been spoken of as the best position for
girls. . . . If the school has become what it is hoped that all reformatories will be
eventually, there will be little difficulty in finding good situations for well-trained girls
who have become trustworthy; and if these are in the immediate neighbourhood, the
school that she can then be sent first on trial, . . . and received back at the school, if
may thus keep up their attachment to it, and esteem it a privilege to be permitted to
join the Sunday afternoon instruction, and occasionally to be associated in other particular gatherings. . . . It is another advantage of placing the girl at service near the
school that she can then be sent first on trial . . . and received back at the school, if
not suitable. But the sudden transition from the regular discipline and necessary
restraint of a school to the freedom of a family is dangerous; for the true character of
a girl is often concealed or curbed while under restraint. The plan has been, therefore,
adopted . . . of renting a small house adjoining the school, where a few older girls are
placed who have already gained a good character, and who are here under little more
control than would be exercised by a judicious mistress in a well-regulated household.
The plan . . . has been an excellent test of the fitness of girls to go out into the world;
two have already left, who have proved themselves worthy of confidence. The house
door is no longer locked; the girls are frequently sent out alone on errands, even to pay
bills to the amount of many pounds. They execute the washing and laundry-work of
the household without any superintendency, and bake, not only for themselves, but for
the school; one is even left at home to take charge of the house and the two young
children of the matron, while she and the other girls attend worship. This confidence
has never in one instance been abused, and a similar plan would probably be always
useful in reformatories. But whatever course is adopted with respect to the destination
of girls on leaving the school, the parties who sent them there in the first place should
not be allowed to forget the moral, if not the legal, responsibility they are under to
make some provision for them on leaving it. The work of a reformatory will be often
thrown away if suitable arrangements are not made for the child on leaving it.

. . . Before concluding, I would urge on the women of England who have not already
any close domestic ties involving prior duties, to do what they can personally in this
work. The distant sufferings of our countrymen have roused to noble and devoted

labour, and women have learnt what they can do, and what they are permitted to do. Let not the "cry of the children" in this humbler, but not less important, sphere be heard in vain. The regeneration of these young girls, whose doom is sealed unless the hand of mercy rescues them, is surely a work which demands the devotion of the highest energies and talents—the consecration of a life. Let not the unremitting, self-denying efforts of "Sisters of Charity" abroad, of devoted Catholic women at home, any longer cast reproach on Englishwomen and Protestants; let us emulate each other in works of Christian love. A noble sphere is here offered, more worthy of the refined, and loving, and true of our sex than the allurements of the world; and the most precious rewards must follow—the joy which is shared by the angels in heaven over each repentant and rescued child—the beloved voice of the Saviour, "Inasmuch as ye have done it unto one of the least of these little ones, ye have done it unto Me."

Octavia Hill, "Organized Work Among the Poor", *Macmillan's Magazine,* XX (1869), 219-226.

Octavia Hill, the granddaughter of the well-known physician and reformer, Thomas Southwood Smith, combined a career as social reformer with that of successful business woman. She was active in the work of the Charity Organization Society, was a member of the Commons Preservation Society, and was one of the founders of the National Trust. She taught classes for women at the Working Men's College, and with her sisters established a school in a working-class district of London. It was, however, chiefly as an imaginative, sympathetic, but firm benefactress of the inhabitants of a London slum that she acquired an international reputation.

Influenced by her grandfather, by the Christian Socialist F. D. Maurice, and by Ruskin, she hit upon an ingenious scheme for helping the poor by involving them in their own rehabilitation rather than making them simply the objects of charity. Ruskin's promise to finance the project caused her to write to her friend, Emma Baumgartner, "I am so happy that I can hardly walk on the ground".[1] Financed at the outset by Ruskin, who also gave her some extremely practical advice, she managed a number of slum buildings so successfully that the Ecclesiastical Commissioners engaged her to manage much of their property in Southwark. By placing her tenants under a regimen based on firmness, kindness, incentives, and rewards, Miss Hill succeeded in making them participate in their own improvement, with a consequent gain in their self-respect. Moreover, this was accomplished so efficiently that the enterprise yielded a respectable profit.

In the article which follows, Miss Hill describes how her method effected dramatic changes in the depressed condition of an average London slum.

[1] C. E. Maurice, *Life of Octavia Hill as Told in Her Letters* (London: Macmillan & Co., Limited, 1914), p. 214.

. . . I feel most deeply that the disciplining of our immense poor population must be effected by individual influence; and that this power can change it from a mob of paupers and semi-paupers into a body of self-dependent workers. It is my opinion, further, that although such influence may be brought to bear upon them in very various ways, it may be exercised in a very remarkable manner by persons undertaking the oversight and management of such houses as the poor habitually lodge in. In support of this opinion I subjoin an account of what has been actually achieved in two very poor courts in London.

About four years ago I was put in possession of three houses in one of the worst courts of Marylebone. Six other houses were bought subsequently. All were crowded with inmates. The first thing to be done was to put them in decent tenantable order. The set last purchased was a row of cottages facing a bit of desolate ground, occupied with wretched dilapidated cow-sheds, manure heaps, old timber, and rubbish of every description. The houses were in a most deplorable condition; the plaster was dropping from the walls; on one staircase a pail was placed to catch the rain that fell through the roof. All the staircases were perfectly dark; the banisters were gone, having been burnt as firewood by tenants. The grates, with large holes in them, were falling forward into the rooms. The washhouse, full of lumber belonging to the landlord, was locked up; thus the inhabitants had to wash clothes, as well as to cook, eat, and sleep, in their small rooms. The dust-bin, standing in the front of the houses, was accessible to the whole neighbourhood, and boys often dragged from it quantities of unseemly objects, and spread them over the court. The state of the drainage was in keeping with everything else. The pavement of the backyard was all broken up, and great puddles stood in it, so that the damp crept up the outer walls. One large but dirty water-butt received the water laid on for the houses; it leaked, and for such as did not fill their jugs when the water came in, or who had no jugs to fill, there was no water. The former landlord's reply to one of the tenants who asked him to have an iron hoop put round the butt to prevent leakage, was, that "if he didn't like it" (i.e. things as they were) "he might leave". . . .

This landlord was a tradesman in a small way of buisness — not a cruel man, except in so far as variableness of dealing is cruelty; but he was a man without capital to spend on improvements, and lost an immense percentage of his rent by bad debts. . . . The arrears of rent were enormous. I had been informed that the honest habitually pay for the dishonest, the owner relying upon their payments to compensate for all losses; but I was amazed to find to what an extent this was the case. Six, seven, or eight weeks' rent were due from most tenants, and in some cases very much more; whereas, since I took possession of the houses (of which I collect the rents each week myself) I have *never* allowed a second week's rent to become due. . . .

As soon as I entered into possession, each family had an opportunity offered of doing better; those who would not pay, or who led clearly immoral lives, were ejected. The rooms they vacated were cleansed; the tenants who showed signs of improvement moved into them, and thus, in turn, an opportunity was obtained for having each room distempered and painted. The drains were put in order, a large slate cistern was fixed, the wash house was cleared of its lumber, and thrown open on stated days to each tenant in turn. The roof, the plaster, the woodwork were repaired; the staircase walls were distempered; new grates were fixed; the layers of paper and rag (black with age) were torn from the windows, and glass was put in; out of 192 panes, only 8 were found unbroken. The yard and footpath were paved.

The rooms, as a rule, were re-let at the same prices at which they had been let before; but tenants with large families were counselled to take two rooms, and for these much less was charged than if let singly; this plan I continue to pursue. In-coming tenants are not allowed to take a decidedly insufficient quantity of room, and no sub-letting is permitted. The elder girls are employed three times a week in scrubbing the passages in the houses, for the cleaning of which the landlady is responsible. For this work they are paid, and by it they learn habits of cleanliness. It is, of course, within the authority of the landlady also to insist on cleanliness of wash houses, yards, staircases, and stair-case-windows; and even to remonstrate concerning the rooms themselves if they are habitually dirty.

The pecuniary result has been very satisfactory. Five per cent interest has been paid on all the capital invested. A fund for the repayment of capital is accumulating. A liberal allowance has been made for repairs; and here I may speak of the means adopted for making the tenants careful about breakage and waste. The sum allowed yearly for repairs is fixed for each house, and if it has not all been spent in restoring and replac-ing, the surplus is used for providing such additional appliances as the tenants them-selves desire. It is therefore to their interest to keep the expenditure for repairs as low as possible; and instead of committing the wanton damage common among tenants of their class, they are careful to avoid injury, and very helpful in finding economical methods of restoring what is broken or worn out, often doing little repairs of their own accord.

From the proceeds of the rent, also, interest has been paid on the capital spent in building a large room where the tenants can assemble. Classes are held there—for boys, twice weekly; for girls, once: a singing class has just been established. A large work class for married women and elder girls meets once a week. A glad sight it is—the large room filled with the eager, merry faces of the girls, from which those of the older careworn women catch a reflected light. It is a good time for quiet talk with them as we work, and many a neighbourly feeling is called out among the women as they sit together on the same bench, lend one another cotton or needles, are served by the same hand, and look to the same person for direction. The babies are a great bond of union; I have known the very women who not long before had been literally fighting, sit at the work-class busily and earnestly comparing notes of their babies' respective history. That a consciousness of corporate life is developed in them is shown by the not infrequent use of the expression "One of us."

Among the arrangements conducive to comfort and health I may mention, that instead of the clothes being hung as formerly out of front windows down against the wall, where they could not be properly purified, the piece of ground in front of the houses is used as a drying-ground during school hours. The same place is appropriated as a playground, not only for my younger tenants, but for the children from the neigh-bouring courts. It is a space walled round, where they can play in safety. Hitherto, games at trap, bat, and ball, swinging, skipping, and singing a few Kinder Garten songs with movements in unison, have been the main diversions. But I have just estab-lished drill for the boys, and a drum and fife band. Unhappily, the mere business con-nected with the working of the houses has occupied so much time, that the playground has been somewhat neglected; yet it is a most important part of the work. The evils of the streets and courts are too evident to need explanation. In the playground are gathered together children habitually dirty, quarrelsome, and violent. They come wholly ignorant of games, and have hardly self-control enough to play at any which have an object or require effort. . . . [We need] the moral influence . . . [of] ladies who will go to the playground, teach games, act as umpires, know and care for the children. . . . Until now, except at rare intervals, the playground has been mainly useful for the fresh air it affords to the children who are huddled together by night in small rooms, in the surrounding courts. The more respectable parents keep them indoors, even in the day-time, after school hours, to prevent their meeting with bad companions.

Mr. Ruskin, to whom the whole undertaking owes its existence, has had trees planted in the playground, and creepers against the houses. In May, we have a May-pole or a throne covered with flowers for the May-queen and her attendants. The sweet luxuriance of the spring-flowers is more enjoyed in that court than would readily be believed. Some months after the first festival the children were seen sticking a few faded flowers into a crevice in the wall, saying, they wanted to make it "like it was the day we had the May-pole."

I have tried, as far as opportunity has permitted, to develop the love of beauty among my tenants. The poor of London need joy and beauty in their lives. . . . They work hard; their lives are monotonous; they seek low places of amusement; they break out into lawless "sprees." Almost all amusements—singing, dancing, acting, expeditions into the country, eating and drinking—are liable to abuse; no rules are subtle enough to prevent their leading to harm. But if a lady can know the individuals, and ask them as her invited guests to any of these, an innate sense of honour and respect preserves the tone through the whole company. Indeed, there can hardly be a more proudly thankful moment than that, when we see these many people to whom life is dull and full of anxiety, gathered together around us for holy, happy Christmas festivities, or going out to some fair and quiet spot in the bright summer time, bound to one another by the sense of common relationship, preserved unconsciously from wrong by the presence of those whom they love and who love them. . . .

All these ways of meeting are invaluable as binding us together; still, they would avail little were it not for the work by which we are connected—for the individual care each member of the little circle receives. Week by week, when the rents are collected, an opportunity of seeing each family separately occurs. There are a multitude of matters to attend to: first there is the mere outside business—rent to be received, requests from the tenant respecting repairs to be considered; sometimes decisions touching the behaviour of other tenants to be made, sometimes rebukes for untidiness to be administered. Then come the sad or joyful remarks about health or work, the little histories of the week. Sometimes grave questions arise about important changes in the life of the family—shall a daughter go to service? or shall the sick child be sent to a hospital? . . .

Sometimes violent quarrels must be allayed. Much may be done in this way, so ready is the response in these affectionate natures to those whom they trust and love. For instance: two women among my tenants fought; one received a dreadful kick, the other had hair torn from her head. They were parted by a lad who lived in the house. The women occupied adjoining rooms, they met in the passages, they used the same yard and wash-house, endless were the opportunities of collision while they were engaged with each other. For ten days I saw them repeatedly: I could in no way reconcile them—words of rage and recrimination were all that they uttered: while the hair, which had been carefully preserved by the victim, was continually exhibited to me as a sufficient justification for lasting anger. One was a cold, hard, self-satisfied, well-to-do woman; the other a nervous, affectionate, passionate, very poor Irish-woman. Now it happened that in speaking to the latter one evening, I mentioned my own grief at the quarrel; a look of extreme pain came over her face; it was a new idea to her that I should care. That, and no sense of the wrong of indulging an evil passion, touched her. The warm-hearted creature at once promised to shake hands with her adversary; but she had already taken out a summons against the other for assault, and did not consider she could afford to make up the quarrel because it implied losing the two shillings the summons had cost. I told her the loss was a mere nothing to her if weighed in the balance with peace, but that I would willingly pay it. It only needed that one of the combatants should make the first step towards reconciliation for the other (who indeed rather dreaded answering the summons) to meet her half-way. They are good neighbours now of some months' standing. . . . It is on such infinitesimally small actions that the success of the whole work rests.

My tenants are mostly of a class far below that of mechanics; they are, indeed, of the very poor. And yet, . . . none of the families who have passed under my care during the whole four years have continued in what is called "distress," except such as have been unwilling to exert themselves. . . . But, for those who are willing, some small assistance in the form of work has from time to time been provided, — not much, but sufficient to keep them from want or despair. The following will serve as an instance of the sort of help given, and its proportion to the results.

Alice, a single woman, of perhaps fifty-five years, lodged with a man and his wife — the three in one room — just before I obtained full possession of the houses. Alice, not being able to pay her rent, was turned into the street, where Mrs. S. (my playground superintendent) met her, crying dreadfully.

It was Saturday, and I had left town till Monday. Alice had neither furniture to pawn, nor friends to help her; the workhouse alone lay before her. Mrs. S. knew that I esteemed her as a sober, respectable, industrious woman, and therefore she ventured to express to Alice's landlord the belief that I would not let him lose money if he would let her go back to her lodging till Monday, when I should return home, thus risking for me a possible loss of fourpence — not very ruinous to me, and a sum not impossible for Alice to repay in the future.

I gave Alice two days' needlework; then found her employment in tending a bed-ridden cottager in the country, whose daughter (in service) paid for the nursing. Five weeks she was there, working, and saving her money. On her return I lent her what more she required to buy furniture, and she then took a little room direct from me. Too blind to do much household work, but able to sew almost mechanically, she just earns her daily bread by making sailors' shirts; but her little home is her own, and she loves it dearly; and, having tided over that time of trial, Alice can live — has paid all her debts too, and is more grateful than she would have been for many gifts. . . .

My tenants are of course encouraged to save their money. It should, however, be remarked, that I have never succeeded in getting them to save for old age. The utmost I have achieved is that they lay by sufficient either to pay rent in times of scarcity, to provide clothes for girls going to service, or boots, or furniture. . . .

One great advantage arising from the management of the houses is, that they form a test-place, in which people may prove themselves worthy of higher situations. Not a few of the tenants have been persons who had sunk below the stratum where once they were known. . . . One man, twenty years ago, had been a gentleman's servant, had saved money, gone into business, married, failed, and then found himself out of the groove of work. When I made his acquaintance, he was earning a miserable pittance for his wife and seven unhealthy children, and all the nine souls were suffering and sinking unknown. After watching and proving him for three years, I was able to recommend him to a gentleman in the country, where now the whole family are profiting by having six rooms instead of one, fresh air, and regular wages.

. . . And yet the main tone of action must be severe, . . . although a deep and silent undercurrent of sympathy and pity may flow beneath. If the rent is not ready, notice to quit must be served; the money is then almost always paid, when the notice is, of course, withdrawn. Besides this inexorable demand for rent (never to be relaxed without entailing cumulative evil on the defaulter, and setting a bad example too readily followed by others) there must be a perpetual crusade carried on against small evils, — very wearing sometimes. . . .

Coming together so much as we do for business with mutual duties, for recreation with common joy, each separate want or fault having been dealt with as it arose, it will be readily understood that in such a crisis as that which periodically occurs in the East End of London, instead of being unprepared, I feel myself somewhat like an officer at the head of a well-controlled little regiment, or, more accurately, like a country proprietor with a moderate number of well-ordered tenants.

For, firstly, my people are numbered; not merely counted, but known, man, woman, and child. I have seen their self-denying efforts to pay rent in time of trouble, or their reckless extravagance in seasons of abundance; their patient labour, or their failure to use the self-control necessary to the performance of the more remunerative kinds of work; their efforts to keep their children at school, or their selfish, lazy way of living on their children's earnings. Could any one, going suddenly among even so small a number as these thirty-four families — however much penetration and zeal he might possess — know so accurately as I what kind of assistance would be really helpful, and not corrupting? And if positive gifts must be resorted to, who can give them with so little pain to the proud spirit, so little risk of undermining the feeble one, as the friend of old standing, — the friend, moreover, who has rigorously exacted the fulfillment of their duty in punctual payment of rent; towards whom, therefore, they might feel that they had done what they could while strength lasted, and need not surely be ashamed to receive a little bread in time of terrible want?

But it ought hardly ever to come to an actual doling out of bread or alms of any kind. During the winter of 1867-8, while the newspapers were ringing with appeals in consequence of the distress prevalent in the metropolis . . . I [arranged] . . . that a small fund (which had accumulated from rents, after defraying expenses and paying interest) should be distributed in gifts to any of the families who might be in great poverty. . . . There were none requiring such help. Now, how did this come to pass?

Simply through the operation of the various influences above described. The tenants never having been allowed to involve themselves in debt for rent. . . , they were free from one of the greatest drags upon a poor family, and had, moreover, in times of prosperity been able really to save. . . .

You may say, perhaps, "This is very well as far as you and your small knot of tenants are concerned, but how does it help us to deal with the vast masses of poor in our great towns?" I reply, "Are not the great masses made up of many small knots? Are not the great towns divisible into small districts? Are there not people who would gladly come forward to undertake the systematic supervision of some house or houses, if they could get authority from the owner? And why should there not be some way of registering such supervision, so that, bit by bit, as more volunteers should come forward, the whole metropolis might be mapped out, all the blocks fitting in like little bits of mosaic to form one connected whole?" . . .

Whoever will limit his gaze to a few persons, and try to solve the problems of their lives, . . . may find it in most cases a much more difficult thing than he had ever thought, and sometimes maybe an impossibility. . . .

Further details as to modes of help must vary infinitely with circumstances and character. But I may mention a few laws which become clearer and clearer to me as I work.

It is best strictly to enforce fulfilment of all such duties as payment of rent, &c.

It is far better to give work than either money or goods.

It is most helpful of all to strengthen by sympathy and counsel the energetic effort which shall bear fruit in time to come.

It is essential to remember that each man has his own view of his life, and must be free to fulfil it; that in many ways he is a far better judge of it than we, as he has lived through and felt what we have only seen. Our work is rather to bring him to the point of considering, and to the spirit of judging rightly, than to consider or judge for him.

The poor of London (as of all large towns) need the development of every power which can open to them noble sources of joy.

CHAPTER V

Education and Emancipation

It was obvious to nineteenth-century feminists, as it had been to Mary Wollstonecraft some sixty or seventy years earlier, that the key with which woman could unlock her shackles was education. Sydney Smith's famous early nineteenth-century essay, "Advice to Young Ladies on the Improvement of the Mind", exposed the superficiality and frivolousness of female education and scoffed at the notion, advanced by opponents of meaningful education for women, that study of a serious kind might prove so distracting to women that their children would be neglected. It was hardly likely, he observed, that a mother would desert her infant for the sake of a quadratic equation.[1]

As late as the 1850's, however, the seductions of mathematics had not yet been made available to women. Most upper-class and some middle-class girls were being educated either by governesses only slightly less ignorant than their pupils; or in small boarding schools where the curriculum was hardly likely to put a strain on even the presumably inferior female brain; or in finishing schools specializing in the application of a fashionable veneer.

The education given at the schools was not only poor; it was very expensive—as much as £500 per year—approximately twice what it cost to send a young man to Eton or Rugby.[2] The object of these schools was to prepare young women for their true vocation: marriage and motherhood. They were taught the social graces—etiquette, dancing, music, singing, drawing, deportment—a smattering of foreign languages, religion, and sometimes even how to swoon in a ladylike fashion.[3] Armed with these accomplishments, it was assumed, young women would be prepared for marriage or, at least, attracting an eligible male.

---

[1] Sydney Smith, "Advice to Young Ladies on the Improvement of the Mind", *Edinburgh Review*, XV (1810), 302.

[2] Cobbe, *Life*, I, 52.

[3] "In a little book, *The Girls' Book of Diversions*, she is taught 'how to faint; the modes of fainting should be all as different as possible and may be made very diverting' ". Cited in Cunnington, *Feminine Attitudes in the Nineteenth Century*, p. 124.

Nobody dreamed that any one of us could in later life be more or less than an "Ornament of Society." That a pupil . . . should ever become an artist, or authoress, would have been looked upon . . . as a deplorable dereliction. Not that which was good in itself or useful to the community, or even that which would be delightful to ourselves, but that which would make us admired in society, was the *raison d'être* of each requirement.[1]

Serious-minded men and women rebelled against this inadequate and wasteful regimen. Attacking the evil at its source meant educating the educators, beginning with the governesses. The Governesses' Benevolent Institution, founded in 1847, attempted to make governesses better teachers so that they could command higher salaries. The next year F. D. Maurice, then professor at King's College, London, collaborated with some of his fellow Christian Socialists in organizing a series of "Lectures for Ladies". This was the origin of Queen's College for Women, whose primary purpose was the training of governesses. One of the pupils, Frances Mary Buss, became the first headmistress of the famous North London Collegiate School for Girls. Another Queen's College alumna, Dorothea Beale, became principal of a girls' school which in 1864 became Cheltenham College for Ladies, the first girls' boarding school modeled on public schools for boys. Bedford College for Ladies, which was similar to Queen's but non-denominational, was established in 1849.[2] Both Bedford and Queen's began to turn out qualified instructors, an immensely important function since one of the chief obstacles to improving the education of girls was the lack of trained teachers. Progress, however, was slow; as late as 1865 a Schools' Inquiry Commission found that teachers in women's schools "have not themselves been well taught, and they do not know how to teach".[3]

In its inquiries into the state of female education, the same Commission revealed: "Want of thoroughness and foundation; want of system; slovenliness and showy superficiality; inattention to rudiments; undue time given to accomplishments, and those not taught intelligently, or in any scientific manner; want of organization".[4] Woman's education, in short, was outrageously expensive and "disgracefully bad".

In fact, if there had been a conspiracy on foot to insure that boys would appear to be cleverer than girls, it could not have been any more effective in achieving that goal than was the existing system of education for women which, according to its feminist critics, made woman "first, man's plaything, and then his slave". From the feminist point of view,

[1] Cobbe, *Life*, I, 55-56. Not surprisingly, Miss Cobbe criticized her formal education as being "shallow and senseless", and "a notable failure".

[2] Among the first students who attended Bedford or Queen's were several who later became active proponents of women's rights, including Barbara Leigh Smith, Adelaide Procter, Sophia Jex-Blake, and Frances Martin.

[3] D. Beale, *Reports issued by the Schools' Inquiry Commission on the Education of Girls* (London: David Nutt, 1869), p. 13.

[4] *Ibid.*, p. 3.

if this humiliating notion of woman's intrinsic inferiority was to be overcome, it would have to be through the educational process. The whole society should be educated to regard woman as not necessarily inferior; but, in addition, woman herself must first demonstrate that she was intellectually capable of getting an education identical to man's.

In 1862 Frances Power Cobbe read a paper before the Social Science Association, meeting that year in London, in which she called for granting university degrees for women—a position which exposed her to "universal ridicule".[1] Not everyone, however, was amused. Emily Davies, soon to emerge as a pioneer in the field, was so impressed that she henceforth devoted her considerable talents to securing higher education for women.

Step by step in the 1860's and 70's the champions of women's education advanced their cause. The opening of Local Examinations to women; the founding of the new college for women at Hitchin (later transferred to Girton), a residential college having the same high standards as Oxford or Cambridge; the establishment of other women's colleges, including the London School of Medicine for Women; the admission to degrees at the University of London—these events opened up for women the possibility of obtaining higher education.

At the same time, opportunities for education on the primary and secondary levels were increasing. Emily Shirreff and her sister, Maria Shirreff Grey, were as committed to improving secondary education as Emily Davies was devoted to higher education. The Shirreff sisters promoted the Girls' Public Day School Company, a venture through which private secondary schools for girls were established and supervised. The importance of this undertaking may be gauged by the comment of a contemporary authority on education and a member of the Schools' Inquiry Commission who wrote: "The establishment of the Girls' Public Day School Company in 1874 . . . perhaps had a larger influence on the improvement of feminine education, than any single measure".[2] Furthermore, the recognition by the state of its responsibility to provide adequate elementary (and later secondary) education—as evidenced by the Education Acts of 1870 and 1902—further narrowed the gap between the education available to boys and that provided for girls. Some feminists, inspired by the work of F. D. Maurice, even endeavored to provide evening classes for working women.

The accomplishments of the feminists who dedicated their efforts to education cannot, of course, be measured in numbers. Their achievement rests rather on their rejection of the very circumscribed role which conventional society approved for a lady. Emily Davies and her friends held out for "a conception of women as human beings, with moral and

[1] Cobbe, *The Duties of Women*, p. 27.
[2] J. G. Fitch, "Women and the Universities", *Contemporary Review*, LVIII (1890), 245.

intellectual claims and responsibilities [both] in the cultivation of their faculties and [in] the direction of their lives''.[1] For such women, education was not merely a process necessary to cultivate whatever mental faculties a woman might have; it was the path by which she might prepare herself for an independent and active life.

"Why Boys are Cleverer Than Girls", *English Woman's Journal*, II (1858), 116-18.

The editors of the *English Woman's Journal*, founded in 1857, devoted a good deal of space to topics, such as employment and education, of particular interest to women. The following selection traces to its source the fallacious notion that girls are congenitally inferior mentally to boys. But while the article succeeds in demonstrating the reasons why girls appear to be less bright than their brothers, the anonymous author's recommendation that women, rather than men, be educated, seems hardly a practicable solution to the problem of providing an adequate education for girls.[2]

We lately asked the clergyman of a neighbouring town, whether the girls in his parish school, were well instructed in arithmetic? "They learn a little of it I believe," said he. We observed that it was of essential importance they should know it thoroughly, as otherwise it would be impossible for them to obtain employment as shop girls. "I fear," he replied, "they can scarcely learn it sufficiently well for that purpose, they have not the natural aptitude for figures that boys possess; when I examine the children at the end of the year, all the boys can answer more or less readily, but only one or two of the girls reply at all."

Conversing further on the subject it appeared that the salary the master who taught the boys received, was seventy pounds a year, while that of the girls' mistress was only twenty. "She is but a poor sick creature," said he, "but what can you expect for so small a salary?" We agreed with him, it was impossible to procure a good teacher for so little pay, but we also thought the want of aptitude in the girls fully explained. We will observe, in passing, that the principle here illustrated extends generally to the education of girls of all ranks, from the peer's daughter to the peasant's, the cost of their instruction seldom amounting to half that of their brothers. [*Editors' note: Conversely, at the higher levels of education the cost of instruction for girls was twice that of their brothers'—not because it was twice as good, but because the enrollment in girls' schools was smaller; consequently, they had to pay more per capita to enable the school to be financially viable.*] It is, therefore, unreasonable to expect them to know half as much, supposing the abilities on both sides to be equal. To return to our school. Let us imagine the contrast between the boys' and girls' compartments.

In one sits the poor sick mistress, whose scanty income hardly provides her with food and decent raiment. Without energy or spirit, she is striving in vain to explain

[1] Maria G. Grey, "The Women's Educational Movement", in *The Woman Question in Europe*, edited by Theodore Stanton (London: Sampson Low & Co., 1884), p. 61.

[2] The author was probably Jessie Boucherett, who, two years later, advocated the same remedy in "On the Obstacles to the Employment of Women", *English Woman's Journal*, IV (1860), 373.

the mysteries of a sum in division, which indeed she scarcely understands herself, to a group of girls who stand around her, their suppressed yawns and weary faces, showing how little interest they feel in their task. And why should they strive to excel? For them there is no prize at the end of the half-year, the prize being given to the best scholar in arithmetic in the whole school, and the girls are well aware that, with their inferior instruction, they have no chance of competing successfully against the boys. Now we will look into the other compartment. There stands the master at his desk, he is a young man, full of life and energy, whose talents have raised him in the world. The son of a small tradesman, he distinguished himself at school, was made a monitor, then a pupil teacher, and finally became a master, earning a larger income than his father, and holding a far higher position in society. He teaches with animation and spirit, the boys are interested and give their whole attention; note the vexation of the lad who could not tell the price of a hundred pair of boots, at thirteen and sixpence each, as quickly as the other boy below him, who is now so triumphantly taking his place at the head of the class. Those who attain the oftenest to this envied position, will at the end of the half year receive a handsome prize, and every boy is ambitious of carrying it off.

We have seen the means of education, let us now glance at the results. A brother and sister have been brought up at this school, and are now about to begin earning their livelihood. The girl is a year the eldest. She can knit and sew very neatly, she can read too, and write slowly and laboriously, and can, with much pains and difficulty, add up the little bill of articles that her mother has bought at the shop. Her brother can read fluently, write a good running hand, and make the most impossible calculations with perfect accuracy without a slate, he also understands book-keeping.

A shop-keeper in the town being in want of an assistant, the brother and sister both apply for the situation. The lad asks six shillings a week wages, the girl only four, and as they have been brought up in the same school, the tradesman supposing them to be equally capable, chooses the cheapest article. The girl goes on trial for a week, but ere she has been an hour in the shop, the master has discovered her deficiencies; she cannot reckon a customer's bill under ten minutes, and if urged to greater speed makes awful blunders. When the day's business is over he dismisses her, and desires that her brother may attend on the morrow in her stead.

He comes, and gives ample satisfaction, proving himself well worth his wages, for he can add up the customers' bills in a moment, and keep accurate accounts, he can also if necessary write a letter for his master in his clerkly hand, and word it well too, for he knows something of grammar. So the tradesman makes philosophical reflections on the natural inferiority of the female intellect, and engages the boy; at the end of the year his wages are raised, and in a few years the young man will be earning eighteen or twenty shillings a week. His sister meanwhile has become a semptress, and goes out sewing for eight pence a day. . . .

If only one sex is to be educated, that sex should surely be the female, for if a man be ignorant he can still earn his bread as a laborer, or soldier, or at the worst go to the backwoods, and hew his road to fortune with the axe; but the ill-educated woman has no resource but her needle, and that often fails to procure the merest necessaries of life.

D. Beale (ed.), *Reports Issued by the Schools' Inquiry Commission on the Education of Girls* (London: David Nutt, 1869), pp. iii-vi, xiv-xix, xxi-xxii, xxiv-xxvii, xxxi-xxxiv.

Dorothea Beale and Mary Frances Buss are the names usually associated with girls' secondary education. Like a number of other women reformers (e.g., Mary Carpenter, Bessie Rayner Parkes), Miss Beale was influenced by her father, a surgeon who was interested in educational and social questions. After being educated at home and at a local school, she and her two elder sisters were sent to a fashionable boarding school in Paris where they stayed until 1848, when the school was closed as a consequence of the revolution of that year. On returning to England, they entered Queen's College, which had just been opened. Later Miss Beale was appointed tutor in mathematics and subsequently head teacher in the school attached to the college. In 1858 she became principal of the Cheltenham Ladies' College, the first proprietary school for girls in England, which had opened four years earlier but was now in danger of failing. Cheltenham prospered to such a degree under her guidance that she achieved a reputation as an outstanding headmistress. Concerned with the poor teaching afforded girls, Miss Beale established in Cheltenham England's first residential training college for secondary school women teachers. The esteem in which she was held as an educator gained for her in 1902, a year before her death, the honorary degree of LL.D., awarded by the University of Edinburgh, which previously had only once conferred that honor upon a woman.

In 1864 Lord Taunton was appointed chairman of the Schools' Inquiry Commission, whose task it was to investigate English secondary education. Emily Davies, recently converted to the cause of feminism by her friend Barbara Leigh Smith Bodichon, pressed the Commission to include in its systematic survey girls' schools, which it originally did not intend to examine. Miss Davies, in addition, provided the Commission with a list of questions which should be asked of the witnesses and a roster of names of people whose testimony on the state of female education would be valuable. Subsequently, she, Dorothea Beale, Mary Frances Buss, and several other women active in the field of education appeared at the hearings, becoming incidentally the first women to testify before a royal commission.

After the hearings were concluded, Miss Beale was given permission to publish a one-volume abridgment of the official report, in order to publicize "the deplorable state of girls' education". Such publicity, it was hoped, would stimulate reform efforts. The following selection is an excerpt from her preface to the volume which summarizes the major findings of the Taunton Commission and documents its conclusion that "the purely intellectual education of girls [was] scarcely attempted, and, when attempted, it [was] a complete failure''[1] By contrast, Miss Beale, as principal of the Cheltenham School for Ladies, presided over a curriculum designed to cultivate the intelligence of her students rather than instructing them in the art of decorous behavior. It was her aim not merely to teach them, as Emily Davies put it, "to be amiable, inoffensive, always ready to give pleasure and to be pleased" (cited in Beale, p. 2), but to give them an education that would prepare them for a meaningful life.

> . . . In England we are always ready to boast of our freedom; to sing in grand chorus — "Britons never will be slaves." There are, however, two kinds of tyranny—one that of law, the other that of society, which we will call custom, fashion. The tyranny of the one is felt most by men, of the other by women. As in the political world tyranny has driven men into revolt, produced servile wars and peasant wars—has degraded the lower natures, and driven into revolt the higher, so has social tyranny—the force of unreasoning custom—exercised a pernicious influence over women. . . . If there is one goddess before whom women bow in blind and abject submission, it is the goddess of fashion. . . .
>
> These remarks have suggested themselves to me, because I believe one great cause of the difficulty we find in reforming the education of girls is the tyranny of custom. It is a pity that the graceful forms should be disfigured by the putting on of ugly clothes; it is worse if the feet of little children are pinched, or their heads flattened, to make them resemble the *élite* of their society; but it is worse still if the mind and character are cramped, and stunted, and distorted. It is because an evil which rests upon a false public opinion can be counteracted only by the creation of a healthy one, that I was anxious these Reports should find their way into the hands of parents and teachers. It will be quite clear to any attentive reader that many elsewhere obsolete practices have been handed down traditionally in Ladies' Schools. Books and plans, upon which our excellent grandmothers were educated, must, it is argued, exercise a beneficial effect upon their descendants. I maintain that we are not following the steps of those cunning housewives, unless we adopt the best methods available. . . .
>
> But the blame does not fall only on books and teachers. The indifference of parents to solid acquirements, the absurdly exaggerated value put upon mechanical skill on the piano, these still stand in the way of improvement. "It is very well," said one, who had accidentally placed her daughter where such traditions were ignored, "it is very well for my daughter to learn something of geology; or to read Shakespeare, but do you not think it of more importance that she should be able to sit down to the piano and amuse her friends?" How often have I been asked what is the use of teaching this or that, and I have been silent; as well might we talk of colours to the blind, as of education to those who are ignorant of its meaning. After reading these reports, no one can doubt that the pupils in hundreds of schools, those whose influence must be great for good or evil, are being fed upon dry bones, their spiritual nature starved, or left to find nourishment where it can. . . .
>
> There is indeed much to justify the most sanguine hope for the future, and perhaps one ground of satisfaction is the extreme badness of the old system; it is so bad that it

---

[1] Millicent Garrett Fawcett, "The Medical and General Education of Women", *Fortnightly Review*, X (1868), 560, citing one of the Taunton Commissioners.

can meet with no champion. The old rubbish about masculine and feminine studies is beginning to be treated as it deserves. It cannot be seriously maintained that those studies which tend to make a man nobler or better, have the opposite effect upon a woman. . . . When a sound system of education has been introduced, people will learn to value rightly ignorant pretentiousness, and that affection of contemptuous superiority which is one of the most decisive tests of ignorance. . . .

I proceed to make a few remarks upon the special subjects of instruction mentioned by the Commissioners. . . .

Music. — Every report is filled with complaints on this subject. Girls who have neither ear, nor taste, are compelled to spend . . . often about one hour out of every four devoted to education, in torturing pianos, and acquiring a mechanical facility, which, in the most favourable cases, enables them to rival a barrel-organ.

We would not say a word against the cultivation of real musical taste; what we regret is the reckless waste of time, money, patience, energy upon hopeless subjects, the diversion of talents which would enable a girl to attain excellence in Science, in Painting, in Literature, to the acquisition of a worthless mechanical facility for using the fingers. . . .

I would make the following suggestions: —

(1) That where there is decided talent, no more than one hour a day should be given to practising.

(2) That parents should cease to attach so exaggerated a value to this accomplishment.

(3) That those who have a natural incapacity, should be allowed to leave off music altogether.

(4) That parents should be led to observe that . . . those whose mind and character is kept in a healthy state by the discipline of a well-balanced course of study, make far more progress even in playing, than those whose power of attention and application is not thus cultivated . . . .

Arithmetic. — We turn next for the sake of contrast to the only branch of the exact sciences usually taught in Girls' Schools, and, . . . we find that whereas one hour in every four of school-work is devoted to exercising the fingers, one in 13 is considered sufficient for exercising the brain in this, often the only branch of science taught to girls. Rarely, however, is arithmetic treated in a scientific way. Rather are the pupils allowed to practise a sort of conjuring, by which they succeed in getting answers, without having the least idea how it is all brought about. . . .

In a few, but very few, schools was the subject taught properly, and in these with very great success. . . .

I have no doubt that an elementary knowledge of mathematical processes and demonstrations would operate most beneficially. We have found a comparatively short training in Euclid greatly improve general work, making it more exact and logical. . . .

. . . Many girls delight in mathematical studies; and, . . . there is no reason why they should not go as far as most schoolboys, and those whose tastes lead them that way, farther still. It is not however so much for the sake of the mathematical knowledge itself (valuable though that be), but for the sake of the mental training, that I think some small portion (say Euclid Book I and elementary Algebra) should be taught in Girls' Schools. This will at least show them what exact reasoning is, and make them more capable of seeing the real drift of any argument.

Language. — I believe few will be prepared to find how very unfavourable is the verdict of the Commissioners on the subject of modern languages. It is supposed that girls at least learn French. . . .

[However,] "the pupil gains," says Mr. Stanton, "no idea of the structure of the language, and acquires a ready habit of talking mere jargon. In one of the upper schools which I examined, and where a resident French governess was kept, not one out of the first 15 girls could, even approximately write into grammatical French, the simplest sentence of a kind which they must have been in the daily habit of using". . . .

The least evil resulting from this, is that a pronunciation is acquired unintelligible to those French people, who have not learnt the language in England, and the habit of speaking ungrammatical and purely British French becomes so fixed, that it is almost impossible to learn the real language afterwards. . . . Learning bad French however is one of the least of the evils connected with this practice. Anything deserving the name of conversation is banished where it is strictly enforced, and so the mind is dwarfed and stunted, and when girls leave school, they are often found unable to talk except upon trivial subjects, and unable to express themselves like rational beings in any language. A second reason for the unsatisfactory results in French is that the teaching is often left in the hands of badly educated foreigners, many of whom would not be allowed to teach in their own country. A third reason is, the pupils themselves have not been trained to accuracy of thought by *any* study, and therefore they carry into their French composition their ordinary habits of inattention and inaccuracy.

I have gradually arrived at a decided conviction that in teaching languages we begin at the wrong end. . . . In grammar we . . . begin with abstract principles, which it is impossible for a child's mind to assimilate. When sentences are first taught and variations made, . . . I have found that children do not pronounce with the usual British accent, and do learn to express themselves in idiomatic French and German. They get to know . . . the sentence-moulds of other languages. Besides, the power of observation is cultivated, they learn to make rules themselves, and their grammatical faculty is developed. . . . I hope we shall eventually teach grammar, as we now teach arithmetic, I mean, give no rules, but induce the learner to find them out. . . .

Science. — In scientific subjects generally, I need hardly say the testimony of the Commissioners is very unfavorable, — it could not be otherwise, when even arithmetic is not understood. The importance of some scientific training has been so eloquently pleaded of late that I need say but little. . . . [According to] Mr. Fitch . . . "Few things . . . are sadder than to see how the sublimest of all the physical sciences is vulgarized in Ladies' Schools. All the grandeur and vastness are eliminated from the study of astronomy; and pupils whose attention has never been directed to one of the great laws by which the universe is governed, think they are learning astronomy, when they are twisting a globe round and round, and solving a few problems in latitude and longitude." . . .

History — To the study of History we should I think attach great importance. . . .

Surely it is well for women, too prone as they are to pay exaggerated regard to the judgments of that social coterie by which they are surrounded, to go sometimes beyond their own circle and their own time, to see how the judgments of the past have been reversed; to learn to realize the past enlarges their sympathies and their charities, and teaches them to distinguish the transitory and the unessential from the lasting and essential. . . .

History and Literature are studies which are intimately associated. Both must be read . . . in large and thoughtful works, if the teaching is to be really fruitful. . . . We must not read merely what other people have said about the writings, we must read the great works themselves. How little the subject is really studied may be seen from the [fact that] . . . "nothing remains of what they have learned often, but a collection of names and dates easily interchanged." I remember a pupil, who entered here at the age of eighteen; being asked when Chaucer lived, she replied, "I think Chaucer lived in the reign of George III", and then added, with characteristic caution, "But it might have been in any other reign."

. . . Some portion of schooltime should be devoted to the reading of English authors. . . . The student of English literature . . . must learn to know each writer, and view his life and writings in connexion with one another and with the times which produced them. He must look for the bearing of the complete book or play, and extract from it the lessons of wisdom. . . .

Do not many of our social follies arise from our inability to conceive and live up to a higher standard than that of the people who surround us? I would that the young should seek the company of the wisest and the best, of those who have the truest title to be called kings of men. . . . I have dwelt at length on the study of history and literature, because I feel the cultivation of a taste for good reading is of the greatest importance to women. . . . By the songs of noble and heroic deeds, the young are animated to live nobly too, and those who have lived on terms of intimacy with the gentle and refined will shrink from vulgarity and coarseness. . . .

When will parents learn that [merely] a year or two at a good school will not educate their daughters. We force plants, but such plants are sickly. We regret it, if a child's body grows too rapidly; yet there are those who think the mind may be forced to do the work of six or seven years in one or two. They do not expect this with boys, why should they with girls?

How often have teachers to grieve over those in whom the seeds of knowledge which have been laboriously planted, and tended, are just beginning to bear abundant fruit. The mind and character are ripening, and it seems as if more were now learnt in a few months than in years before; then the girl reaches 17 or 18, . . . and friends enquire how it is she is still at school, and think it is time for her to "come out." A little later, and she would have gained a power of thought and independent study. A taste for good reading would have been formed; a love perhaps of some special branch of science. She would have reached an age when one might look for her to find work, and in a sphere of her own. Now years are likely to intervene between school and marriage; she is too young, and her character too unformed for her to be of use as a teacher, or in works of charity. She falls perhaps into a state of depression, and her health suffers, . . . she is ennuyée, and she must have excitement; and as the appetite for wholesome food fails, the desire for stimulants is increased, — foolish novels, silly conversation, petty scandal, sensational dresses, &c., &c., these are the husks upon which a noble character is sometimes reduced to feed. . . .

. . . A father insures his life because he feels in his own case the uncertainty of the future. A good education is a sort of insurance for his daughter; a wealth which cannot so easily take to itself wings and fly away. For this reason, as well as from the higher motives already urged, I would strongly advise parents to take advantage of the University examinations now open. A certificate may one day be of great use; it is clear that it will, before long, be impossible in England, as it is now on the Continent, for any one to obtain employment as a teacher, without some such attestation. And lastly, why should it be thought dishonorable for a woman to earn money. If she is married or has home duties, let her not neglect these; but if she has none, why should she not obey the precept of St. Paul, and labour, "that she may have to give that needeth." . . .

Who has not seen the little maiden's face glow with pleasure, when allowed to render some trifling service, "to help mamma," and surely the love of helpfulness is not, or ought not to be extinguished, as years advance. It is this feeling which gives a joy, a dignity to our lives. . . .

. . . Let us resolve to make ourselves fit, and to live for our work, never fancying that our education is finished. Those who might be real teachers, often fail, because they do not give themselves wholly to it; if they would spare no pains, they would learn that a reward is to be found in the work itself, and then, though it be most imperfect, much of it wood, hay, stubble, they will sometimes hear a gentle voice saying, "She hath done what she could". . . .

Mrs. William [Maria G.] Grey, *On the Special Requirements for Improving the Education of Girls* (London: William Ridgway, 1872), pp. 24-28.

In several books and articles Maria G. Grey and her elder sister, Emily Shirreff, reform-minded daughters of an admiral, addressed themselves to the questions inherent in the movement to improve the education of girls of the middle and upper classes, an education that was generally acknowledged to be even worse than that of the lower classes. In 1851, they had co-authored *Thoughts on Self Culture,* which, they explained, contrasted with other recent treatises on that subject, because their book had been designed as a practical, rather than a theoretical, guide to education. In attempting to show precisely *how* the task of self-improvement was to be accomplished, *Thoughts on Self Culture* included chapters on the development of mental training, methods of study, and the cultivation of conscience and imagination.

The conclusions of the Taunton Commission and, subsequently, the publicity given to those findings by the appearance of Dorothea Beale's report of the proceedings, impelled Mrs. Grey to take a more active role on behalf of women's education. The following selection, taken from a paper which was originally read before the Social Science Association in October 1871, is particularly interesting because it correlates the prevailing social ideals (regarding marriage, for example) with the narrow education reserved to girls. It was after this paper was presented, incidentally, that Mrs. Grey announced her intention to form a National Union whose aim would be to provide secondary education for girls of all social classes (see pp. 130-2).

. . . This brings me to the last of the requirements I have mentioned for improving female education, i.e. that women should have an object to work for, and on this I must crave your patience to listen to a few words, for though not a portion of education it influences it throughout.

It is true that women have the highest object of all, the attainment of excellence for its own sake; but that, like the attainment of knowledge for its own sake, affects only the small minority of either sex, the upper 10,000 of the human race, who are alone capable of conceiving and pursuing a high ideal with a disinterested passion. The average, — and it is always the average we must consider, — are incapable of this, and require lower and more commonplace motives to stimulate them to exertion. These motives are supplied to boys by the necessity of working for their maintenance. They are brought up in the knowledge that they will have to choose a profession, and that their success in life will depend on their doing their work well, whatever it may be. Girls, on the contrary, of the classes we are dealing with, are brought up to think their education of no consequence, except as fitting them to take their place in their own social sphere. They are taught explicitly, or implicitly, that marriage is the only career open to them, and they learn but too quickly that success in that career does assuredly not depend on their efforts at self-improvement.

. . . So long as marriage is . . . the only aim of a girl's life, and her education regulated with the sole view of making her pleasing to marrying men, so long will all attempts at improvement fail, except with the few capable of rising above the average tone of thought and feeling. . . . All who hold the higher and truer view [must] urge upon parents, and upon society, that marriage should not be the first object of a woman's life, any more than of a man's: that girls should be trained from childhood, to the idea that they, like their brothers, must take their share of the work of life; that their education should prepare them by the formation of good intellectual and moral habits, to perform it well; — that they should be not only allowed, but induced to work for their own maintenance, where the circumstances of their parents make an independent provision for them impossible, and that when those circumstances place them above the necessity of working for a provision, they should hold themselves bound to help, and train themselves to help efficiently in doing the unpaid work of the world, where the harvest is so plentiful and the labourers so few.

How much women would gain in worth and dignity, how rapidly their education would improve, if such views were prevalent, scarcely need be pointed out. All the want of thoroughness, the showy superficiality which degrade it now, would disappear before the necessity of real preparation for real work, and the ends being clearly understood and accepted, the means would not long be wanting.

Let it not be supposed that I undervalue marriage, or that I want to broach some wild theory of feminine independence; so far from it, I hold that only in the union of man and woman is human life perfect and complete. I would not wish, even if it were possible, to make women independent of men, but neither do I wish them to sit in half-starved, or luxurious idleness, waiting, or worse still, planning for husbands by whom they are to be raised to the single dignity possible to them.

Mr. Anthony Trollope, in one of his late novels, mentions as a true anecdote, that in a family of three maiden ladies, the youngest always took precedence of her sisters, and on a stranger asking the reason why, the elder sister meekly replied, "Matilda once had an offer of marriage." I would put an end to the state of society in which such an anecdote is not only possible, but where similar ones would be common, if people generally spoke and acted as they feel; a state of society in which it can be said with perfect truth of large numbers of women, in the words of one of the heroines of the same novel: — "They're just nobodies. They are not anything particular to anybody, and so they go on living till they die. . . . A man who is a nobody can perhaps make himself somebody, or at any rate he can try; but a woman has no means of trying. She is a nobody, and a nobody she must remain. She has her clothes and her food, but she isn't wanted anywhere. . . . People put up with her, and that is about the best of her luck. If she were to die, somebody, perhaps, would be sorry for her, but nobody would be worse off. She doesn't earn anything, or do any good. She is just there, and that is all."

Is that a fate for a human being with a heart and soul and intellect, and the capabilities within her of using them, if allowed, in adding to her own welfare and that of others, a fate to be condemned solely because she is not born with the charm or the cunning to win a husband? I recommend the novel I have quoted to the consideration of all who think women have nothing to complain of, when they are neither beaten nor starved, and who advise them as their only wise policy, "to rest and be thankful."

My advice is very different. Let us be thankful indeed that there is, at last, a feeling awakening in the country, that the women who desire education ought to have it placed within their reach. Let us be thankful, — we cannot be too thankful, — to the many generous and able men who, in the spirit of true chivalry, are helping our weakness with their strength. Let us be thankful too that our own tongues are unloosed, and that we are not only allowed but invited, as I have been on this occasion, to plead our own cause before the public; but let us not rest, — no, not for an instant, — till we have won for women the right and the means to the highest culture of which their nature is capable, — not that they may gratify an unwomanly spirit of selfish ambition and rivalry, but that they may become more worthy and more fit to do the noble work God has given them to do.

Millicent Garrett Fawcett, "The Education of Women of the Middle and Upper Classes", *Macmillan's Magazine,* XVII (1868), 511-17.

Millicent Garrett Fawcett was active in reforming female education and attempting to obtain female suffrage, but it was the latter which, as we shall see, ultimately absorbed most of her energies. She was affected by the struggle of her elder sister, Elizabeth Garrett, to obtain a medical degree, and by her contact with Elizabeth's friend and ally, Emily Davies. Subsequently she was influenced by her husband, Henry Fawcett, M.P., professor of economics at Cambridge, and his friend, John Stuart Mill, both of whom were advocates of higher education for women. She became part of a Cambridge group, whose members held their first meeting in her drawing room and organized a series of Lectures for Women. This led to the formation of the Association for Promoting the Higher Education of Women and subsequently to the founding of Newnham Hall, which in 1880 became the second college for women at Cambridge.

In Mrs. Fawcett's view, the intellectual impoverishment of women of the upper and middle classes was the result of their inferior education. Schools for girls emphasized worthless "accomplishments", such as music and foreign languages, which were taught so superficially as to insure, at best, no more than a mediocre command of these subjects. Instruction in mathematics and science was offered only at an elementary level. Not only did these schools deliberately avoid teaching subjects of real value; their headmistresses regarded any attempt to get them to improve their curricula as a brazen intrusion into their private affairs. Until the proprietors of these educational sanctuaries dedicated to the perpetuation of female ignorance could be made to offer their pupils an education comparable to that afforded boys, no significant improvement in the position of women could be expected.

. . . When such phrases as "national education," and "the education of the people," are made use of, it is usually implied that they mean the extension of education to the working classes; and it is also implied when the reform of national education is spoken of, that the only part of the nation whose education is neglected, and which therefore needs reform, is that part which receives the designation of "the lower orders." We think that the education of women in the middle and upper classes is at least as important, almost as much neglected, and that it needs even more strenuous efforts to effect reform in it. For scarcely any one now openly opposes, in theory, the education of the poor; but with regard to women, before substantial and national reform is effected in their education, an immense amount of opposition, prejudice, and undisguised hostility must be overcome. . . .

The effect of this lack of mental training in women has been to produce such a deterioration in their intellects as, in some measure, to justify the widely-spread opinion that they are innately possessed of less powerful minds than men, that they are incapable of the highest mental culture, that they are born illogical, created more impetuous and rash than men. This it is at present, owing to the want of education amongst women, impossible absolutely to disprove. If this inferiority really exists, society must abide the consequences; but in this case, surely, everything which education could do should be done to produce in women the highest mental development of which they are capable; whereas, the present system of education heightens and aggravates the difference between the intellectual acquirements of men and women.

The belief, however, in the innate inferiority of women's minds, though it is impossible from want of sufficient data to prove its absurdity, we do not for one instant hold. All reasoning from analogy points to the fallacy of such a belief. . . . Let any man, however gifted and whatever intellectual distinction he may have attained, consider what the state of his mind would have been, had he been subjected to the treatment which ninety-nine out of a hundred of the women of his acquaintance have undergone. . . .

. . . At about eighteen, when a boy is just beginning his university career, a girl is supposed to have "completed her education." She is too often practically debarred from further intellectual progress by entering into a society where pleasure, in the shape of balls, fêtes, &c., engrosses all her time; or, hers being a country life, and it being her supposed duty to be what is called domesticated, she devotes her life to fancy needlework, or to doing badly the work of a curate, a nurse, or a cook. If she does attempt to carry on her education by means of reading, many almost insuperable difficulties beset her. . . .

The principal reform, therefore, which it is desirable to carry out in women's education is their admittance to all the sources of mental and moral development from which they have hitherto been excluded. Let all, both men and women, have equal chances of maturing such intellect as God has given them. Let those institutions which were originally intended to provide an education for girls as well as boys be restored to what their founders intended. . . . Many charitable institutions for the purpose of providing an asylum for a certain specified number of old men and women, were endowed with land which was not at the time considered more than sufficient to provide for their support. Owing to the immense increase in the value of land, the property of these charities has been found much more than adequate to fulfil the intentions of their founders. The surplus property has frequently been appropriated to found, not schools for boys and girls, but schools for boys only. It is indisputably unjust, the property having been left for the benefit for both sexes, that one sex only should reap the advantage of its increased value.

We should therefore wish to see equal educational advantages given to both sexes; to open all the professions to women; and, if they prove worthy of them, to allow them to share with men all those distinctions, intellectual, literary, and political, which are such valuable incentives to mental and moral progress. . . .

. . . One examination has been opened to them, and with great success. The Cambridge local examinations have been held at Cambridge, and boys and girls have both been examined there, in different rooms, but at the same time, without the least difficulty or inconvenience resulting; and if it is safe and practicable thus to examine boys and girls of sixteen or seventeen years of age, what are the insuperable difficulties which attend their examination at nineteen and twenty-one?

In these days religions disabilities are fast becoming obsolete; we trust that university reformers . . . will continue the attack with even increased vigour against sexual disabilities. . . .

To describe the consequences of this increased diffusion of sound mental training in a few words, we conceive that it would add as much as any other proposed reform to the general happiness and welfare of mankind. In the first place, every woman who had had the advantage of sound mental training, could make the best possible use of her special faculties or talent, simply because education would have discovered what those faculties or talents were, and with this assistance she would have a much greater chance than at present of finding and occupying her proper sphere. For woman's—the same as man's—sphere is precisely that situation in which she is doing the highest and best work of which she is capable. This is a high standard, and one which, with every advantage society can afford, is too frequently found unattainable; nevertheless, it is one to which all educational schemes should aspire, and their approach to, or neglect of it, should be deemed the only valid test of worth.

We also confidently believe that with the possession of mental culture and development women would gain much of that public spirit and sense of the importance of public duties, the lack of which now so frequently pains us. It could no longer then be said with impunity in a public place—and it was said last year in the House of Commons—that a woman, if she had a vote, would sell it to the man who could offer her the highest bribe; and we should then no longer hear, what was far worse, this accusation smilingly acknowledged to be just, at least of themselves individually, by women on whom the important social duty had devolved of training the tender minds of children. . . .

Of those who say that education will unfit women to fulfil the duties of wives and mothers, we ask if ignorance . . . and an utter incapability of comprehending the chief interests of her husband's life are qualities which so eminently conduce to domestic happiness. . . .

It would also be a considerable pecuniary advantage if married women were able to assist their husbands in their business or profession. Of course, there are cases where this would be impracticable; but there are hundreds of cases where, if the woman had been properly trained, she could with great ease render the most valuable assistance to her husband. . . . If women were accustomed to enter into this sort of partnership with their husbands they could also carry on his business or profession in case of his sickness or death: in the latter case, the burden of a heavy life insurance, which a thoughtful husband feels bound to lay upon himself in order to form some provision for his family, would be rendered to a great extent unnecessary, and much destitution and misery would be avoided. . . .

Important, however, as is the claim of married women to an improved education, the burden of an ill-cultivated mind falls much heavier on unmarried women, for they are as devoid as married women of general interests, without having an occupation found for them in the direction of a household, or the care of children. . . .

. . . It is not too much to say that one of the great curses of society is the enforced idleness of such a large proportion of its members as is formed by the women who have nothing to do. We say enforced idleness, for we believe it to be enforced by bad education. . . . If we are forced to the conclusion that the present training of women tends to produce creatures like Becky Sharp or Amelia Osborne, it is the duty of all who care for the welfare of mankind to strive earnestly after every reform that may effect an improvement in that training. The first thing to be sought is education, . . . for following close upon improved education must come the extension to women of those legal, social, and political rights, the withholding of which is felt, by a daily increasing number of men and women, to be unworthy of the civilization of the nineteenth century.

Emily Davies, "Special Systems of Education for Women", (1868), reprinted in *Thoughts on Some Questions Relating to Women* (Cambridge: Bowes & Bowes, 1910), pp. 118-37.

Like her younger friend, Millicent Garrett Fawcett, Emily Davies was concerned with obtaining both higher education and votes for women but, unlike Mrs. Fawcett, to whom the franchise eventually became all-important, Miss Davies concentrated her efforts on opening the universities to women.

A number of factors, apparently coincidental, combined to push Miss Davies, the small, mild daughter of a rural clergyman, into the forefront of the movement to provide higher education for women. In the 1850's through her theologian brother, John Llewelyn Davies (a co-founder of the Working Men's College), she became acquainted with the Christian Socialists, Maurice, Kingsley, and Ludlow, who were actively promoting the cause of female education. In 1858, while vacationing in Algeria, she met Madame Bodichon, who introduced her to the ladies of the *English Woman's Journal* and the Society for the Employment of Women, a branch of which she later established in her native parish of Gateshead. She was caught up in Elizabeth Garrett's battle to gain admission to the University of London so as to qualify for a medical degree and, after hearing a paper by Frances Power Cobbe in 1862 on the entrance of women to universities, Miss Davies organized a committee to work toward that end. Her position was strengthened by the publication of the *Report of the Schools' Inquiry Commission*, which clearly documented the de-

plorable state of female education. But recognition of the need to improve that education was not enough for, even among those who accepted the necessity for change, there were fundamental and often irreconcileable differences of opinion concerning the nature of a new and improved education for the female sex. Should, for example, the education of girls of the middle and upper classes be analogous to that of their
brothers? Or, on the other hand, should young women be trained in a
manner decidedly different from that of young men, giving careful consideration to the feminine mind, mission, and moral obligations? Rejecting the latter notion, Miss Davies, in the following selection, pleads for
a common standard of competence by which to judge the academic
accomplishments of men and women.

Among the controversies to which the movement for improving the education of
women has given rise, there is one which presses for settlement. The question has
arisen and must be answered—Is the improved education which, it is hoped, is about
to be brought within reach of women, to be identical with that of men, or is it to be as
good as possible, but in some way or other specifically femine? The form in which the
question practically first presents itself is—What shall be the standards of examination?
. . . The controversy may be assumed to be between two parties. . . .

Of these two parties, one regards it as essential that the standards of examination for
both sexes should be the same; the other holds that they may without harm—perhaps
with advantage—be different. . . .

The latter course is urged on the ground that there are differences between men and
women which educational systems ought to recognize; or . . . at any rate the conditions of women's lives are special, and ought to be specially prepared for; or there is a
latent feeling of repugnance to what may appear like an ungraceful, perhaps childish,
attempt to grasp at masculine privileges—an idea which jars upon a refined taste.
Considerations of this sort, resting mainly upon sentiment or prejudice, can scarcely
be met by argument. It is usually admitted that we are as yet in the dark as to the
specific differences between men and women—that we do not know how far they are
native, and to what extent those which strike the eye may have been produced by artificial influences—that even if we knew much more than we do about the nature of the
material to be dealt with, we should still have much to learn as to the kind of intellectual discipline which might be most suitable. Nor have we as yet any trustworthy evidence . . . as to the manner in which the differences of the work in life to which men
and women respectively are said to be called, could be met by corresponding differences in mental training. The arbitrary differences established by fashion seem to
have been directed by the rule of contraries rather than by any intelligent judgment.
Practically, what we come to is something like this—People who want to impose a special system have . . . a vague impression that as certain subjects and methods have
been in a manner set apart for women ever since they can remember, there is most
likely something in them which distinguishes them either as suitable to the female
mind, or as specially useful to women in practical life. To discover how much of truth
there may be behind this opinion would be a tedious and difficult task. It may be
enough to remark that experience seems to be against it. It is precisely because the
special system, as hitherto tried, has proved a signal failure, that reform is called for. . . .

The immediate controversy turns . . . upon examinations — examinations regarded as a controlling force, directing the course of instruction into certain channels; pronouncing upon the comparative value of subjects, fixing the amount of time and attention bestowed upon each, and to some extent guiding the method of teaching; wholesomely stimulating. . . . We want an examination which can be worked beneficially. . . . We want an examination for which candidates will be forthcoming. Finally, we want an examination which will sift. We do not want to have certificates of proficiency given to half-educated women. There are examinations which will do this already within reach. . . .

. . . An examination by men of high repute will carry more weight than one by men unknown, and . . . an examination by an official body such as a university, will be more readily believed in than one by any self-constituted board, however respectable. But supposing these two points secured, is a new examination conducted by competent examiners appointed by a university all that is to be desired? Will an unknown standard having expressly in view candidates drawn from a limited and notoriously illiterate class [i.e., female], be worth much . . .? The most highly cultivated women would not care to submit themselves to an ordeal in which to fail might be disgrace, but to pass would be no distinction. The mere fact of its special character would in itself repel them. That the greatest of female novelists should have taken the precaution to assume a masculine *nom de plume* for the express purpose of securing their work against being measured by a class standard, is significant of the feeling entertained by women. Right or wrong, wise or foolish, here is at any rate a fact to be recognized. . . . An examination limited to a class, and with which the *élite* of that class will have nothing to do, is not likely to command very high respect. . . .

The kind of result which is likely to follow from an . . . examination [which has been designed exclusively for women] . . . may be conjectured from the advice given by a schoolmistress in reference to the Cambridge Local Examinations. Complaining of the vexatious demands for a degree of attainment in arithmetic not commonly reached in girls' schools, she remarked briefly, ''I would have all that expunged.'' The suggestion that one advantage of these examinations might consist in the pressure brought to bear in favour of unpopular subjects, was met by the rejoinder, "But why press an unpopular subject which is of no use in after-life?"

The tendency of examinations to adjust themselves to studies is a consideration of great importance. . . . The Cambridge Local Examinations furnish a case in point. In the first examination to which girls were admitted, 90 per cent. of the senior candidates failed in the preliminary arithmetic. Fortunately, the standard was fixed by references to an immense preponderance of boy candidates, and it was understood that the girls must be brought up to it. Extra time, and probably better teaching, aided by greater willingness on the part of the pupils, who had been made aware of their deficiency, were devoted to the unpopular and "useless" subject. In the next examination, out of the whole number of girls only three failed in it.

Other reasons for desiring a common standard, of a more subtle character, can scarcely be apprehended perhaps in their full force without personal experience. Probably only women who have laboured under it can understand the weight of discouragement produced by being perpetually told that, as women, nothing much is ever to be expected of them, and it is not worth their while to exert themselves — that they can write lively letters, full of graphic description and homely touches, but that anything like original research or profound learning is not for them to think of — that whatever they do they must not interest themselves, except in a second-hand and shallow way, in the pursuits of men, for in such pursuits they must always expect to fail. Women who have lived in the atmosphere produced by such teaching know how it stifles and chills; how hard it is to work courageously through it. Every effort to improve the education of women which assumes that they may, without reprehensible ambition, study the same subjects as their brothers and be measured by the same standards, does something towards lifting them out of the state of listless despair of themselves into which so many fall. Supposing that the percentage of success attained by women should be considerably less than that of men, the sense of discouragement thus engendered would be as nothing compared with the general self-distrust produced by having it taken for granted that they are by nature disqualified to stand the ordinary tests. To make the discovery of individual incompetence may be wholesomely humbling or stimulating, as the case may be, but no one is the better for being told, on mere arbitrary authority, that he belongs to a weak and incapable class. And this, whatever may be the intention, is said in effect by the offer of any test of an exclusively female character. . . .

Emily Davies, "Some Account of a Proposed New College", (1872), reprinted in *Thoughts on Some Questions Relating to Women* (Cambridge: Bowes & Bowes, 1910), pp. 84-107.

In 1866, as an outgrowth of a meeting of the Schoolmistresses' Association, which she had founded and which included in its membership Dorothea Beale, Octavia Hill, and Frances Mary Buss, Emily Davies decided on a new strategy. Since the University of London could not be persuaded to accept women as candidates for degrees, she now proposed to give women a residential college of their own—one that would offer an education equal to that provided for men by Oxford and Cambridge. This intention (which was ultimately realized by the founding of Girton College) evoked opposition and ridicule when it was announced at the Social Science Congress in 1868, in a paper in which Miss Davies discussed the new venture to which she and Madame Bodichon were by now fully committed (and to which the latter had made a contribution of £1,000 and subsequently left a legacy of £10,000). After considering— and rejecting—possible alternatives to the establishment of a new college (for example, the teaching of university subjects at home or the conversion of existing secondary schools into institutions of higher learning), Miss Davies turned to more general considerations. In the following excerpt she reviews the benefits that will accrue, both to individuals and society, from the extension of higher education to women.

. . . But here we arrive at the fundamental question, whether, after all, light is better than darkness—whether a moderately ignorant person cannot discharge the plain duties of life just as well as the most highly educated—whether in trying to work women up to an exalted pitch of mental superiority, we might not be making sacrifices of health, refinement of manners, and the minor morals, for which no intellectual gains could compensate. . . .

First, let us be clear as to what the alternative is. Let it be distinctly understood that the choice is not between a life wholly given up to study, and a life spent in active domestic duty. The dilemma thus stated is untrue on both sides; for while on the one hand, giving to women the opportunity of a complete education does not mean that they will thereupon spend all their lives in reading, so, on the other, denying them education does not mean that they will occupy themselves in household affairs. The young unmarried women of the present generation are not called upon to take an active part in household work. It is needless to insist on this, for every one knows it, and yet there is an undertone of lamentation and reproach as the admission is made. There is nothing for them to do, we confess; and yet somehow we have a feeling that they ought to be doing it. We sigh, and say—Yes, domestic employments are gone out of fashion. But why have they gone out of fashion? There are two reasons—the increase of wealth, and the supply of domestic wants by machinery. . . . The fact is patent, . . . unless we came to dismissing the servants . . . a healthy young woman will find no adequate pull upon her energies in the domestic employments of a well-to-do household. . . . None of us—or only a very few people, the quality of whose optimism is somewhat strained—profess to be satisfied with the present manner of life of young women of the wealthy class. The young lady of the world is universally condemned. . . . We are all agreed that the sooner she is abolished the better.

But what are we to have in her place? That is the question. We are quite ready, it may be said, to crush the gay trifler, but we are not prepared to accept in her stead the pale-faced student, poring over miserable books. We want healthy, happy, dutiful English women; and we are persuaded that if women take to College, and examinations, and diplomas, and the rest, they will be unhealthy, unhappy, undutiful, and worst of all—American.

But what if it should be found that it is through the process of poring over books in due season, with moderation, and under wise guidance—that health, and happiness, and dutifulness, and the many good things which go to make an English lady of the highest type, will most surely come?

What is so conducive to health and happiness as regular, interesting occupation? Who are so likely to see the true poetry which lies in the discharge of the humblest duties as those whose minds are fitly balanced, their imaginations withdrawn from vanities, and occupied with pure visions? What is so likely to give gentleness, simplicity, and real refinement, as an orderly, melodious, disciplined life, possessing a genuine dignity which does not need to support itself by defiance? . . .

If, indeed, higher education is regarded merely as the acquirement of an unusual quantity of information—information which may happen to prove useful, or may not—there is much reason for scepticism as to its practical value. So long as education is treated only as a means of getting on in the world, nothing is easier than to show that women for whom the getting on has been done by other people do not want it. But it is not as a means of getting on that University education is recommended. The object of the new College is not to enable women to make money, though that may probably be among the results indirectly attained. It has a wider scope. It has been said of education that its business, "in respect of knowledge, is not to perfect a learner in all or any one of the sciences, but to give his mind that freedom, that disposition, and those habits, that may enable him to obtain any part of knowledge he shall apply himself to, or stand in need of, in the future course of his life." This will be the aim of the College work. It will not be specifically directed towards changing the occupations of women, but rather towards securing that whatever they do shall be done well. Whether as mistresses of households, mothers, teachers, or as labourers in art, science, literature, and notably in the field of philanthropy, so largely occupied by women, their work suffers from the want of previous training. They have to do for themselves in mature life . . . what ought to have been done for them in their youth. They are required to inflict upon themselves the discipline, and to gain for themselves the knowledge, which ought to have come to them as part of their education. Their youth is unduly cut short. They are expected to be grown up at eighteen. And . . . they *do* grow up, at any rate in the sense that they cease to grow any more. Many a woman is as childish and undeveloped at twenty-eight as she was at eighteen. She has missed the intermediate stage of discipline between the necessary restraint of childhood and early youth, and the undivided responsibility which is the burden of mature years. Is it said that the education of life is more than that of books? That is most true. And if there is any stage in our history at which it is of primary importance that the education of life . . . should be wisely adjusted so as to favour healthy growth, it is surely during the transition period of youth. It is not natural to be "finished" at eighteen. It is when the school period has passed that the mind and character are ready to receive the kind of teaching and discipline which are wanted as a preparation for standing alone. . . .

A few words may here find place with respect to the effect of mental cultivation on health. That a heartless, mechanical routine must be morally and spiritually deadening is not difficult to see, but it seems to be commonly supposed that to the physical constitution it is rather strengthening than otherwise. It is, in fact, often taken for granted, that though for women who have only themselves to think of, it may be a good thing to have some intellectual resources, for *mothers* there is nothing like good sound ignorance. A stolid indifference to the higher interests of life, complete absorption in petty cares, is supposed to produce a placid, equable animal state of existence, favourable to the transmission of a healthy constitution to the next generation. We have persuaded ourselves that Englishmen of the present day are such a nervously excitable race, that the only chance for their descendants is to keep the mothers in a state of coma. The fathers, we think, are incurable. Their feverish energy cannot be controlled. We give them up. But there is hope for the future if only mothers can be kept out of the vortex.

But are we, indeed, so morbidly spiritual and intellectual as this notion assumes? Is it because their minds are overwrought, because they have thrown themselves with too great ardour into literary and scientific pursuits, that men and women display so much eagerness in making and spending money? Is it not rather that men heap up and women squander, as a diversion from an insupportable dullness, incapable of higher pleasures? . . .

. . .It cannot be denied that an institution for women, professing to give something equivalent to an Oxford or Cambridge education, is a new thing, and public bodies will think it only right to wait till it has succeeded, before doing much to help it on. . . . The initiative must be taken by private persons, and something like a start must be made before any definite application can be preferred for grants from public funds. When the first step shall have been taken, and a nucleus formed, there is little doubt that benefactions in various shapes will accrue. In this point of view, every contribution to such an undertaking as the new College will have a kind of reproductive power. Those who take part in promoting the scheme at its present stage, not only help to bring a useful institution into existence, —they are putting their hands to a work which will by-and-by be carried on to far larger issues. It was begun in faith and hope in more difficult times than ours. Those who went before have prepared the way; we profit by their labours. It is for us to do our part, while handing on the task to the generations yet to come.

Maria G. Grey, "The Women's Educational Movement", in *The Woman Question in Europe,* edited by Theodore Stanton (London: Sampson Low & Co., 1884), pp. 30-63.

By the mid-1880's feminists had made sufficient progress to justify the publication of a volume which summarized accomplishments in various fields. In this volume (edited by the son of the prominent American feminist, Elizabeth Cady Stanton), Maria G. Grey wrote an account of the movement on behalf of the education of women in England, noting that whereas "forty years ago the question of women's education did not exist", within the last twenty years, it had "taken its place among the public and active interests of the day" (p. 31).

The excerpt which follows is a survey of the steps taken to provide education for girls in secondary schools and colleges. Although the founding of the Girls' Public Day School Company, designed to aid in the establishment of secondary schools, was, in large measure, the creation of Maria Grey and Emily Shirreff, the interests of these two sisters in the field of education spread far beyond their commitment to secondary school instruction for women. Miss Shirreff, who was one of the founders of the Froebel Society and its president for many years, published several works on the kindergarten system and the philosophy of education. She and Mrs. Grey initiated plans for the training of secondary school teachers which culminated in the establishment of the Maria Grey Training College. Both women frequently prepared papers to be delivered at meetings of the Social Science Association, and published a number of articles on education in contemporary journals.

. . . Miss Emily Davies, . . . being dissatisfied with these imperfect substitutes [lectures and courses for women on an informal basis] for the higher education given to men by a university college course, had conceived the bold idea of giving to women a precisely similar education, under similar conditions of college life; to be tested at its close by the same examination as that by which the university tests its under-graduates. The idea was, of course, scouted at first, and many even of the best friends of women's education opposed it, on the ground that, considering the great and recognized imperfection of the existing university system, it was unwise to adopt it in founding a wholly new institution for the other sex. Miss Davies, whose singular clearness of judgment, tenacity of purpose, and untiring energy, specially fitted her for the task she had undertaken, maintained the ground she had taken up, i.e., that the question of woman's fitness for the higher education, represented by the university course, could be fairly solved only by submitting the women students to precisely the same course, under precisely the same tests, as the men. . . . In October, 1869, the college for women, organized in all respects as one of the Cambridge colleges and getting its tuition from Cambridge tutors, was opened in a small hired house at Hitchin, with five students. In 1873, it was removed to Girton, close to Cambridge, where proper buildings had been erected for it from funds raised by subscriptions and donations, which constitute its only endowment. . . . To quote . . . Lady Stanley of Alderley: . . . "Girton is in all respects a college on the old model. The students have their own rooms for private reading, their class-rooms for lectures, their public dining-hall; and if no grand old library is theirs, much earnest enthusiasm for study has proved them worthy of richer opportunities than they yet possess. The university did not recognize, nor has it yet recognized in any official sense the existence of the women's college, but the help and favor of individual members has never failed. The teaching has been Cambridge teaching; and the Girton students have been yearly examined from the same papers, and under the same conditions as the under-graduates, both for the previous examinations, and for examinations for degrees, with or without honors."

Side by side with Girton, another institution has grown up in Cambridge, which has met the educational wants of numbers of women to whom Girton, with its strict collegiate organization, high standard of matriculation and also higher terms, would have been inaccessible. In 1870, a system of lectures for women was established. . . . The educational opportunities thus offered soon attracted students from various parts of the country. . . . In 1873, the Association for Promoting the Higher Education of Women in Cambridge was formed, and Newnham Hall was built for the reception of the rapidly increasing number of students. . . . The success of Newnham Hall has equaled that of Girton; and though the first object of both Association and Hall was to afford students thorough preparation for the Cambridge Higher Local Examinations, many of them have desired and obtained more advanced instruction, and have shared the privilege granted to the Girton students of informal examination in the Tripos subjects. In 1880, a further step was taken. The Association and Newnham Hall were amalgamated as Newnham College; a second building was added to accommodate the largely increased number of students, remaining under the superintendence of Miss Clough, to whose initiative in the first instance, and unwearied care throughout, the College mainly owes its present prosperity. . . .

It will be seen that all these various movements for the education of women sprang up sporadically as it were, supported, indeed, in large measure by the same active and devoted group of friends to the cause, but having no connection and no bond of common action. . . . The need of some wider organization which should offer the means of communication and cooperation to all throughout the three kingdoms interested or actively concerned in the movement, pressed with great force on the mind of the present writer, and in June, 1871, she brought before a meeting of the Society of Arts . . . a scheme for a national society affording the desired means of co-operation between all workers in the cause. . . . The new organization took definite shape under the name of the National Society for Improving the Education of Women of All Classes; shortened afterward into Women's Education Union. . . . The objects of the society were as follows: (1) To bring into communication and co-operation all individuals and associations engaged in promoting the education of women, and to collect and register, for the use of members, all information bearing on that education. (2) To promote the establishment of good schools, at a moderate cost, for girls of all classes above those provided for by the Elementary Education Act. (3) To aid all measures for extending to women the means of higher education after the school period, such as colleges and lectures for women above eighteen, and evening classes for women already earning their own maintenance. (4) To provide means for training female teachers, and for testing their efficiency by examinations of recognized authority, followed by registration according to fixed standard. (5) To improve the tone of public opinion on the subject of education itself, and on the national importance of the education of women.

After a lapse of eleven years we venture to affirm that those objects have in the main been attained. . . . The Union, by giving scholarships to successful candidates in the various examinations open to girls in the three kingdoms; to be held at some place of higher education, gave an impulse to the latter, and set an example which was largely followed afterward by other bodies. By public and drawing-room meetings . . ., by the publication of papers, by memorials and deputations bringing concentrated influence to bear wherever questions affecting the interests of women's education were being decided, the Union carried on with unwearied energy and no little success its work of propagandism. . . .

Of its two principal achievements, the formation of the Girls' Public Day School Company and of the Teachers' Training and Registration Society, I must speak with somewhat more detail, as both were initiatory movements of great and far-reaching importance. . . .

The reader will have perceived that up to this time the efforts of the supporters of the movement had been mainly directed to obtaining higher education for women, as the continuation and supplement of school education. But a greater and more pressing want, as shown by the Reports of the Schools Enquiry Commission, was that of good schools to prepare girls not only for this higher education, which must always be the privilege of the few, but for the work and duties of life incumbent on all. It was to supply this want that the Central Committee of the Women's Education Union first turned their attention. . . .

It was Miss Buss's original creation, the North London Collegiate School, that the Women's Education Union took as their model. . . . In July, 1872, this company was formed under the title of the Girls' Public Day School Company (limited), and its first school was opened at Durham House, Chelsea, in November of the same year. The experiment of a public, undenominational school [open to anyone who could pay the tuition] for girls of the middle and upper classes, was an entirely novel, and by many held to be a perilously bold one. . . . At this date, only ten years and a half from its commencement, [the Company] has twenty-three schools at work in London and the provinces, giving a thoroughly good education to an aggregate of over four thousand scholars, at a maximum fee of £15 a year; and before the end of 1882, two more will be opened. . . . The Girls' Public Day School Company has thus satisfactorily solved the problem of providing good and cheap education for girls of the classes above those attending the public elementary schools, on terms insuring a fair interest on the capital invested in them. Nor should the beneficent action of the company be measured by its own schools only. Its example has been largely followed throughout the country; schools of the same type have been established by independent local bodies in various places, and it may be safely predicted that, in the course of a few years, no town with a sufficient population to maintain a school will remain unprovided with one, either by the Girls' Public Day School Company, or by some local agency of a similar nature. . . .

The Women's Education Union having thus provided schools, next turned its attention to the training of teachers. In the case of teachers of elementary schools, the necessity for training had been admitted long before. . . . But the equal necessity of such training for higher-grade teachers was by no means admitted, and the very fact that it was required for elementary school-masters caused it to be looked upon as the stamp of an inferior grade of teachers. . . .

The Women's Education Union took up the question in 1876, and . . . formed a Society for the Training and Registration of Teachers. . . . Teachers of both sexes were contemplated by the Society, but the Council felt that the first claim upon them was that of women, always at a disadvantage in regard to means; and in May, 1878, their first Training College for Teachers in Middle and Higher Schools for Girls was opened. . . . The College opened with only four students, but the numbers rapidly increased, . . . and the efficiency of its training has been most satisfactorily tested by the success of the students at the Cambridge University Examinations in the Theory, History and Practice of Education. . . .

It must be noted, as marking the great advance already made in public opinion by the women's claim to educational equality, that in this examination no difference is made between the male and female candidates, the conditions of admission, standard, and certificate being precisely the same for both. This brings me to the last and culminating success of the movement—the admission of women to University degrees. . . .

It was natural that the University of London, from its modern origin and constitution, and consequent freedom from ancient tradition and social prejudice, should take the lead in this bold innovation; but it is another proof of the rapid advance of public opinion on the subject, that within two years the ancient University of Cambridge should have followed the example. . . .

Great as this step is, it still falls far short of the position of the University of London as regards equality between men and women. Cambridge has conferred that equality only in respect of the Tripos Examination, but it has not acknowledged women as members of the University. . . . We may, however, be satisfied with this partial result, knowing well that the wedge, already inserted so deeply, will not fail to be driven home before long. Perhaps Oxford, which, though always moving more slowly than Cambridge in the cause of women's education, has made each concession more thorough when granted at last, . . . may again better the example of the sister University by granting in full what Cambridge is doling out piecemeal: the admission of women to all the privileges of the University on equal terms with the other sex. . . .

Frances Martin, "A College for Working Women", *Macmillan's Magazine*, XL (1879), 483-88.

In 1854 F. D. Maurice founded the London Working Men's College for manual workers who had at least the rudiments of an education. He was aided in this venture by Kingsley, Ruskin, Dante Gabriel Rossetti, and other idealistic middle-class intellectuals. In a period when the Mechanics' Institutes were markedly declining because of their unrealistic expectations, Maurice's school was a success, probably because it provided instruction of a practical nature. Frances Martin, one of the first graduates of Queen's College (of which Maurice was a principal founder) and a number of kindred spirits carried on his tradition by offering evening classes in an institution established in his memory in

1874, a College for Working Women. The men and women who organized the school were concerned with more than education; just as Octavia Hill attempted to improve not merely the housing but the quality of life of the slum-dwellers in her charge, so Miss Martin and her associates strove to provide, in addition to instruction, a healthy and constructive alternative to the temptations of the London slums. Thus education was considered valuable not only as a source of personal gratification, but, in addition, as a vehicle of social regeneration.

Five years ago a few ladies and gentlemen took a house in Fitzroy Street, and opened it as a *College for Working Women.* They use the term *College* in accordance with its primary meaning as a *Collection* or *Assembly,* and have made the College a place of assembly for women employed during the day.

Women who earn their living have few opportunities for self-improvement; and yet the means of remedying a defective education, or supplying the want of any education whatever, would often enable them to improve their own position and that of others depending upon them.

Many women in London are young, friendless, and solitary. They lack the stimulus and interest of social life, rational entertainment, and intellectual pursuit. If they supply the want of these in the way that so many learn to do, or deaden their craving for them, they do it at a terrible cost. The College in Fitzroy Street steps in to meet their need, and helps to make their lives bright and good.

When the work of the day is over, when the shops are closed and the tired shop-women are free; when the young milliners and dressmakers have completed their task, and the female bookkeepers, telegraph clerks, and post-office clerks leave their desks; when the gold and diamond polishers, the burnishers and gilders, the machinists and bootmakers quit the noisy workrooms; when the hospital nurse, the lady's-maid, the cook, and the housemaid have their evenings out, and the weary teacher closes her books for the day, some two hundred of them find their way to the place of assembly, the collection of women in Fitzroy Street.

That which impels them most strongly is the need of instruction. They want to improve. . . . They have earned their own living almost from childhood, and any rudiments of instruction they may have received are almost effaced. They hear of the College, and come to see what it can do for them. . . .

There are many who come because they are "ashamed" of not being able to write, or because some one has told them that if they knew how to read they would like books. . . .

About one-third of those who join the collection of women in Fitzroy Street are learning to read and write. The remaining two-thirds attend classes in grammar, arithmetic, bookkeeping, history, geography, drawing, physiology, hygiene, French, Latin, German, singing; in fact, any subject they wish to study, of which the committee approves, and for which a voluntary teacher can be found. And thus it comes to pass that from October to July every room in the house is occupied by a class of students on every night of the week save Saturday. All the College teachers are unpaid.

Many of these ladies and gentlemen are professional teachers, trained to their work and educated for it; coming when the labours of the day are over to give the best they have for the love of service, and as a voluntary ministration to the need of others. . . .

Such work should be undertaken not by those who are willing to come out on fine evenings when they have nothing else to do, but by a far more earnest and sympathetic class of helpers. . . . The pupils who await them have not been kept back by wind or snow, by rain or frost; they have come long distances on foot in the cold of winter, or after the trying heat of a summer's day; they are tired, exhausted, often depressed at the hopelessness of the task they have undertaken, the almost insurmountable barrier of ignorance which impedes progress, and if they learn anything from a teacher, they learn much more than he professes to teach. They learn that life is, and ought to be, something more than mere living. . . .

The College is a collection of students. It seeks to supply the need of instruction and improvement felt by a few women in every class. But it does more than this: it seeks to promote culture, to teach habits of prudence and forethought; it gives thoughtful women an opportunity of meeting each other and forming valuable friendships, and it offers healthy and rational entertainment as a recreation to the older, and a means of guiding and forming the tastes of its younger members.

. . . Examinations are held within its walls, free of cost to students, who can obtain certificates and prizes. There are free lending and reference libraries, open to students every night in the week except Saturday. . . . There are now about 600 volumes in the library, and more than a hundred readers. Wholesome fiction is freely supplied, and is greatly in request; there is also a fair demand for poetry, biography, history, and travels. . . .

The occupations of the students and members during one year are as follows: —

Artificial flower, feather, and toy-makers	5
Bookbinders, folders, and compositors	6
Bookkeeper	1
China painters, gilders, japanners, hair workers	7
Clerks and newspaper agent	4
Domestic servants	30
Embroiderers, lace milliners, and jewelcase liners	8
Hospital nurses	9
Machinists	18
Needlewomen, dress and mantle-makers, milliners, &c.	107
Shopwomen	26
Stationers, tobacconist, and fancy trades	6
Surgical-instrument makers	4
Teachers and pupil-teachers	38
No occupation stated [Nearly all employed in housework or needlework at their own homes.]	107
	376

. . . Too much stress cannot be laid on the importance of making the classrooms, the coffee-room, the reading-room, the hall and staircase, and office beautiful. Beautiful objects should greet the tired eyes and weary brain, and refresh them. The knowledge that this beauty has been provided by the loving service of others will revive many a drooping heart and spirit.

Moreover, how shall the temptations of this great city and its lighted halls be neutralised save by the efforts of those who join together to withdraw the young from the dull and lonely lives which so often betray them to ruin? If kind friends are ready with bright, loving welcome, they will find it easy to lead young women to love that which is good and noble, and to be contented with wholesome, happy entertainments. . . .

The students, whose small fees for classes and membership often represent sharp economy, and who give time and attention after the work of the day is over; and the teachers, who, in addition to time and money and thought for the educational part of the work, devote so much generous care to bringing beauty in art, music, and literature home to their pupils, have between them made the College all that it is, and will make it all that it hopes to become. . . .

CHAPTER VI

Women and Work

Throughout the Victorian era, the employment of women of the upper and middle classes was largely regarded as improper, for the notion of the ideal Victorian lady still held sway. It was assumed that the guardian of morality, the defender of virtue, and the presiding divinity of the hearth should not allow herself to be tainted by contact with less elevating pursuits, particularly those of a commercial nature. Work outside the home and perfect womanhood were held to be incompatible. It is true that as early as the 1840's, Sarah Stickney Ellis had taken the very advanced position (all the more remarkable in the light of her usually conventional views) that the entrance of women into the workaday world—even for a lady of good family—should not be considered degrading.[1] That, however, was a minority view; in general, society was critical of ladies who worked for money. Thus, although the idea of educating women was winning at least some approval in the 1860's, the suggestion that they be employed aroused pained protests. As one observer noted, education was acceptable; employment was not.[2]

On the other hand, nineteenth-century feminists, in their rebellion against the stereotype of the Angel in the House, favored education for women, not only for its own sake, but also as a means of securing employment.[3] To those who believed that work was "knowledge put into practice", it was absurd to accept the concept of education for women and to reject what appeared to be the logical corollary. It seemed to them equivalent to putting an edge on a blade and then refusing to use it, or getting steam up in a locomotive and declining to open the throttle. Education without application, in short, was waste.[4]

The woman of good family most in need of opportunities for employment was she whom widowhood or loss of investments had placed in reduced circumstances. Practically the only situation available to her

[1] Ellis, *The Women of England*, p. 104.
[2] Emily Shirreff, "College Education for Women", *Contemporary Review*, XV (1870), 55.
[3] Jessie Boucherett, "On the Education of Girls, with Reference to their Future Position", *English Woman's Journal*, VI (1860), 217-24.
[4] E. P. Ramsay Laye, "Women and Careers", *Englishwoman's Review*, LXI (1878), 197-98.

(if in fact one could be found) was that of governess, a position characterized by misery and some loss of social status. "No class of men can
compete with the governess in wretchedness", asserted Bessie Rayner
Parkes in 1859.[1] The degraded condition of the helpless women who
were forced to become governesses by economic need, lack of training
for any useful occupation, and a pathetic desire to retain the appearance of respectability, Miss Parkes described as the "plague spot" of
English society. Of course, governesses did not constitute the most depressed group of English working women, but to the middle and upper
classes who employed them they were the most conspicuous. Moreover,
the lot of the governess, even if it did not actually match the deprivation
of working women of the lower classes, was dismal enough: long hours,
meager wages, lack of job security, and fear of dismissal without references. In addition, the problems of governesses were compounded by
the undeniable fact that the market for their services, as a contemporary observed, was "glutted by the introduction of an inferior article";
many governesses were "worth nothing, and anything they [earned] in
that capacity [was] too much".[2]

Two different institutions were established to remedy the pitiful plight
of these women. The promoters of Queen's College, as we have seen,
wished to improve the educational level of governesses. In addition, the
Governesses' Benevolent Institution, founded in 1841, attempted after a
belated start to assist "privately and delicately" ladies "in temporary distress", by providing a number of modest annuities to retired governesses
and by establishing, as early as 1849, an asylum for the aged among
them.

Such types of assistance, valuable as they were to individuals, were
mere palliatives. The essential problem remained — a legacy of society's
insistence on preserving feminine purity from the contamination of the
real world. But, according to feminists, employment for women represented not contamination, but preservation. The extent to which middle-
class feminists were interested in the question of women's employment
may be gauged by the fact that so many of them wrote books and articles
which dealt specifically with this question.[3] But some feminists attempted
to do more than this. In order to provide women of the middle and
upper classes with an alternative to becoming a governess, heretofore
the only acceptable occupation for a lady, Bessie Rayner Parkes, Barbara

---

[1] Bessie Rayner Parkes, "The Market for Educated Female Labor", *English Woman's Journal*, IV (1859),
149. Cf. Emily Faithfull's account of a governess who in a "small backroom in Drury Lane, literally starved
to death, having previously sold every scrap of furniture to purchase food". See "Miscellanea", *Victoria
Magazine*, XXIII (1874), 69-70.
[2] Mary Calverley, "Who Teaches Our Little Ones?" *Good Words*, XIX (1878), 391. The author goes on
to plead for the certification of governesses in order to raise teaching standards.
[3] Barbara Leigh Smith Bodichon, *Women and Work* (1857); Bessie Rayner Parkes, *Essays on Women's Work*
(1865); Josephine Butler, ed., *Woman's Work and Woman's Culture* (1869); Emily Faithfull, *Women's Work*
(1871); Louisa Twining, *Women's Work, Official and Unofficial* (1887); Emily Pfeiffer, *Women and Work* (1888).

Bodichon, Jessie Boucherett, and Adelaide Procter launched a movement with the goal of enabling such women (superfluous in both a social
and economic sense) to live by their own endeavors. Utilizing organizations like the Society for Promoting the Employment of Women and the
Social Science Association, publications such as the *English Woman's
Journal,* and enterprises such as the Victoria Press[1], feminists labored to
provide middle-class spinsters, widows, and wives of bankrupts with
some means of earning their own livings and leading decent lives. Women
of this class were therefore encouraged to seek careers in journalism,
literary work, science, the arts, the civil service, and particularly medicine, since women, as Emily Davies argued in the early 1860's, had a
natural inclination to doctoring. Moreover, Miss Davies asserted, they
were intellectually and physically equal to the demands that would be
made on them by a medical education or by the subsequent practice of
medicine.

     Feminists believed that women must be employed, as physicians or in
any other capacity, for reasons other than economic ones. There were
women, economically secure, who needed positions to rescue them from
the boredom, the emptiness, and the frustration of what was at most a
"half-life".[2] Some bold spirits went so far as to assert that holding a job
was not incompatible with the wedded state, although that was far from
being a typical feminist attitude.

     For most women, however, the question was academic. Harriet
Martineau observed in 1859, "In [former] days . . . the supposition was
true which has now become false, . . . that every woman is supported . . .
by her father, her brother, or her husband. . . ."[3] The census of 1851
had revealed that hundreds of thousands of single, lower-class women
were supporting themselves as domestics, millhands, or agricultural
laborers. Some of these women too, it was argued, ought to be prepared
for other occupations appropriate to their station.

     Those who were condemned to remain at the base of the industrial
pyramid were to be helped by encouraging them to form unions, or by
expanding the Factory Acts, although feminists like Emma Paterson
and Henry Fawcett opposed such legislation on the grounds that limiting women's working hours would be detrimental to their interests, since

---

     [1] See M. M. H., "A Ramble with Mrs. Grundy: A Visit to the Victoria Printing Press", *English Woman's
Journal,* V (1860), 269-72.

     [2] Barbara Leigh Smith Bodichon, *Women and Work* (New York: C. S. Francis & Co., 1859), p. 39; Laye,
"Women and Careers", p. 199. There were, of course, critics who insisted that middle-class ladies who
worked were guilty of depriving their less fortunate sisters of jobs. In such cases, it was maintained, "the
remuneration earned [was] little to the rich woman, but [might] mean bread to the poor one". One conclusion to be drawn from this type of thinking was that ladies should seek only unpaid work. See, for example,
"Work and Women", *Westminster Review,* CXXXI (1889), 278. In actual fact, however, middle-class women
did not compete with lower-class women for the same jobs.

     [3] Harriet Martineau, "Female Industry", *Edinburgh Review,* CCXXII (1859), 297. It was this article
which inspired Jessie Boucherett to establish a society "to introduce women into new employments". See
Boucherett, "On the Obstacles to the Employment of Women", pp. 361-75.

employers would prefer to hire men who, not being restricted by the Factory Acts, could work longer hours.[1]

The efforts of feminists to improve the condition of all segments of the female population, it must be said, met with only limited success. The entrance of middle-class women into the professions, for example, was so rare as to justify its being regarded as mere tokenism. But an evaluation of the feminists' record of achievement must take into consideration their attempts to erase the notion that the sole occupation of women must be marriage and motherhood, attempts which made it possible for some women at least to see themselves in another dimension — as thinkers and doers, rather than as parasites and breeders. In view of the opposition to this attitude — an opposition based on the conviction that the wide-scale employment of women must lead ultimately to moral degeneration and the destruction of society — feminists had some right to be pleased with their progress.

Barbara Leigh Smith Bodichon, *Women and Work* (New York: C. S. Francis & Co., 1859), pp. 22-25, 27-28, 30.

One can almost say that, with her background and family connections, it would have been difficult for Barbara Leigh Smith Bodichon *not* to be a reformer. A first cousin of Florence Nightingale; the eldest daughter of Benjamin Leigh Smith, the Radical member for Norwich; the granddaughter of William Smith, an M.P. who had favored the abolition of slavery and the reform of Parliament; she moved in the society of the leading reformers and philanthropists of the day, including Harriet Martineau, Richard Cobden, W. J. Fox, and Joseph Parkes.

Physically attractive, a talented artist, intelligent, public-spirited, generous (she became the chief benefactress of Girton College), she was the acknowledged leader of "the ladies of Langham Place", a group that included the Misses Craig, Boucherett, Parkes, Procter, and the other ladies of the *English Woman's Journal* and the Society for the Employment of Women. Her pamphlet, *A Brief Summary in Plain Language of the Most Important Laws Concerning Women* (1854) was discussed by the Law Amendment Society and played a part in the debate that eventually led to the passage of the Married Women's Property Act. In *Women and Work* (first published in 1857) she stressed the need to open more occupations to women for the sake of their mental and bodily health,

---

[1] The support by the Factory Acts Reform Association (representing the men's unions) of further protective legislation for women seemed to bear out Mrs. Paterson's and Professor Fawcett's charge that the men were attempting to exclude women from the labor force. It seemed apparent to others, however, that because shortening the hours of women would necessarily have the same effect on the hours of the men working with them, "the men's unions aimed, not at the exclusion of women in order to work longer themselves, but at the virtual shortening of their own hours by setting this law in motion for the women". B. L. Hutchins and A. Harrison, *A History of Factory Legislation*, 2nd ed. rev. (London: P. S. King & Son, 1911), p. 187.

and pointedly observed that Queen Victoria's domestic concerns did not prevent her from fulfilling her public obligations; working women, she suggested, might similarly be able to arrange their lives so as to satisfy both the needs of their households and the demands of their jobs. Asserting that no human being had the right to be idle, Madame Bodichon justified the employment of women on religious, moral, social, and practical grounds.

> . . . Women *do* want work, and girls must be trained for professions. . . .
>
> Ask the thousands of soldiers who passed under the consoling hands of Florence Nightingale and her noble band, what profession wants women! The profession of nursing wants women, and they will have them. . . .
>
> Ask the emigrants who went out to Australia year after year under the careful and wise system of Caroline Chisholm's colonization, how women can organize and what professions they should fill. I think they would answer, "As organizers of colonization, emigration, secretaries to colonies," &c., &c.
>
> Ask those interested in the reform of juvenile criminals. They will say, "Mary Carpenter is appointed by nature to be establisher and inspector of such schools. Women are wanted in the vast vocation of reformation." . . .
>
> Perhaps there is no profession which so calls for women as that of medicine. In New York there are three very eminent female physicians, and a hospital established through the exertions of Dr. Elizabeth Blackwell, into which women are received as students.
>
> In Boston, Dr. Harriet K. Hunt has practised for twenty years. In Philadelphia, Dr. Ann Preston is professor of physiology to the Female Medical College. But in England, Jessie Meriton White attempted in vain to obtain a medical education. She applied to fourteen London hospitals, and was refused by all. The London University, the most liberal community in England, refused to admit her as a candidate to the matriculation examination. In fact there is no way of obtaining a diploma in England.
>
> In prisons and workhouses women are much needed. An earnest quiet woman in such places has more power than a strong man. . . .
>
> Women can be designers for art, manufacture, and, with proper training, show themselves remarkably apt at ornamentation. All that appertains to interior architecture is especially woman's province, though there is no reason at all why a woman should not build a cathedral if she has the instruction and the genius.
>
> There is no reason why women in England and America should not make as good watches as the women of Switzerland. The watch-making men of course, are against it, and persecute all who begin; this is natural, but let some thousands of the 50,000 women of London, who are working for under six pence a day, enter this new profession, and the persecution will cease.
>
> Of the profession of teacher, we can say what Webster said of the law—"There is always room above." For well trained teachers there is a great demand—below them is no room—nothing but starvation. . . .
>
> . . . Young women begin to ask at the age of sixteen or seventeen, 'What am I created for? Of what use am I to be in the world?" According to the answer is often the destiny of the creature.
>
> Mothers! the responsibility lies with you: what do you say in answer? I fear it is almost always something to this purport: "You must marry some day. Women were made for men. Your use is to bear children; to keep your home comfortable for your

husband. In marriage is the only respectable life for woman." . . .

Love is not the end of life. It is nothing to be sought for; it should come. If we work, love may meet us in life; if not, we have something still, beyond all price.

Oh young girls! waiting listlessly for some one to come and marry you; wasting the glorious spring time of your lives sowing nothing but vanity, what a barren autumn will come to you! You are trying hard to make yourselves agreeable and attractive by dress and frivolity, and all this time your noblest parts lie sleeping. Arouse yourselves! Awake! Be the best that God has made you. Do not be contented to be charming and fascinating; be noble, be useful, be wise.

To many of you the question comes direct, whether you will accept a dependent, ornamental and useless position, or an independent and hard working one. Never hesitate for one moment; grasp the hand that points to work and freedom. Shake the hand with thanks of refusal, which offers you a home and "all the advantages of city society until you are married." Say that you prefer to pay your own way in the world, that you love an honorable independence better than to live on charity, though gilded with all the graces of hospitality and affection. Plan for yourselves a life of active single blessedness and usefulness. Be sure this is nobler and happier than many married lives, and not a hell at all, as some tell you; and is the way, too, to secure a happy marriage, if that is your destiny. . . .

. . . Fathers have no right to cast the burden of the support of their daughters on other men. It lowers the dignity of women; and tends to prostitution, whether legal or in the streets. As long as fathers regard the sex of a child as a reason why it should not be taught to gain its own bread, so long must women be degraded. Adult women must not be supported by men if they are to stand as dignified rational beings before God. Esteem and friendship would not give nor accept such a position; and Love is destroyed by it. How fathers . . . can give up their daughters to be placed in such a degrading position, is difficult to understand. . . .

Bessie Rayner Parkes, "The Market for Educated Female Labor", *English Woman's Journal,* IV (1859), 145-52.

At the 1859 meeting of the Social Science Association in Bradford, Bessie Rayner Parkes read a paper dealing with the plight of the forlorn army of governesses, whose ranks were swollen by middle-class ladies untrained for any gainful occupation. The excerpt which follows is particularly valuable in a number of ways. First, as evidence of the pitiable state of governesses, Miss Parkes cited the records of the Governesses' Benevolent Institution, and described ten typical cases of ladies who, after a lifetime of service, were now destitute. Second, the solution which Miss Parkes proposed was typical of the thinking of those feminists of the *English Woman's Journal* or the Society for Promoting the Employment of Women. Like Miss Parkes and Madame Bodichon, they believed that it was the responsibility of middle-class fathers to prevent their daughters from becoming governesses, to provide for them by buying life insurance, and, above all, to train them in vocations that would provide them a livelihood.

. . . The theory of civilised life in this and all other countries . . . is that the women of the upper and middle classes are supported by their male relatives: daughters by their fathers, wives by their husbands. If a lady has to work for her livelihood, it is universally considered to be a misfortune, an exception to the ordinary rule. All good fathers wish to provide for their daughters; all good husbands think it their bounden duty to keep their wives. All our laws are framed strictly in accordance with this hypothesis; and all our social customs adhere to it more strictly still. We make no room in our social framework for any other idea, and in no moral or practical sphere do the exceptions more lamentably and thoroughly prove the rule. Women of the lower class may work, *must* work, in the house, if not out of it — too often out of it! But among us, it is judged best to carefully train the woman as the moraliser, the refiner, the spiritual element. . . .

. . . [This would be ideal] if the theory of a material provision for all educated women were humanly possible, *which it is not.*

It is not possible! . . . Educated women must work. . . .

The aristocracy are rich enough to make some invariable, though scanty, provision for their female members, but the middle class is at the mercy of a thousand accidents of commercial or professional life, and thousands and thousands of destitute educated women have to earn their daily bread . . . . Probably every person present has a female relative or intimate friend whom trade-failures, the exigencies of a numerous household, or the early death of husband or father has compelled to this course; it is in the experience of every family.

Of course the first resource of these ladies is teaching; nothing else is obviously present to them. Now listen to the result. The reports of the Governesses' Benevolent Institution, one of the largest charities and most efficient organisations for the assistance of industry which exist in the kingdom, reckon fifteen thousand governesses as an item in our population! Fifteen thousand educated women, chiefly single or widowed, unsupported by their male relations, and in innumerable cases obliged to support *them*. . . .

But it may be said, "Well, fifteen thousand is a large number; but if an equivalent number of families require teachers, and can afford to pay good salaries, it is mere sentimentality to regret that these ladies are forced to work."

. . . If any one wants to learn the truth about the condition of the educated working woman in England, let him consult the reports of the Governesses' Benevolent Institution. It is divided into several branches of usefulness. There is a Home for the disengaged at 66, Harley-street, London, and an elaborate system of Registration, by which last year fifteen hundred names were entered, and eleven hundred obtained situations. It may be recorded as a passing fact that the hall-book of the house, where Home and Register are jointly located, should record the visitors of one year as twenty-four thousand. There is a Provident Fund for the securing of annuities, of which we are told that the first payment, by a lady contracting for one of these annuities, was paid on the 20th of June, 1843, and that the amount now invested is £177,292 10s. 3d. There is also a fund out of which Elective Annuities are created, and a system of temporary assistance managed by a committee of ladies. The applications for this, in 1858, were eight hundred and thirty-eight, and the grants four hundred and ninety-three, to the extent of £1,346 8s. 8d. The total number of applications have been ten thousand three hundred and thirty-four; of grants, five thousand five hundred and seventy-one; and the total amount of gifts, £14,284 12s. 4d. Lastly, there is an Asylum for Aged

Governesses at Kentish Town; it contains twenty-two apartments duly filled.

My hearers will consider these statistics as a somewhat astounding revelation of the need of assistance in which women stand. What should we think of educated men, after long lives of honest and industrious labor, sank into such depths of poverty that they required wholesale help by hundreds and thousands; for the total number of cases in nine years, to which the society has been useful, is twenty-six thousand five hundred and seventy-one.

Let us now see how and why these unhappy women endure such misery. We have roughly the means of ascertaining; for every May and every November an election occurs to the annuities, and I find one hundred and forty-five cases of candidates printed in the list for last May, of whom some three or four only could receive an annuity. I take the first ten cases, hap-hazard, of those who have in different years been elected; they read in this wise: —

"No. 1. Miss S. M. A., aged fifty-nine. 1856. Father a colonel, in active service until Waterloo. Governess upon his death, and that of an only brother. Assisted relations to the utmost of her power. Frequent illnesses have consumed her savings; is now in very delicate health. Earned only £10 in the past year.

"No. 2. Mrs. S. A., aged sixty-eight. 1857. Father a large calico printer; her mother having impoverished herself to assist her son's speculations, she gave up the whole of her property to her and became a governess; and to the same purpose devoted all her earnings. Is now entirely dependent upon the kindness of her friends.

"No. 3. Mrs. A. A., aged sixty-six. 1858. Compelled to leave home by the embarrassment of her father, whom she assisted with nearly the whole of her salary. The foreclosure of a mortgage upon her property has rendered her entirely dependent upon two daughters who keep a small school. Is very deaf, has lost one eye, and suffers from great pain and weakness, arising from a threatening of an internal complaint.

"No. 4. Miss F. A., aged sixty-one. 1848. Engaged in tuition since nineteen, her father, a merchant, having left seven children unprovided for. Constantly assisted various members of her family, and still has a niece dependent upon her. Sight and hearing much impaired; only dependence a small day-school.

"No. 5. Miss M. A., aged seventy-four. 1848. Left home upon her father's failure. Fourteen years in one family. Devoted most of her salary to the support of an aged parent and an afflicted brother and sister. Supported afterwards an elder sister. Only income an annuity of £10 from a charitable institution.

"No. 6. Miss M. J. A., aged fifty-nine. 1852. One of sixteen children; left home in consequence at fifteen years of age. With two sisters, supported her father for many years, also an orphan niece. Impaired sight and infirm health have obliged her to subsist entirely upon a small legacy, now utterly exhausted. Mental derangement daily increases under the pressure of perfect destitution, having no means from any quarter.

"No. 7. Miss E. A., aged fifty-eight. 1851. Her father died when she was very young; and her mother's second husband ruined the family. Greatly assisted her mother and sister. Being long crippled from a fall, and having some years since lost the use of her right arm and foot, is not only incapable of self-support, but entirely helpless.

"No. 8. Mrs. O. S. G. B., aged fifty-seven. 1858. Father a captain in the army.

Her husband, a surgeon, died suddenly, having made no provision for her and two children. Assisted her mother for some years. She, suffering from chronic bronchitis and sciatica, and a daughter, also in very ill health, are without certain income, being dependent upon the letting of her apartments.

"No. 9. Miss E. B., aged sixty-five. 1849. Left home, her father having become involved; supported him till 1846, and her aged and sick mother till 1834, and for the last nine years assisted in bringing up a niece. Sight and hearing both failing, and suffers from spasmodic affection of the heart. No income whatever.

"No. 10. Miss H. B., aged sixty-one. 1851. One of six daughters; left home, her parents' means being injured by mining speculations. Assisted them during twenty years, and educated some of her nieces when settled in a school, where her parents and a helpless invalid sister resided upon very slender means. In very delicate health, and has no income."

Here you see are ten cases of most deplorable destitution, arising from the most ordinary causes. Would to God there were any thing remarkable in them; but fathers fail and brothers speculate every day, and the orphan nephews and nieces are left to the unmarried as a legacy from the beloved dead; and in families of sixteen children all must work: there is nothing unusual here; and it is also amply proved that the savings of the average governess cannot support her in her old age. The very highest class of governess is highly paid, just because there are so few; if the number increased they would not command great salaries, and the pittance accorded to the average is an irrefragable fact.

Surely then in a country where the chances of provision for women are so frightfully uncertain, parents in the middle classes ought, —

Firstly, to train their daughters to some useful art, however humble,

Secondly, to repress all desire of forcing them into tuition, because it is more "genteel",

Thirdly, to insure their lives when they cannot lay by money for their female children. . . .

. . . The one conclusion which I desire to enforce is, that in all cases it is the *fathers* who are morally responsible for their daughter's welfare. Let each father consider how he can best provide, whether by giving her a special training, by saving money, or by insurance. One or the other he is bound to do; sacredly and morally bound. He has no right, in a country like England, to risk her future on the chances of marriage which may never be fulfilled.

Bessie Rayner Parkes, "Association for Promoting the Employment of Women", *English Woman's Journal*, IV (1859), 54-59.

As long as society held to the twin assumptions that women would find husbands to support them, and, moreover, that work outside the home was unsuitable for middle- and upper-class women, the future, as Bessie Rayner Parkes saw it, held nothing for many English ladies save single wretchedness, genteel poverty, or both. In order to provide women with a more attractive option—employment and independence—a committee was formed (July 1859) out of which developed the Society for Promoting the Employment of Women. Several months later, the

Society became affiliated with the National Association for the Promotion of Social Science. The following selection is an excerpt from the article that announced the formation of the new society to the readers of the *English Woman's Journal.* It includes the initial statement prepared by the committee, which summarizes the goals of the new organization.

. . . As editors of the only representative Journal the working portion of our sex has, we have within the last two years been brought face to face with the overwhelming difficulties which await all classes and grades of women—from the seamstress to the artist and literary woman—who have their bread to earn. Difficulties so harassing to mind and body, so insuperable save by an amount of sustained courage, perseverance, privation, and fatigue, —such as men face once in their lives, as in the trenches before Sebastopol, and rest upon the laurels thereof ever after, —that, having witnessed them, we no longer wonder to find our hospitals, madhouses, and workhouses, magdalens [rehabilitation homes for prostitutes], and penitentiaries, filled to overflowing with the victims.

Yet, what is it we working women ask? What is it we are made to think and feel through every fibre of the frame with which it has pleased God to endow us as well as men, and for the maintenance of which in health, ease, and comfort, we, with men, have equal rights?

It is work we ask, room to work, encouragement to work, an open field with a fair day's wages for a fair day's work; it is injustice we feel, the injustice of men, who arrogate to themselves all profitable employments and professions, however unsuited to the vigorous manhood they boast, and thus, usurping women's work, drive women to the lowest depths of penury and suffering.

We are sick to our hearts of being told "women cannot do this; women must not do that; they are not strong enough for this, and that, and the other:" while we know and see every hour of our lives that these arguments are but shams; that some of the hardest and coarsest work done in this weary world is done by women, while, in consequence of usurped and underpaid labor, they are habitually consigned to an amount of physical endurance and privation from which the hardiest man would shrink appalled.

In the May [1869] number of this Journal we gave, in ''Warehouse Seamstresses,'' *a chronicle of facts,* by one who was herself for a time a seamstress; listen to what she says about women's work and women's wages in one of the few fields allowed her, and then ask yourselves where are the men who could or *would* endure such work as this?

"One word about remuneration, yet I hardly know what that word is to be. The piece workers earn, by working all the day, half the night, and half the sabbath, from six shillings to a pound a week. The pay depending less on labor and time than on the kind of work. I have known women earn twenty-five shillings per week for some eight or nine weeks in succession, then fifteen, twelve, eight, or five, according to the time of the season. Many, many weeks the best hands will not average five shillings, and inferior ones, two or three; several months in the year they will earn even less. On an average perhaps, mantle makers, straw hands, and flower makers will get six shillings weekly, while inferior workers and skirt hands, brace hands, etc., will earn four.

"But the toil—oh, the toil! Not for a fair day's work do they realise these amounts— by a fair day's work I mean, that a woman shall sew unremittingly ten hours, *not twenty.* Who can describe the state of mind and body consequent on having sewn twenty hours per day for six weeks? *No one, yet there are thousands who know exactly.*"

In the current number we give another paper from the same hand, *a record of facts again:* "Infant Seamstresses," — poor babes, and yet more hapless mothers! May every parent who reads this record lay it to heart, and join in the good work of helping women to help themselves. God knows the need is sore! This Association, as yet in its infancy, is a direct and immediate channel whereby the many may help the few to overcome some among the numerous difficulties which beset the working woman. A working Committee it already has, and funds only are needed to enable it to carry out the admirable objects it has in view, which we cannot do better than give in its own recently printed statement.

"That there exists a great want of employment for women, throughout England, and more especially in London, is no longer a contested point.

"The extent of the distress thus produced, and the best methods of remedying it, are still matters of doubt, but no one will be found bold enough to deny the suffering, or to assert that the means now in action for its relief, have proved sufficient for the purpose.

"A plan for the prevention of this distress, and of the many evils arising from it, has been formed by a Society, called 'The Society for Promoting the Employment of Women'. . . .

"It appears from the census [of 1851] that there are two millions of unmarried women in England, who work for subsistence. It is of no use to tell these persons that domestic life is the best position for them, and that a woman never appears to such advantage as in her husband's home, for they have no husbands belonging to them, and though any individual of the number may marry, yet the proportion of two million of single women must remain for ever, gradually increasing with the numbers of the population. These must be their own bread winners, and earn money in some way or other, unless they are contented to take up their abode for life in the union workhouse.

"The three great professions open to receive them — Teaching, Domestic Service, and Needlework — are over-crowded to such a degree as to render competition excessive, and to beat down wages to a point at which it is difficult to live, so that we hear of maids of all-work earning from three to six pounds a year, (a sum barely sufficient to furnish them with the scantiest raiment, and which makes any attempt at laying by money, against old age or a time of sickness, utterly impossible;) or, more cruel still, till we read of women toiling for sixteen hours a day at their needles, and earning fourpence! . . .

"As is natural under these circumstances, the workhouses are full of able-bodied women; the parish officers, urged on by the overtaxed ratepayers, treat them with rigor, affecting to believe that their idleness is voluntary, and so drive them forth into the world to live as best they may. And all this misery is inflicted on them for no fault, but that of having come into a world where there is no employment for them.

"But can this state of things be natural? Could Providence have created several thousand superfluous women for the purpose of rendering them useless burdens on society, as inmates of our prisons, workhouses, and charitable institutions? Or is it that there is something wrong in our social arrangements, whereby they are unfairly deprived of occupations that were intended for their peculiar benefit?

"If this want of employment extended to the men, it would be a sign that the country was in a state of decadency, but happily this is not the case, for everywhere we hear how high their wages are.

"Government is obliged to raise the bounties for soldiers and sailors, or they could procure none, and even then finds it difficult to obtain enough, occupations for men being so plentiful, and so well remunerated. From the colonies, letters declare they are at a stand still for want of workmen. 'We want nothing,' says a paper from Cape Town, 'but more men, more carpenters, more blacksmiths, more bricklayers. If we had twice as many as at present, they would all find full employment.' Is it not somewhat strange, that, while men's labor is in such demand, women should experience a difficulty (often amounting to an impossibility) in earning a living by honest industry? That, while in some departments of labor, men will only work three days a week, because in that time they can earn enough to provide food for their families and the means of drunkenness for themselves, women should be glad to work sixteen hours a day for fourpence?

"Surely there must be something wrong in this disproportion, something unnatural, and that was never intended. . . .

"It is the intention of the society to establish a large School for girls and young women, where they may be specially trained to wait in shops, by being thoroughly well instructed in accounts, book keeping, etc.; be taught to fold and tie up parcels, and perform many other little acts, which a retired shopwoman could teach them. The necessity of politeness towards customers and a constant self-command, will also be duly impressed upon them. Girls educated in this school would be capable of becoming clerks, cashiers, and ticket-sellers at railway stations.

"It is also contemplated to establish workshops in connection with the school, where the girls might be taught other trades, — trades well suited to women, but now almost exclusively in the hands of men, such as printing, hairdressing, etc., for instance, and possibly even watchmaking. As the means of the Society increased, so would the number of workshops, and the variety of trades taught.

"No girl would be admitted to either school or workshop, who did not bring with her a certificate of good character from the clergyman of her parish, or from two respectable householders; she must also bring a certificate of health from a medical man, as it would be a waste of time and money to instruct feeble or sickly girls in trades that require a considerable degree of strength for their exercise.

"Nevertheless, the weakly would benefit by the plan, by being relieved from the competition of their stronger sisters in needlework, teaching, and whatever other resources for the feeble there may exist.

"We are aware that instruction cannot be given to all who require it; twenty schools would not suffice for that; but when it is proved that women are capable of these employments, a demand for them will spring up, which will compel a change in our present one-sided system of education. Our workshops, too, will lead to considerable benefits, and will greatly increase the number of occupations open to women. Thus, if we send out a dozen young women as accomplished ladies' hair-dressers, other girls will speedily be apprenticed to them; and in a few years the dozen will have become hundreds.

"It is also the intention of the Society to render their office a depôt for information of every kind relating to the employment of women. Curious and interesting facts will be collected. Extracts from newspapers, pamphlets, and speeches on the subject, will be gathered together, and kept for the inspection of members of the Society. . . ."

Jessie Boucherett, "The Industrial Movement", in *The Woman Question in Europe,* edited by Theodore Stanton (London: Sampson Low & Co., 1884), pp. 90-107.

Although the interests of Jessie Boucherett, Adelaide Procter, and Bessie Rayner Parkes encompassed many aspects of the Woman Question, these ladies were concerned, in particular, with the problem of employment. They rejected the notion—so dear to the hearts of Victorian status-seekers—that work, for a lady, was incompatible with the ideal of Perfect Womanhood, and they devoted their considerable talents to opening new occupations to women. But they took a realistic view of the value of their efforts, and recognized that their main contribution to the cause must be the formation of a favorable public opinion, "for it is the public and not the Society that must find employment for women. All that can be done by a Society is to act as pioneer". . . .[1] In the following selection, Jessie Boucherett (see p. 74), one of the founders of the Society for the Employment of Women and its prime mover, summarizes the accomplishments of twenty-five years.

In 1845, Thomas Hood, shortly before his death, wrote the well-known "Song of the Shirt". . . . The pathos of the "Song" roused public sympathy strongly, and an impression became general that the condition of working women of the lower class was not what it ought to be, and that it would be well if something could be done to raise their wages. This impression, though vague and impracticable, was of great use, for it not only turned the minds of philanthropists toward the subject, but it prepared the way for any efforts that might be made to introduce women into new occupations. . . .

From another quarter, about the same time, attention was called to the distress existing amongst educated gentlewomen. The Governesses' Benevolent Institution was started in 1841. . . . [It] is now one of the largest charities in London, and gives pensions to 243 aged governesses, besides affording other relief. . . .

A considerable number of people having thus become impressed with the unhappy condition of women who had to earn their bread, whether as teachers, or needlewomen, some efforts were made to relieve their distress by introducing them into new occupations. . . .

A most successful effort was made . . . to introduce women into the telegraph service, as is shown in the following extract from the *Englishwoman's Journal* of December 1859: ". . . About six years ago Mr. Ricardo, M.P., the then chairman of the International and Electric Telegraph Company, heard of a young girl, the daughter of one of the railway stationmasters, who had for three years carried on day by day the whole of the electric telegraph business for her father, and that too with great intelligence and correctness. The idea then suggested itself of training and employing women as clerks for the telegraph company. . . . Opposition was of course naturally enough shown by the clerks of the establishment, but the experiment was permitted to proceed, and Mrs. Craig, the present intelligent matron, appointed to instruct in her own room eight pupils on two instruments. At first the instruments in one room were worked by

[1] "Report of the Society for the Employment of Women", *National Association for the Promotion of Social Science, Transactions,* 1860, p. xx.

young men, and the instruments in the other by young women, and it seemed as though the directors were pitting them against each other, establishing a kind of industrial tournament, to see which description of laborer was worthiest. . . . At Founder's Court alone, upward of ninety young women are . . . in active employment, the whole of the actual working of the instruments having fallen into their hands. The committee are now perfectly satisfied that girls are not only more teachable, more attentive and quicker eyed than the men clerks formerly employed, but have also pronounced them more trustworthy, more easily managed, and, we may add, more easily satisfied with lower wages. So well pleased are they, indeed, with the result of their experiment, that about thirty more women are now employed at the branch offices, . . . and eventually there is no doubt they will fill posts in all the branch offices in England."

The success thus foretold has been far more than attained. The government took possession in 1870 of the electric telegraphs of the country, and the staff employed by the companies passed into the hands of the Postmaster General. By good fortune, or more correctly speaking, by the mercy of Providence, Mr. Scudamore . . . was favorable to the employment of women. He retained the women clerks whom the company had employed and even added to their number. Before that time, women had often been employed by local postmasters in country towns as assistants, but they had never been employed by the government. Under Mr. Scudamore women were employed in London as post-office counter-women as well as telegraphists. . . . The success which attended the employment of women in the minor duties of postal work, encouraged . . . the experiment of employing women of higher education as clerks in the discharge of work of a superior sort. . . . It was no doubt owing to the very successful results of the experiment, as regards the Telegraph Clearing-House, of employing female clerks that Lord John Manners . . . was induced to recruit certain branches of the savings bank department with ladies, intrusting to them that simpler kind of work which hitherto had for the most part been allotted to boy clerks. And, so far as can be learnt, there has been no cause to regret the step taken in this direction. The employment of females has also been tried since 1873 in the Returned Letter office, where they have been engaged . . . in returning the ordinary correspondence that the Post Office has not been able to deliver. No better proof of the capacity of females for certain kinds of clerk work could be afforded than the emphatic testimony . . . by the Controller of the Returned Letter office, who stated that their employment in that office had been a "perfect success." They have, he continues, "completely surpassed my expectations. They are very accurate, and do a fair quantity of work; more so, in fact, than many of the males who have been employed in the same duty." . . .

Let us now return to the earlier period and trace the course of other efforts to find suitable employment for women.

In 1855 a pamphlet appeared entitled, "Women and Work," written by Miss Leigh Smith, now Madame Bodichon. This work gained some attention, and in 1857 a small monthly publication called the *Englishwoman's Journal,* was established by Madame Bodichon and others interested in the condition of women. Miss Bessie Parkes was the editor of the new periodical, around which gathered a small but earnest circle of sympathizers. A reading-room for women was opened in the house which contained the office of the *Journal,* and from this small office and humble reading-room have grown almost all the great women's movements of the present day. . . .

In April, 1859, an article was published in the *Edinburgh Review* on the industrial position of women. It must have had a wide effect, and inspired many with a desire to assist women to earn their livelihood. It gave me the idea of establishing a society, the object of which should be to introduce women into new employments. I had seen the *Englishwoman's Journal,* and I applied to the editor for advice and assistance, and by her was introduced to the reading-room, where I was made acquainted with Miss Ade-laide Procter, the poet, who became my coadjutor. As she had many friends in London and considerable influence, we succeeded in drawing a few people together, and opened, in 1859, a very humble room over a shop, as the office of the Society for Promoting the Employment of Women. It was shortly afterward removed to 19 Langham Place, where the *Journal* office and reading-room had already been established. The Asso-ciation for the Promotion of Social Science . . . gave us its support; the Earl of Shaftes-bury, whose name was a tower of strength, became our president, and, with a committee of twenty-two members, we made a beginning. The first trade we thought of was printing, but thinking it probable that such an undertaking would succeed better in private hands, we apprenticed five girls to Miss Emily Faithfull, who started the Victoria Press. This undertaking did not, I believe, become a commercial success, but it com-pletely proved that women were good type-setters. Many women were taught the trade, and several printing offices now employ women as type-setters. . . . A women's·print-ing office is now established . . . of which Mrs. Paterson is the manager. The women are not merely type-setters, but they work at the higher branches of the trade as well. . . .

The society was always desirous of teaching girls to become commercial clerks and book-keepers. . . . As soon as it was found that instructed women were capable of doing the work, several employers taught their own daughters, nieces or other depen-dents, how to keep their accounts. Sometimes an employer who had engaged one of our clerks would take other girls and have her to teach them the business. In this way the number of women clerks and book-keepers has increased with great rapidity, and to-day there is almost an unlimited field of employment for women in this direction. A girl, who is a good arithmetician, writes a good hand, and obtains a certificate for double entry, is sure of a situation, and if in addition she learns to write shorthand, she may aspire to a superior position. . . .

In 1876, Miss Crosby . . . opened an office under the auspices of the Society for the Employment of Women for tracing plans for engineers and architects. Ladies are found to do the work well. . . .

The society has started women in various other trades. . . . A register is kept at the office, 22 Berners Street, from which competent women can be obtained in the follow-ing capacities: secretaries, readers, clerks, book-keepers, copyists, canvassers, wood engravers and carvers, art decorators, proof-readers, printers, lithographers, law writers, upholsterers, hair-dressers, waitresses, gilders, lace-cleaners, linen markers, and needle-women. . . .

It is not intended in this paper to enumerate all the efforts which have been made of late years to assist women to earn a better livelihood. . . . For instance, the great sub-ject of sisterhoods and nursing institutions is altogether omitted, although the number of poor ladies who are earning their livelihood in a noble and useful manner in these establishments must be very large. However, I will give a brief account of some of the trades open to women which have not already been mentioned.

Wood-engraving, it is said, is not a favourite employment with Englishmen, and the best work is done by foreigners, who reside in England for the purpose of illustrating our newspapers and books. Three years ago the City of London Guilds opened a wood-engraving school . . . to which girls as well as boys are admitted. Few boys attend, but there are twelve girls, who like the work and have aptitude for it. Some are already skilled enough to earn money. . . .

In the article already referred to, which appeared in the *Edinburgh Review* in 1859, mention was made of the oppression of the women engaged in china-painting in Worcestershire, who were forbidden by their fellow-workmen to use hand-rests in painting, lest they should be able to rival men in skill of execution. This statement has often been vehemently denied, and equally often reasserted. It appears, however, to have been true, and I am by no means certain that the abuse has even now been put an end to in the great factories in Staffordshire and Worcestershire. In London, however, means have been found of evading the difficulty. Mr. Minton set up a workshop where women were taught china-painting and received employment if they proved skilful. His workshop some years ago was burnt down and not rebuilt, but many women had meanwhile learnt the art and furnaces had been erected for baking their wares. A large number of women are now engaged in the trade . . . . As Mr. Doulton's factory of pottery in Lambeth, one woman was employed as an experiment in 1871; at the present time (1882) more than two hundred are employed there. . . .

Several years ago the Misses Garrett set up as house-decorators and have met with great success. Some other ladies have followed their example. It is a trade well suited to women who possess taste, business capacity and capital.

A few educated women are now being taught how to dispense medicines, and Miss Clarke keeps a chemist shop in London.

The subjoined table, taken from the former censuses, will be found of some interest.

Comparison of the census of 1861 with that of 1871, as regards the employment of women in various branches of industry in England and Wales.

OCCUPATIONS	NUMBER IN 1861.	NUMBER IN 1871.
Civil Service	1,931	3,314
Law stationers	21	51
Painters and artists	853	1,069
Photographers, including assistants	168	694
Commercial clerks, accountants, etc.	404	1,755
Saleswomen (not otherwise described)	1,055	1,721
Drapers and assistants	11,993	19,112
Hosiers and haberdashers	2,126	4,147
Shopwomen	4,520	8,333
Apprentices	185	743
Stationers	1,752	3,004
Booksellers and publishers	952	1,077
Printers	419	741
Hair-dressers and wigmakers	501	1,240
Gilders	74	234

It will perhaps be asked whether what has been done has had any perceptible effect in lessening the distress among women. As far as regards women of the higher classes who are obliged to earn their bread, I confess that in my opinion no improvement has taken place in their condition, but rather the contrary. The number of applicants for pensions at the Governesses' Benevolent Institution still far exceeds the number of pensions, and every charitable effort to give assistance to ladies brings to light an innumerable host of helpless women, chiefly composed . . . of the widows and daughters of officers, clergymen and professional men who are left destitute or nearly so. The explanation of the anomaly is that the efforts made to obtain increased employment for ladies have been more than counteracted by other causes. The excellent day-schools which have been established . . . have almost put an end to the occupation of the daily governess, and have greatly diminished the demand for resident governesses. At the same time a great increase has been made in the number of ladies seeking employment by the political troubles in Ireland. The widows and daughters of many landed proprietors there have lost the incomes which were supposed to be secured to them on the rentals of the estates. The rents not being paid, the income naturally stops, and some of these ladies have been reduced to such poverty as to have been compelled to take refuge in the work-house. Those who are capable of teaching seek for situations as governesses, and thus the profession of the teacher becomes more overcrowded than ever. Gentlewomen are also now exposed to competition from the ex-pupil teachers in board-schools, who often become nursery governesses. Hence the salaries of ordinary governesses have fallen, and it is only highly superior, accomplished or musical governesses who are still able to obtain good salaries. I may here remark that the competition would have been even keener if the industry of a large number of ladies had not been turned into other channels. The position of poor gentlewomen, bad as it is, would have been still worse if no efforts had been made to assist them. . . .

With regard to the women of the working classes, it appears to me that their condition has improved of late years. The great number of women who earn their livelihood in shops and factories has caused the wages of servants and needle-women to rise. The pay for plain sewing is still too low, and sad stories of destitute needle-women sometimes appear, but I believe that they are rarer than they used to be. . . .

The cause of this improvement is that there is less competition for employment among women of the working classes than was formerly the case, and this enables them to make better terms for themselves. There being less competition is probably due partly to the opening of new occupations to women and partly to emigration. Many men emigrate rather than submit to low wages, and employers prefer to accept women at lower wages in numerous easy occupations. This emigration is most beneficial. The emigrant himself is far happier engaged in some manly out-of-door pursuit in the colonies than he could have been while following a sedentary feminine trade in England. He probably marries, and thus three individuals are directly benefited by his emigration—the emigrant himself, his wife, and the woman who has taken his place in the old country. . . . Women in England owe much to the high spirit of the men who so bravely go forth to spread wider the area of civilization, thus taking on themselves the rough work of the world, and leaving space for their sisters to follow less laborious occupations at home.

Emily Davies, "Female Physicians", (1861), reprinted in *Thoughts on Some Questions Relating to Women* (Cambridge: Bowes & Bowes, 1910), pp. 19-27.

Medicine was the field that feminists particularly wanted to have opened to women. The legal profession and the Church might some day allow ladies to enter their ranks, but the prospects for the employment of women in the near, if not the immediate, future seemed brightest in the medical profession. Nevertheless, the problems inherent in society's acceptance of women doctors were formidable, in view of the widespread belief that medicine as a career for ladies was indecent, revolting, and somewhat freakish, pursued only by females who were presumably unsexed creatures. Even those who actively sought to further women's education (F. D. Maurice, for example) usually recoiled at the notion of lady doctors.[1] Popular opinion was not the only obstacle in the 1860's. Since English universities did not then admit women, a medical education leading to a degree in medicine was denied them. Although Elizabeth Blackwell, who had won her degree from an American university in 1849, managed to have her name put on the British Medical Register in 1859, by the following year all those who held foreign medical degrees were excluded from the Register.

Dr. Blackwell's accomplishment, of course, aroused admiration from those feminists who sought to expand employment opportunities for women. One of the early issues of the *English Woman's Journal* paid tribute to Dr. Blackwell, and in 1859 Barbara Bodichon and Bessie Parkes supported Dr. Blackwell's series of lectures designed to encourage women to enter the medical profession. Dr. Blackwell later recorded that "the most important listener [during the first lecture] was the bright, intelligent young lady whose interest in the study of medicine was then aroused—Miss Elizabeth Garrett".[2] During the next few years as Elizabeth Garrett tried to prepare herself for admission to the medical profession, she was in constant correspondence with Emily Davies, who "entered into every detail and every step in her friend's career".[3] Emily Davies' interest in medicine as a profession for women was only in part the result of her friendship with Elizabeth Garrett; in addition, Miss Davies was, in the early years of her association with the Langham Place ladies, particularly concerned with the problem of women's employment.[4] In an article, written in 1861 and published in the *English Woman's Journal,* and in a paper presented the following year at the meeting of the National Association for the Promotion of Social Science, Miss Davies suggested that the practice of medicine was an "eminently

[1] In *Lectures to Ladies on Practical Subjects* (1855), Maurice made clear his views: "I hope, by this language, I have guarded against the suspicion that I would educate ladies for the kind of tasks which belong to our professions. . . . The more pains we take to call forth and employ the faculties which belong characteristically to each sex, the less it will be intruding upon the province which, not the conventions of the world, but the will of God, has assigned to the other". Cited in Ray Strachey, *"The Cause": A Short History of the Women's Movement in Great Britain* (Port Washington, New York: Kennikat Press, Inc., 1928), pp. 168-69.

[2] Elizabeth Blackwell, *Pioneer Work in Opening the Medical Profession to Women* (London and New York: Longmans, Green & Co., 1895), p. 218. Source Book Press Reprint, 1970.

[3] Barbara Stephen, *Emily Davies and Girton College* (London: Constable & Co. Ltd., 1927), p. 57. Stephen has reprinted the letters from Elizabeth Garrett to Emily Davies (pp. 58-68).

[4] See in particular "Letters to a Daily Paper, Newcastle-on-Tyne, 1860", and "Northumberland and Durham Branch of the Society for Promoting the Employment of Women", reprinted in *Thoughts on Some Questions Relating to Women* (Cambridge: Bowes & Bowes, 1910), pp. 1-18, 28-33. AMS Reprint, 1973.

suitable" profession to be opened to ladies.[1]

The notion that training as a physician would incapacitate a woman for marriage and motherhood, she maintained, was baseless. Her response to those who illogically objected to female physicians but approved of female nurses was that nursing was essentially a menial occupation altogether inappropriate for ladies of the middle and upper classes.[2] The real obstacle, as she saw it, was not the difficulty of providing medical education for women; it was persuading eligible women to defy the social pressures of the day and to run the risk of appearing as singular, strange, and (of course!) unladylike. In short, it was the responsibility of women themselves to crumble the cake of custom and make the idea of "women-physicians" socially acceptable. The chief difficulty, in fact, was not, as Miss Davies imagined, the reluctance of women to present themselves for degrees in medicine, but the hostility of the medical profession itself, whose members, with a few honorable exceptions, fought bitterly in the courts and Parliament to keep their ranks solidly masculine (see Chapter IX).

. . . "A Physician of twenty-one years' standing," in the English Woman's Journal of last month . . . [raises] the question . . . whether there is anything in the practice of medicine by women which must necessarily contravene [the laws of our physical and moral nature].

"A Physician" asks us to consider the question under two aspects, corresponding to two main elements which determine the choice of a young man in selecting a profession: his own aptitude and the sphere into which his profession may throw him. First, as to aptitude, . . . I scarcely suppose that the most vehement objectors to female physicians would argue that, as a class, women have less taste for Medicine than men. An ignorant love of doctoring is one of the recognized weaknesses of women.

Their intellectual and physical incapacity requires to be proved by "something more stringent than the dogmatic opinion of any writer." Whether the mental powers of women are on the whole equal to those of men is a wide and difficult question, on which it is needless to enter, inasmuch as we claim only the right to exercise such powers

[1] "Female Physicians", and "Medicine as a Profession for Women", reprinted in *Thoughts on Some Questions Relating to Women*, pp. 19-27, 34-40.

[2] Emily Davies, like other middle-class feminists, maintained that "the profession [suitable for a lady] should not involve the sacrifice of social position". Consequently, nursing could not be considered a suitable occupation — the salary of a hospital nurse was "less than the wages of a butler or groom", and, furthermore, the social status of a nurse was "too nearly allied to that of an upper servant". "Medicine as a Profession for Women", p. 37. Cf. Bessie Rayner Parkes, "A Year's Experience in Woman's Work", *National Association for the Promotion of Social Science, Transactions*, 1860, pp. 811-19.

Occasionally it was suggested that middle-class ladies become nursing *supervisors*, while lower-class women would discharge the more ordinary duties on the hospital wards. See Warrington Haward, "Ladies and Hospital Nursing". *Contemporary Review*, XXXIV (1879), 490-503. Certainly the training of nurses was regarded not only as a means of providing care for the sick and suffering, but, in addition, as an opportunity to employ part of the surplus female population of the lower classes. See, for example, "Training-Schools for Nurses", *Fraser's Magazine*, X (1874), 706-13.

Eventually, of course, nursing took on the status of a profession to which a middle-class woman might aspire. See Lee Holcombe,"Women in White: The Nursing Profession", in *Victorian Ladies at Work: Middle-Class Working Women in England and Wales, 1850-1914*, Archon Books (Hamden, Conn.: The Shoe String Press, Inc., 1973), pp. 68-102.

as we possess, be they great or small. "A Physician" speaks of the previous training medical students have received as boys, as if it were impossible that girls should receive the same. But is not some training of this sort just what women want? . . .

That lady students, entering upon the course without preliminary training, do so at an immense disadvantage, we are quite ready to admit. It is perhaps the strongest point in our case, as regards mere power, both physical and intellectual, that women have been able to do so much while debarred from the advantages of early education open to most men.

"Supposing the difficulties of the student's life surpassed, you then come to the troubles and difficulties of incipient practice." And here the physical weakness of women is the argument. That, as a whole, men are stronger than women, no one denies; but does that justify us in assuming that every individual man is stronger than any individual woman? We learn from "A Physician" what our own observation confirms, that many members of the medical profession are feeble in constitution and scarcely fit for the struggle of life; but we do not therefore condemn them to complete inaction, nor do we propose any regulation for limiting the profession to men of herculean frames. On the other hand, we learn from our own observation, though not from your correspondent, that in various parts of the country women of the lower classes go through an amount of labour under which a gentleman would probably break down. I have myself been told by an eyewitness, that in Staffordshire, women are doing, "not men's work, but horses' work;" and it is an unquestionable fact, that in manufactures where women and girls are employed, the low, rough, exhausting work is given over to them, while the higher branches, in which some intelligence is required, are reserved for men. The same may be said of brick-making and other laborious outdoor work. Let it not be supposed that we look with satisfaction upon this overtasking of the physical strength of women. . . . But we do think that while women are showing themselves to be capable of such an amount of physical exertion, the comparatively far easier career of a physician should not be closed to us on the ground of physical weakness. It is remarked, that "unless she can cope with men in all the various branches of medical inquiry and practice, she will, in the race of life, necessarily go to the wall; and the struggle, which will be unavoidable, must be to the stronger." Be it so. Women are so much in the habit of going to the wall, that the position will not alarm them by its novelty, and their fate will only be the same as that of all members of the professions who are not able to cope on equal terms with their superior brethren.

As we look round upon medical men, we cannot help observing many physicians and surgeons who do not appear to be superior in ability to average women; and as for many years, only women somewhat above the average in mental and physical strength will dare to think of entering the profession, perhaps they would *not* always go to the wall. . . .

"A Physician" proceeds to inquire, "Is there a proper field for the employment and support of female physicians?" We unhesitatingly reply that all diseases to which women and children are liable would naturally come within the province of the female physician, and surely that is a domain wide enough, without encroaching upon the sphere of men. But your correspondent is confident that ladies would not consult female doctors. On this point my experience is widely different from his. I can well believe that ladies, being suddenly questioned, would reply at once that they would not have confidence in a woman. Hastily assuming that the female physician would be either a shallow, superficially taught lady, or a sort of superior nurse, they naturally feel that they would prefer the services of an able and experienced man. But ladies who have had time to think, are almost unanimous in declaring that if they could secure the attendance of equally well-educated women (and this can be certified by a Degree), they would give them the preference. I speak not from hearsay, but from actual personal knowledge, when I say that this feeling is much stronger among refined women of the poorer classes who are more at the mercy of young men and the inferior order of practitioners. The feeling is strongest of all among young girls. I believe that to many of them the sympathy and tenderness of a woman would be absolutely more curative than the possibly superior skill of a man—of which, indeed, they often refuse to avail themselves.

Finally, your correspondent inquires from whence you would draw your supply of females who are to study medicine and become physicians? To which I reply, from whence do we draw our supply of governesses? Of them there appears to be an abundant, nay an excessive supply. A female medical student need not "devote herself heart and soul to celibacy." She might indeed exercise a more independent choice, because she would not be driven into marriage by the mere longing for some satisfying occupation; but if suitable marriage came in her way, her profession need be no hindrance. . . . This question of marriage, in fact, amounts to this, — Are all women to be shut out from any and every method of earning money by honest and intelligent work lest they should grow too independent of their natural supporters, or are they to be encouraged and urged to use their gifts as those who must give account? It is beginning to be believed that women have certain gifts of hand, and that it is not unfeminine to use them. Let us hope that in a generation or two it will also be admitted that they have heads, and that this being so, it is their bounden duty "sincerely to give a true account of their gift of reason, to the benefit and use of men." How they may best labor to this end, can surely be satisfactorily proved only by experience. There may be much confident assertion on both sides, but till the experiment has been fairly tried, we have no right to decide positively that women can or cannot go through the medical course uninjured; that they will or will not find patients . . . .

Robert Wilson, "AESCULAPIA VICTRIX", *Fortnightly Review,* XXXIX (1886), 18-33.

Sophia Jex-Blake and the other women—Isabel Thorne, Edith Pechey, Matilda Chaplin, and Helen Evans—who managed to obtain admission in 1869 to the medical program at the University of Edinburgh, applied themselves so successfully to their studies that they carried off a number of prizes and honors, bruising male vanity to such an extent that in 1870 they found themselves in the center of a riot organized by hostile students who were incited by some of the faculty. They were protected, however, by a small number of sympathetic male students, one of whom, Robert Wilson, enlisted the help of a friend, "Micky O'Halloran, . . . leader of a formidable band, known as the 'Irish Brigade' . . . [of] some thirty or forty men", who formed an escort for the beleaguered women. Even after the riot had subsided they had to contend with threats of physical violence, hisses, shouts of "whore", and jibes that "they'd never do it if they could get married".[1]

Writing in 1886, Robert Wilson described the difficulties which had beset English women aspiring to become physicians in the 1860's and noted the salutary change in public opinion which had taken place in less than twenty years.

. . . Little more than ten years ago the mere suggestion that a woman might be encouraged to practice medicine simply horrified decent people. It seems but as yester-day since in the streets of Edinburgh ladies were insulted and rabbled on their way to a medical lecture-room. Now, however, this foolish prejudice scarcely exists, whether because most of those who entertained it have died out or grown wiser it is hard to say. Englishwomen study medicine and surgery in London without let or hindrance, in their own College, under professors of high distinction. Armed wtih formidable diplomas, and laden with academic laurels, they go forth each year in goodly numbers to prac-tice their art. . . . As for "the world" which once declared that such an extension of "Woman's sphere" must bring down the social fabric with a crash, it looks on unmoved, fearing the "crash" as little as a mimic earthquake in a sensational stage play. . . .

. . . Miss Jex Blake, in the spring of 1869, induced the superior authorities of the University of Edinburgh to allow her, Miss Edith Pechey, Mrs. Thorne, Miss Chaplin, and Mrs. De Lacy Evans, to matriculate in the Faculty of Medicine. The story of their career is not one which in the telling brings much credit to that enterprising seminary of science. Edinburgh seems to have tolerated its lady students while they could be considered merely as enthusiastic amateurs willing to submit to an increased scale of fees for the gratification of a foolish crotchet. But when it became clear from the ability and zeal with which they carried on their studies that they not only meant to graduate, but were certain to pass their examinations, a curious change occurred. Chill indif-ference gave place to hot hostility. A powerful faction among the professors raised a legal objection to their position, and a decision of the Court of Session finally prevented them from finishing their course. . . . Miss Jex Blake and her fellow-students accord-ingly migrated to London.

In London they began their work under happy auspices. They at once gained the support of Mrs. Garrett Anderson, M.D., well known in society as a medical practi-tioner, whose idea, however, was that some of the existing institutions should be utilized for teaching medical women. When this was found to be impracticable, the view of Mrs. Thorne . . . prevailed. This view was that medical women should set up in London a College for themselves. . . .

. . . In the Autumn of 1874 . . . there was no place in the United Kingdom where a woman could attend lectures qualifying her for a medical diploma. No general hos-pital would give her the necessary clinical instruction. She could nowhere obtain admission to qualifying examinations, for the only licensing body that did not profess to have the right to exclude women as women — the Society of Apothecaries — made it a condition of their admission that they must study at schools which they were not allowed to enter. . . . In three short years all these wants were supplied by the efforts of those who founded the School of Medicine in Henrietta street: qualifying instruction was given by its professors; clinical teaching and hospital practice were obtainable at the

---

[1] Cited in Edythe Lutzker, *Women Gain a Place in Medicine* (New York: McGraw-Hill Book Company, 1969), pp. 79, 88.

Royal Free Hospital; the examinations of the King and Queen's College of Physicians in Ireland and of the great London University were thrown open to ladies. And all this work, involving an apparently forlorn contest with professional prejudice and constituted authority, was done quietly, with unruffled temper, without any passionate popular agitation, or any strident appeals for public sympathy. . . .

It may fairly be asked, What has the Governing Body to show for the money they have spent? Few persons in their position can show so much. There is, for example, the equipment of the school itself—its lecture-rooms and teaching apparatus, its skilfully arranged and selected museum, its serviceable little library and laboratory, its quiet, cosy reading-rooms and tea-room, its dissecting-room—spacious, airy, and scrupulously clean and fresh—and its recreation-ground, where part of the garden of the old house has been turned into a lawn-tennis court. Unlike most medical schools on which twenty times as much money has been lavished, the Medical College for Women does not invest student-life with a maximum of ugliness and discomfort. Within its walls life is, indeed, bright and pleasant, and work, though hard, is arranged with great ingenuity, so as to lighten its pressure on teachers and taught. It has no residential hall, nor is it desirable perhaps that it should have any. The tendency of all professional study is narrowing, and the students of the Henrietta Street school are accordingly encouraged to live in association with ladies who are preparing for other pursuits. Indeed, the Governing Body, in pursuance of this policy, have freely thrown open their scientific lectures to non-professional students, and in time the value of this concession will be highly appreciated. This school is the only place in England where a woman who is studying art can be taught practical anatomy, without a training in which it is as ridiculous for her to draw or model the figure as for a man to build a steam-engine without knowing mechanics. Something must also be placed to the credit of the school on account of the tokens of gratitude that so often come from patients in the Royal Free Hospital who have benefited by the tender ministrations and watchful skill of clinical students, whose gentle hands are ever swift in doing good. People who demand "results" might also be referred to the reports received at varying intervals of the doings of these *alumni* of the school who have gone forth as missionaries to distant lands, and where, amidst grievous hardships, they ply their noble craft in honourable exile. But other "results" more obviously practical may be noted. There is, for example, the system of hospital instruction which the school has organised. This seems most thorough, for not only must every lady student "walk the hospital" during the legally prescribed term, but she has also to serve as a clerk and a dresser for three months to each of the physicians and surgeons, both in the out-patient and in-patient departments. She must further officiate as a clerk in the special departments of ophthalmic surgery, pathology, and diseases of women, and in her third year of study she must take a course of practical midwifery at a special lying-in hospital. Even a stupid woman could hardly emerge from all this practical tuition without knowing the routine work of her profession a great deal better than the majority of young men in the large schools, who have no such golden opportunities for gaining experience open to them. The statistics of attendance and the academic honours won by the students of the Henrietta Street school may also be cited here as attesting the solidity of the work it has done. Since the institution was opened in 1874 one hundred and fifty students have been admitted. Forty-one of these now hold diplomas from the King and Queen's Colleges of Physicians in Ireland. The school has sent to the examinations of the University of London thirteen students, of whom two have taken gold medals, and five have graduated in honours. . . .

. . . So far, I think, I have proved that the school has done a marvellous amount of solid work on the slenderest resources. Now I come to another point. Was the work worth doing? Was it needed?

Happily events have simplified the business of answering this last question. That women *are* practising medicine with much popular acceptance and success both in private practice and in dispensaries and hospitals proves the reality of the need or demand for their services. The existence of this demand is due to a delicacy of senti- ment which it would be barbarous to ignore and brutal to crush, so that the Henrietta Street school requires little vindication on this head. . . .

. . . Why should we debar a woman from supporting herself by a calling the prac- tice of which . . . is naturally in accord with her cultured sympathies and her intel- lectual tastes? Why should we deem her amply provided with a field for her energies in the arts when she does not inherit . . . Rosa Bonheur's colour-sense, George Eliot's intellect, Mrs. Browning's lyric inspiration, or even, like Sarah Bernhardt, a nervous system that can at will be turned into a magnificent instrument of dramatic emotion? Probably few medical women will ever rival the achievements of a Harvey, a Cullen, a Sydenham, or a Simpson; indeed, only four of them, Mrs. Garrett Anderson, Mrs. Hoggan, Miss Agnes McLaren, and the late Mrs. Chaplin Ayrton have as yet contri- buted anything very noteworthy to scientific literature. But their academic "record" proves that they have, at all events, the ordinary amount of brain-power possessed by nine-tenths of the better educated members of their profession. The world is not so rich in medical genius that it can afford to despise the chance of evolving so rare a pro- duct, even from feminine assiduity and capacity. It seems to me we cannot be too cautious about discouraging gifted women from making the most of whatever capacities they may have, especially if they be guided by pure aims, high ambitions, and culti- vated intelligence.

After all, Humanity wins nothing by forcing those who cannot entirely fill their lives with family interests, to crush their cravings for other activities, unless, indeed, these be in themselves demoralising. But no educated and unprejudiced person nowadays believes that medical practice or study must necessarily demoralise a lady. The service of the sick has in all ages had a strange but seemingly natural fascination for women, and it is simply contrary to commonsense to suppose that a woman must needs be un- sexed by such service, unless it be utterly divorced from scholarly culture and scientific knowledge. Yet this is precisely what we are asked to believe by the curious folk who would persuade us that they would rather "lay their daughters in their coffins" than see them enter a sick-room. . . .

Emily Pfeiffer, *Women and Work* (London: Trübner & Co., 1888), pp. 9-11, 45-50, 142-43.

Although Emily Pfeiffer, largely self-educated, achieved a measure of fame through several volumes of poetry published in the 1870's and 1880's, her interests were not confined to literature. She advocated changes in woman's dress, and left substantial legacies to be used to pro- mote higher education for women. Her main concern, improving the social and economic position of women, is evident in various articles that she wrote for leading periodicals, and that were incorporated in her book, *Women and Work,* issued in 1888. In that volume, Mrs. Pfeiffer addressed herself to problems such as the opening of socially suitable occupations to ladies; she attacked the assumption that women were physiologically incapable of working; and she called for the improvement of conditions and wages of women who were already part of the labor force. In the following excerpt, Mrs. Pfeiffer indicates what she considers to be the major solution to the problems of working women: trade unionism.

. . . The fair picture, which as a picture we all know so well (I am about to quote from a recent address), of "the man going forth to his work and to his labour, and the woman waiting at home to welcome him back and lend her ear to his doing or suffering" . . . has lately been recalled to the attention of a large audience, and reproduced approvingly by the most weighty organs of the press. If this picture was ever largely taken from life, it has certainly now little worth as a truthful representation of the condition of the toiling masses. That which we look back upon as the age of chivalry, to a partial view of which it would seem originally to owe its existence, has long passed, and in its palmiest hour the queens of beauty, those who, sitting on high above the heat and dust of the conflict, graced victory with a wreath or a smile, were few, while the hard-handed Joans and Jills were many, and more hopelessly underfoot even than the strugglers of to-day.

. . . As a considerable amount of indolence and inertia is characteristic of human nature generally, we can hardly err in assuming that the vast majority of women would still prefer to be sheltered from, not to say lifted above, the rude battle of life, and to have their part in it taken by some man to whom the fight might prove an agreeable stimulant. But it may not be. If all that has been changed, it would be well for the sentimentalist to remember that the change has been effected not so much by women—certainly not by the rank and file of them—as in their despite. If in large numbers they are seen to be pressing forward, and endeavouring to force and to fit themselves for new spheres of labour, it is not that their choice lies between work and ease, but between work and work. . . .

The man as the providence of the woman, the woman as the rewarder of labour and strife, is undoubtedly a tempting representation; but it is condemned as out of keeping with the stern realism of the age. Let us hope that, as a compensation for the loss of this fair dream, some higher form of good, some more potent idea of beauty, may arise out of the hardier conditions which, whether we like them or not, we are compelled to accept. In any case, the more reasonable among women are agreed not to squander time and energy in vain regret for a state of things which no available power could now make to be even a working hypothesis. It is time that the often very clever men, who still flourish the faded banner of chivalry, together with the less reasonable or less vitally interested among women, should copy the resignation of those most deeply concerned, and cease to maintain any figment of argument on grounds of fancy which the hard facts of modern life must often make to seem absurd. . . .

. . . The woman-worker, standing alone and unaided, is beset on every side with difficulty, if not with injustice and exaction. . . .

Not only is the unfortunate woman compelled by the requirements of her family to work at home, ground down to famine wages, but the middleman, who is ordinarily a sort of taskmaster and shopkeeper together, requires that she shall take out the miserable pittance of her labour in articles of food and clothing, on which his profits are often exorbitant, and of the bad quality of which she stands too much in his power to complain.

The under-paid "assistants" in certain shops are compelled, for the honour and glory of the establishment, to wear silk dresses, which taking an undue portion of their pay, they are often driven to eke out their existence in a manner to which the temptation stands only too near. [*Editors' note: Mrs. Pfeiffer then cites a letter from the Rev. Horsley, chaplain to the Clerkenwell prison.*]

"It is useless to insist on the temptation to crime and to prostitution which is the consequence of insufficient wages. The least of the evils which beset the sempstress is the temptation to pawn the work confided to her, together with the coverings and other articles of her poverty-stricken dwelling. I ardently hope that success may crown your efforts to introduce organization into women's work, to raise them out of their despair, and afford help to their ignorance in combating the jealousy and selfishness of male workers, and the farming of the labours by that tribe of intermediaries who are nourished at their expense."

This, then, is the point to which all inquiry into the justly remunerative conditions of the labour of at least that portion of the sex which is the poorest and most helpless, must carry us. Trade-unions, such as abound for men, supplementing a more perfect technical training, are the sorely needed remedies for the evils which beset the unassisted efforts of women. . . .

Women even more than men have need of the protection which association can alone afford. A man in his own strength may hold out with no worse a prospect than that of slow starvation. For him there is temptation in many forms, it is true, but not that one gulf darker than death ever open to women in the weakness and dizziness of despair. It is for them that there exists the fatal attraction of a precipice, approached by degrees as over the rounded brow of a hill, which ultimately yawns and plunges the victim into a pit of such horror as has no parallel in the life of any other of God's creatures.

The following are a few of the aids which would accrue to women through association: —

Help in times of crisis and commercial depression.
Facility of information in regard to the labour market, and the wages in different localities.
Safeguard against the accumulation of labour at any one point.
Encouragement given to a high quality of work by the maintenance of a standard of excellence.
Succour to the sick, together with the comfort and moral force arising from the sense of human relation and sympathy, &c., &c.

It might be supposed that benefits so unquestionable, of which I am far from having exhausted the list, might be safely trusted to commend themselves; but, as I have already indicated, the whole course of life, the whole dependent past of women, has been such as to render them averse to united action among themselves; and it may be justly feared that, until this disinclination, or, where not positive disinclination, inertia has been overcome, the progress of the movement already inaugurated by philanthropists must be slow.

The first union for the protection of working-women from the exactions of employers had birth in New York as far back as 1871. . . .

This first union in New York was followed in London, at some little distance of time, by the Woman's Protective and Provident League, founded by Mrs. Paterson, with the advantage of possessing Mrs. Fawcett as permanent president of its meetings. To this, various other unions for the protection of special industries have succeeded, both in London and the provinces.

It is in vain, if it were not worse than vain, that Acts of Parliament should regulate the hours of work. The working-women are aware of the disadvantage under which legal limitation places them, and unscrupulous employers disobeying the law would stand in little fear of being denounced by those whose keenest desire is that their services shall be retained at any price.

It is association, therefore, which can alone be looked to for effective protection. We have seen that such societies are already at work amongst us, but it is to be regretted that they are yet far from having enlisted adherents in numbers commensurate with the benefits they offer. It is clearly not enough that helpful souls from without the industrial ranks should have organised these societies; in order that their advantages should be fully enjoyed, it is above all needful that the perceptions of women and girls shall be open to their recognition. I naturally conclude that the subject has been touched from time to time in lectures delivered to working women, but I think that a ground should be laid for the enforcement of the lesson in all schools established for girls of the industrial class. Those who have to gain their living by the labour of their hands should be left to no haphazard acquaintance with the means best fitted to ensure success in a struggle of such difficulty. . . .

Granting, as we must if we fairly face the facts, that the new forms in which the burthen of life are being accepted by the weaker sex are rather laid upon its needier members than chosen by them, of what avail are such questions . . . as to "whether it be well that our women should be equipped and encouraged to enter the battle of life shoulder to shoulder and on equal terms with men"? We know too well that in ever-increasing numbers they have to enter into the battle, whether they like it or not. The question, thus so far settled for us, resolves itself into the simpler one of *terms*. Shall women be driven to the fight, in which no allowance will be made for their heavier burthens, *un*equipped and *dis*couraged — the disadvantages inherent in sex being set up as the starting-point for increased and arbitrary disabilities? or shall the terms of contract be made as equal as the peculiarities of the case permits? [*sic*] . . .

Emilia F. S. Dilke, "Benefit Societies and Trade Unions for Women", *Fortnightly Review*, XLV (1889), 852-56.

Nineteenth-century English society presents a number of examples of upper- and middle-class women who, without becoming in the least degree radical, spurned the role of Angel in the House, and devoted themselves to improving the condition of working women through trade union organization. Emilia Francis Strong, who married Mark Pattison, rector of Lincoln College, Oxford and, who, after his death, became the wife of Sir Charles Dilke, a prominent member of the "Little England" school, was one of this group. A friend of George Eliot, immersed in literature, the study of languages, painting, and art criticism, conducting what amounted to a salon, she managed at the same time to be an active member of the Women's Provident and Protective League, which

EMILY DAVIES IN ACADEMIC DRESS, reproduced by courtesy of
Girton College, Cambridge

MADAME BODICHON BY EMILY M. OSBORN, reproduced by courtesy of
Girton College, Cambridge

THE RIGHT HON. SIR CHARLES AND LADY DILKE, reproduced
by courtesy of the Mansell Collection.

THE HON. MRS NORTON, reproduced by courtesy of the Mansell Collection.

Emma Paterson had founded on her return from the United States in 1874, and which subsequently became the Women's Trade Union League. She frequently spoke on labor questions affecting women, on providing technical education for women, and in favor of female suffrage.

Emma Paterson, who also came from a middle-class background, devoted the greater part of her brief life (she died at 38) to promoting unions for women. She was instrumental in organizing the National Union of Working Women, which founded a number of unions in various trades. She was the first woman delegate to the Trade Union Congress in 1875. She became a printer and the manager of the Women's Printing Society at Westminster, which her husband had founded, and was active in union affairs almost literally until the day of her death.

The members of the Women's Protective and Provident League, which consisted originally of upper middle-class sympathizers with working-class women, were convinced that the only way these women could materially improve their status was through trade union organization. In the following article Lady Dilke discusses Emma Paterson's ideas and her role as the founder of the Women's Protective and Provident League.

Seventeen or eighteen years ago, I went into the office of the Society for the Promotion of Women's Suffrage to see the Secretary, Emma Smith, who, I heard, had just been dismissed from her post by the Committee. The news I found was true.

"The ladies have complimented me on my zeal," she said, "but they say my bodily presence is weak and my speech contemptible; so I must make room for some one who can represent them better. I've saved a little money, and I'm going to America to see for myself how the women's friendly societies work there. You know, I don't think the vote the only panacea for all the sufferings of the weaker sex. I am a working woman myself" (she was a printer by trade), "and my work for this society has brought me into contact with large bodies of women in other trades, so when I have picked up some hints on the other side of the Atlantic, I hope to induce Englishwomen to try whether they cannot help themselves, as men have done, by combination."

In 1874, some time after her return, Miss Smith, who, I think, had then married Mr. Paterson, a printer, like herself, wrote to me claiming the fulfilment of my promise of help. She explained that her scheme was to collect all those of her friends who had money or time to give, into a body to be called, "The Women's Protective and Provident League." The object of the league was to be the formation of trade societies amongst women; the money collected was to be applied to the maintenance of an office, to defraying the expenses of public meetings, the cost of printing rules, and other matters incidental to the work of organisation. The societies themselves, when formed, were to remain fully independent in the management of their own business and strictly self-supporting. She added that a society was already formed amongst the women engaged in bookbinding, and that she had good hope of speedily establishing several others.

From that day until the day of her death — due in great measure to her incessant and unselfish labours in the cause she had taken up — I never ceased to have full knowledge of Mrs. Paterson's plans, and I worked with her whenever I could. The formation of the "Society of Women engaged in Bookbinding" was, as she had hoped, instantly followed by the formation of those for Women Upholsteresses and for the Shirt- and Collar-makers, and although the movement has never been taken up to any great extent throughout the country, it has secured some measure of success, for there are now twelve women's unions existing, if not flourishing, in London alone, and the number of women enrolled as members of trade societies in England and Scotland is, I believe, between seven and eight thousand.

At first Mrs. Paterson and her friends did not dare to call these societies "unions" for the word "union" had an evil sound in the ears of those to whom it seemed obviously associated with acts of wicked violence and intimidation. Things have, however, altered so much in these respects that the league has now fearlessly changed its name, and styles itself, "The Women's Trades Union Provident League" — a title which admirably sums up the purposes of its existence. Unionism is, indeed, a very big question with far-reaching issues. . . . There is, however, no necessity to touch on these matters in dealing with the possibilities which it offers to helpless women of helping themselves. The unions, in their capacity of trade organisations, simply tend to procure better wages for the employed; whilst in discharging the functions of insurance societies, they relieve their members from the pressure of unforeseen risks and accidents, against which individual thrift and prudence cannot protect them. It is a matter of notoriety that there are some of these bodies so powerful, and so well able to provide against all contingencies, that no member has ever been known to receive parish relief; and although the present wages obtained by women in most of the trades in which they are employed do not admit of their keeping up the rate of subscriptions which men are able to meet, yet it is found that very substantial aid can be afforded them from the modest payments which they are able to make to their own societies. I know a "baster" in a country factory who, out of her wages of five shillings a week, has been for several years steadily contributing her weekly twopence. She is a single woman, wholly dependent on her own exertions for a living; and all those who know the poor will understand that, to one in her position, it was a boon beyond words to feel that she was secured from the horror of a pauper's funeral; and knew that in sickness or out of work she had made certain, by her weekly sacrifices, of receiving at least a few shillings every week.

Next after these advantages, which are best appreciated by the old, may be reckoned the wholesome influence which membership in a union exercises over the young. There is no greater source of mischief with girls than long periods of "out of work," they demoralise men; they ruin young women. Now, the regular visits and words of interest from the member of her society's committee who is entrusted with the duties of payment of out-of-work or sick allowance are not only a great check on evil courses, but they give to our girls a sense of protection, which is heightened by the sense of union with a large body having common interests and cares. "I feel," said a girl to me, "that I am now part of something larger than myself!" And this consciousness of increased value and importance is not only a moral influence and safeguard, but offers us the means of arousing the stolid misery of our suffering and labouring sisters, and of educating them by bringing them into touch with the great industrial and social problems by which they are affected. . . .

. . . Theoretically, I suppose most of us would agree with John Stuart Mill that "the natural division of labour is that a man goes out to earn the wages, and the woman stays at home to make the home comfortable and to see after the children," and the feeling that this is the most natural division of labour influences us immensely in the practical question of wages; for the man is popularly regarded and paid as the bread-winner, who is answerable for the maintenance of others besides himself, whilst the woman's labour, however constant and fruitful, is only looked on as something by which she may supplement his earnings. The consequence of this is that women are either employed at inferior wages on the inferior branches of the trades, or too frequently become the tools of unscrupulous employers, who use them as cheap labour to bring down the just demands of the men, who are husbands and fathers. We are thus placed in a dilemma at the very outset of our attempts to organise women's labour, for, whilst on the one hand we are anxious to strengthen the hands of the men and prevent women from being an additional drag upon them in the labour market, we know that women are not in a position at present to demand equal payment with men, nor would they be supported by public opinion if they put forth such a demand as part of a programme to be vigorously enforced. They are not, as a rule, the bread-winners; nor, as a rule, can they work as hard or as long as men.

In this respect, therefore, as in several others, it seems advisable to go carefully and tentatively to work. Wherever we can induce men to admit women, who are working in the same trade, to their unions, we encourage the women to take advantage of existing organisations, but this can only be done where the wages they receive enable them to pay the same contributions as those paid by the men. It is only where we find that the men have no union existing or available, that we strive to induce the women to "form" on their own account. Wherever they form an independent union we lay down no hard and fast rules, but endeavour to adapt the general outlines of a trade society to the peculiarities which, as I have said, characterise women's labour. . . .

When I see women here in London wasting themselves, their time and their money on costly schemes of all sorts, which end perhaps in underselling the shops; or busied in fostering an unfair competition between patronised and unpatronised workers, which simply results in putting money into the pockets of the buyers, I could cry for shame and vexation. Alms and patronage, these idols of the drawing-room, make the labours of the trades unionist heavier tenfold. And, after all, what we want is not so much money as personal help. Personal influence in carrying on this kind of work means everything. If only the richer, idler, abler women amongst us would come out and help! Teach these poor souls to trust you; show cause why they should, by honestly attempting to understand the complicated difficulties of their labouring lives, and you will find that this gospel of self-defence, which is also one of self-sacrifice, goes to the heart of all those who are truly familiar with the cruel hardships of the working woman's life.

CHAPTER VII

"Criminals, Idiots, Women, and Minors"

It was not mere hyperbole to say, as some outspoken critics did, that women in Victorian England possessed as few personal rights as convicted felons, the feeble-minded, and the young. If anything, the inferior position of women was even more hopeless than that of the other three categories of the legally disqualified or incompetent because woman's position was sanctioned not only by the law, by custom, by science, and by public opinion, but by Christian tradition as well: "A man shall cleave to his wife, and they twain shall be one flesh".[1] The Common Law, as we have seen, echoed the Bible, holding that the joining of two individuals in marriage literally created a single entity, the husband in effect enveloping (or as some put it, swallowing) the wife. It followed, then, that the rights and privileges which a woman had enjoyed before marriage were henceforth unnecessary; she was now under the protection of her husband, who would exercise *his* rights and privileges on behalf of both of them.

This built-in ambivalence, which demanded a degree of objectivity not ordinarily found in mere mortals (even Victorian husbands), obviously operated to the wife's disadvantage whenever her interests conflicted with those of her spouse. Furthermore, the notion that a wife had no legal existence apart from that of her husband probably encouraged some men to think of their wives merely as possessions. It should come, therefore, as no surprise to learn that a few men of the lower classes actually sold their wives: "In 1881 a wife was sold at Sheffield for . . . a quart of beer".[2] There is a scattering of such instances, the prices charged ranging from a few shillings to an ox. These arrangements, of course, were neither usual nor legal, but the mere fact of their existence is indicative of how fully a woman was considered to be subject to her husband. Given that implicit premise, it is understandable that many men, especially those of the lower classes, imposed on their

[1] Matthew 19:15.

[2] "Wife-selling", *All the Year*, LV (1884), 259. See also H. W. V. Temperley, "The Sale of Wives in England in 1823", *History Teachers' Miscellany*, III (1924), 66-68.

wives physical abuse of a particularly "violent or cruel manner". Despite the fact that the husband's right to chastise his wife, once sanctioned by the law, had earlier been abolished, in the nineteenth century women were being not only beaten, but mangled, choked, mutilated, blinded, burned, and trampled on by their husbands.[1]

The obvious way to end these outrages was to get to the root of the evil— the law itself. "To a woman . . . who . . . has never committed a Crime; who fondly believes that she is not an Idiot; and who is alas! only too sure she is no longer a Minor",[2] it seemed incongruous that she be lumped with the legally incompetent. Not surprisingly, in an age devoted to progress, a dedicated handful of English women would move to change the laws which condemned them to a permanent state of inferiority. Starting in 1857, the efforts of feminists in this direction were aided by the Law Amendment Society and the newly-formed Social Science Association, which began to lobby for legislation on divorce, property rights, child custody, wife-beating, and other topics suggested by Barbara Leigh Smith in her pamphlet, *A Brief Summary in Plain Language of the Most Important Laws Concerning Women* (1854).

Partly as a result of their activities a number of laws were enacted, but much of this legislation fell short of feminist expectations. Parliament, for example, passed several acts which attempted to protect wives from physical abuse, but the courts continued to deal leniently with wife-beaters. Although two earlier Married Women's Property Acts conferred a number of property rights on a wife, not until the passage of the Act of 1882 did married women obtain the same right to own, control, and dispose of property as that heretofore enjoyed only by single women.[3] Some progress was made in modifying the law regarding divorce. Prior to 1857 a divorce had been possible only through a private Act of Parliament. Such a procedure was open, of course, only to the rich, and as a practical matter almost exclusively to males. There had been only four divorces granted to women in approximately 150 years; two of them were based on proof of incest, and the circumstances of the other two were probably equally unusual. Although a divorce was made more easily obtainable after 1857, it was still very difficult for a woman to secure one, even if she was able to pay the necessary expenses. A man could obtain a divorce on the grounds of his wife's adultery, whereas the husband's adultery, even when it was a public scandal, was considered insufficient grounds for divorce; either cruelty, bigamy, incest, or deser-

---

[1] Cobbe, *Life*, II, 534.

[2] Cobbe, "Criminals, Idiots, Women, and Minors", p. 778.

[3] The passage of the Married Women's Property Act of 1870, which deprived husbands of their former absolute powers over their wives' property, was followed by the introduction of a bill, probably inspired by a combination of masculine spite, fear, and outrage, which would theoretically have compelled every married woman employed in a factory to work only half-time. See IGNOTA, "The Present Legal Position of Women in the United Kingdom", *Westminster Review*, CLIII (1905), 520.

tion had also to be proved (leading one commentator to estimate that
this requirement conferred on 99% of all male adulterers immunity to
an action for divorce).[1] The rationale for this discrimination was essentially that which Dr. Johnson had set forth for Boswell's benefit: adultery
was a graver offense for a woman than for a man, because an adulteress
might produce a spurious heir to her husband's estate. Moreover, since
a woman was, in a sense, the property of her husband, her sexual relations with another man were an infringement of his property rights: she
had become damaged goods.[2] Finally, a man whose wife made him a
cuckold (a word, interestingly enough, for which there is no feminine
equivalent) was subjected to ridicule, whereas a wife whose husband was
unfaithful was the object of sympathy. Dr. Johnson's observation, "wise
married women don't trouble themselves about the infidelity in their
husbands",[3] could not possibly have been worded to apply to "wise married men".

Since even most feminists implicitly conceded that adultery was more
reprehensible in the female than in the male, it is easy to see why the
courts dealt more rigorously with women involved in divorce suits than
with men. In suits for separation or divorce, for example, proved or
acknowledged adultery on the part of a husband who was also guilty of
cruelty, did not preclude his being awarded custody of the children because, under the Common Law, they belonged not jointly to both parents, but exclusively to him. An adulterous wife, on the other hand, was
automatically denied custody of, and often access to, her children.

Even after the passage of the Custody of Infants Act (1886), the adulterous father, but not the adulterous mother, could obtain custody of
the children. Adulterous spouses aside, despite the passage of several
acts purporting to improve the position of women in regard to their
rights of visitation and custody, the legal position of a mother was still
vastly inferior to that of her husband, who in 1884 was described as able
to "deprive her at any moment, out of mere caprice, or out of malice, of
all her natural maternal rights".[4]

These anomalies indicate the influence of Blackstone's dictum, which
was still tacitly accepted, that a wife had no existence independent of
her husband's. Blackstone, in a memorable passage, had maintained
that the very disabilities under which a woman labored were devised to
protect her interests and hence were evidence of the favoritism that
women enjoyed under English law. To one critic who obviously did not
regard women as the spoiled darlings of the English Common Law, the

---

[1] "The Bill for Divorce", *Quarterly Review*, CII (1857), 287.

[2] Keith Thomas, "The Double Standard", *Journal of the History of Ideas*, XX (1959), 195-216.

[3] *Boswell's Life of Johnson*, edited by George Birkbeck Hill, 6 vols. (Oxford: Clarendon Press, 1887), III, 406.

[4] Frances Elizabeth Hoggan, *The Position of the Mother in the Family*, (Manchester: A. Ireland & Co., 1884), p. 9.

argument was specious and hypocritical:

> The notion of the unity of the husband and the wife, meaning thereby the
> suspension of the wife and the lordship of the husband, seems from the first to
> have been particularly agreeable to the race of English lawyers, tickling their
> grim humour and gratifying their very limited sense of the fitness of things. When-
> ever they approached the subject a grin seems to have spread itself over their
> liberal expanse of countenance. How pleasantly, how goodhumouredly does
> Blackstone . . . handle the theme. . . . Blackstone, we know, wrote his famous
> book with a bottle of port by his side; and we would wager a dozen that after
> [describing women as the sex singularly favored by English law], he sipped his
> glass and chuckled.[1]

The concept of merged identity, declared the Law Amendment Society, "must be reckoned among legal fictions, which have no foundation in fact, but are mere convenient modes of speech, invented by lawyers, and used for particular purposes".[2] The particular purpose, in this instance, was to insure the subjection of women by invoking the notion that husband and wife blended into one existence when, as a matter of fact, the provisions of the Common Law concerning matrimonial relations were precisely those which belonged to the relation of "master and bondwoman".[3] The female slave could not own property, make a contract, leave her master's domicile, or assert a claim to her own children. And the Victorian wife, for the larger part of the nineteenth century, was almost equally impotent. Understandably, then, feminists were forced to the conclusion that, in general, the legal reforms of the nineteenth century had not substantially improved the position of women; and this failure only reinforced their conviction that it was unrealistic to expect a parliament composed exclusively of men to legislate in the interests of women. Lord Chief Justice Coleridge, speaking in the House of Commons, concurred; the "state of the law . . . as regards women", he charged, "was more worthy of a barbarian than a civilised State". The law, in his opinion was "in many respects wholly indefensible".[4] To Coleridge, as to most feminists, it had become obvious that erasing the inequities from which women suffered required an assault on the masculine monopoly of political power. Women, in short, must have the vote.

But there were women in England whom no vote could help, whose status was quite literally barbarous, and whose treatment by the law was based on conceptions derived from experience with animals: they were prostitutes, and "prostitutes, like animals, had no legal personalities".[5] The Contagious Diseases Acts of the 1860's, which were based on that

---

[1] Augustine Birrell, "Women under the English Law", *Edinburgh Review*, CLXXXIV (1896), 324.
[2] "The Property of Married Women", *Westminster Review*, LXVI (1856), 186.
[3] *Ibid.*, p. 187.
[4] Cited in M. M. Blake, "The Lady and the Law", *Westminster Review*, CXXXV (1892), 364.
[5] F. B. Smith, "Ethics and Disease in the Later Nineteenth Century: The Contagious Diseases Acts", *Historical Studies*, XIV (1971), 119.

principle, provide a melancholy example of man's inhumanity to woman.

T. E. Perry, "Rights and Liabilities of Husband and Wife", *Edinburgh Review*, CV (1857), 181-205.

Sir Thomas Erskine Perry had a distinguished career in the public service in two hemispheres. In his twenties, he was interested in political reform, and became honorary secretary of the National Political Union, a middle-class organization which worked for the passage of the Reform Bill of 1832. He founded the Parliamentary Candidate Society, whose object was to secure the election of properly qualified candidates to the House of Commons. A lawyer and law reporter, he was the co-author of several volumes of law reports. He was appointed a judge of the Bombay Supreme Court, and was Chief Justice from 1847 to 1852. Perry bore his share of the white man's burden with grace and dignity, and achieved a reputation for fairness and impartiality that led to the establishment, by his Indian admirers, of a professorship of law in his name. Elected to Parliament in 1854, he took a liberal, anti-imperialist position on Indian affairs, and strongly urged that Indians be admitted to positions in the civil service. In 1856 he took up the cause of another class suffering from discrimination—married women—and moved for a bill that would give them a voice in the disposition of their property. The next year he sponsored a bill to amend the property law on their behalf. That Perry's concern for the plight of women powerless to control their own property was justified, is indicated by the examples cited in the following selection.

. . . No father can secure an independent provision for his daughter; no woman, whatever the amount of her personal estate may be, can rescue it from her future husband, unless an attorney be at hand to frame the requisite provisions which shall evade the grasp of the Common Law. . . .

. . . To all who marry without any previous settlement, the Common Law, applies in all its harshness. We are enabled to give a few examples of the operation of the law amongst the industrious classes. . . .

. . . An industrious woman in Belgravia having been deserted by her husband, set up in business as a lady's shoemaker, and met with great success; but after three years' attention to her trade, the husband, discovering that there was something to be got, suddenly made his appearance, swept off the furniture and the stock-in-trade, collected the outstanding debts, and again disappeared with his paramour. Again and again this operation has been performed. . . .

Here is another case of the same class detailed in a letter by a lady:—

"I was in Paris in 184- on a visit to Dr. and Mrs. B., who took me to a milliner . . . [who] was a great favourite with English visitors. Her husband was a great profligate, and lived separate from her. . . . Some English ladies of rank promised Madame M. good patronage if she settled in London, and in an evil hour for her prospects she determined to do so. She was very successful, and very careful; but her husband found out her abode, and, to her horror and surprise, collected all her monies due, seized everything she possessed, and, turned adrift in the world, she returned to just and equitable France. 'Oh! . . .' she exclaimed to me before she went, 'how can you live in such a country as this?' "

If we descend lower in the social scale, we shall find innumerable cases of the tyranny and injustice which the law now allows a husband to exercise over his wife's acquisitions. The husband, in the following instance, ought to have been sent to the treadmill; but, according to law, he was only doing what he would with his own: —

"A respectable woman . . . having been many years in service, had saved a considerable sum of money, when she was sought in marriage by a man of suitable age and plausible manners, and their wedding shortly took place. She had given her 'bankbook' to her husband, but on the very day of the wedding he said to her, 'I have not such good health as I used to have, and do not feel equal to supporting a wife; therefore I think you had better go back to service.' The woman . . . in a state of indignation, replied, 'Very well, I *will* go back to service immediately, but give me back my bank-book.' 'Why,' replied he, 'as I don't feel able to work just now, I require the money, but you can go as soon as you like.' So she turned away too heart-broken to speak, left the vagabond, who had gone through the marriage ceremony as the only legal means of obtaining her money, and, returning to service, has never seen him since. I had all this from her own lips."

We will mention another case which illustrates the rights of the husband to dispose of *his* property by will: —

"A lady whose husband had been unsuccessful in business established herself as a milliner in Manchester. After some years of toil she realised sufficient for the family to live upon comfortably; the husband having done nothing meanwhile. They lived for some time in easy circumstances after she gave up business, and then the husband died, bequeathing all his wife's earnings to his own illegitimate children. At the age of sixty-two she was compelled, in order to gain her bread, to return to business."

. . . It may be said, and we believe with justice, that the cases we have been citing are exceptional. In the great majority of cases, good sense, good feeling, deference to public opinion, undoubtedly operate upon husbands to prevent their exerting the powers given them by law to selfish purposes. But the question naturally arises, Why should the law in such exceptional cases give the husband powers so easily to be abused?

From the statements we have made as to the law, we think that few will be disposed to deny that some change is required. It is not consistent with justice that a man should acquire a large fortune with his wife, and be allowed by law to bequeath it the day after his marriage to his illegitimate children. It is not consistent with justice that a man, whose misconduct has been such as to compel his wife to quit his roof, should be enabled by law to retain the whole of her property, and appropriate all her subsequent acquisitions. It is not consistent with justice that when a wife is enabled to earn a large income, the husband by law should have the power of squandering it without any means open to the wife of securing the least provision for herself and children.

No one, we think, will deny that cases such as these are scandals to our law, and if they are rectified and provided for in other codes, why are they not so by the law of England? . . .

"Petition for the Married Women's Property Act", reprinted in "The Property of Married Women", *Westminster Review*, LXVII (1856), 184-85.

The following document, a petition presented to Parliament in 1856, constitutes the first collective protest of women against the injustice of the English law.

In 1854 Barbara Leigh Smith had written a pamphlet, *A Brief Summary in Plain Language of the Most Important Laws Concerning Women,* which set forth the case for reforming the law, particularly as it affected women. Through a family friend, the Recorder of Birmingham, Matthew Davenport Hill, Miss Leigh Smith's pamphlet was presented to the Law Amendment Society, among whose members were Lord Brougham and George W. Hastings, the founders of the Social Science Association, with which the Law Amendment Society was later to merge.

At a public meeting of the Law Amendment Society, a number of ladies, including Miss Leigh Smith, Bessie Rayner Parkes, Mary Howitt, Maria Rye, and Anna Jameson, formed a committee for the purpose of securing signatures to a petition drawn up by Miss Leigh Smith, calling for an act that would give married women the same rights over their property as those enjoyed by single women. The petition was submitted to Parliament in 1856, but a resolution in its favor, presented by Thomas Erskine Perry in the House of Commons, was withdrawn for tactical reasons. Nevertheless, although this attempt to obtain remedial legislation had been aborted, the petition, in another respect, had borne fruit: "people interested in the question were brought into communication in all parts of the kingdom, and . . . the germs of an effective movement were scattered far and wide".[1] Eventually seventy petitions similar to this one were submitted in support of the Married Women's Property Bill, and in all, about 24,000 signatures were collected. That impressive array of strength, however, was not yet enough to persuade the House of Commons to change the existing property laws.

To the Honourable the House of Peers [and Commons] in Parliament assembled. The Petition of the undersigned Women of Great Britain, Married and Single, Humbly Sheweth—That the manifold evils occasioned by the present law, by which the property and earnings of the wife are thrown into the absolute power of the husband, become daily more apparent. That the sufferings thereupon ensuing, extend over all classes of society. That it might once have been deemed for the middle and upper ranks, a comparatively theoretical question, but is so no longer, since married women of education are entering on every side the fields of literature and art, in order to increase the family income by such exertions.

That it is usual when a daughter marries in these ranks, to make, if possible, some distinct pecuniary provision for her and her children, and to secure the money thus

[1] Parkes, *Essays on Woman's Work,* p. 60.

set aside by a cumbrous machinery of trusteeship, proving that few parents are willing entirely to entrust the welfare of their offspring to the irresponsible power of the husband, to the chances of his character, his wisdom, and his success in a profession.

That another device for the protection of women who can afford to appeal, exists in the action of the Courts of Equity, which attempt, within certain limits, to redress the deficiencies of the law; but that trustees may prove dishonest or unwise in the management of the funds entrusted to their care, and Courts of Equity may fail in adjusting differences, which concern the most intimate and delicate relation of life. . . .

That if these laws often bear heavily upon women protected by the forethought of their relatives, the social training of their husbands, and the refined customs of the rank to which they belong, how much more unequivocal is the injury sustained by women in the lower classes, for whom no such provision can be made by their parents, who possess no means of appeal to expensive legal protection, and in regard to whom the education of the husband and the habits of his associates offer no moral guarantee for tender consideration of a wife.

That whereas it is customary, in manufacturing districts, to employ women largely in the processes of trade, and as women are also engaged as semstresses, laundresses, charwomen, and in other multifarious occupations which cannot here be enumerated, the question must be recognised by all as of practical importance. . . .

. . . That for the robbery by a man of his wife's hard earnings there is no redress, — against the selfishness of a drunken father, who wrings from a mother her children's daily bread, there is no appeal. She may work from morning till night, to see the produce of her labour wrested from her, and wasted in a gin-palace; and such cases are within the knowledge of every one.

That the law, in depriving the mother of all pecuniary resources, deprives her of the power of giving schooling to her children, and in other ways providing for their moral and physical welfare; it obliges her, in short, to leave them to the temptations of the street, so fruitful in juvenile crime.

That there are certain portions of the law of husband and wife which bear unjustly on the husband, as for instance, that of making him responsible for his wife's debts contracted before marriage, even although he may have no fortune with her. Her power also, after marriage, of contracting debts in the name of her husband, for which he is responsible, is too unlimited, and often produces much injustice.

That in rendering the husband responsible for the entire maintenance of his family, the law expresses the necessity of an age, when the man was the only money-getting agent; but that since the custom of the country has greatly changed in this respect the position of the female sex, the law of maintenance no longer meets the whole case. That since modern civilisation, in indefinitely extending the sphere of occupation for women, has in some measure broken down their pecuniary dependence upon men, it is time that legal protection be thrown over the produce of their labour, and that in entering the state of marriage, they no longer pass from freedom into the condition of a slave, all whose earnings belong to his master and not himself.

That the laws of various foreign countries are in this respect much more just than our own, and afford precedent for a more liberal legislation than prevails in England; — and your Petitioners therefore humbly pray that your Honourable House will take the foregoing allegations into consideration, and apply such remedy as to its wisdom shall seem fit—and your Petitioners will ever pray. [*Editors' note: Among the 24 signers were: Anna Blackwell, Elizabeth Barrett Browning, Mrs. Carlyle, Mary Cowden Clarke,*

Mrs. Gaskell, Anna Jameson, Harriet Martineau, Bessie Rayner Parkes and Barbara Leigh Smith.]

Frances Power Cobbe, "Criminals, Idiots, Women, and Minors", *Fraser's Magazine,* LXXVIII (1868), 777-94.

Sir Thomas Erskine Perry, whose resolution in favor of a Married Women's Property bill had, as we have seen, been withdrawn in 1856, returned to the fray in 1857 with a bill which he introduced in May of that year. It survived its second reading, but became a casualty of the campaign to pass the Marriage and Divorce Act, which by including a provision protecting the property rights of women whose husbands had deserted them, diverted votes that would have gone to Perry's bill. Something had been gained, however; even though the Marriage and Divorce Act fell far short of what the Law Amendment Society had hoped for in regard to property rights, it at least established the principle that *some* women had a legal right to dispose of their own property.

Not until the formation in 1867 of the Married Women's Property Committee, led by Elizabeth Wolstenholme and Ursula Mellor Bright, and numbering the formidable France Power Cobbe among its members, was the effort to pass a property bill renewed. Miss Wolstenholme had been associated with Emily Davies in the work of the Schools' Inquiry Commission, before which she testified on the subject of female education, and was active in behalf of women's suffrage. Mrs. Bright was the wife of Jacob Bright, a radical M.P., who had long been involved in the struggle for women's rights. Just as the ladies associated with Barbara Leigh Smith's petition committee a dozen years earlier had appealed for the support of the Law Amendment Society, in 1867 the Married Women's Property Committee appealed to the Social Science Association, with which the Law Amendment Society was now merged. In 1868 a committee of the Social Science Association that had been appointed to consider the question, presented the draft of a bill which was submitted to Parliament, where it won the support of John Stuart Mill and other prominent advocates of women's rights. The proposed bill called for giving married women rights over their property comparable to those enjoyed by single women. In 1869, when victory seemed assured, Bessie Rayner Parkes, now Mrs. Belloc, wrote to Barbara Bodichon: "How wonderful to know the Married Women's Property Bill *has passed the Commons!* Thus ends, my dear, one chapter of what was once our life endeavour".[1] Mrs. Belloc's exultation, unfortunately, was premature. The bill as rewritten by the Lords and passed, because of the lateness of the session, by a reluctant Commons, was almost a travesty of the original measure. It was not until 1882 that an Act which met the expectations

---

[1]Mrs. Belloc Lowndes, *"I, too, Have lived in Arcadia"* (London: Macmillan & Co. Ltd., 1941), p. 101.

of the ladies of the Married Women's Property Committee was finally passed.

The following selection is an excerpt from a widely reprinted article that secured the reputation of Frances Power Cobbe as an ardent, outspoken, and witty advocate of women's rights. Writing as the campaign to pass the Social Science Association-sponsored property bill was getting under way, Miss Cobbe suggested that the union of two human beings in marriage was—at least in England—most analogous to the relationship between two tarantulas in a bell jar: "When one of these delightful creatures is placed under a glass with a companion of his own species, a little smaller than himself, he forthwith gobbles him up" (p. 789).

. . . Had [a] visitor heard for the first time upon his arrival on earth of another incident of human existence—namely, *Marriage,* it may be surmised that his astonishment and awe would also have been considerable. To his eager inquiry whether men and women earnestly strove to prepare themselves for so momentous an occurrence, he would have received the puzzling reply that women frequently devoted themselves with . . . singleness of aim to that special purpose; but that men, on the contrary, very rarely included any preparation for the married state. . . . But this anomaly would be trifling compared to others which would be revealed to him. "Ah," we can hear him say to his guide as they pass into a village church. "What a pretty sight is this! What is happening to that sweet young woman in white who is giving her hand to the good-looking fellow beside her, all the company decked in holiday attire, and the joy-bells shaking the old tower overhead? She is receiving some great honour, is she not? The Prize of Virtue, perhaps?"

"Oh, yes," would reply the friend; "an honour certainly. She is being Married." After a little further explanation the visitor would pursue his inquiry:

"Of course, having entered this honourable state of matrimony, she has some privileges above the women who are not chosen by anybody? I notice her husband has just said, 'With all my worldly goods I thee endow.' Does that mean that she will henceforth have the control of his money altogether, or only that he takes her into partnership?"

"*Pas precisement,* my dear sir. By our law it is *her* goods and earnings, present and future, which belong to him from this moment."

"You don't say so? But then, of course, his goods are hers also?"

"Oh dear, no! not at all. He is only bound to find her food; and truth to tell, not very strictly or efficaciously bound to do that."

"How! do I understand you? Is it possible that here in the most solemn religious act, which I perceive your prayer book calls 'The Solemnisation of Holy Matrimony,' every husband makes a generous promise, which promise is not only a mockery, but the actual reverse and parody of the real state of the case: the man who promises giving nothing, and the woman who is silent giving all?"

"Well, yes; I suppose that is something like it, as to the letter of the law. But then, of course, practically—"

"Practically, I suppose few men can really be so unmanly and selfish as the law warrants them in being. Yet some, I fear, may avail themselves of such authority. May I ask another question? As you subject women who enter the marriage state to such very severe penalties as this, what worse have you in store for women who lead a dissolute life, to the moral injury of the community?"

"Oh, the law takes nothing from them. Whatever they earn or inherit is their own. They are able, also, to sue the fathers of their children for their maintenance, which a wife, of course, is not allowed to do on behalf of *her* little ones, because she and her husband are one in the eye of the law."

"One question still further — your criminals? Do they always forfeit their entire property on conviction?"

"Only for the most heinous crimes; felony and murder, for example."

"Pardon me; I must seem to you so stupid! Why is the property of the woman who commits Murder, and the property of the woman who commits Matrimony, dealt with alike by your law?"

Leaving our little allegory and in sober seriousness, we must all admit that the just and expedient treatment of women by men is one of the most obscure problems, alike of equity and of policy. Nor of women only, but of all classes and races of human beings whose condition is temporarily or permanently one of comparative weakness and dependence. In past ages, the case was simple enough. No question of right or duty disturbed the conscience of Oriental or Spartan, of Roman or Norman, in dealing with his wife, his Helot, his slave, or his serf. "Le droit du plus fort," was unassailed in theory and undisturbed in practice. But we, in our day, are perplexed and well nigh overwhelmed with the difficulties presented to us. What ought the Americans to do with their Negroes? What ought we to do with our Hindoos? What ought all civilized people to do with their women? . . .

At the head of this paper I have placed the four categories under which persons are now excluded from many civil, and all political rights in England. They were complacently quoted this year by the *Times* as every way fit and proper exceptions; but yet it has appeared to not a few, that the placed assigned to Women among them is hardly any longer suitable. To a woman herself who is aware that she has never committed a Crime; who fondly believes that she is not an Idiot; and who is alas! only too sure she is no longer a Minor, there naturally appears some incongruity in placing her, for such important purposes, in an association wherein otherwise she would scarcely be likely to find herself. But in all seriousness, the question presses, Ought Englishwomen of full age, at the present state of affairs, to be considered as having legally attained majority? or ought they permanently to be considered, for all civil and political purposes, as minors? . . .

. . . Of course it is not pleasant to women to be told they are "physically, morally, and intellectually inferior" to their companions. . . . For a proud and gifted woman to be told that she is in every possible respect inferior to the footman who stands behind her chair, can hardly be thought pleasing intelligence. Nevertheless, women are foolish to be angry with the man who in plain words tells them straightforwardly that in his opinion such is the case. After all he pays them a better compliment than the fop who professes to adore them as so many wingless angels, and privately values them as so many dolls. In any case all such discussion is beside our present aim. [*Editors' note: Miss Cobbe then proceeds to discuss the legal disabilities of a married woman deriving from the fact that her "personal property at the time of her marriage, or whatever she may afterwards earn or inherit, belongs to her husband". After summarizing the stock arguments based on grounds of Justice, Expediency, and Sentiment, Miss Cobbe thoroughly refutes the allegations.*]

. . . What in the first place, [is] the Justice of giving all a women's property to her husband? The argument is, that the wife gets an ample *quid pro quo. Does* she get it under the existing law? That is the simple question.

In the first place, many husbands are unable, from fault or from misfortune, to maintain their wives. . . .

. . . When all that a woman possesses in the present and future is handed over unreservedly by the law to her husband, is there the smallest attempt at obtaining security that he on his part *can* fulfil that obligation which is always paraded as the equivalent, namely, the obligation to support her for the rest of her life? Nay, he is not so much as asked to promise he will reserve any portion of her money for such purpose, or reminded of his supposed obligation. If he spend [£]10,000 of her fortune in a week in paying his own debts, and incapacitate himself for ever from supporting her and her children, the law has not one word to say against him.

But waiving the point of the *inability* of many husbands to fulfil their side of the understood engagement, one thing, at all events, it must behoove the law to do. Having enforced her part on the woman, it is bound to enforce his part on the man, *to the utmost of his ability.* The legal act by which a man puts his hand in his wife's pocket, or draws her money out of the savings' bank, is perfectly clear, easy, inexpensive. The corresponding process by which the wife can obtain food and clothing from her husband when he neglects to provide it—what may it be? Where is it described? How is it rendered safe and easy to every poor woman who may chance to need its protection? When we are assured that men are always so careful of the interests of the women for whom they legislate, that it is quite needless for women to seek political freedom to protect themselves, we might be inclined to take it for granted that here, if anywhere, here where the very life and subsistence of women are concerned, the legislation of their good friends and protectors in their behalf would have been as stringent and as clear as words could make it. We should expect to find the very easiest and simplest mode of redress laid open to every hapless creature thus reduced to want by him to whom the law itself has given all she has ever earned or inherited. Nay, seeing the hesitation wherewith any wife would prosecute the husband with whom she still tries to live, and the exceeding cowardice and baseness of the act of maltreating so helpless a dependent, it might not have been too much had the law exercised as much severity in such a case as if the offender had voluntarily starved his ass or his sheep, and the Society for the Prevention of Cruelty to Animals were his prosecutors.

But this is the imaginary, what is the actual fact? Simply that the woman's remedy for her husband's neglect to provide her with food, has been practically found unattainable. The law which has robbed her so straightforwardly, has somehow forgotten altogether to secure for her the supposed compensation. Since 1857, if the husband altogether forsake his home for years together, the wife may obtain from the magistrate a protection order, and prevent him from seizing her property. But, if he come back just often enough to keep within the technical period fixed as desertion, and take from her everything she may have earned, or which charitable people may have given her, then there is absolutely no resource for her at all. . . . When the poor wretch, . . . perhaps on the point of bearing a child to the wretch who is starving her, goes to the magistrate to implore protection,—what answer does she receive? She is told that he cannot hear her complaint; that she cannot sue her husband, as he and she are one in the eye of the law. [*Editors' note: Included in a footnote at this point is the following illustration which demonstrates quite clearly that a wife's claim to support was not enforceable.*] A horrible instance in point occurred near Gainsborough, in Lincolnshire. The evidence given on the inquest was published in the *Lincolnshire Chronicle,* July 5, 1863.

The parish surgeon wrote thus to the clergyman of the parish, who was also a magistrate: —

"Dear Sir, — I have to-day seen Mrs. Seymour. I found her in a wretchedly weak state. She is nursing a baby, which office she is not able to perform effectually from her exhausted condition. Her husband, she says, does not allow her the necessaries of life, which he, in his position, could find if he liked. Without some means be taken to provide her with good diet, &c., or to make her husband do so, she must die of starvation at no very distant period. If you could, in your official capacity, help the poor creature, you would confer a great blessing on the poor woman, and oblige yours faithfully,

J. C. SMALLMAN."

The clergyman found, however, that he had no power as a magistrate to take cognisance of the case, unless the [Poor Law] guardians would give the wife relief, and prosecute the husband; and this they declined to do. In vain did the poor half-starved wretch appear before them, and pray to be admitted into the workhouse. She was refused admission on the ground that her husband earned good wages; and so she went home, and after lingering awhile, probably fed now and then by her neighbours, she died. The husband escaped without any punishment whatever. The jury who tried him [*men,* of course!] gave him the benefit of a doubt as to the cause of his wife's death, and acquitted him. . . .

So much for the Justice of the Common Law. What now shall we say to its Expediency? The matter seems to lie thus. Men are generally more wise in worldly matters; more generally able and intelligent, and their wives habitually look up to them with even ridiculously exaggerated confidence and admiration. Such being the case, it would naturally happen, were there no law in the case, that the husband should manage all the larger business of the family. The law then *when the husband is really wise and good* is a dead letter. But for the opposite cases, exceptions though they be, yet alas! too numerous, where the husband is a fool, a gambler, a drunkard, and where the wife is sensible, frugal, devoted to the interests of the children, — is it indeed expedient that the whole and sole power should be lodged in the husband's hands; the power not only over all they already have in common, but the power over all she can ever earn in future? Such a law must paralyse the energy of any woman less than a heroine of maternal love. How many poor wives has it driven to despair, as one time after another they have been legally robbed of their hard won earnings, who can calculate? One such hapless one, we are told, when her lawful tyrant came home as usual, drunk with the spoils of her starving children, took up some wretched relic of their ruined household and smote him to death. She was a murderess. In former times she would have been burnt alive for "petty treason" for killing her lord and master. But what was the law which gave to that reckless savage a power the same as that of a slaveholder of the South over his slave? . . .

. . . It is the alleged *helplessness* of married women which, it is said, makes it indispensable to give all the support of the law, *not* to them, but to the stronger persons with whom they are unequally yoked. "Woman is physically, mentally, and morally inferior to man." Therefore it follows — what? — that the law should give to her bodily weakness, her intellectual dulness, her tottering morality, all the support and protection which it is possible to interpose between so poor a creature and the strong being always standing over her? By no means. Quite the contrary of course. The husband being already physically, mentally, and morally his wife's superior must in justice receive from the law additional strength by being constituted absolute master of her property. . . .

Such is the argument from the feebleness of women to the expediency of weakening any little independent spirit they might possibly found on the possession of a trifle of money. "To him that hath shall be given, and he shall have more abundantly; but from her that hath not, shall be taken away even that which it seemeth she has a right to have." The text is a hard one, in an ethical point of view.

But the great and overwhelming argument against the *Expediency* of the Common Law in this matter is the simple fact that no parent or guardian possessed of means sufficient to evade it by a marriage settlement ever dreams of permitting his daughter or ward to undergo its (supposed) beneficial action. . . . How then can it be argued that the same rule is generally considered expedient yet invariably evaded by all who have means to evade it? . . .

. . . The only persons for whom the existing law is expedient are fortune-hunters, who, if they can befool young women of property so far as to induce them to elope, are enabled thereby to grasp all their inheritance. Were there no such law as the cession of the wife's property on marriage, there would be considerably fewer of those disgusting and miserable alliances where the man marries solely to become possessed of his wife's money.

But, as we have said already, there is an argument which has more force in determining legislation about marriage than either considerations of Justice or of Expediency. It is the sentiment entertained by the majority of men on the subject; the ideal they have formed of wedlock, the poetical vision in their minds of a wife's true relation to her husband. . . . Let us try to fathom this sentiment, for till we understand it we are but fighting our battles in the dark. It is not this — that a woman's whole life and being, her soul, body, time, property, thought, and care, ought to be given to her husband; that nothing short of such absorption in him and his interests makes her a true wife; and that when she is thus absorbed even a very mediocre character and inferior intellect can make a man happy in a sense no splendour of endowments can otherwise do? Truly I believe this is the feeling at the bottom of nearly all men's hearts, and of the hearts of thousands of women also. There is no use urging that it is a gigantic piece of egotism in a man to desire such a marriage. Perhaps it is natural for him to do so, and perhaps it is natural for a great number of women to give just such absorbed adoring affection. . . .

So far all is plain and natural, but the question is this: Supposing such marriages to be the most desirable, do men set the right way about securing them, by making such laws as the Common Law of England? Is perfect love to be called out by perfect dependence? Does an empty purse necessarily imply a full heart? Is a generous-natured woman likely to be won or rather to be alienated and galled by being made to feel she has no choice but submission? Surely there is great fallacy in this direction. The idea which we are all agreed ought to be realised in marriage is that of the highest possible Union. But what *is* that most perfect Union? Have we not taken it in a most gross commercial sense, as if even here we were a nation of shopkeepers? . . .

To sum up our argument. The existing Common Law is not *Just,* because it neither can secure nor actually even attempts to secure for the woman the equivalent support for whose sake she is forced to relinquish her property.

It is not *Expedient,* because while in happy marriages it is superfluous and useless, in unhappy ones it becomes highly injurious; often causing the final ruin of a family which the mother (if upheld by law) might have supported single-handed. It is also shown not to be considered expedient by the conduct of the entire upper class of the country, and even of the legislature itself in the system of the Court of Chancery. Where no one who can afford to evade the law fails to evade it, the pretence that it is believed to be generally expedient is absurd. . . .

Lastly, it does not tend to fulfil, but to counteract, the *Sentiment* regarding the marriage union, to which it aims to add the pressure of force. Real unanimity is not produced between two parties by forbidding one of them to have any voice at all. The hard mechanical contrivance of the law for making husband and wife of one heart and mind is calculated to produce a precisely opposite result.

The proposal, then, to abolish this law seems to have in its favour Justice, Expediency, and even the Sentiment which has hitherto blindly supported the law. . . .

Pearce Stevenson [Caroline Norton], *A Plain Letter to the Lord Chancellor on the Infant Custody Bill* (London: James Ridgway, 1839), pp. 11, 42-44, 46-47, 108-12, 115.

In 1836 George Norton, a London lawyer and former Tory M.P., brought suit against Lord Melbourne, the Whig prime minister, whom he accused of having seduced his wife, Caroline. Mrs. Norton, a granddaughter of Richard Brinsley Sheridan, was a noted beauty who moved in the highest circles of English society, as befitted a lady whose childhood had been spent at Hampton Court. It is possible that her husband, even though he encouraged her social activities for reasons of his own, resented her achievements as poet, author, musician, and successful hostess, and that his accusations were politically motivated as well. His charges were practically laughed out of court, Melbourne was acquitted, and Mrs. Norton was vindicated, but—human nature being what it is—left with a tarnished reputation. The Nortons' stormy marriage continued to deteriorate, and they soon separated, waging a bitter struggle for the custody of their children over a period of several years. Aided by influential friends, Mrs. Norton devoted herself to winning support for a measure, the Infant Custody Bill, which would at least enable mothers to petition the Court of Chancery to grant them the right to visit older children and, in some cases, give them temporary custody of their children under seven years of age. The Infant Custody Bill became law in 1839, partly because of the effect of a pamphlet, the famous *Plain Letter to the Lord Chancellor,* which had first appeared in 1838, and which was an eloquent plea on behalf of the Bill. The name of the author, Pearce Stevenson, was a pseudonym which Mrs. Norton adopted for the occasion. The vehemence, indignation, and sense of outrage evident in the selection that follows, reflect the trials to which she had been, and continued to be, subjected by her vindictive husband, who employed all available legal devices to frustrate her attempts to secure the custody of her children.

. . . A woman may bear cheerfully the poverty which anomalies in the laws of property may entail upon her; and she may struggle patiently through an unjust ordeal of
shame [in a divorce suit]; but against the inflicted and unmerited loss of her children
she *cannot* bear up; . . . she will still hold *that* injustice to stand foremost, distinct,
and paramount above them all. . . . It is in the single point of *her children* that she is
entirely without remedy; it is in the single point of her children that her innocence or
her ill-usage avail nothing: how then can *this* be rated with instances in which it is
expressly understood that she *will* be protected if she can prove herself blameless and
ill-used? . . .

[In the discussion on the Infant Custody Bill,] . . . the idea that a sinful *mother*
should be allowed to look upon, speak to, or caress the children of an injured husband,
was monstrous, was incredible, and called forth eloquent and proud rebukes . . . :
but the idea that a sinful *father* should in any way be interfered with, or prevented
from disposing of his children as best suited his vengeance or his caprice, was quite
incomprehensible to the defenders of his "*right.*" Truly this is straining at a gnat and
swallowing a camel; to be so outrageously shocked at the sinful *female* parent seeing
her child at chance intervals, and to be perfectly contented that the sinful *male* parent
should live with it, have authority over it, and never part from its society! . . . Vice, in
the shape of the miserable and degraded mother, is viewed with stern and merciless
abhorrence; but vice, in the shape of the husband's mistress, is contemplated with
indulgence. . . .

. . . Consider . . . the established *certainty*, that bad fathers have wrested their
children from blameless wives, to force a disposition of property in their own favour,
or to gratify a brutal spirit of vengeance; that to a blameless mother, her diseased and
dying child has been refused; that from a blameless mother's care her innocent offspring has been transferred to the home of a wanton. . . .

. . . But the question is, on what principle the legislature should give a man this
power to torment; this power to say to his wife "You shall bear blows, you shall bear
inconstancy, you shall give up property, you shall endure insult, and *yet* you shall
continue to live under my roof, *or else* I will take your children, and you shall never
see them more"? Or, on what principle, if his victim leaves him, he is to say with hard
and insolent triumph, "She shall return to her home, or weep her heart out; I make no
promise—I admit no man's right to interfere—I care not what truth there may be in
her complaints of my conduct; all I say is, that either she shall *return*, or she shall
never again see or hear of her children." . . .

. . . Who could believe that honest and honourable men would gravely argue that
it is a fit state of the law, and one which had better not be altered, which permits a
cruel or adulterous husband to take his children from the mother who bore and reared
them, and give them to any stranger he pleases, himself the only judge under what
circumstances this cruelty shall be inflicted!—his own bad and revengeful passions the
only guide to a selection of the guardianship which is to influence the destiny of his
child! Who could believe that, after it was shown what this admission of *nominal custody* had led to, it would be gravely argued that it would be a pity to disturb the general
rule which gave all fathers power to do the like? Who could believe that, because it is
the duty of a wife to show rational and proper submission to her husband, it would
therefore be gravely argued that she has no more claim to the children she may have
by him, than the female of some dumb animal to the calves, foals, or puppies bred for
their owner? Who could believe that the same law, which refuses to assist the father to

regain possession of his son at the age of fourteen, will authorize the seizure from the mother (by any stratagem or violence) of an infant under that age, for the purpose of being delivered to one who perhaps entertains aversion both to mother and child; it may be to one whose interest it is that the child should not exist? Who could believe that, because there are loose, profligate wives in this world, as well as loose, profligate husbands, it would be gravely argued that *no* woman, however clear the case of ill-usage, however monstrous the circumstances of wrong, should have any chance of redress, by being made an exception from this bitter law of her country? . . .

. . . If [a woman's] marriage is indissoluble because *she* has not misconducted herself, and yet the offspring of the marriage is held to belong to the party who *has* misconducted himself, would it not require the religious resignation of a martyr to prevent a woman from reasoning thus within herself: "My marriage is made a mockery of that holy tie, through no fault of mine; my children are taken from me, though I have never done anything to deserve it; I am condemned by the law to punishment without committing any crime and I am viewed by society with harshness and distrust on account of a position I cannot help. . . ."

. . . If the general understanding throughout Great Britain is to be, that men may execute in the privacy of their own houses such tyranny as they would not dare to inflict on the meanest of their fellow-subjects anywhere else; if it be declared that children, sent by heaven as a blessing and bond of peace, are to be considered chiefly as a means and instrument in the hand of the father to compel his wife to endure all things meekly; if it be declared that the fair face of some smiling wanton shall not only seduce a husband from his wife, but shall replace to her child the image of his exiled mother, whose petition for redress is unheard:—If this *is* to be the declaration of this law—why, we can only wonder that such should be the decision of a Christian legislature in the nineteenth century. . . .

The Hon. Mrs. [Caroline] Norton, *A Letter to the Queen on Lord Chancellor Cranworth's Marriage and Divorce Bill,* 3rd. ed. (London: Longman, Brown, Green & Longmans, 1855), pp. 8-13, 16, 28-29, 31, 76-79, 84-86, 96, 126-28, 145-46, 154-55.

Although, as we have seen, the jury established Mrs. Norton's innocence in the suit brought against Lord Melbourne, Mr. Norton—acting completely within the law—exacted a brutal revenge. The ordeal to which he subsequently subjected her eloquently testifies to the "non-existence" of married women. Having "learned the English law piece-meal by suffering under it" (p. 145), Mrs. Norton was only too aware that she could not ask for her rights because, as she put it, "I have no rights. I have only wrongs."[1]

The chief of those wrongs was that she could not free herself from her husband's absolute control of her property. Mrs. Norton was neither a feminist nor a reformer; what she wanted was simply protection from her husband's arbitrary power. She did not like "strong-minded women" (a label that might aptly describe her), and she rejected the notion that

[1] Cited.in Jane Grey Perkins, *The Life of the Honourable Mrs. Norton* (New York: Henry Holt & Company, 1909), p. 232.

the sexes were equal. Conventional as she was in this respect, her personal problems forced her to take a radical position on the subject of divorce, making her a reformer despite her reluctance to assume that role. The following selection is taken from a pamphlet, *A Letter to the Queen*, which Mrs. Norton wrote when Parliament was considering the subject of divorce. Her account of what happened to her property clearly shows the injustice which had to be endured by a woman who was separated from her husband, but who, in the years before 1857, could not obtain a divorce.

. . . A married woman in England has *no legal existence:* her being is absorbed in that of her husband. Years of separation or desertion cannot alter this position. Unless divorced by special enactment in the House of Lords, the legal fiction holds her to be *"one"* with her husband, even though she may never see or hear of him.

She has no possessions, unless by special settlement; her property is *his* property. Lord Ellenborough mentions a case in which a sailor bequeathed "all he was worth" to a woman he cohabited with; and afterwards married, in the West Indies, a woman of considerable fortune. At this man's death it was held, —notwithstanding the hardship of the case, —that the will swept away from his widow, in favour of his mistress, every shilling of the property. It is now provided that a will shall be revoked by marriage: but the claim of *the husband* to all that is his wife's exists in full force. An English wife has no legal right even to her clothes or ornaments; her husband may take them and sell them if he pleases, even though they be the gifts of relatives or friends, or bought before marriage.

An English wife cannot make a will. She may have children or kindred whom she may earnestly desire to benefit; —she may be separated from her husband, who may be living with a mistress; no matter: the law gives what she has to him, and no will she could make would be valid.

An English wife cannot legally claim her own earnings. Whether wages for manual labour, or payment for intellectual exertion, whether she weed potatoes, or keep a school, her salary is *the husband's.* . . .

An English wife may not leave her husband's house. Not only can he sue her for "restitution of conjugal rights," but he has a right to enter the house of any friend or relation with whom she may take refuge, and who may "harbour her,"—as it is termed, — and carry her away by force, with or without the aid of the police.

If the wife sue for separation for cruelty, it must be "cruelty that endangers life or limb," and if she has once forgiven, or, in legal phrase, *"condoned"* his offences, she cannot plead them; though her past forgiveness only proves that she endured as long as endurance was possible.

If her husband take proceedings for a divorce, she is not, in the first instance, allowed to defend herself. She has no means of proving the falsehood of his allegations. She is not represented by attorney, nor permitted to be considered a party to the suit between him and her supposed lover, for "damages". . . .

If an English wife be guilty of infidelity, her husband can divorce *her* so as to marry again; but she cannot divorce the husband *a vinculo* [a complete divorce, as distinguished from a separation], however profligate he may be. No law court can divorce in England. A special Act of Parliament annulling the marriage, is passed for each case. The House of Lords grants this almost as a matter of course to the husband, but not to the wife. In only four instances (two of which were cases of incest), has the wife obtained a divorce to marry again.

She cannot prosecute for a libel. Her husband must prosecute; and in cases of enmity and separation, of course she is without a remedy.

She cannot sign a lease, or transact responsible business.

She cannot claim support, as a matter of personal right, from her husband. . . .

She cannot bind her husband by any agreement, except through a third party. A contract formally drawn out by a lawyer, — witnessed, and signed by her husband, — is *void in law;* and he can evade payment of an income so assured, by the legal quibble that "a man cannot contract with his own wife".

Separation from her husband by consent, or for his ill usage, does not alter their mutual relation. He retains the right to divorce her *after* separation, — as before, — though he himself be unfaithful.

Her being, on the other hand, of spotless character, and without reproach, gives her no advantage in law. She may have withdrawn from his roof knowing that he lives with "his faithful housekeeper": having suffered personal violence at his hands; having "condoned" much, and being able to prove it by unimpeachable testimony: or he may have shut the doors of her house against her: all this is quite immaterial: the law takes no cognisance of which is to blame. As *her husband,* he has a right to all that is hers: as *his wife,* she has no right to anything that is his. As her husband, he may divorce her (if truth or false swearing can do it): as his wife, the utmost "divorce" she could obtain, is permission to reside alone, — married to his name. The marriage cermony is a civil bond for him, — and an indissoluble sacrament for her; and the rights of mutual property which that ceremony is ignorantly supposed to confer, are made absolute for him, and null for her. . . .

In Scotland, the wife accused of infidelity defends herself as a matter of course, and as a first process. . . .

In Scotland, the property of the wife is protected; rules are made for her "aliment" or support; and her clothes and "paraphernalia" cannot be seized by her husband.

In Scotland, above all, the law *has* power to divorce *a vinculo,* so as to enable *either* party to marry again; and the right of the wife to apply for such divorce is equal with the right of the husband; that license for inconstancy, take out under the English law by the English husband, — as one of the masculine gender, — being utterly unknown to the Scottish courts.

This condition of the English law; its anomalies, its injustice, its actions for damages . . . and its perpetual contradictions, have long marked it out for reform. . . .

. . . Why is England the only country obliged to confess she cannot contrive to administer justice to women? Why is it more difficult than in France? Why more difficult than in Scotland? Simply because our legists and legislators insist on binding tares with wheat, and combining all sorts of contradictions which they never will be able satisfactorily to combine. They never *will* satisfy, with measures that give one law for one sex and the rich, and another law for the other sex and the poor. Nor will they ever succeed in acting on the legal fiction that married women are "non-existent," and man and wife are still "one," in cases of alienation, separation, and enmity; when they are about as much "one" as those ingenious twisted groups of animal death we sometimes see in sculpture; one creature wild to resist, and the other fierce to destroy.

Nor does all this confusion arise, because the law is professedly too weak for the necessary control which would prevent it. The law is strong enough when it interferes with labour, — with property, — with the guardianship of children, — with the rights of speculative industry. We find no difficulty in controlling the merchant in his factories, the master with his apprentices, nor in the protection of persons in all other dependent positions. We find no difficulty in punishing the abuse of power, or discovered crime. It suffices that it be proved that wrong was committed, and punishment follows as a matter of course. . . .

. . . Is [the law] able to protect the poorest, the meanest, the most apparently helpless persons in the realm, and not able to protect women? Are the only laws in England "so surrounded with difficulty" that they cannot possibly be re-modelled to any pattern of equal justice, the laws between man and wife?

I think not. I think if men would approach them with the same impartial wish to make rules of protection, that is brought to bear on other subjects, they would find the same facility in applying those rules. . . .

Why should there be no tribunal of control over these "vacillating" husbands who refuse to abide by written pledges, and make promises "for the opportunity of breaking them"? Why is the absurd fiction of "non-existence," to be kept up *in law,* when *in fact,* two alienated parties exist, with adverse interests, struggling and antagonistic? . . .

. . . I wrote two pamphlets: one, "On the Separation of Mother and Child;" the other, "A Plain Letter to the Chancellor, by Pierce [*sic*] Stevenson, Esq." The [*British and Foreign Quarterly*] Review . . . attributed to me a paper I did *not* write, and never saw; "On the Grievances of Woman"; and boldly setting my name, in the index, as the author,—proceeded, in language strange, rabid and virulent, to abuse the writer; calling her a "SHE-DEVIL" and a "SHE-BEAST." No less than one hundred and forty-two pages were devoted to the nominal task of opposing the Infant Custody Bill, and in reality to abusing *me.* Not being the author of the paper criticised, I requested my solicitor to prosecute the Review as a libel. He informed me that being a married woman, I could not prosecute of myself; that my husband must prosecute: my husband — who had assailed me with every libel in his power! There could be no prosecution: and I was left to study the grotesque anomaly in law of having my defence made *necessary,* — and made *impossible,* — by the same person. . . .

In 1851, my mother died. She left me (through my brother, to guard it from my husband) a small annuity, as an addition to my income. Mr. Norton first endeavored to claim her legacy, and then balanced the first payment under her will, by arbitrarily stopping my allowance. I insisted that the allowance was secured, by his own signature, and these other signatures, to a formal deed. He defied me to prove it—"as, by law, man and wife were one, and could not contract with each other; and the deed was therefore good for nothing."

. . . I do not receive, and have not received for the last three years, a single farthing from [my husband]. He retains, and always has retained, property that was left in my home — gifts made to me by my own family on my marriage, and to my mother . . . — articles bought from my literary earnings,—books which belonged to Lord Melbourne. . . .

[Mr. Norton] receives from my trustees the interest of the portion bequeathed me by my father, who died in the public service. . . .

I have also (as Mr. Norton impressed on me, by subpoenaing my publishers) the power of earning, by literature, — which fund . . . is no more legally mine than my family property.

. . . I cannot divorce my husband, either for adultery, desertion, or cruelty; I *must* remain married to *his name; he* has, in right of that fact (of my link to his name), a right to everything I have in the world — and I have no more claim upon *him,* than any one of your Majesty's ladies in waiting who are utter strangers to him! . . .

I am, as regards my husband, in a worse position than if I had been divorced. . . . I am *not* divorced, and I cannot divorce my husband; yet I can establish no legal claim upon him, nor upon any living human being! . . .

. . . If Mr. Norton, a magistrate and member of the aristocracy, had cheated at a game of cards in one of the clubs of London, all England would have been in a ferment. Nay, even if he had refused to pay a "debt of honour" — to a *man* — it would have been reckoned a most startling and outrageous step! But, because the matter is only between him and his wife, — because it is "only a woman," — the whole complexion of the case is altered. Only a woman! whom he can libel with impunity, to find a loophole for escape or excuse.

I declare, upon the holy sacraments of God, that I was *not* Lord Melbourne's mistress; and, what is more, I do not believe (and nothing shall ever make me believe), that Mr. Norton ever thought that I was. In that miserable fact is the root of all my bitterness, and of all his inconsistency! He never had a real conviction (not even an unjust one), to make him consistent. He wavered, because he was doing, not what he thought necessary and just, but what he imagined would ''*answer:*'' and sometimes one thing appeared likely to answer and sometimes another. He thought the course he took respecting me and my children, in 1836, would answer; and so far it did answer, that he is two thousand a-year the richer. He thought his defence to the tradesman's action, in 1853, would answer; and so far it did answer, that he is five hundred a-year the richer. But he never *believed* the accusations on which he has twice founded his gainful measures of expediency. He acknowledged he did not believe them, to others who have published his acknowledgement.

It ought not to be *possible* that any man, by mock invocations to justice, should serve a mere purpose of interest or vengeance; it ought not to be *possible* that any man should make "the law" his minister, in seeking not that which is just, but that which may "answer". . . .

I have, as I said before, learned the English law piecemeal, by suffering under it. My husband is a lawyer; and he has taught it me, by exercising over my tormented and restless life, every quirk and quibble of its tyranny; of its *acknowledged* tyranny; — acknowledged, again I say, not by wailing, angry, despairing women, but by Chancellors, ex-Chancellors, legal reformers, and members of both Houses of Parliament. And yet nothing is done! indeed, when the Solicitor-General, May 10th, in this session, informed the House that the delayed Marriage Bill would be brought forward "as soon as the House had expressed an opinion on the Testamentary Jurisdiction Bill,'' there was a good-humoured laugh at the very vague prospect held out, — but nobody murmured; for nobody greatly cared when it should come on; or whether it ever came on at all.

Nevertheless, so long as human nature is what it is, some marriages must be unhappy marriages, instead of following that theory of intimate and sacred union which they ought to fulfil: and the question is, therefore, what is to be the relation of persons living in a state of alienation, instead of a state of union, — all the existing rules for their social position being based on the first alternative, — namely, that they *are* in a state of union, — and on the supposition that marriage is indissoluble, though Parliament has now decided that it is a civil contract? Divorced or undivorced, it is absolutely necessary that the law should step in, to arrange that which is disarranged by this most unnatural condition. It becomes perfectly absurd that the law which appoints the husband legal protector of the woman, should not (failing him who has ceased to be a protector, and has become a very powerful foe) itself undertake her protection. She stands towards the law, by an illustration which I have repeatedly made use of, — in the light of an ill-used inferior; and she is the *only* inferior in England who cannot claim to be so protected.

. . . Let the recollection of what I write, remain with those who read; and above all, let the recollection remain with your Majesty, to whom it is addressed; the one woman in England who *cannot* suffer wrong; and whose royal assent will be formally necessary to any Marriage Reform Bill which the Lord Chancellor, assembled Peers, and assembled Commons, may think fit to pass, in the Parliament of this free nation; where, with a Queen on the throne, all other married women are legally "NON-EXISTENT."

J. W. Kaye, "The Non-Existence of Women", *North British Review*, XXIII (1855), 536-62.

The publication of Caroline Norton's *Letter to the Queen,* and, concurrently, Parliament's discussion of the need for reform of the marriage and divorce laws gave rise to a number of articles in contemporary journals on this topic. The author of one such article, published in the *North British Review,* was J. W. Kaye, a sometime lawyer, professional writer, and military historian, who had spent a good part of his life in India. Having sympathetically read Mrs. Norton's pamphlet, he subsequently wrote several articles demonstrating the legal injustices from which women suffered. Kaye's analysis of the insurmountable problems involved in obtaining a divorce in the years before Parliament passed the Marriage and Divorce Act of 1857, is instructive, but even more significant, is his awareness of the social consequences of the "non-existence" of women.

. . . In England, the first step towards a divorce, is an action for damages, on the part of the husband, against the supposed paramour of the wife. As in these proceedings, the wife is "non-existent," and cannot appear by counsel to defend herself, the chances are that the whole case is prejudged against her, before she has the power of saying a word in her own defence. It is true that her paramour may defend her; but it is not his interest to do so, except by shewing that the husband has offended against his wife, and does not enter Court "with clean hands". But so long as a money-value is set upon the love and fidelity of the woman, it is rather the policy of the defendant's counsel to make it appear that she was a bad than that she was a good wife. The tariff of damages is of course regulated in accordance with the supposed value of the chattel of which the husband is deprived, and it is the professional duty of the defendant's counsel to make this chattel appear as valueless as he can. Now this, which is, we believe, peculiar to the English law, is an injustice at the very outset to the woman. Her character, her position, her very means of subsistence are at stake. She is virtually, though non-existent and unrecognised, on her trial; but she is not permitted to say a word in her own defence. The matter is settled between the two men, as though it were one with which she has nothing to do. It need not be said that if another woman steal *her* life-partner, the damage which she has sustained is not triable by judge, or assessable by jury. There is no pecuniary compensation by law established for her. That idea the world considers as simply too preposterous for a moment's consideration. Doing or suffering wrong, women are "non-existent." The law decrees that they cannot injure each other. . . . It is the perfection of the English law that the only person for whom there is no protection is a virtuous and injured woman.

. . . Facility of divorce would not necessarily produce frequency of divorce. . . . Women, except in cases of grievous, long-continued, and complicated wrong, will not rush to the emancipating tribunal; but it does not follow on that account that such a tribunal ought not to exist. It would be no valid argument against the abolition of slavery . . . that there are many good masters, and that thousands of slaves would not practically demand their freedom if it were to be legally declared. The legal remedy ought still to exist. . . .

It may be said, "But redress is open to the woman—she may sue for a divorce, and having obtained it, she may profit by her own industry." Ostensibly, the law promises divorce in such cases; but practically she denies it. Divorce is for the rich; not for the poor. For the man; not for the woman. If there were any tribunal to which an injured woman could betake herself and say,—"I come before you with an empty purse but a full heart. I have no money wherewith to propitiate the divinity of justice; for the law allows me to possess none. I have only my wrongs to lay at your feet. My husband has deserted me. He is wasting his substance on a strange woman. But he will not suffer me to eat in peace the bread which I have earned with my own hands. He comes to me in my loneliness—vaunts himself my husband—and takes from me the wages of my industry. I now ask to be permitted to eat in quietness the bread which I have earned. I ask that, having ceased to be protected by my husband, I may be protected against my husband. I ask to be dissolved of my allegiance to him—to cease to be a part of him—to bear my own name and to work for myself." If there were any tribunal, we say, to which an Englishwoman could betake herself, needing only the utterance of such solemn words as these to call forth the prompt response, "Stand forth and prove it," then might it be asserted that redress is open to the woman. . . .

. . . It is obvious, that so long as the dissolution of the marriage contract is almost an impossibility, and the marriage contract is what it is, the larger and more important section of the women of England must be legal nonentities. That the effect of this is to limit the aspirations, to paralyze the energies, and to demoralize the characters of women, is not to be denied. . . . We make women what they are—we make them weak, and complain that they are not strong—we reduce them to dependence, and then taunt them with being incapable of independent action. . . . We reduce them to the lowest possible level, keep them there, and revile them for not mounting higher. . . .

This theory of the non-existence of women pursues its victims from the school-room to the grave. Trained from the first to be dependent upon men, they pass through different stages of dependence, and at the last find that they cannot bequeath to another man the ring on their finger, which they may have worn from their earliest girlhood, or the Bible in which they first learnt to spell. To attain and preserve a condition of independence, it is necessary that they should abide in a state of singleness, which is, more or less, a state of reproach. . . . And it is often the perception of this which drives women into matrimony without any assurance, sometimes scarcely even with a hope, of domestic happiness. What else are they to do? If they continue in their singleness, having been educated for non-existence, they are incapable of acting for themselves. They are fit, indeed, only to be absorbed.

And thus it is that this legal fiction of the non-existence of married women sits as a curse upon married and single alike. It taints from first to last the stream of their life. And Heaven only knows what a crop of misery is the rank result. As society is at present constituted, women are educated not to do, but to suffer. . . .

"The Law in Relation to Women", *Westminster Review,* CXXVIII (1887), 698-710.

The following selection is an indictment (by an anonymous author who identifies herself only as a woman) of the English legal system as it affected women even after the passage of the Guardianship of Infants Act of 1886 and the slightly less recent Married Women's Property Acts. Although the author placed the greatest emphasis on the unjust treatment of women in regard to divorce and child custody, she was concerned with other aspects of the legal discrimination of which women were the victims. The plight of English women was, in her view, inescapable while they were dependent on men for relief from their oppression. Even Lord Selbourne, who in another document will be quoted as favoring the principle that a mother *"had natural rights in her children not less than those of the father",* in this excerpt is shown to have participated in a decision which was a gross denial of a woman's right to the custody of her children. It was futile, maintained the author, to depend on masculine chivalry and good intentions to improve the legal condition of women; the single effective cure was political representation, and that could be secured only by giving women the vote.

. . . Any one who applies his mind to the state of the law, even at the present day, as between man and woman, will be astonished and horrified to find how completely the female interest is sacrificed whenever it happens to clash with that of the male. . . .

The first and most glaring injustice to women that strikes the eye of an impartial critic is the law of divorce in England, by which our legislators were not ashamed to enact, so late as 1857, that no amount of infidelity on the part of a husband should entitle a wife to divorce unless it were joined with cruelty. . . . To refuse her the right of divorce while granting it to her husband is deliberately to draw an unjust distinction between the two, and to affirm that what he can do almost with impunity is in her case to be visited with the severest penalties. . . . To deny her the right to obtain divorce is almost to recognize a privilege in the husband to commit adultery. It certainly indicates an opinion that infidelity on his part is a small matter, and one which the wife would do well to say nothing about, and it gives the husband a sense of immunity from punishment which encourages him to continue in a course of profligacy, if so disposed. . . .

As an instance of a wife's failure to obtain divorce take the following case, in the year 1866 . . . which has the more weight as the decision was affirmed by the House of Lords on appeal. A wife petitioned for dissolution of marriage on the ground of adultery and cruelty. Evidence was given of *repeated* acts of adultery committed by the husband in the town near which they were living, at a time when he was cohabiting with his wife. This was not denied. Evidence of the wife as to cruelty was that he had sworn at her, that he took up the poker and said, "I will dash your brains out" (when no one else was in the room); that he threw a brush at her; that he hung up in his room the picture of a lady with whom he had been intimate, and refused to remove it, though it caused her great pain; that on one occasion, in their bedroom, he took up a pillow, threatened to smother her, and put it over her face; that she threw it off and went to the door, when he swung her back, and bolted it. This was denied, but no evidence was led in defence. The judge-ordinary found that there was no appreciable bodily harm inflicted on the petitioner, still less any injuries calculated to interfere with her health or permanent safety. As she threw off the pillow at once, he could not have intended to smother her. *Held,* that cruelty was not proved, and therefore only judicial separation was granted on ground of adultery. Appeal taken to House of Lords. . . . Appeal dismissed. . . .

. . . Our male legislators deliberately laid down the principle in 1857, that let a man be as profligate as he likes, let him break his marriage vow again and again, yet his unhappy spouse shall not be entitled to shake him off; but the utmost alleviation of her misery that shall be allowed her, is the gracious permission to live separately from him. . . . [Furthermore] let the wife be as innocent as day and the husband as guilty as night, it by no means necessarily follows that she is to have the custody of her children. . . . In a leading case, . . . a wife obtained separation on account of her husband's infidelity, and the Court of Session in Scotland gave her the custody of her five children; but the House of Lords partially reversed the decision, and gave the father the custody of the boys, and the mother that of the girls only. In giving judgment Lord Cairns said:

". . . Where a wife established her title either to divorce or separation it was either matter of course, or almost a matter of course, that that should carry with it for her the custody of the children, and that having shown good cause for severing the conjugal tie, she, not being herself in fault, should not be amerced or punished by being deprived of the custody of her children."

That a person who is not in fault should not be punished one would have thought a very excellent doctrine, but that, it appears, is quite a delusion; for Lord Cairns continues:

"My Lords, I should greatly regret that any general rule so sweeping, and as it appears to me so inconvenient in its working, should be laid down on a subject of this description. . . . It appears to me the duty of the Court . . . to consider the whole circumstances of the particular case before it."

Lord O'Hagan said: ". . . The father's right to the guardianship of his child is high and sacred. . . ."

Lord Selbourne concurred with Lords Cairns and O'Hagan. Now, the facts of this case, and which were held as proved by their Lordships, were as follows: — A gentleman of wealth and position seduced a girl of seventeen who was in his house in the position of nurse to his children. Both before and after doing so he accused his wife (falsely in the judgment of the Court) of being given to drinking, and four months after the seduction had taken place he wrote to his wife telling her that as the children grew up they would be "warned against her and her sinful untruthful ways, and that, painful though the duty might be, he would not have them (the children) either misled or contaminated by the neglect of it.'' The best commentary on the man's conduct is to be found in the opinions expressed by the judges in the Court below. The Lord President of the Court of Session said:

"I need hardly say that a husband who has added to the sin of adultery, committed within the sacred precincts of his own house, with a young girl in his own service, the further sin against matrimonial life of bringing wilfully false charges against the moral character of his wife, and threatening as he has done, to bring up his children in the belief of these false charges against their mother, is unfit to have the custody of his pupil children."

Lord Deas said: "We have here not only adultery, accomplished by what I may call seduction under trust, but we have disclosed to us a malignant design, deliberately formed and perseveringly persisted in, on the part of the husband, to ruin the character and credit of his wife, and an intention, declared in his letter of 15th May 1871 — not to this hour retracted — to bring up his children in the belief that she had been guilty of the charges he falsely brought against her."

Even Lord Cairns in the Court above said: "The conduct of the husband in making these charges was that of an obstinate, overbearing, tyrannical man, drawing conclusions from insufficient premises, and blindly refusing to be undeceived in ideas which he had once entertained." Yet this "obstinate, overbearing, tyrannical man," this "seducer under trust," was considered a more fitting person to have the custody of his sons than their innocent mother! . . .

It appears, then, to be settled law both for England and Scotland that the innocent wife may be punished by the loss of her children, in the discretion of the Court; and certainly in Scotland, in cases of separation for cruelty, it appears to be the rule rather than the exception. Here is a Scotch case so monstrous that we feel constrained to give the particulars. . . . A wife obtained separation on account of cruelty. There were five children, the eldest of age, the youngest a girl of four. The wife asked for the custody of all, which was refused; but the Lord Ordinary gave her the youngest. On appeal this was reversed, and the child, like the rest of the family, was handed over to the father. In giving judgment, Lord Deas said: "The defender (i.e., the husband) frequently used bad language towards his wife, addressing her by such epithets as 'blackguard,' 'fool,' 'liar.' It is proved that in 1862 he locked her into the drawing-room, and behaved in a very violent manner, which so greatly alarmed her that she escaped by the window. . . . In 1869 it is proved that the defender struck the pursuer several violent blows upon the head with his clenched fist. She fell, and was taken up insensible, and continued in a helpless state for some time afterwards." Lord Deas was in favour of granting separation, but refusing even the custody of the youngest child. Lord Ardmillan agreed, and said: "The rule, as a general rule, is settled; and notwithstanding his conduct to the mother, we have no reason to dread injury to the health or morals of the child. *To leave his wife with the defender were to subject him to an influence exciting and tempting him to violence towards her. To leave his little child in his house is, or may well be, to introduce a soothing influence to cheer the darkness and mitigate the bitterness of his lot, and bring out the better part of his nature.*" The utter disregard of, and profound contempt for, the feelings of the wife displayed in the last sentence would be amusing, if we could forget the suffering of the victim. Observe that even the separation is granted, not as a protection to her, but rather because "to leave her with her husband were to subject him to an influence exciting him to violence". She must therefore be removed; but his little girl of four will be left with him, in the hope that its "soothing influence" will prevent him breaking any more heads than his wife's, and as a means "to cheer the darkness and mitigate the bitterness" which his own vile temper has produced. That a learned judge should give vent to such sickly sentimentality and unmitigated nonsense as this is surely strong proof that he had great difficulty in giving any reason for his judgment at all. Here is a poor lady, who on one occasion is so frightened by her husband's violence that she jumps out of a window, who is frequently addressed in the vilest language, and who finally is knocked down insensible; and her reward is, that not one of her five children is allowed to live with her, while her husband, instead of getting six months' hard labour, is rewarded by obtaining the custody of all his children, and by the apparent commiseration and pity of the Bench. The desirability of "cheering the darkness and mitigating the bitterness" of the wife's lot does not seem to have crossed the judicial mind at all, and the poor lady obtains absolutely no redress except the privilege of living separate from the brute who had so abused her. . . .

It thus appears clear that both in England and Scotland the custody of the children by no means necessarily falls to the innocent wife. . . . What the practice *ought* to be, is not difficult to see. It should be a clear and definite rule that the innocent party, whether husband or wife, who has succeeded in an action against a spouse, should "*not* be amerced or punished,*"* to use the language of Lord Cairns, by the loss of his or her children. . . .

Matilda M. Blake, "The Lady and the Law", *Westminster Review,* CXXXVII (1892), 364-70.

By 1892, because of recent changes in the law, the courts could not practice to the same degree, the glaring discrimination of which Caroline Norton had been the victim in the 1830's. Nevertheless, the position of English women under the law—particularly with regard to the custody of their children and their property rights—justified the charge that, as late as 1891, it seemed comparable in some respects to slavery. The following excerpt from "The Lady and the Law", by Matilda M. Blake, who, like the anonymous author of the preceding article, advocated female suffrage as the only cure for the evil, illustrates the fact that English law still systematically treated women as inferior beings—to such an extent that a pregnant sow had a better chance of being attended to by a licensed practitioner than the vast majority of pregnant English women had.

. . . It may be useful to bring before the public eye a few of the crying points of injustice in that law of England which Lord Coleridge [Chief Justice of the Court of Queen's Bench] characterises as "more worthy of a barbarian than a civilised State". . . .

Let us begin with what men are never tired of defining as the one paramount function and duty of women—motherhood—and see how a mother's interests, wishes, and what one would suppose to be inalienable rights, are protected by laws in the making of which they have no voice.

Much was done for the mother by the Custody of Infants Act of 1886, but in passing through the Houses of Parliament the Bill was mutilated and rendered imperfect. It by no means establishes equality between the parents. . . .

As the Bill stands, the father can appoint a guardian or guardians to act after his death jointly with the mother, however faultless she may be; whereas the mother can only provisionally appoint such a guardian or guardians to act jointly with the father after her death; and the Court, after her death, will only confirm such an appointment in case it is clearly shown that the father is, *for any cause whatever,* unfit to be the sole guardian of the child.

How small is the mother's power with this proviso may be demonstrated by pointing out that the adulterous life of the father does not disqualify him from claiming custody of the children during the wife's lifetime, provided he does not bring them in contact with his mistress. . . .

Yet the father who is invested with such enormous powers is allowed, if he pleases, to will every farthing that he possesses away from his children, and to leave them helpless and destitute for the community to maintain. We have it on the authority of Chief Justice Cockburn, as an established fact, "that, except under the Poor Laws, there is no legal obligation on the part of the father to maintain his child". . . .

Let us now take the case of the unmarried mother. Whether married or unmarried, a mother is bound to maintain her children. If no contract of marriage has been signed, the mother has discretionary power, within twelve months of the child's birth, to institute proceedings against the father on her own behalf in a court of summary jurisdiction; and if her evidence is corroborated by further testimony "in some material particular"—often cases are dismissed on the ground that there are no witnesses to the act!— she can recover from him a sum varying from sixpence to five shillings a week during the time that she is herself liable in law for the maintenance of her child; not a penny more, however rich the father may be; and this is for *herself*—he has *no* legal obligations whatever to the child. If the mother dies, his liability ceases. Nor is the case altered if he voluntarily admits the paternity, and brings up the child; he can repudiate it when he chooses. . . .

The mothers on whom this sole responsibility is cast may be but a day over sixteen years of age—the law does not protect them beyond it; though they would be held minors in regard to any property belonging to them until they are twenty-one, they are able to "consent" to their own degradation, and the parents and guardians of a girl over sixteen have no remedy against her seducer.

We will now glance at the legal hardships of the wife. It is to be hoped that the decision in the Clitheroe case (1891) has purged from the law of England, once and for all, the reproach of upholding a slavery as absolute as any that ever was inflicted on the negro race by giving the husband right or property in the person of his wife. . . . Yet although in 1891 it was decided that a husband had no right to use violence of any kind on his wife's person, nor to imprison her, and that such rights had never existed, the popular view is, undoubtedly, that both chastisement and imprisonment are the natural prerogative of the husband; and the sentences given for violent assaults by husbands on their wives at police and sessional courts are evidently guided by such a theory of the marriage relationship. Cases might be quoted by scores in which the killing of wives is brought in as manslaughter, and punished by a few years' (or even months') imprisonment.

. . . The Maintenance in case of Desertion Act of 1886 allows a deserted wife to summon her husband for alimony, and authorises magistrates to appoint a sum (in no case to exceed *40s.*) to be paid weekly by a man for the support of his family. This is the extent of the liability of the husband and father for the maintenance of his wife and family, though his income may be thousands annually—just sufficient to keep them off the parish, and no more; for the Act directs the Court, in adjusting the amount to be paid by the husband, to make allowance for the wife's earnings.

Such is the legal value of the promise made by the husband at the altar: "With all my worldly goods I thee endow.'' Moreover, a wife who has property is equally bound to maintain her husband. The Married Women's Property Act of 1882 has, however, made it no longer possible for the bridegroom to say to his bride on returning from church: ''What's mine is my own; what is yours is mine''. Yet, much as that Act did for women—being the deathblow to the old status of *coverture*, by which the individuality of the wife was entirely merged in that of the husband, and she became his "chattel"—it has limitations which need correction. . . .

The greatest wrong of all which the law inflicts upon wives is the maintenance of the Divorce Act of 1857 (to Scotland's honour, be it said, not sanctioned over the Border), which enables a man to obtain divorce by proving simple adultery, but refuses the like relief to the wife of an adulterous husband, unless she can prove in addition that her husband treated her with *legal* cruelty, or has deserted her for a term of two years, virtually condoning adultery as permissible to men; and which further insults and degrades the wife by treating her as the property of the husband, whom it enables to claim money compensation for the loss of his goods from the co-respondent.

In 1887 Mr. Justice Butt pronounced a decree of judicial separation [but not a divorce] in a case in which, after a married life of eleven days, the husband left his wife, coolly informing her that he intended to return to a woman with whom he had lived previously. This case illustrates clearly the cruelty of the law. Here is an innocent woman tied for life to a man who had broken his vows in the most insulting manner, she being left in the anomalous position of being neither maid, wife, nor widow. If she had waited two years in the hope of establishing desertion, she would all that time have been at the mercy of the husband, who could, if it pleased him, have claimed conjugal rights.

Again, the cruelty which must be added to adultery to entitle a wife to a divorce must show ''danger to life and limb.'' Considerable brutality and refined mental torture will yet escape this definition.

Another instance in which the law presses hardly on women is in the distribution of intestate estates. . . .

In the case of personal property: if the intestate die leaving *wife only, no blood relations*—half to wife, half to Crown; *wife, no near relations*—half to wife, rest to next of kin in equal degree to intestate, or their legal representatives; *wife and children*— one-third to wife, the rest to children and issue of dead children; *wife and father*— half to wife, half to father.

If, however, it is the wife who dies, leaving *husband and children*—all to husband. The Crown claims no share in this instance; it is the widow only that it mulcts. Neither have the wife's next of kin, her father or mother, or sisters or brothers, any claim— nor even the children she has risked death to bring into the world; while the widower into whose hands it falls has the right to will every penny of it away from them if he chooses.

In the case of real property, if intestate die leaving *wife only, no blood relations*— one-third to wife for life, rest to Crown, copyholds to the lord of the manor; *husband and children*—husband for life, afterwards to the eldest son or only child; *mother, brothers and sisters*—all to eldest brother; *brother and wife*—one-third to wife for life, rest to brother; *father's father and mother's mother*—all to father's father.

These contrasts will show the spirit of the law. . . .

The civil position of women by the law of this country is on a par with criminals, paupers, and lunatics; and that men do not regard their interests as their own is very abundantly shown by the samples of our laws given above.

Some 656,000 women are engaged in our textile trades alone; but a single line in a Factory Act could snatch the bread from thousands of working women at a stroke. Men are continually interfering with the labour of women, making arbitrary regulations often entailing great hardships, and putting female labour at a disadvantage against male labour, which is free from like restrictions. . . .

Again, legislation for those who cannot give force to their own wishes is often quite mistaken and disastrous in its consequences to them, when meant most kindly; while matters that much need regulation are neglected.

As an instance of such neglect we may take the non-registration of mid-wives. Physicians, surgeons, and chemists have long been compelled to prove their competency by holding diplomas. In 1878 Parliament enacted in the interest of the public that no one should practise or assume the title of *dentist* without holding a diploma which guaranteed his efficiency. In 1883 the same action was taken with regard to veterinary surgeons. No protection is accorded to English mothers, who are without any assured means of ascertaining that the midwives they employ are in any way qualified for the responsible duties they undertake. It is estimated that seven births out of ten are attended by midwives only. . . .

The greatest of all wrongs inflicted on women by the law of England is the denial of Parliamentary vote! this rectified, all other hardships would right themselves by the simple action of their enfranchisement.

Benjamin Scott, F.R.A.S., *A State Iniquity: Its Rise, Extension and Overthrow* (London: Kegan Paul, Trench, Trübner & Co., Ltd., 1890), pp. 14-17, 19-22, 31, 33-41, 99-104, 114, 116, 184-92, 227-30.

It is difficult to imagine legislation more brazenly sexist, even in the context of the times, than the Contagious Diseases Acts of 1864, 1866, and 1869, which authorized the police to subject prostitutes plying their trade in the vicinity of army camps and naval stations to medical examinations, and to confine them to hospitals if they were found to be diseased. Despite the pretense of concern for the prostitutes themselves, the real objective of the Acts was to provide a pool of "clean" females for the sexual gratification of soldiers and sailors in certain "protected" areas.

Alarmed by the appallingly high incidence of venereal disease among members of the armed forces and the consequent impairment of their military effectiveness, the framers of these Acts had succeeded in slipping the first two inconspicuously through a somnolent Parliament which was not aware that it had in effect approved the adoption of procedures similar in some respects to those practiced in France and a number of other Continental nations which had brought prostitution under government supervision and regulation. Subsequently, however, this legislation, which treated women like sexual chattels, was aggressively supported by the Association for the Extension of the Contagious Diseases Acts, by a majority in Parliament, and by leading figures in the Church, the medical profession, the universities, and the military establishment.

Opposed to the Acts were devout laymen, humanitarians of every persuasion, feminists, libertarians, and militant members of the working
classes.

The campaign to repeal the Acts was led in Parliament by James
Stansfeld. But the person who mobilized public opinion in support of
repeal and who, in particular, organized the women of England on a
truly national scale, was a beautiful, dynamic, heroic, and eloquent
woman, Josephine Butler, who dared to discuss openly such topics as
prostitution and venereal disease:

> Women have been told that they must be silent on this subject. Can the soul of my
> sister be defiled, and my own soul not be the worse for it? It cannot; unless indeed I
> rise up in wrath for her redemption, and through the long toils and pains and
> anguish of my life I render back to God my soul for hers (p. 113).

Mrs. Butler carried her crusade to a number of European nations
where prostitution was legalized. At a public meeting in Paris, replying
to the argument of an official that the toleration of prostitution was a
social necessity, she dared to say, "If prostitution is an institution of
public safety such as should be organized by Government, even the Ministers, the Prefect of Police, the high functionaries and the doctors who
defend it fail in their duty if they do not consecrate to it their own
daughters!"[1]

The combination of Josephine Butler's missionary efforts and James
Stansfeld's resolute parliamentary leadership resulted in the repeal of
the Contagious Diseases Acts in 1886. Benjamin Scott, the author of the
document which is excerpted below, was himself an active worker, as his
vehemence indicates, in the cause of repeal.

... On June 20th, 1864, Lord Clarence Paget, the Secretary to the Admiralty,
introduced a "Bill for the Prevention of Contagious Diseases at certain Naval and
Military Stations". It happened that at that time the public mind was in a state of
alarm at the ravages of disease among CATTLE, and Parliament had passed various Acts
of a stringent character, under the title of "Contagious Diseases (Animal) Acts."
The short title of this Act was: —
"CONTAGIOUS DISEASES PREVENTION ACT, 1864."
It craftily cloaked a measure which would otherwise have been distasteful to the public,
if not to Parliament. There were few people outside Parliament who did not suppose
it was another Animals' Act. ...

The Bill passed all its stages rapidly, and without evoking any controversial discus-
sion, and received the Royal assent on July 29th. It applied to Portsmouth, Plymouth,
Woolwich, Chatham, Sheerness, Aldershot, Colchester, Shorncliffe, the Curragh,
Cork, and Queenstown, and was to endure for only three years. It was to be executed
by a special body of Metropolitan Police, under the control of the Admiralty and War
Offices, and not subject to the control of the *local* authorities.

THE ACT PROVIDED

for the certifying of hospitals wherein women infected with venereal disease might be

---

[1] Cited in A. S. G. Butler, *Portrait of Josephine Butler* (London: Faber & Faber Ltd., 1954), p. 118.

officially housed. The Act provided only for women declared to be common prostitutes, no provision was made for the cure of diseased *men*, or their *wives*, or for their innocent *children* inheriting disease. . . .

It was an Act to enforce the physical exploration of prostitutes, in order to see whether any fornicator had so injured her as to make her dangerous material for the use of other fornicators. . . .

There was no whisper of opposition in the country, whilst an Association for extending the operation of the Act which existed under the patronage of the medical profession went to and fro in the country representing the Act to be a *benevolent endeavour* to aid and save the wretched women of the garrison towns. The Act of 1864 would expire in 1867, and the members of this Association wished it to be replaced by a more stringent Act. . . .

The Bill [which] received the Royal assent on June 11th, 1866 . . . was to come into operation on September 30th of that year, when the Act of 1864 was to expire. Like its forerunner, it was entitled "An Act for the Better Prevention of Contagious Diseases at certain Naval and Military Stations".

IT EXTENDED THE AREAS

of the places named in the Act of 1864 (adding the town of Windsor to the number), and the powers to appoint Surgeons and to make regulations for Lock Hospitals, the power to detain women supposed to be infected with venereal disease, the penalty for harbouring a *diseased* prostitute, and conferred the power to

ENFORCE A PERIODICAL SURGICAL EXAMINATION

of the persons of women whom the police *believed* to be "common prostitutes" (a phrase always undefined) by summary proceedings before a Magistrate. . . . It provided that any woman might subject herself to such periodical examinations for a year by signing a form. This Act, in addition to the lesser changes, founded a

"REGISTER OF PROSTITUTES,"

and instituted regular periodical examinations of them. . . .

The Regulationists were satisfied with the system as created by the Act of 1866, but they were dissatisfied with the *extent* of its application. They wished it to be extended to the whole country. . . .

. . . A Bill was introduced into the House of Lords by Lord Northbrook, was rapidly driven through both Houses, and received the Royal assent on August 11th, 1869. This was

THE LAST REGULATION ACT.

It added six more places, viz., Canterbury, Dover, Gravesend, Maidstone, Winchester, and Southampton, to the places named in the Act of 1866, making 18 in all, and increased the areas of those places. It tightened the meshes of the previous Act in a few particulars, but there was little that could be done to make the system more complete. All that was wanted was to make it *universal*.

The system was not a complex one. It may be stated in a few sentences. It formed a special body of police, whose duty it was to force all prostitutes in the areas named to be surgically examined once a fortnight, and as to this end they must make investigation into the habits of all women of the humble classes; they were clothed as civilians, that they might the better make close scrutiny as private detectives. A Register of the women examined was kept, from which no woman could remove her name without formal permission, and any woman ordered to be examined, who refused to regularly submit herself to physical examination, might be imprisoned. Women condemned by the examining surgeons as diseased with a venereal disease were immediately interned in hospitals, where they were detained as prisoners. Brothels were recognized, and not interfered with, if women having the particular disease were not permitted to remain in them. The system was intended to save soldiers and sailors, if possible, from catching these diseases, without limiting their intercourse with prostitutes. And the system dealt with those diseases only as they were to be found in the bodies of *women,* each of whom it regarded as outside the pale of human society, as, in the words of Mr. Lecky, "the priestess of humanity, blasted for the sins of the people," and sought to keep each priestess fitted to perform her sacrificial functions. . . .

THE TASK OF THE POLICE

was to strain every energy to discover clandestine prostitutes and those women who occasionally committed fornication, to bring them, together with the self-advertising harlots, by persuasion or compulsion, to attend periodical surgical examinations, and having securely locked up those diseased in hospitals, to set the rest free to pursue again the practice of vice. . . .

To bring the women to the surgical examinations the police had to obtain a "voluntary submission", or the order of a magistrate. The signing of a

"VOLUNTARY SUBMISSION"

form was the method almost exclusively adopted.

The Act of 1866 in providing for voluntary submission seems to have intended that the form should be signed by women, who freely admitting they were prostitutes, would *willingly* submit to the consequent examinations. Therefore the Act provided no punishment for refusal to be examined after such submission. But, in fact, the women would not attend the examinations. They had to be *compelled,* and to make the submission effective the Act of 1869, by section 6, gave to it the same effect as a magistrate's order. Thereafter the woman who signed the submission form was registered as a prostitute, and if she refused to be surgically examined every fortnight, or if she refused to go into the hospital when ordered to do so, might be *imprisoned with hard labour.* It was a self-inflicted sentence accepted by the State as binding without investigation. . . .

The alluring nature of the inquiries before the magistrates was evidenced by the invariable crush to get a place in the court when such a case was to be heard. At those times prostitutes and men and youths jostled each other in rough play, and vied with each other in making suggestive observations.

Having been made subject to the Acts, the woman's name was entered upon a police Register (upon which were found the names of quite young children as being "common prostitutes"), and she was ordered to report herself once a fortnight to the police inspector, who passed her on to the examining room for examination by the appointed surgeon.

THE FORTNIGHTLY SURGICAL EXAMINATIONS

were the life of the system. Thither the eyes of the special police always turned, and thither every purpose they had tended.

The examining-room was in some places at a certified hospital, but in most places at a house taken for the purpose. Usually this house was in a bye-street, with the houses of poor respectable people beside and opposite to it. *In one case it faced a factory where many girls were employed.* The women had to attend between eleven and two o'clock. The sensation created in the neighbourhood was

A GROSS PUBLIC SCANDAL.

Some of the women arrived in carriages or cabs attended by officers of the Army or

Navy, or by other men, who awaited their return from the examination-room, for if they were passed as sound, the first subsequent intercourse with them was considered safe for the men. Roughs were accustomed to gather about the place of examination, and lavish their gibes and coarse jokes upon the women as they entered and left. The nature and objects of the examinations were openly and freely discussed, not only by adults, but also by young boys and girls; little children

PLAYED AT EXAMINATION

in the open streets! The women awaited their turns in a waiting-room, their names having been entered by the police in the order of their arrival. A number of women of every grade, the worst and the best mingled together, and the scenes which took place were not all of a seemly character.

A nurse was present at the examinations. If a woman was suffering from a natural periodical flux, the surgeon might order her, as though she were a criminal, to be *compulsorily confined* for five days, or until she could be examined, in a certified hospital, where she might be subjected to solitary confinement in a cell, on bread and water diet, if she committed a breach of its rules. . . .

The time occupied in each examination, including preparing for it, was on the average from three to five minutes. There was no common code of instructions for the guidance of examining surgeons. Originally the Admiralty issued instructions to examining surgeons to use the speculum, but these instructions were withdrawn, and they were merely told to satisfy themselves that the women were properly examined. Some specula are very liable to cut in a rapid use of them, the expanding one, for instance, and one medical man, giving evidence on this point, said of any kind of speculum, "if not judiciously managed, a rough introduction might create an abrasion." Some women complained that they had been wounded by the examination.

The speculum ought to be have been properly cleansed and disinfected after each successive use of it. Syphilis is easily transmitted, and the greatest care is required in the cleansing of the instruments; this was often impossible. For instance, evidence was given of 200 examinations in a day. . . .

It was alleged that enough care was not taken by the examining surgeons to thoroughly cleanse and disinfect their specula between their examinations. If this were so, compulsory examination would mean, as no doubt it did, *compulsory infection.* . . .

If, upon examination, a woman was found to be affected with disease, the surgeon gave her a certificate to that effect, stating the certified hospital in which she was to be placed. The police took her straight from the examination-room to the hospital. This was a source of bitter complaint amongst the women. They were taken away suddenly to hospitals a long distance away, sometimes from Southampton to Portsmouth, or from Maidstone to Chatham, and often from Aldershot, Chatham, Canterbury, Deal, Dover, Shorncliffe, and other places to the London Lock Hospital. They had no opportunity afforded them of making any arrangements for a prolonged absence from their homes, though they were often kept in hospital for several months. Many of them had children, for whose support it was necessary to make some provision; and many lived in lodgings, with no one to care for their effects in their absence. They had good cause to complain. When they returned they found children neglected or put into the workhouse, and a big accumulation of rent; or their homes broken up; or their lodgings let to others, and their goods sold to pay for the arrears of rent.

THE HOSPITAL REGULATIONS

were stringent and severe. They were, in fact, *prisons* for the punishment of·disease.

Thus, at Devonport, and Portsmouth, one of the rules was, that a woman interned there could only receive one letter per week, and that only after it had been read by the Chaplain. In 1874, Emily Hayes was sent to the Portsmouth Hospital, though she protested that she was not diseased. Mr. Harfield, a solicitor, went to the hospital, and asked to see her as her legal adviser. He was *refused admission,* and a letter he sent informing her of the power she possessed of appealing to a magistrate was withheld from her during the several weeks she was detained there, and was *only given to her just before she was discharged and was leaving the hospital.* No criminal would have been so cruelly treated. . . .

. . . The certified hospitals were *state prisons* for the women condemned by the examining surgeon *without power of appeal.* Some of the women were confined in cells for considerable periods by the mere orders of the hospital authorities, and without any judicial intervention. And yet many were sent

INTO THESE PRISONS IN PERFECT HEALTH.

Four surgeons at the Devonport Hospital reported that "*numerous cases* have been admitted to the hospital from time to time in which no symptoms of contagious diseases have been found present on their admission to hospital."

Every woman upon the Register, whether she had ceased to be a prostitute or not, *even though she had married in the meantime,* was subjected to imprisonment if she failed to attend the periodical surgical examinations. Some of the recorded instances were peculiarly cruel. Susan White, having been induced to sign a "voluntary" submission retreated to one of the Homes of the London Rescue Society, where her conduct was exceedingly good. Presently she left the Home *to be married* from her mother's house at Dover, and there she was apprehended by the police, and imprisoned for fourteen days *with hard labour* for not having attended the fortnightly examinations! The cogent evidence of her complete reformation failed to placate the police, who thoroughly understood that the object of their employ was *not* the rescue of the fallen from an immoral life, but the supply of prostitutes to the State. . . .

WOMEN COMBATANTS—THE WOMEN'S PROTEST.

Other means not availing, it became necessary to rouse the women of England to oppose the Contagious Diseases Acts. The nature of the Acts made it necessary and just, but at the same time indescribably difficult for women to publicly refer to and actively combat the Acts and the system created by them. Men avoided the subject as much as they could, and preferred to let the Acts exist rather than incur the frowns of incredulous people by stating in public the disgusting details of the system. The press only broke its almost uniform and perpetual silence by publishing occasionally some officially communicated paragraph, which asserted in words or in figures that the Acts were conferring incalculable benefit on the men and women of the districts wherein they were in operation.

The two great political parties eschewed the question until towards the close of the struggle for repeal, when the Liberal party adopted the principle of repeal and accepted the votes of Repealers. With but one or two exceptions, none of the party leaders ever referred to the question in or out of the House of Commons, save to answer the question, which, in course of time, was frequently put, "Will you vote for the repeal of the Contagious Diseases Act?"

. . . Because the managers of the parties looked askance on the repeal movement, the rank and file of the parties did the same.

Repealers had everything against them in the world of politics. The Acts were in existence; by the few who knew of them they were regarded as military ordinances necessary to the maintenance of the Army and Navy; they were carried by a Liberal Government, they were publicly supported by the leaders of both parties, and by military and naval men, by several Bishops and many Clergymen, by some Nonconformist divines, and by crowds of doctors. They had the silent acquiescence of the press, even of the religious press, and they had the protection of the universal silence about them because the discussion of them savoured of nastiness.

The Repealers themselves were, at the outset, a small band of persons, who had to study the system and make known the facts as they discovered them. They were of no great influence in the country, and were regarded and spoken of by politicians as sentimental faddists. It was clear that to obtain the repeal of the Acts, some new force was required in public affairs; that force was

THE VOICE OF THE WOMEN.

. . . Already, before the repeal movement began, women of great ability and of exalted character had been claiming and winning for their sex a higher education. In the painful struggle for repeal they entered as moralists into the political arena, and won a great victory for themselves, for their sex, and for the morality of the nation. . . .

. . . A woman was the only one who [had] called public attention to the proposals of the Regulationists before the Act of 1864, though the articles in the *Daily News* in 1863, written by MISS HARRIET MARTINEAU, seem to have attracted little attention at the time. In 1869 that lady was infirm and incapable of active exertion, but she made herself heard once more on the subject. She wrote to the *Daily News* four letters, over the signature

"AN ENGLISHWOMAN,"

in which she renewed her protest against the regulation system. They appeared in that paper just at the close of the year 1869, and it was intended that they should be followed by a formal Women's Protest. . . .

This protest [published on New Year's Day, 1870] was drawn up by Miss Martineau, and was signed by many honoured women, amongst whom were HARRIET MARTINEAU, FLORENCE NIGHTINGALE, MARY CARPENTER, and JOSEPHINE BUTLER.

As it set forth the principles upon which *women* entered into the struggle, and upon which . . . the struggle was maintained unvarying to the end, we insert it. It was as follows: —

We, the undersigned, enter our solemn PROTEST against these Acts—

1st. — Because, involving as they do, such a momentous change in the legal safeguards hitherto enjoyed by women in common with men, they have been passed, not only without the knowledge of the country, but unknown to Parliament itself; and we hold that neither the Representatives of the People, nor the Press, fulfill the duties which are expected of them, when they allow such legislation to take place without the fullest discussion.

2nd. — Because, so far as women are concerned, they remove every guarantee of personal security which the law has established and held sacred, and put their reputation, their freedom, and their persons absolutely in the power of the Police.

3rd. — Because the law is bound, in any country professing to give civil liberty to its subjects, to define clearly an offence which it punishes.

4th. — Because it is unjust to punish the sex who are the victims of a vice, and leave unpunished the sex who are the main cause, both of the vice and its dreaded consequences; and we consider that liability to arrest, forced surgical examination, and (where this is resisted) imprisonment with hard labour, to which these Acts subject women, are punishment of the most degrading kind.

5th. — Because, by such a system, the path of evil is made more easy to our sons, and to the whole of the youth of England; inasmuch as a moral restraint is withdrawn the moment the State recognizes, and provides convenience for, the practice of a vice which it thereby declares to be necessary and venial.

6th. — Because these measures are cruel to the women who come under their action — violating the feelings of those whose sense of shame is not wholly lost, and further brutalising even the most abandoned.

7th. — Because the disease which these Acts seek to remove has never been removed by any such legislation. The advocates of the system have utterly failed to show, by statistics or otherwise, that these regulations have, in any case, after several years' trial, and when applied to one sex only, diminished disease, reclaimed the fallen, or improved the general morality of the country. We have, on the contrary, the strongest evidence to show that in Paris and other continental cities where women have long been outraged by this forced inspection, the public health and morals are worse than at home.

8th. — Because the conditions of this disease, in the first instance, are moral, not physical. The moral evil through which the disease makes its way separates the case entirely from that of the plague, or other scourges, which have been placed under police control or sanitary care. We hold that we are bound, before rushing into the experiment of legalising a revolting vice, to try to deal with the *causes* of the evil, and we dare to believe that with wiser teaching and more capable legislation, those causes would not be beyond control.

This protest (to which thousands of names were subsequetly added) was rightly regarded at the time of its publication to be of such importance that news of it was telegraphed to every place where the Acts were in operation, and it attracted the attention of the chiefs of the *police des moeurs* of Paris and other Continental cities. . . .

. . . The great difficulty experienced by Repealers was to get information of the system to the people. . . . The newspapers, the organized means of disseminating information, either excluded all reference to the subject, or inserted the Army and Navy Medical Reports and the Reports of Captain Harris, of the Metropolitan Police, which claimed great moral and physical advantages from the existence of the Acts. Some publications, notably *The Saturday Review,* not only recited the praises of the Acts, but also flung offensive and filthy epithets at the opponents of them. . . .

. . . A meeting was held (on January 19th, 1870), at which "the Metropolitan Anti-Contagious Diseases Acts Association" was formed. . . .

Mr. Robert Charleton moved, and Professor F. W. Newman seconded, the first resolution, which was — "That the extension of the so-called Contagious Diseases Acts to the civil population of the United Kingdom would be highly inexpedient, inasmuch as the provisions and operations of the Acts are entirely contrary to the first principles of English law and custom, are inimical to morality and destructive of liberty, without being at the same time effectual for the prevention of disease; and this meeting is further of opinion that

THE ACTS ALREADY PASSED SHOULD BE REPEALED."

. . . There existed in 1873 at least a dozen different societies in the United Kingdom, working in accord for the Repeal of the Acts. . . .

On Nov. 11th, 1874, the Northern Counties' League held a conference and a public meeting at Bradford, which was addressed by Mr. Stansfeld, Mrs. Butler, and others. Such conferences and meetings were being held frequently in various parts of the country, under the auspices of the different societies for repeal; but this conference is specially referred to, as affording an

EXAMPLE OF MRS. BUTLER'S ELOQUENCE,

for it was the spirit that breathed through her words which had made the movement what it was, and which subsequently raised it to the height of its great success. . . .

MRS. BUTLER SAID—

"Others will have practical questions to bring before you. I hope it will not be considered impractical, however, if I dwell for a few minutes on that which it is needful for us all to think of frequently—the far-reaching character of our movement, and the radical nature of the principles which it involves. . . . The question which we have raised in this nineteenth century, lies at the root of all that most vitally affects the life of nations, and the progress of the human race. Looking back over the five short years of our labours, we cannot but be struck by seeing how, under the energizing influence of a searching test-question addressed to the consciences of men, the field of our operations has widened, and the evil has deepended, since the time when we first challenged public opinion on this root question of human life—the true relation of the sexes. . . .

. . . It is manifest that on all sides it begins to be felt that the principle is to be decided whether male profligacy, at the expense of women, is to be condoned, excused, and darkly perpetrated, or to be sternly condemned and pertinaciously resisted. This question has got to be answered—to be answered first by England, before Europe and the whole world. The answer to this question involves the sweeping away of that whole corrupt fabric of injustice and inequality in matters moral, and in the relations of men and women, upon which, alone, was it possible for men to erect this

LAST ABOMINATION OF LEGALIZED VICE AND SLAVERY.

In the answer to this question is involved the expulsion from men's minds of the radical and woe-working error that a woman was made *for man*, and not, equally with himself, for God—a being, not permitted merely, but morally bound before God to command the uses of her soul, alone, upon the threshold of her individual being, to appear and answer before God, with no sacrilegious and impotent interposition of man, for vicarious responsibility or selfish protection.

"When, in the whole course of the life and teaching of Him whom we call Lord and Master, do we find Him subjecting women to the will, government, or caprice of men, or in any way sanctioning the notion that superior physical strength is to constitute the ultimate appeal in deciding the relations to each other of immortal and spiritual beings? When do we find Him assigning her a place as a mere minister to the male sex, for his convenience or pleasure, or even for his highest good, save in the sense in which we are all divinely called to minister to, and not to hinder each other's moral and spiritual growth? When do we ever find Him showing such a partiality for the stronger sinner, man, as to 'stamp out' the remotest possibility of moral recovery, or the feeblest sparks of lingering humanity, in the most wretched of outcast women, in order that the

STRONGER SINNER MIGHT SIN WITHOUT SUFFERING?

On the contrary, be it observed, His dealings with women, even more emphatically than with men, expressed a setting free, a loosing of bonds, an elevation to equality of dignity with man; not by increasing the weight of her skull, or adding strength to her muscles, but by bestowing wisdom, humanity, holiness, and power. . . . Contagious Diseases Acts, framed for the careful superintendence of women devoted to the systematic service of the lusts of men, will disappear from the face of the earth, together with their originators and patrons, when we shall have succeeded in bringing our accepted and conventional morality

FACE TO FACE WITH JESUS OF NAZARETH. . . .

There is no time to lose, for the work of corruption is rapid, and will not be counteracted by efforts made in the few spare moments of men who are so taken up with their money-making, their dinner-parties, their church and chapel affairs, and their own family matters, as to have neither time nor money to spare for this pressing cause. Each day,

MORE AND MORE APPALLING EVIDENCE

reaches us that the regulation system creates horrors far beyond those which it is supposed to restrain. . . .

"Vice once stimulated by this atrocious system, imagines and dares all unutterable things; and such things perplex with misery the lives of parents of missing children in continental cities, and daunt the courage of rulers, and madden the moral sense, and gnaw the conscience of whole orders of sinners and sufferers of whom we can form no conception here. We shall have entered upon our national decline whenever we slacken our efforts in opposing such a system. . . .

". . . We hear much *talk* about Christianity, we want the reality now. . . .

". . . In the contest against slavery in America, men and women gave up fortune, home, friends, and life itself. The system against which we contend is one which has as deeply corrupted the life of nations as Negro Slavery has done; the evil we oppose is rooted in a *yet more cruel negation of human brotherhood, and a more immoral violation of the principle of liberty.* . . .

"The Victory, which may not be near, but which is *certain*, will be not merely the repulse of an attack by the enemy of all good, but a turning point in the history of our country and the world. Our battle belongs to a great and extensive field of spiritual war; we are standing at a key position, and are called to promote a revival of faith on the earth, with higher views of righteousness and purity. No matter, if we, the pioneers, lay our bones in the dust, others will pass over them to victory. Let us remember the cry of the Crusaders (and ours is a better crusade),

'GOD WILLS IT, GOD WILLS IT!' "

[*Editors' note: The author then traces in detail the efforts over the next twelve years of Mrs. Butler and Mr. Stansfeld as well as those of the various societies organized to secure repeal. In March 1886 Mr. Stansfeld once again introduced a bill calling for the repeal of the Contagious Diseases Acts. Passed by both Houses of Parliament, the bill was signed by the Queen on April 16, 1886.*]

REPEAL HAD FINALLY TRIUMPHED. . . .

The victory of the Repeal party was thus final and complete. They had done something more than blot out the stain of these Acts upon the Statute Book. So said Mr. Stansfeld in his speech which ushered in the triumph of Repeal. . . .

He said: "I have spoken of our seventeen years' work. Our difficulties have been enormous—from the nature of the subject, from the unwillingness of this House, or a former House, to entertain it, from the unwillingness of the Press to ventilate it in their columns. But there is one sense, and that the highest sense, in which I make no complaint. Very early in this movement, I came to the conclusion that it was not desirable to seek to obtain a

TOO SPEEDY OR A MERE TACTICAL SUCCESS,

. . . because I knew what the object was for which I, and hundreds and thousands of other men and women in this country, had determined to make every necessary sacrifice, for any necessary number of years, to accomplish; and that it was not merely the repealing of these Acts, but something far deeper, far higher, far more momentous than that: it was the arousing and the awakening of the popular mind to the dangers, and the degradations, and the crimes of the growing sexual vice of this country. . . . I have the strongest conviction that when we shall have turned from this hopeless legislation, and repealed, and rejected, and destroyed it . . . I believe each and all of us will become conscious of a great relief—become conscious of the possession of a new and higher ideal, a new and sustaining and well-grounded hope, a general rise in the moral health of the community, and in the spirit of true manliness—

A SPIRIT WHICH WILL RESPECT WOMEN, EVEN WHEN UNREFORMED

and that will be our permanent justification and reward for the course we have adopted."

Thus fell in Great Britain the GIANT INIQUITY—the State-recognition, regulation, and sanitation of a degrading vice. . . .

CHAPTER VIII

"Votes for Women, Votes for Donkeys, Votes for Dogs!"[1]

It is usually assumed that the women's suffrage movement began with those indomitable ladies, the Pankhursts. Although it is true that the drive for the vote achieved a spectacular notoriety while they dominated it from 1903 onward, the movement owed its origins to more decorous parents almost four decades earlier.

The demand for the franchise had, in fact, a long history. Even in the first half of the nineteenth century, voices had been raised in favor of giving women the vote. In the late 1830's, some Chartists, as we have seen, advocated the inclusion of women in the demand for universal suffrage; Richard Cobden, the guiding spirit of the Anti-Corn Law League, publicly announced in 1845 his support of voting rights for women; a few years later, the Sheffield Association for Female Franchise was born, and its members (one of whom was Anne Knight of Chelmsford, a Quaker who had issued in 1847 the first leaflet on women's suffrage) vowed to rectify the injustices arising out of the exclusion of women from politics. But, while all of these actions evidence concern for the representation of women, none provided a carefully reasoned, intellectual argument which would justify the extension of political rights to women. Nor was there any need to do so, for that task had been masterfully accomplished in 1825 when William Thompson, a Benthamite and socialist, published his *Appeal of One Half the Human Race, Women, Against the Pretensions of the Other Half, Men.* This was a rejoinder to an article on government written by another disciple of Bentham, James Mill, for the 1823 Supplement to the *Encyclopaedia Britannica.* Mill took the Benthamite position that the best form of government was representative democracy. But, while the corollary to that would seem to be (since Bentham maintained that all individuals were equally important) a vote for everybody, male and female alike, both Bentham and Mill drew back from that logical implication of their doctrine.

Bentham's advocacy of universal suffrage was somewhat theoretical;

[1] An anonymous street boy, cited in Katherine Roberts, *Pages from the Diary of a Militant Suffragette* (Letchworth and London: Garden City Press Limited, Printers, 1910), p. 13.

while he acknowledged its necessity, he felt that it was not yet expedient to give women the vote. Mill, on the other hand, attempted to reconcile his belief in political democracy with the contradictory notion that all individuals (i.e., women and children) whose interests were supposedly represented by their husbands or fathers, might "without inconvenience" be denied political rights. This position infuriated Thompson, who demanded that Mill retract his discriminatory statements. When he refused, Thompson wrote his impassioned *Appeal,* which called for complete equality of the sexes in every sense of the word—politically, economically, socially, and even sexually!

Obviously, Thompson's arguments, which in some respects might be considered radical even by today's standards, were too advanced for the times. It is likely, in fact, that the advocacy of equal rights for women coming from so tainted a source was actually prejudicial to that cause. At any rate, almost nothing of a practical nature contributing to the advancement of women's political rights was accomplished for nearly forty years. By the 1860's, however, some of the feminists who had heretofore devoted their energies to law reform, social work, education, and employment, now proceeded to agitate for woman's suffrage. Political change was in the air. The reform bill of 1866 was being debated by Parliament. In that year John Stuart Mill presented to the House of Commons "The Ladies' Petition", which called for giving women exactly the same voting rights as those enjoyed by men. He also made several speeches in Commons in favor of political equality, for which he was ridiculed and abused by his fellow parliamentarians. The Reform Bill of 1867, of course, made neither mention of women nor concessions to them; their claims were simply ignored.

Mill was not altogether alone in his support of feminist aspirations. A few other eminent men came out in favor of emancipation. For example, the renowned Christian Socialist, Charles Kingsley, in an article published in 1869, asked:

> Who will say that Mrs. Fry, or Miss Nightingale, or Miss Burdett Coutts, is not as fit to demand pledges of a candidate at the hustings on important social questions as any male elector; or to give her deliberate opinion thereon, in either House of Parliament, as any average M.P. or peer of the realm? And if it be said that these are only brilliant exceptions, the rejoinder is, What proof have you of that? You cannot pronounce on the powers of the average till you have tried them. These exceptions rather prove the existence of unsuspected and unemployed strength below.[1]

Kingsley, like many other feminists, came to believe that only through getting the franchise would the other goals of the woman's movement — employment and education — be achieved.

But Mill and Kingsley were exceptions. Most of the prominent men of the period, and practically all the leading politicians, regarded the

[1] "Women and Politics", p. 558.

granting of the vote to women as either preposterous, subversive, immoral, or impractical. Nevertheless, a small but dedicated band of women, led by such ladies as Millicent Garrett Fawcett, Lydia Becker, and Helen Blackburn, went on writing pamphlets, editing journals, conducting drawing-room discussions, giving lectures, and holding mass meetings. These activities, in addition to those of local women's suffrage societies which had been established in the late sixties, prepared the groundwork for the change which would eventually take place—but it was a hard and at times apparently thankless task. It was made more difficult by the opposition not only of the male establishment, which could have been expected, but of many prominent women of the period who were vehemently opposed to equal rights for their sex. There were even more women, of course, who were simply indifferent to the question.[1]

Not only had feminists failed in their attempts to secure the vote by the end of the century, but, to some observers, they seemed to be confronted by obstacles even more formidable than those they had faced twenty-five or thirty years earlier. The division of opinion among suffragists as to whether the projected franchise should include married women; the death of the indefatigable Lydia Becker; the dogged opposition of the leadership of both political parties (in particular, that of Mr. Gladstone), and the fact that in the intervening years the electorate had grown from about 1,000,000 to more than 6,300,000 (leaving sex the sole ground for exclusion), moved one frustrated suffragist to describe the position of women as more "obnoxious and painful" than before.[2]

The movement for female suffrage was about to enter a new phase, characterized by tighter organization, stricter discipline, and increased aggressiveness. Richard M. Pankhurst, a Manchester socialist who had for years been active in support of women's rights, was joined in this

[1] In 1905 Emily Davies observed that, even among the graduates of women's colleges, "comparatively few seriously object to it [women's suffrage], but also that not many care about it". Miss Davies traced the apathy to "pre-occupation with other interests". See "The Women's Suffrage Movement", reprinted in *Thoughts on Some Questions Relating to Women*, p. 201. Annie Besant, on the other hand, suggested that the indifference of women to the franchise was due to something more fundamental: The "bitterest curse of oppression" is that "it crushes out in the breast of the oppressed the very wish to be free. . . . Habit, custom make hard things easy. If a woman is educated to regard man as her natural lord, she will do so". *The Political Status of Women*, 3rd ed. (London: Freethought Publishing Company: n.d.), pp. 7-8.

[2] IGNOTA, "Women's Suffrage", *Westminster Review*, CXLVIII (1897), 364. Two years later this same observer recorded the bitterness felt during the 1890's by those women "who had given many of the best years of [their] lives" to the cause of female emancipation, but who nevertheless "were told by young men — men who were in their cradles whilst some of us were working hard to secure the very rights which they claimed to have freely given us — how men had out of their boundless generosity given to us (that is, to the married women of us) the right to our own property, and also some right to the custody of our own children. To those of us present . . . it seemed that these men ought rather to have asked our pardon for the usurpation and slow restitution of these human and social rights than to have claimed credit for that which they never lifted a finger to do". IGNOTA, "Privilege v. Justice to Women", *Westminster Review*, CLII (1899), 128. She maintained subsequently that the years after 1884 had witnessed an increase in "masculine degradation", which, furthermore, had "so corrupted and perverted human sentiment that there [was] far less enthusiasm or effort now for any wise or just social reform than there was fifteen years ago". "Woman's Lost Citizenship", *Westminster Review*, CLIX (1903), 512-13.

cause by his wife, Emmeline, and later by their daughters, Christabel and Sylvia. Finding the Manchester Suffrage Society too moderate for their tastes, the Pankhursts founded the Women's Social and Political Union in 1903 and agitated for a government-sponsored bill which should grant "Votes for Women". Becoming convinced, after repeated disappointments, that only a show of force would compel the government to make any concessions, the Pankhursts embarked on a program of steadily increasing militancy, which alienated not only large segments of the general public, but even those women who had led the movement through its gradualist, non-violent phase. Freely expending blood, sweat, tears, and petrol, the Pankhurst ladies and their militant cohorts committed arson, smashed shop windows, damaged *objets d'art,* violated the sanctity of the postal system, provoked the police into arresting them, refused to eat when confined to jail, had to be forcibly fed, tempted violent death (and in Emily Davison's case, actually suffered it), and kept London in an uproar. These tactics were based on the assumption that getting the vote was all-important, because there could be no effective change in the position of women until they gained political rights. (To their opponents, of course, political rights for women — given their numerical superiority — would inevitably lead to a gynocracy, which no upstanding Englishman — red-blooded or not — could contemplate without his gorge rising.) The consequence of the Pankhursts' single-minded concentration on getting the vote was that activities on behalf of other social causes were held to be an unjustifiable diversion of energies which could be most profitably employed in the battle for the vote.

While it is debatable whether this strategy was effective in advancing the cause of women's suffrage in the long run, there seems little doubt that in the years prior to the outbreak of World War I, the movement was an utter failure.

[Harriet Taylor], "Enfranchisement of Women", *Westminster Review,* LX (1851), 150-61.

John Stuart Mill and Harriet Taylor, whom he met in 1830 when she was the wife of John Taylor, and married in 1851 after Taylor's death, enjoyed a relationship which was the subject of gossip by their contemporaries and is still a matter of interest to scholars. It is generally assumed that while they were profoundly devoted to one another, their attachment was primarily intellectual.

According to Mill, Mrs. Taylor was a unique combination of spiritual and intellectual resources so profound that she was literally a paragon of all the virtues. Her influence on Mill was undoubtedly great, but it is difficult to determine exactly what her share was in the publications, such as the *Political Economy,* that Mill referred to as their "joint production".[1] But there is an article, obviously the product of an incisive mind, which appeared anonymously in the July 1851 issue of the *Westminster Review,* and which is now accepted as her work. Mill later acknowledged that she had been the source of many of the ideas he advanced in *The Subjection of Women,* which was published in 1869, eighteen years after her article appeared. In fact, her views on such subjects as the employment of women were more explicit and radical than those of Mill. She assailed society's narrow definition of the female role, which effectively imprisoned women in her "proper sphere", thereby excluding her from professional activities and civic responsibilities and, unlike those of her contemporaries who argued for a partial improvement in the position of women, she called for nothing less than complete emancipation, with the object of enabling women to function as the equals of men in every respect: socially, legally, and politically.

. . . There has arisen in the United States . . . an organised agitation on a new question . . . new, and even unheard of, as a subject for public meetings and practical political action. This question is, the enfranchisement of women; their admission, in law, and in fact, to equality in all rights, political, civil, and social, with the male citizens of the community.

. . . The agitation which has commenced is not a pleading by male writers and orators *for* women; . . . it is a movement not merely *for* women, but *by* them. . . . On the 23rd and 24th of October last, a succession of public meetings was held at Worcester, in Massachusetts, under the name of a "Women's Rights Convention," of which the president was a woman, and nearly all the chief speakers women; numerously reinforced, however, by men, among whom were some of the most distinguished leaders in the kindred cause of negro emancipation. . . .

That the promoters of this new agitation take their stand on principles, and do not fear to declare these in their widest extent, without time-serving or compromise, will be seen from the resolutions adopted by the Convention . . . [which proclaim that every qualified human being should have a voice in legislation; that those who are taxed should be directly represented; that women are entitled to vote and should be eligible for office; that all persons, regardless of sex or color, should be equal in law and in the exercise of their civil and political rights; that women should be afforded opportunities for commercial and professional employment; that the education of women must necessarily be a failure until they are given political rights; and that married women should have property rights identical to those of their husbands].

. . . That women have as good a claim as men have, in point of personal right, to the suffrage, or to a place in the jury-box, it would be difficult for anyone to deny. It cannot certainly be denied by the United States of America, as a people or as a community. Their democratic institutions rest avowedly on the inherent right of everyone to a voice in the government. Their Declaration of Independence, framed by the men who are still their great constitutional authorities—that document which has been from the first, and is now, the acknowledged basis of their polity, commences with this express statement:—

---

[1] F. A. Hayek, *John Stuart Mill and Harriet Taylor* (Chicago: The University of Chicago Press, 1951), p. 118.

"We hold these truths to be self-evident: that all men are created equal; that they are endowed by their Creator with certain inalienable rights; that among these are life, liberty, and the pursuit of happiness; that to secure these rights, governments are instituted among men, deriving their just powers from the consent of the governed."

We do not imagine that any American democrat will evade the force of these expressions by the dishonest or ignorant subterfuge, that "men," in this memorable document, does not stand for human beings, but for one sex only; that "life, liberty, and the pursuit of happiness" are "inalienable rights" of only one moiety of the human species; and that "the governed," whose consent is affirmed to be the only source of just power, are meant for that half of mankind only, who, in relation to the other, have hitherto assumed the character of *governors*. The contradiction between principle and practice cannot be explained away. A like dereliction of the fundamental maxims of their political creed has been committed by the Americans in the flagrant instance of the negroes. . . . It was fitting that the men whose names will remain associated with the extirpation, from the democratic soil of America, of the aristocracy of colour, should be among the originators, for America and for the rest of the world, of the first collective protest against the aristocracy of sex; a distinction as accidental as that of colour, and fully as irrelevant to all questions of government.

Not only to the democracy of America, the claim of women to civil and political equality makes an irresistible appeal, but also to those radicals and chartists in the British islands, and democrats on the Continent, who claim what is called universal suffrage as an inherent right, unjustly and oppressively withheld from them. For with what truth or rationality could the suffrage be termed universal, while half the human species remain excluded from it? To declare that a voice in the government is the right of all, and demand it only for a part — the part, namely, to which the claimant himself belongs — is to renounce even the appearance of principle. The chartist who denies the suffrage to women, is a chartist only because he is not a lord; he is one of those levellers who would level only down to themselves.

Even those who do not look upon a voice in the government as a matter of personal right, nor profess principles which require that it should be extended to all, have usually traditional maxims of political justice with which it is impossible to reconcile the exclusion of all women from the common rights of citizenship. It is an axiom of English freedom that taxation and representation should be co-extensive. Even under the laws which give the wife's property to the husband, there are many unmarried women who pay taxes. It is one of the fundamental doctrines of the British constitution, that all persons should be tried by their peers: yet, women, whenever tried, are tried by male judges and a male jury. To foreigners the law accords the privilege of claiming that half the jury should be composed of themselves; not so to women. Apart from maxims of detail, which represent local and national rather than universal ideas; it is an acknowledged dictate of justice to make no degrading distinctions without necessity. In all things the presumption ought to be on the side of equality. A reason must be given why anything should be permitted to one person and interdicted to another. But when that which is interdicted includes nearly everything which those to whom it is permitted most prize, and to be deprived of which they feel to be most insulting; when not only political liberty but personal freedom of action is the prerogative of a caste; when even in the exercise of industry, almost all employments which task the higher faculties in an important field, which lead to distinction, riches, or even pecuniary independence, are fenced round as the exclusive domain of the predominant section . . . , the

miserable expediencies which are advanced as excuses for so grossly partial a dispensa-
tion, would not be sufficient, even if they were real, to render it other than a flagrant
injustice. While, far from being expedient, we are firmly convinced that the division
of mankind into two castes, one born to rule over the other, is in this case, as in all
cases, an unqualified mischief; a source of perversion and demoralization, both to the
favoured class and to those at whose expense they are favoured; producing none of the
good which it is the custom to ascribe to it, and forming a bar, almost insuperable
while it lasts, to any really vital improvement, either in the character or in the social
condition of the human race. . . .

We deny the right of any portion of the species to decide for another portion, or any
individual for another individual, what is and what is not their "proper sphere." The
proper sphere for all human beings is the largest and highest which they are able to
attain to. What this is, cannot be ascertained, without complete liberty of choice. . . .
To interfere beforehand by an arbitrary limit, and declare that whatever be the genius,
talent, energy, or force of mind of an individual of a certain sex or class, those faculties
shall not be exerted, or shall be exerted only in some few of the many modes in which
others are permitted to use theirs, is not only an injustice to the individual, and a detri-
ment to society, which loses what it can ill spare, but is also the most effectual mode of
providing that, in the sex or class so fettered, the qualities which are not permitted to
be exercised shall not exist. . . .

. . . If those who assert that the "proper sphere" for woman is the domestic, mean
by this that they have not shown themselves qualified for any other, the assertion evinces
great ignorance of life and of history. Women have shown fitness for the highest social
functions, exactly in proportion as they have been admitted to them. By a curious
anomaly, though ineligible to even the lowest offices of state, they are in some countries admitted to the highest of all, the regal; and if there is any one function for which
they have shown a decided vocation, it is that of reigning. Not to go back to ancient
history, we look in vain for abler or firmer rulers than Elizabeth; than Isabella of
Castile; than Maria Teresa; than Catherine of Russia; than Blanche, mother of Louis
IX. of France; than Jeanne d'Albret, mother of Henri Quatre. There are few kings on
record who contended with more difficult circumstances, or overcame them more
triumphantly, than these. . . .

Concerning the fitness, then, of women for politics, there can be no question: but
the dispute is more likely to turn upon the fitness of politics for women. When the
reasons alleged for excluding women from active life in all its higher departments, are
stripped of their garb of declamatory phrases, and reduced to the simple expression of
a meaning, they seem to be mainly three: the incompatibility of active life with maternity, and with the cares of a household; secondly, its alleged hardening effect on the
character; and thirdly, the inexpediency of making an addition to the already excessive
pressure of competition in every kind of professional or lucrative employment.

The first, the maternity argument, is usually laid most stress upon: although (it
needs hardly be said) this reason, if it be one, can apply only to mothers. It is neither
necessary nor just to make imperative on women that they shall be either mothers or
nothing; or that if they have been mothers once, they shall be nothing else during the
whole remainder of their lives. Neither women or men need any law to exclude them
from an occupation, if they have undertaken another which is incompatible with it.
No one proposes to exclude the male sex from Parliament because a man may be a
soldier or sailor in active service, or a merchant whose business requires all his time

and energies. Nine-tenths of the occupations of men exclude them *de facto* from public life, as effectually as if they were excluded by law; but that is no reason for making laws to exclude even the nine-tenths, much less the remaining tenth. The reason of the case is the same for women as for men. There is no need to make provision by law that a woman shall not carry on the active details of a household, or of the education of children, and at the same time practise a profession or be elected to parliament. Where incompatibility is real, it will take care of itself: but there is gross injustice in making the incompatibility a pretense for the exclusion of those in whose case it does not exist. And these, if they were free to choose, would be a very large proportion. The maternity argument deserts its supporters in the case of single women, a large and increasing class of the population; a fact which, it is not irrelevant to remark, by tending to diminish the excessive competition of numbers, is calculated to assist greatly the prosperity of all. There is no inherent reason or necessity that all women should voluntarily choose to devote their lives to one animal function and its consequences. Numbers of women are wives and mothers only because there is no other career open to them, no other occupation for their feelings or their activities. Every improvement in their education, and enlargement of their faculties—everything which renders them more qualified for any other mode of life, increases the number of those to whom it is an injury and an oppression to be denied the choice. To say that women must be excluded from active life because maternity disqualifies them for it, is in fact to say, that every other career should be forbidden them in order that maternity may be their only resource.

But secondly, it is urged, that to give the same freedom of occupation to women as to men, would be an injurious addition to the crowd of competitors, by whom the avenues to almost all kinds of employment are choked up, and its remuneration depressed. This argument, it is to be observed, does not reach the political question. It gives no excuse for withholding from women the rights of citizenship. The suffrage, the jury-box, admission to the legislature and to office, it does not touch. It bears only on the industrial branch of the subject. . . .

The third objection to the admission of women to political or professional life, its alleged hardening tendency, belongs to an age now past, and is scarcely to be comprehended by people of the present time. There are still, however, persons who say that the world and its avocations render men selfish and unfeeling; that the struggles, rivalries and collisions of business and of politics make them harsh and unamiable; that if half the species must unavoidably be given up to these things, it is the more necessary that the other half should be kept free from them; that to preserve women from the bad influences of the world, is the only chance of preventing men from being wholly given up to them.

There would have been plausibility in this argument when the world was still in the age of violence; when life was full of physical conflict, and every man had to redress his injuries or those of others, by the sword or by the strength of his arm. Women, like priests, by being exempted from such responsibilities, and from some part of the accompanying dangers, may have been enabled to exercise a beneficial influence. But in the present condition of human life, we do not know where those hardening influences are to be found, to which men are subject and from which women are at present exempt. . . . If there are hatred, malice, and all uncharitableness, they are to be found among women fully as much as among men. In the present state of civilization, the notion of guarding women from the hardening influences of the world, could only be realized by secluding them from society altogether. . . .

But, in truth, none of these arguments and considerations touch the foundations of the subject. The real question is, whether it is right and expedient that one-half of the human race should pass through life in a state of forced subordination to the other half. . . .

Barbara Leigh Smith Bodichon, *Reasons for the Enfranchisement of Women* (London: n.p., 1866), 6-10, 12.

The membership list of the Kensington Society, a discussion group created specifically to consider questions of importance to women, reads like a Who's Who of prominent feminists. Charlotte Manning was the president, Emily Davies, the secretary, and the approximately fifty members included Madame Bodichon, Isa Craig, Jessie Boucherett, Frances Power Cobbe, Dorothea Beale, Mary Frances Buss, Elizabeth Garrett, Sophia Jex-Blake, Helen Taylor, and Elizabeth Wolstenholme, all of whom had distinguished themselves in various aspects of the struggle to improve the position of women. At the first meeting of the society in May 1865, Emily Davies proposed a question which was taken up at the next meeting, in November of that year: *"Is the extension of the Parliamentary suffrage to women desirable, and if so, under what conditions?"* Barbara Bodichon, like the true daughter of a father (Benjamin Leigh Smith) who had fought for the Reform Bill of 1832, submitted a paper, which the ladies of the society overwhelmingly endorsed, calling for the extension of the franchise to women. Before the paper was discussed, Emily Davies had suggested to Madame Bodichon that a few semantic changes, based on her understanding of male psychology, would be desirable:

> I don't think it quite does to call the arguments on the other side "foolish." Of course they *are*, but it does not seem quite polite to say so. I should like to omit the paragraph about outlawry. You see, the enemy always maintains that the disabilities imposed upon women are not penal, but solely intended for their good, and I find nothing irritates men so much as to attribute tyranny to them. I believe many of them do really mean well, and at any rate as they say they do, it seems fair to admit it and to show them that their well-intended efforts are a *mistake,* not a crime. Men cannot stand indignation, and tho' of course I think it is just, it seems to me better to suppress the manifestation of it. . . .[1]

Thus tutored, the Kensington Society ladies organized London's first women's suffrage committee, whose members sought support for their cause by collecting signatures on petitions which were subsequently presented to the House of Commons. The next year Madame Bodichon presented her ideas more formally at the Manchester meeting of the Social Science Association, in a paper from which an excerpt is given below.

[*Editors' note: Madame Bodichon has already discussed several arguments for giving*

---

[1] Stephen, *Emily Davies and Girton College*, p. 108.

women the vote based on "considerations of justice and mercy".] . . . There remain to be considered those aspects of the question which affect the general community. And among all the reasons for giving women votes, the one which appears to me the strongest, is that of the influence it might be expected to have in increasing public spirit. Patriotism, a healthy, lively, intelligent interest in everything which concerns the nation to which we belong, and an unselfish devotedness to the public service, — these are the qualities which make a people great and happy; these are the virtues which ought to be most sedulously cultivated in all classes of the community. And I know no better means at this present time, of counteracting the tendency to prefer narrow private ends to the public good, than this of giving to all women, duly qualified, a direct and conscious participation in political affairs. Give some women votes, and it will tend to make all women think seriously of the concerns of the nation at large, and their interest having once been fairly roused, they will take pains, by reading and by consultation with persons better informed than themselves, to form sound opinions. As it is, women of the middle class occupy themselves but little with anything beyond their own family circle. They do not consider it any concern of theirs, if poor men and women are ill-nursed in workhouse infirmaries, and poor children ill-taught in workhouse schools. If the roads are bad, the drains neglected, the water poisoned, they think it is all very wrong, but it does not occur to them that it is their duty to get it put right. These farmer-women and business-women have honest sensible minds and much practical experience, but they do not bring their good sense to bear upon public affairs, because they think it is men's business, not theirs, to look after such things. It is this belief—so narrowing and deadening in its influence—that the exercise of the franchise would tend to dissipate. The mere fact of being called upon to enforce an opinion by a vote, would have an immediate effect in awakening a healthy sense of responsibility. There is no reason why these women should not take an active interest in all the social questions—education, public health, prison discipline, the poor laws, and the rest—which occupy Parliament, and they would be much more likely to do so if they felt that they had importance in the eyes of Members of Parliament, and could claim a hearing for their opinions.

Besides these women of business, there are ladies of property, whose more active participation in public affairs would be beneficial both to themselves and the community generally. The want of stimulus to energetic action is much felt by women of the higher classes. It is agreed that they ought not to be idle, but what they ought to do is not so clear. Reading, music and drawing, needlework, and charity are their usual employments. Reading, without a purpose, does not come to much. Music and drawing, and needlework, are most commonly regarded chiefly as amusements intended to fill up time. We have left, as the serious duty of independence and unmarried women, the care of the poor in all its branches, including visiting the sick and the aged and ministering to their wants, looking after the schools, and in every possible way giving help wherever help is needed. Now education, the relief of the destitute, and the health of the people, are among the most important and difficult matters which occupy the minds of statesmen, and if it is admitted that women of leisure and culture are bound to contribute their part towards the solution of these great questions, it is evident that every means of making their co-operation enlightened and vigorous should be sought for. They have special opportunities of observing the operation of many of the laws. They know, for example, for they see before their eyes, the practical working of the law of settlement—of the laws relating to the dwellings of the poor—and

many others, and the experience which peculiarly qualifies them to form a judgement
on these matters, ought not to be thrown away. We all know that we have already a
goodly body of rich, influential working-women, whose opinions on the social and political questions of the day are well worth listening to. In almost every parish, there are,
happily for England, such women. Now everything should be done to give these valuable members of the community a solid social standing. If they are wanted, and there
can be no doubt that they are, in all departments of social work, their position in the
work should be as dignified and honourable as it is possible to make it. Rich unmarried
women have many opportunities of benefitting the community, which are not within
reach of a married woman, absorbed by the care of her husband and children. Everything, I say again, should be done to encourage this most important and increasing
class, to take their place in the army of workers for the common good, and all the
forces we can bring to bear for this end are of incalculable value. For by bringing women
into hearty co-operation with men, we gain the benefit not only of their work, but of
their intelligent sympathy. Public spirit is like fire: a feeble spark of it may be fanned
into a flame, or it may be very easily be put out. And the result of teaching women
that they have nothing to do with politics, is that their influence goes towards extinguish-
ing the unselfish interest — never too strong — which men are disposed to take in public
affairs.

Let each member of the House of Commons consider, in a spirit of true scientific
inquiry, all the properly qualified women of his acquaintance, and he will see no reason why the single ladies and the widows among his own family and friends should not
form as sensible opinions on the merits of candidates as the voters who returned him to
Parliament. When we find among the disfranchised such names as those of Mrs. Somerville, Harriet Martineau, Miss Burdett Coutts, Florence Nightingale, Mary Carpenter,
Lousia Twining, Miss Marsh, and many others scarcely inferior to these in intellectual
and moral worth, we cannot but desire, for the elevation and dignity of the parliamentary system, to add them to the number of electors. . . .

It was said by Lord Derby, in his speech on entering upon the office of Prime Minister
last Session, in reference to Reform—that "there were theoretical anomalies in our
present system which it was desirable, if possible, to correct; but there were classes of
persons excluded from the franchise who had a fair claim and title, upon the ground
of their fitness to exercise the privilege of electors; and that there was a very large class
whom the particular qualifications of the Act of 1832 excluded." I venture to submit,
that the exclusion of female freeholders and householders from the franchise is an
anomaly which it is very desirable, and not impossible, to correct; that there is no
class of persons having a fairer claim and title upon the ground of their fitness to exercise the privileges of electors; and that whatever may be deemed expedient with
regard to other classes, this class, at any rate, should not be excluded by the particular
qualifications of the Reform Act of the future.

John Stuart Mill, *The Admission of Women to the Electoral Franchise*
(London: Trübner & Co., 1867), pp. 3-6, 14-16.

The origins of John Stuart Mill's concern with female suffrage were
several: his admiration for William Thompson (the author of an *Appeal of
One Half the Human Race,* etc.), his contacts with the Saint-Simonians,
and — above all — the influence of Harriet Taylor, whose own interest in
the subject derived from her association with the noted (and subsequently

notorious) Unitarian divine, William Johnson Fox.[1] It was Mrs. Taylor who changed Mill from a theoretical believer in woman's suffrage to an active campaigner on behalf of that cause.

Mill announced his support for the enfranchisement of women during the election of 1865, when he was a successful candidate for a seat representing Westminster. In June 1866 he presented to the House of Commons a petition, signed by almost 1,500 sympathizers (including Frances Power Cobbe, Harriet Martineau, Emily Shirreff, Barbara Leigh Smith Bodichon, Jessie Boucherett, Emily Davies, and Elizabeth Garrett), in support of female suffrage. The next year Mill moved in the House of Commons an amendment to the second Reform Bill which, by substituting "person" for "man", would have given the vote to women in boroughs who were rated householders or £10 lodgers. The House was prepared to greet the amendment "with all the deference due to so great a thinker",[2] but not to give it the necessary votes. It lost — 196 to 83.

That deference, however, was not in evidence on May 20, 1867, when Mill addressed the House of Commons on behalf of female suffrage. This speech, which many of Mill's critics alleged was evidence of a decline in his intellectual powers, if not his actual sanity, was, in fact, a telling indictment of the glaring injustices daily perpetrated on English women. What Mill said was not new, but his arguments were so eloquent and logical that it is difficult to see how even his adversaries could have failed to be affected by them. But their bias was equal to the challenge.

. . . There is nothing to distract our attention from the simple question, whether there is any adequate justification for continuing to exclude an entire half of the community, not only from admission, but from the capability of being ever admitted within the pale of the Constitution, though they may fulfil all the conditions legally and constitutionally sufficient in every case but theirs. Sir, within the limits of our Constitution this is a solitary case. There is no other example of an exclusion which is absolute. If the law denied a vote to all but the possessors of £5000 a year, the poorest man in the nation might — and now and then would — acquire the suffrage; but neither birth, nor fortune, nor merit, nor exertion, nor intellect, nor even that great disposer of human affairs, accident, can ever enable any woman to have her voice counted in those national affairs which touch her and hers as nearly as any other person in the nation.

. . . We should not, capriciously and without cause, withhold from one what we give to another. . . . To lay a ground for refusing the suffrage to any one, it is necessary to allege either personal unfitness or public danger. Now, can either of these be alleged in the present case? Can it be pretended that women who manage an estate or conduct a business, — who pay rates and taxes, often to a large amount, and frequently from their own earnings, — many of whom are responsible heads of families, and some of whom, in the capacity of schoolmistresses, teach much more than a great number

---

[1] Fox's radical views were promulgated through the *Monthly Repository*, a literary and political journal to which both Harriet Taylor and Mill contributed articles. In an essay entitled "A Political and Social Anomaly", published in 1832, Fox boldly enunciated his feminist views. See *Monthly Repository*, XI (1832), 637-42.

[2] M. Ostrogorski, *The Rights of Women* (London: Swan Sonnenschein & Co., 1893), pp. 41-42.

of the male electors have ever learnt, — are not capable of a function of which every male householder is capable? Or is it feared that if they were admitted to the suffrage they would revolutionize the State, — would deprive us of any of our valued institutions, or that we should have worse laws, or be in any way whatever worse governed, through the effect of their suffrages? No one, Sir, believes anything of the kind.

And it is not only the general principles of justice that are infringed, or at least set aside, by the exclusion of women, merely as women, from any share in the representation; that exclusion is also repugnant to the particular principles of the British Constitution. It violates one of the oldest of our constitutional maxims — a doctrine dear to reformers, and theoretically acknowledged by most Conservatives — that taxation and representation should be co-extensive. Do not women pay taxes? Does not every woman who is *sui juris* contribute exactly as much as the revenue as a man who has the same electoral qualification?

The House, however, will doubtless expect that I should not rest my case solely on the general principles either of justice or of the Constitution, but should produce what are called practical arguments. . . . Practical arguments, practical in the most restricted meaning of the term, are not wanting; and I am prepared to state them, if I may be permitted first to ask, what are the practical objections? . . . [That] politics are not women's business, and would distract them from their proper duties: Women do not desire the suffrage, but would rather be without it: Women are sufficiently represented by the representation of their male relatives and connexions: Women have power enough already. . . . [*Editors' note: Taking each of these objections in order, Mill proceeded logically to demolish them. This, for example, is how he disposed of the argument that women's interests were more than adequately looked after by men.*]

But at least, it will be said, women do not suffer any practical inconvenience, as women, by not having a vote. The interests of all women are safe in the hands of their fathers, husbands, and brothers, who have the same interest with them, and not only know, far better than they do, what is good for them, but care much more for them than they care for themselves. Sir, this is exactly what is said of all unrepresented classes. The operatives, for instance: are they not virtually represented by the representation of their employers? Are not the interest of the employers and that of the employed, when properly understood, the same? To insinuate the contrary, is it not the horrible crime of setting class against class? Is not the farmer equally interested with the labourer in the prosperity of agriculture, — the cotton manufacturer equally with his workmen in the high price of calicoes? Are they not both interested alike in taking off taxes? And, generally, have not employers and employed a common interest against all outsiders, just as husband and wife have against all outside the family? And what is more, are not all employers good, kind, benevolent men, who love their workpeople, and always desire to do what is most for their good? All these assertions are as true, and as much to the purpose, as the corresponding assertions respecting men and women. . . . Workmen need other protection than that of their employers, and women other protection than that of their men. I should like to have a return laid before this House of the number of women who are annually beaten to death, kicked to death, or trampled to death by their male protectors: and, in an opposite column, the amount of the sentences passed, in those cases in which the dastardly criminals did not get off altogether. I should also like to have, in a third column, the amount of property, the unlawful taking of which was, at the same sessions or assizes, by the same judge, thought worthy of the same amount of punishment. We should then have an arithmetical estimate of the value set by a male legislature and male tribunals of the murder of a woman, often by torture continued through years, which, if there is any shame in us, would make us hang our heads. . . . This is the sort of care taken of women's interests by the men who so faithfully represent them. . . .

Lydia E. Becker, "Female Suffrage", *Contemporary Review*, IV (1867), 307-16.

It would not be much of an exaggeration to say that, if Barbara Bodichon was the prophetess of the woman's suffrage movement, Lydia Becker was its high priestess. True, Miss Becker had another interest — science, on which she was sufficiently informed to enable her to correspond with Darwin on botanical questions — but, from the moment she was inspired by hearing Madame Bodichon's paper on woman's suffrage at the Social Science Association's meeting in 1866, she devoted her life almost single-mindedly to that cause.

Early in 1867 she organized the Manchester Women's Suffrage Committee, which merged with similar groups to form the Manchester National Society for Women's Suffrage. This Society, of which Miss Becker was the secretary, and Richard Pankhurst, Jacob Bright, and Elizabeth Wolstenholme were members, organized "the first public meeting ever held in support of the female franchise . . . on 14th April 1868".[1] At this meeting, Lydia Becker moved a resolution (and scandalized conventional opinion, which considered such an act unladylike), that called for the vote to be granted to women on the same terms it was granted to men.

In 1870 Miss Becker became editor of the *Woman's Suffrage Journal*, which published the details of all speeches made, both inside and outside Parliament, on the subject of female suffrage. Adopting the tactics used earlier in the century by the Anti-Corn Law League, she organized mass meetings, door-to-door canvassing and the circulation of petitions. She took a very active part in supervising and coordinating parliamentary efforts to secure the franchise for women and became an accomplished lobbyist. Contributing to her efforts to secure the vote for women were her activities as a member of the Manchester School Board, to which she was elected eight consecutive times. The lesson was obvious: if a woman could vote and hold elective office in Manchester, how could she be denied that right in Westminster?

The excerpt which follows is from the article, "Female Suffrage", which appeared in the *Contemporary Review* for March 1867 and won Miss Becker a national reputation. It is a good example of her lucid and trenchant style.

The action taken by Mr. J. S. Mill in the House of Commons on behalf of the free-

[1] Roger Fulford, *Votes for Women* (London: Faber & Faber Ltd., 1957), p. 73.

holders and householders, the petition for whose enfranchisement he presented, raises a question of very great importance to women, and to the community of which they form the numerical majority. . . .

Hitherto the difficulty has been to get the question of the political rights of individuals of the female sex recognised as one open to discussion at all. The advocate has not been allowed to come into court. It has been assumed that the male sex, by a sort of divine right, has the exclusive privilege of directing the affairs of the community; and any serious claim made by the other half of the human race, to a share in controlling its destinies, has been met, not by argument showing the groundlessness or inexpediency of the demand, but by a refusal to entertain it, as if it were something intrinsically absurd. . . .

It surely will not be denied that women have, and ought to have, opinions of their own on subjects of public interest, and on the events which arise as the world wends on its way. But if it be granted that women may, without offence, hold political opinions, on what ground can the right be withheld of giving the same expression or effect to their opinions as that enjoyed by their male neighbours? To individual men the law says, "All of you whose rental reaches the prescribed standard shall have your political existence recognised. You may not be clever nor learned, possibly you do not know how to read and write. Still you know your own wants and wishes better than others know them for you; you have a stake in the country, and your interests ought to be consulted; you contribute directly to the national revenue a certain proportion of your property or earnings, and you shall enjoy in return a small share of direct political power, for the exercise of which, according to the best light you possess, you shall be legally responsible to no one."

But to individual women the law says, "It is true that you are persons with opinions, wants, and wishes of your own, which you know better than any other can know for you; we allow that your stake and interest in the country are equal to that of your next-door neighbour, and that your intelligence is not inferior to that of great numbers of male voters; we will tax your property and earnings as we see fit, but in return for your personal contribution to the national revenue you shall not possess the minutist fraction of personal political power; we will not allow you to have the smallest share in the government of the country of which you are a denizen, nor any voice in the making of the laws which determine the legal and political status of persons of your sex."

Now can any man who feels that he would not like to be addressed in language of this sort, seriously believe that women do like it? Surely there is no such difference in the feelings of persons of opposite sexes as to make language which would sound mortifying and unjust to one set of persons, seem agreeable and equitable to another set. . . .

. . . Where is the consistency or propriety of saying to [women], "Open your eyes to what is going on in the world, think for yourselves on the subjects that engage public attention, and when you have taken pains to inform yourselves on the topics of the day, and on the merits of the various questions that stir the mind of the nation, your opinions shall be treated as worthless, your voices counted as nothing, and not a point of independent standing-ground shall be given to one of you from which you may endeavour to give effect to the strongest desire or opinion that may influence you." Is not this style of dealing with the opinions women are encouraged to form, something after the manner of the famous recipe for treating a cucumber—Carefully prepare the fruit, adjust the proportions of the seasoning, and when all is done, and the dish dressed to perfection, open the window and fling it away!

The question should be fairly put, and honestly answered, Ought the wishes and opinions of women to be allowed any political influence at all, any weight whatever in the general councils of the nation? It is for those who answer this question in the affirmative to show cause why they should not be permitted to exercise whatever influence it is thought right they should possess, in a direct, straightforward manner.

But many who allow that women's voices ought to count for something in estimating public opinion, say that the proper manner for them to exercise power in the State is through the influence they possess over the minds of their male relatives — when they happen to have any — and that this indirect method of making their opinions known ought to satisfy them. This may sound plausible, but the legal measure of influence accorded under this arrangement to the opinions of women of independent position is found, on examination, to vanish to a nullity. By what process can the votes of men be made to represent the opinions of women? Is a man bound, before giving his vote, to consult the wishes of the woman or women on whose behalf, as well as his own account, he is supposed to be acting? Each individual voter can give but one voice — his own; that voice represents the sentiments of a single mind. It adds nothing to the weight of this voice in choosing a representative, that any number of his female neighbours coincide in the views of the elector; and if they do not so coincide, far from representing their wishes, he is thwarting them. If, then, the opinions and wishes of women ought to have any political influence whatever, a channel should be open to them for expressing them independent of the votes of men, for these may or may not represent their opinions truly. . . .

The case of persons excluded from the franchise solely on account of their sex, is essentially different from that of male persons shut out by the operation of the existing electoral law. In the latter case the disability is not inherent, but accidental, and may be overcome by the efforts of the individual, without change in the law. If a man is not an elector to-day, he may be one to-morrow; his exclusion carries no stigma of supposed mental or moral incapacity to form a judgment in political matters, and is no logical bar to his making himself as fully acquainted with them as his tastes and circumstances permit. His acquisition of a vote would be simply the adding another name to the electoral roll, and would possess no special interest for other men.

But the admission of female freeholders and householders to the privilege of voting would enfranchise, not simply the individual voters, but the whole sex. Every woman in the land would have an immediate accession of personal dignity, for she would belong to a class no longer denied the logical right to hold political opinions. Though she might not happen to possess the requisite qualification for a vote, personal exclusion from political power would lose its sting, for it would cease to imply presumed mental incapacity for its exercise. English women would be relieved from the mortifying consciousness, that while feeling no moral nor intellectual inferiority to the generality of the men of their own families, or whom they meet in society, and unable to perceive any difference between men's and women's manner of judging, or sentiments on public affairs, — except such as may be attributed to individual differences of tastes and circumstances, — the opinions of their male aquaintances are respected, as forming a legitimate portion of the motive power of the State, while their own are rejected, as only women's, and therefore not to be taken into account. It is to this feeling, and not to any unworthy desire to interfere in party squabbles, that the movement of women for enfranchisement is to be attributed. . . .

R. M. Pankhurst, "The Right of Women to Vote Under the Reform Act,
1867", *Fortnightly Review*, X (1868), 250-54.

Dr. Richard Marsden Pankhurst, the socialist husband of Emmeline
and father of Christabel and Sylvia Pankhurst, had a broad and increasingly radical range of interests: he was at various times a member of the
Social Science Association, the Association for the Reform and Codifi-
cation of the Laws of Nations, the Fabian Society, the Manchester Repub-
lican Club (of which he was a founder), and the Independent Labor
Party. It is understandable that, although he had a brilliant mind, his
attempts to be elected to the House of Commons were unsuccessful: his
religious and political beliefs were unorthodox; he was an agnostic and
advocated the abolition of the House of Lords; and tact was not his strong
point.

Pankhurst was particularly concerned with improving the position of
women. He drafted the Women's Disabilities Removal Bill of 1870 and
the Married Women's Property Bill of 1882, joined the Manchester
Society for Women's Suffrage when it was founded by Lydia Becker,
and acted as counsel in advancing the claims of women to the franchise
under the provisions of the Reform Act of 1867. As we have seen, John
Stuart Mill had failed to obtain the substitution in the language of that
Act, of "person" for "man". Subsequently, Dr. Pankhurst was no more
successful in contending, in a legal action, that "man", as it was employed
in the Act, was a generic term comprising both sexes, and that, consequently, women had the right to vote. Citing Magna Carta and the
opinions of such legal authorities as Coke and Romilly, Pankhurst sought
to prove that the language of the Act could be interpreted only as conferring the vote on *both* men and women. It was an ingenious argument
but, as the almost five thousand Manchester women who tried to place
their names on the voters' register had discovered, the courts did not
take it seriously.

. . . The question of the electoral right of women has assumed a new aspect since
the passing of the Reform Act of last year. It is proposed to submit a short statement
of some of the grounds and reasoning in accordance with which it is contended that,
under "The Representation of the People Act, 1867," all women who are *sui juris,* and
possess the necessary qualification, are entitled to vote in the election of members of
Parliament. . . .

The intention of the Act can only be collected from its language. The intention of
the Legislature is represented, is expressed, by the language of the Legislature. The
golden rule in the interpretation of an Act of Parliament, as of all written instruments,
is that its intention is to govern its construction; and what is its intention is to be ascertained from the meaning of the language used. In the present case the Legislature has
granted the electoral franchises to "every man." The simple question is, what, according to the intention of the Act, is the legal value of the expression "every man."

It is submitted that women are within the intention and definition of the Act for the following reasons: —

(1) The franchises are granted not, as in the case of the Act of 1832, to "every male person," but to "every man."

(2) Everywhere throughout the Act the equivalent terms for "every man" are such as would, without doubt, comprehend women. . . .

(3) The word "man," and its equivalent "homo," are in good English and Latin generic, and include man and woman.

(4) As to the legal value of the words "man" and "homo," respectively—

(a) The term "homo," in classical jurisprudence and juridical science, has no necessary reference to sex; it means human being, and comprehends man and woman. . . .

(b) In the law of England, the word man is used generically to include man and woman in cases arising under the common and statute law.

The expression, "No free man—*nullus liber homo*," of the Great Charter, comprehends women as well as men. Lord Coke (2 inst. 45) says, "*Homo* doth extend to both sexes, men and women." By 3 Hen.VII.c.1, it is enacted that the heir of *him* slain shall have the appeal; and Coke (4 Rep. 46) says, "The heir of a woman shall have the appeal." By 25 Edw.III., the killing of a master is made treason; "this extends by construction to the mistress."—Powlter's case, 11 Rep.34. It may, indeed, be affirmed generally, but particularly where political rights are concerned, that words which may appear to be only of masculine value are used generically. . . .

(5) By express statutory enactment, the word "man" has been distinctly constituted a technical expression, a term of art. By Lord Romilly's Act, 13 & 14 Vict. c.21, s.4, it is enacted that "in all Acts, words importing the masculine gender shall be deemed and taken to include females, unless the contrary as to gender is expressly provided."

In "The Representation of the People Act, 1867," there is no proviso to the contrary; therefore the statutory value must be given to the word "man," and the rights granted by the Act extended to women.

Much has been made of the history of the passage of the Act through Parliament as an index of the intention of the Legislature. It is perfectly clear, whatever be the nature of the facts of that history, that they cannot be considered in the interpretation of the Act. The facts, however, do not warrant an adverse inference. Before the Bill went into committee, the attention of Parliament was called to the terms of Lord Romilly's Act; and on the 28th of March, Mr. Denman, Q.C., asked whether, having regard to that Act, it was the intention of Government to confer the franchise upon women as well as men. In reply, Mr. Disraeli stated he believed there was a proviso excluding Lord Romilly's Act. But there was no such proviso in the Bill, and there is none in the Act. On the 20th of May, Mr. Mill moved that the word "person" should be substituted for the word "man," but it was rejected. Finally, on the 12th of July, Parliament refused to adopt Mr. Powell's amendment to substitute the expresion "male person" for the term "man." Therefore, as to the history of the passage of the Act, the case stands thus: — The Legislature, being in possession of the expression "male person" employed in the Act of 1832, rejected it, and deliberately, and with full knowledge of its legal value, used the term "man;" but declined to construe the term in express words, leaving term "man". Therefore, as to the history of the passage of the Act, the case stands the land, guided by the common rules of interpretation.

On the whole, then, as to this part of the argument, it is affirmed that women are within the intention of the Act, because they are within the meaning of the language by which that intention is expressed. . . .

"The Political Disabilities of Women", *Westminster Review*, XCVII (1872), 50-60.

Persons enfranchised by the Reform Act of 1867 were subject to an increase in the rates they were assessed for poor relief, on the theory that the grant of the vote compensated for the higher taxes. In practice, however, as George Orwell might have put it, all ratepayers were equal, but some ratepayers (male) were more equal than other ratepayers (female), since the latter found that they indeed were required to pay the increased rates, but were denied the vote. The author of the following selection points out that woman's political status was, in the eyes of the law, actually inferior to that of criminals, idiots, and the insane. Some authorities, in fact, went so far as to equate the legal condition of women, so far as the right to vote was concerned, with that of dogs or horses.

. . . We, who make this claim for the enfranchisement of women, do so from the feelings and for the reasons which have led other classes of the comunity to make the same claim, and we ask that our claim shall be decided by the same principles which have guided the judgment of the Legislature in the case of others. In making this demand we are, however, met at the outset with the allegation that the same principles of justice are not applicable to both sexes — that the claim which is just when made by a man, is unjust when made by a woman — that when men say that the Government has no moral right to hold them responsible to laws enacted without or against their consent, nor to tax the fruits of their labour without giving them a voice in the imposition and disbursement of such taxation, their complaint is just and reasonable, and deserves attention; but that when women say the same thing, their complaint is unjust and absurd, and must be suppressed. . . .

The theory on which the right of voting under the new Reform Act is ostensibly based is that of giving a vote for every household or home. Mr. Disraeli stated in the House of Commons that by the Act regulating the franchise, the House gave it, and intended to give it, to every householder rated for the relief of the poor. But when this declaration comes to be practically tested, it is found that about one-seventh of the ratepayers in every borough are adjudged to be out of the pale of representation. This happens though they are taxed to the same extent as the others, and, moreover, have been subjected to the special burdens imposed by the ratepaying clauses of the Representation of the People Act, for which the vote conferred by that Act was confessedly offered as an equivalent. A woman would be not only derided, but punished, who refused to obey a law on the ground that "man" did not include "woman," that "he" did not mean "she," and that therefore she was not personally liable for contravening any Act so worded. Accordingly, though the "occupiers" and "owners" who come under the operation of the ratepaying clauses of the Reform Act were referred to throughout by masculine pronouns only, women were made to pay the increased rates thereby imposed. These clauses bore with distressing severity on thousands of poor women, as we gather from police reports which appeared in London and other newspapers. At Hackney in one day more than six thousand persons, mostly women, were summoned for non-compliance with them; and at Lambeth, we are told that several poor women applied to Mr. Elliott for his advice how to save their "things" from being seized by the parish authorities for rates under these clauses. Mr. Elliot did not appear to have any power to help them, and the applicants left, lamenting that they were likely to have all their "things" taken for rates for the right to vote under the new Reform Act. But when women came into court to claim the vote conferred on the occupiers who were fined, they discovered that *"words importing the masculine gender" were held to include women in the clauses imposing burdens, and to exclude them in the clauses conferring privileges, in one and the same Act of Parliament.* [Italics added]

One of the excuses alleged for excluding women from the right of voting, is a desire to save them from the unpleasantness of contact with a crowd during the conduct of an election. But no one proposes to force women to record their votes, and if they did not like the crowd, they would have full liberty to stay away and exempt themselves from the operation of the votegiving clauses. But there was no escape from the operation of the ratepaying clauses; and under these, thousands of poor women were dragged from their homes, and haled before the magistrate, for no wrong that they had done, but solely by the operation of an Act from the benefits of which they were excluded under the pretext of exempting them from an unpleasant duty. . . .

The political position of women under the existing law has been compared to that of minors, criminals, lunatics, and idiots. But a little examination will prove that the status of persons of all these classes would be considerably lowered were it reduced to that of women. Minority, if a personal, is merely a temporary disqualification. A householder who is a minor will in time come into the enjoyment of his vote. But adult women are kept throughout their lives in the state of tutelage proper to infancy. They are never allowed to grow up to the rights of citizenship. As Justice Probyn said, "Infants cannot vote, and women are perpetual infants." Criminals are also only temporarily disqualified. During the debate on the Bill of 1867, Lord E. Cecil proposed a clause providing that persons who had been sentenced to penal servitude for any offence should be incapable of voting. Mr. Gladstone objected to the clause because "a citizen ought not to bear for life the brand of electoral incapacity." Another member objected to "extending a man's punishment to the whole of his life." The clause was finally negatived. But the brand of life-long electoral incapacity, which was thought too severe for burglars and thieves, is inflicted without scruple on rational and responsible human beings, who have never broken the law, for the sole crime of womanhood. Parliament deems an ex-garotter morally competent to exercise the franchise, whilst it rejects the petition of Florence Nightingale. So much for the moral standard required for the exercise of the suffrage. Let us now see what the law says to lunatics. In a legal textbook we find the following statement: — "With regard to a lunatic who, though for the most part he may have lost the sound exercise of his reason, yet sometimes has lucid intervals, it seems that the returning officer has only to decide whether at the moment of voting the elector is sufficiently *compos mentis* to discriminate between the candidates and to answer the questions, and take the oath if required in an intelligible manner." But the law never allows that a woman can have a lucid interval during which she is sufficiently *compos mentis* to discriminate between the candidates, and to comply with the formalities incident to recording a vote. Thus it places her mentally below lunatics, as it does morally below felons. The courts have a very kindly consideration for the electoral rights of idiots, as a case quoted by Mr. Rogers [a legal authority] will show. He states that the voter had no idea of the names of the candidates but he had of the side on which he wished to vote. He seems to have been unable to answer the ordinary questions, and the returning officer rejected the vote of this idiot; but on appeal the decision was reversed, and the vote held to be good. Mr. Rogers states that it is difficult to determine since the decision in the "Wigan Case," what degree of drunkenness need to be shown in order to disqualify an elector. It is a question of fact for the returning officer to decide; and with respect to persons deaf, dumb, and blind, he says, that "although it is difficult to believe that such persons should have understanding, still if such a person can show by signs or otherwise that he knows the purpose for which he has come to the poll, and can also comprehend the obligation of an oath, and the temporal dangers of perjury, it is conceived that a returning officer would not be justified in refusing his vote." It will be seen by these extracts that those who compare the political status of women to that of criminals, lunatics, and idiots, give too favourable a view of the facts. The true comparison is that which was used by Mr. Justice Byles in the Court of Queen's Bench, when he likened the political condition of women to that of dogs and horses. After indignantly scouting the claims of woman to humanity: "I will not," said the Judge, "allow that woman can be man, unless in a zoological treatise, or until she is reduced to the condition of fossil remains," he proceeded to level the political rights of woman to those of the domestic animals. He would not even allow her to be "something better than his dog, a little dearer than his horse," but assumed the absolute identity of the political rights of all three. The case was that of 1600 ratepayers, who had been placed on the register by the overseers of Salford, and who had been struck off by the revising barrister without inquiry, merely because they bore such names as Mary, Hannah, &c. No objection was raised by any one to these names, though they had been published in the usual way. The mayor, the overseer, and the public generally concurred in the propriety of retaining them, and the representatives of both Liberals and Conservatives in the Revision Court did their best to keep them on the register, but in vain. Though the revising barrister expressed doubts as to whether he had a right to expunge the names, he said he should do so. This decision was appealed against, and the counsel was arguing that the revising barrister had exceeded his jurisdiction in striking off the names of persons not objected to, and the description of whose qualification was good on the face of it, when he was interrupted by the Judge asking whether he meant to say that if the barrister found the name of a dog or a horse on the register, he would not be justified in striking it off. This sudden question rather staggered the learned counsel, who had evidently up to that time not looked upon his clients as exactly on a level with brutes; but he could only follow the Judge's lead, and reply that in case a man happened to be called Ponto or Dobbin, he did not see why he should lose his vote.

In the election petition at Oldham, where a scrutiny was demanded, one set of objections turned on alleged legal incapacity of the voters. These comprised some aliens, some minors, and one woman, who, being upon the register, had recorded her vote. Mr. Justice Blackburn decided that the objections to the aliens and the minors should have been taken before the revising barrister, and that it was then too late to challenge the votes on the ground of legal incapacity, but a woman was not a man at all, and he should strike off her vote at once. . . . We hereby perceive what a mere fetish sex becomes according to the principles of English law. The attributes that distinguish man from the beasts are speech, reason, moral responsibility, and religious faith. Out of these attributes springs the capacity for political functions, for knowledge and experience, and for the formation of a stable, regular government. Yet in seeking the proper basis of a qualification on which to rest the possession of political power, men deliberately reject as insufficient all those attributes of reason and conscience which raise humanity above the brutes, and select one [mere masculinity] which they have in com-

LYDIA E. BECKER, reproduced by courtesy of the Central Library, Manchester.

ELIZABETH GARRETT ANDERSON, 1889, reproduced by courtesy of the
Mansell Collection.

MILLICENT GARRETT FAWCETT, c. 1895, reproduced by courtesy of the
Mansell Collection.

EMMELINE PANKHURST, 1885, reproduced by courtesy of the Illustrated
London News.

mon with these. . . .

Emmeline Pankhurst, *My Own Story* (London: Eveleigh Nash, 1914),
pp. 37-38, 45-51, 57-62, 149-53, 156, 158-59, 268-69.

Brought up in Manchester by parents with enlightened views, Emmeline
Goulden Pankhurst maintained that her childhood experiences were
instrumental in the later pursuit of her mission to secure the franchise
for women. Her father and mother were so passionately interested in
the condition of slaves in America, that selections from *Uncle Tom's
Cabin* were read to the young Emmeline as bedtime stories. In addition,
the Gouldens were engaged in woman's suffrage activities; Emmeline
herself was only fourteen years old when she attended her first suffrage
meeting and heard the famous Lydia Becker speak. After marriage and
the birth of her children, Mrs. Pankhurst continued to take part in at
least some outside activities. As she explained, "Dr. Pankhurst did not
desire that I should turn myself into a household machine" (p. 13). She
and her husband were founders of the Women's Franchise League, an
organization which, by its support of voting rights for *all* women, was
distinguished from most suffrage societies; while in London, Mrs. Pankhurst sat on the committee which was organized to secure the passage of
a Married Women's Property Act, and she worked with Annie Besant,
who at that time was organizing working women so that they could undertake effective strikes.

Back in Manchester after 1893, Mrs. Pankhurst was elected to the
Board of Poor Law Guardians, where she found the men on the board
"guardians, not of the poor, but of the rates" (p. 24). Her work to
improve the conditions in the Manchester workhouses for "these poor,
unprotected mothers and their babies" was formative: "I thought I had
been a suffragist before I became a Poor Law Guardian, but now I
began to think about the vote in women's hands not only as a right but
as a desperate necessity" (p. 28). After the death of her husband in 1898,
Mrs. Pankhurst assumed the position of Registrar of Births and Deaths.
Her duties in this capacity, which included the registering of illegitimate
children of young girls, reinforced in her mind the belief that women
and children were society's victims. Also instrumental in the development of the idea that women *must* gain the franchise was Mrs. Pankhurst's tenure as a member of the Manchester School Board. In this
work she saw firsthand the discrimination, both in pay and workload,
suffered by the female teachers. For Mrs. Pankhurst and her two daughters, Sylvia and Christabel, the securing of the women's franchise became
the single remedy by which the many abuses of women would be cured.

The following selection from Emmeline Pankhurst's autobiography
was largely written, as she put it, "in camp between battles", when the
war to win the vote had not yet been won. Mrs. Pankhurst describes the

mission of the Women's Social and Political Union, the tactics employed by its members, and, in addition, the special problems which they encountered in their efforts to secure votes for women.

. . . In the summer of 1902—I think it was 1902—Susan B. Anthony paid a visit to Manchester, and that visit was one of the contributory causes that led to the founding of our militant suffrage organisation, the Women's Social and Political Union. During Miss Anthony's visit my daughter Christabel, who was very deeply impressed, wrote an article for the Manchester papers on the life and works of the venerable reformer. After her departure Christabel spoke often of her, and always with sorrow and indignation that such a splendid worker for humanity was destined to die without seeing the hopes of her lifetime realised. "It is unendurable," declared my daughter, "to think of another generation of women wasting their lives begging for the vote. We must not lose any more time. We must act."

. . . At a recent annual conference of the [Labor] party . . . we determined to organise a society of women to demand immediate enfranchisement, not by means of any outworn missionary methods, but through political action.

. . . In October, 1903 . . . I invited a number of women to my house in Nelson-street, Manchester, for purposes of organisation. We voted to call our new society the Women's Social and Political Union. . . . We resolved to limit our membership exclusively to women, to keep ourselves absolutely free from any party affiliation, and to be satisfied with nothing but action on our question. Deeds, not words, was to be our permanent motto. . . .

The Women's Social and Political Union had been in existence two years before any opportunity was presented for work on a national scale. The autumn of 1905 brought a political situation which seemed to us to promise bright hopes for women's enfranchisement. . . . The country was on the eve of a general election in which the Liberals hoped to be returned to power . . . .

. . . We determined to address ourselves to those men who were likely to be in the Liberal Cabinet, demanding to know whether their reforms were going to include justice to women.

We laid our plans to begin this work at a great meeting to be held in Free Trade Hall, Manchester, with Sir Edward Grey as the principal speaker. . . . Late in the afternoon on the day of the meeting, we cut out and made a small banner with the three-word inscription: "Votes for Women." Thus . . . there came into existence the present slogan of the suffrage movement around the world.

Annie Kenney and my daughter Christabel were charged with the mission of questioning Sir Edward Grey. They sat quietly through the meeting, at the close of which questions were invited. Several questions were asked by men and were courteously answered. Then Annie Kenney arose and asked: "If the Liberal party is returned to power, will they take steps to give votes for women?" At the same time Christabel held aloft the little banner that every one in the hall might understand the nature of the question. Sir Edward Grey returned no answer to Annie's question, and the men sitting near her forced her rudely into her seat, while a steward of the meeting pressed his hat over her face. A babel of shouts, cries and catcalls sounded from all over the hall.

As soon as order was restored Christabel stood up and repeated the question: "Will the Liberal Government, if returned, give votes to women?" Again Sir Edward Grey ignored the question, and again a perfect tumult of shouts and angry cries arose. Mr.

William Peacock, chief constable of Manchester, left the platform and came down to the women, asking them to write their question, which he promised to hand to the speaker. They wrote: "Will the Liberal Government give votes to working-women? Signed, on behalf of the Women's Social and Political Union, Annie Kenney, member of the Oldham committee of the card- and blowing-room operatives." They added a line to say that, as one of 96,000 organised women textile-workers, Annie Kenney earnestly desired an answer to the question.

Mr. Peacock kept his word and handed the question to Sir Edward Grey, who read it, smiled, and passed it to the others on the platform. They also read it with smiles, but no answer to the question was made. Only one lady who was sitting on the platform tried to say something, but the chairman interrupted by asking Lord Durham to move a vote of thanks to the speaker. Mr. Winston Churchill seconded the motion, Sir Edward Grey replied briefly, and the meeting began to break up. Annie Kenney stood up in her chair and cried out over the noise of shuffling feet and murmurs of conversation: "Will the Liberal Government give votes to women?" Then the audience became a mob. They howled, they shouted and roared, shaking their fists fiercely at the woman who dared to intrude her question into a man's meeting. Hands were lifted to drag her out of her chair, but Christabel threw one arm about her as she stood, and with the other arm warded off the mob, who struck and scratched at her until her sleeve was red with blood. Still the girls held together and shouted over and over: "The question! The question! Answer the question!"

Six men, stewards of the meeting, seized Christabel and dragged her down the aisle, past the platform, other men following with Annie Kenney, both girls still calling for an answer to their question. On the platform the Liberal leaders sat silent and unmoved while this disgraceful scene was taking place, and the mob were shouting and shrieking from the floor.

Flung into the streets, the two girls staggered to their feet and began to address the crowds, and to tell them what had taken place in a Liberal meeting. Within five minutes they were arrested on a charge of obstruction and, in Christabel's case, of assaulting the police. Both were summonsed to appear next morning in a police court, where, after a trial which was a mere farce, Annie Kenney was sentenced to pay a fine of five shillings, with an alternative of three days in prison, and Christabel Pankhurst was given a fine of ten shillings or a jail sentence of one week..

Both girls promptly chose the prison sentence. . . .

Of course the affair created a tremendous sensation, not only in Manchester, where my husband had been so well known and where I had so long held public office, but all over England. The comments of the press were almost unanimously bitter. Ignoring the perfectly well-established fact that men in every political meeting ask questions and demand answers of the speakers, the newspapers treated the action of the two girls as something quite unprecedented and outrageous. They generally agreed that great leniency had been shown them. Fines and jail-sentences were too good for such unsexed creatures. "The discipline of the nursery" would have been far more appropriate. One Birmingham paper declared that "if any argument were required against giving ladies political status and power it had been furnished in Manchester." Newspapers which had heretofore ignored the whole subject now hinted that while they had formerly been in favour of women's suffrage, they could no longer countenance it. The Manchester incident, it was said, had set the cause back, perhaps irrevocably.

This is how it set the cause back. Scores of people wrote to the newspapers expressing sympathy with the women. The wife of Sir Edward Grey told her friends that she considered them quite justified in the means they had taken. It was stated that Winston Churchill, nervous about his own candidacy in Manchester, visited Strangeways Gaol, where the two girls were imprisoned, and vainly begged the governor to allow him to pay their fines. On October 20, when the prisoners were released, they were given an immense demonstration in Free-Trade Hall, the very hall from which they had been ejected the week before. The Women's Social and Political Union received a large number of new members. Above all, the question of women's suffrage became at once a live topic of comment from one end of Great Britain to the other.

We determined that from that time on the little "Votes for Women" banners should appear wherever a prospective member of the Liberal government rose to speak, and that there should be no more peace until the women's question was answered. We clearly perceived that the new Government, calling themselves Liberal, were reactionary so far as women were concerned, that they were hostile to women's suffrage, and would have to be fought until they were conquered, or else driven from office.

We did not begin to fight, however, until we had given the new Government every chance to give us the pledge we wanted. Early in December the Conservative Government had gone out, and Sir Henry Campbell-Bannerman, the Liberal leader, had formed a new Cabinet. On December 21 a great meeting was held in Royal Albert Hall, London, where Sir Henry, surrounded by his cabinet, made his first utterance as Prime Minister. Previous to the meeting we wrote to Sir Henry and asked him, in the name of the Women's Social and Political Union, whether the Liberal Government would give women the vote. We added that our representatives would be present at the meeting, and we hoped that the Prime Minister would publicly answer the question. Otherwise we should be obliged publicly to protest against his silence.

Of course Sir Henry Campbell-Bannerman returned no reply, nor did his speech contain any allusion to women's suffrage. So, at the conclusion, Annie Kenney, whom we had smuggled into the hall in disguise, whipped out her little white calico banner, and called out in her clear, sweet voice: "Will the Liberal Government give women the vote?"

At the same moment Theresa Billington let drop from a seat directly above the platform a huge banner with the words: "Will the Liberal Government give justice to working-women?" Just for a moment there was a gasping silence, the people waiting to see what the Cabinet Ministers would do. They did nothing. Then, in the midst of uproar and conflicting shouts, the women were seized and flung out of the hall.

This was the beginning of a campaign the like of which was never known in England, or, for that matter, in any other country. . . .

To account for the phenomenal growth of the Women's Social and Political Union after it was established in London, to explain why it made such an instant appeal to women hitherto indifferent, I shall have to point out exactly wherein our society differs from all other suffrage associations. In the first place, our members are absolutely single minded; they concentrate all their forces on one object, political equality with men. No member of the W.S.P.U. divides her attention between suffrage and other social reforms. We hold that both reason and justice dictate that women shall have a share in reforming the evils that afflict society, especially those evils bearing directly on women themselves. Therefore, we demand, before any other legislation whatever, the elementary justice of votes for women.

There is not the slightest doubt that the women of Great Britain would have been enfranchised years ago had all the suffragists adopted this simple principle. They never did, and even to-day many English women refuse to adopt it. They are party members first and suffragists afterward; or they are suffragists part of the time and social theorists the rest of the time. We further differ from other suffrage associations, or from others existing in 1906, in that we clearly perceived the political situation that solidly interposed between us and our enfranchisement.

For seven years we had had a majority in the House of Commons pledged to vote favourably on a suffrage bill. The year before, they had voted favourably on one, yet that bill did not become law. Why? Because even an overwhelming majority of private members are powerless to enact law in the face of a hostile Government of eleven cabinet ministers. The private member of Parliament was once possessed of individual power and responsibility, but Parliamentary usage and a changed conception of statemanship have gradually lessened the functions of members. . . .

This, then, was our situation: the Government all-powerful and consistently hostile; the rank and file of legislators impotent; the country apathetic; the women divided in their interests. The Women's Social and Political Union was established to meet this situation, and to overcome it. . . .

There was little formality about joining the Union. Any woman could become a member by paying a shilling, but at the same time she was required to sign a declaration of loyal adherence to our policy and a pledge not to work for any political party until the women's vote was won. This is still our inflexible custom. Moreover, if at any time a member, or a group of members, loses faith in our policy; if any one begins to suggest that some other policy ought to be substituted, or if she tries to confuse the issue by adding other policies, she ceases at once to be a member. Autocratic? Quite so. But, you may object, a suffrage organisation ought to be democratic. Well the members of the W.S.P.U. do not agree with you. We do not believe in the effectiveness of the ordinary suffrage organisation. The W.S.P.U. is not hampered by a complexity of rules. We have no constitution and by-laws; nothing to be amended or tinkered with or quarrelled over at an annual meeting. In fact, we have no annual meeting, no business sessions, no elections of officers. The W.S.P.U. is simply a suffrage army in the field. It is purely a volunteer army, and no one is obliged to remain in it. Indeed we don't want anybody to remain in it who does not ardently believe in the policy of the army. . . .

. . . We adopted Salvation Army methods and went out into the highways and the byways after converts. We threw away all our conventional notions of what was "ladylike" and "good form," and we applied to our methods the one test question, Will it help? Just as the Booths and their followers took religion to the street crowds in such fashion that the church people were horrified, so we took suffrage to the general public in a manner that amazed and scandalized the other suffragists.

We had a lot of suffrage literature printed, and day by day our members went forth and held street meetings. Selecting a favourable spot, with a chair for a rostrum, one of us would ring a bell until people began to stop to see what was going to happen. What happened, of course, was a lively suffrage speech, and the distribution of literature. Soon after our campaign had started, the sound of the bell was a signal for a crowd to spring up as if by magic. All over the neighbourhood you heard the cry: "Here are the Suffragettes! Come on!" We covered London in this way; we never lacked an audience, and best of all, an audience to which the woman-suffrage doctrine was new. We were increasing our favourable public as well as waking it up. Besides these street meetings, we held many hall and drawing-room meetings, and we got a great deal of press publicity, which was something never accorded the older suffrage methods. . . .

. . . It will be remembered that . . . Miss Wallace Dunlop had been sent to prison for one month for stamping an extract from the Bill of Rights on the stone walls of St. Stephen's Hall. On arriving at Holloway on Friday evening, July 2nd [1909], she sent for the Governor and demanded of him that she be treated as a political offender. . . . [She] informed him that it was the unalterable resolution of the Suffragettes never again to submit to the prison treatment given to ordinary offenders against the law. Therefore she should, if placed in the second division as a common criminal, refuse to touch food until the Government yielded her point. It is hardly likely that the Government or the prison authorities realised the seriousness of Miss Wallace Dunlop's action, or the heroic mould of the Suffragettes' character, . . . and the prison authorities did nothing except seek means of breaking down her resistance. The ordinary prison diet was replaced by the most tempting food. . . . Several times daily the doctor came to feel her pulse and observe her growing weakness. The doctor, as well as the Governor and the wardresses argued, coaxed and threatened, but without effect. The week passed without any sign of surrender on the part of the prisoner. On Friday the doctor reported that she was rapidly reaching a point at which death might at any time supervene. Hurried conferences were carried on between the prison and Home Office, and that evening . . . Miss Wallace Dunlop was sent home, having served one-fourth of her sentence, and having ignored completely all the terms of her imprisonment.

On the day of her release the fourteen women who had been convicted of window breaking received their sentences, and learning of Miss Wallace Dunlop's act, they, as they were being taken to Holloway in the prison van, held a consultation and agreed to follow her example. Arrived at Holloway they at once informed the officials that they would not give up any of their belongings, neither would they put on prison clothing, perform prison labour, eat prison food or keep the rule of silence. . . .

. . . Several days after they had gone to prison, . . . the visiting magistrates arrived, and the mutineers were sentenced to terms of seven to ten days of solitary confinement in the punishment cells. In these frightful cells, dark, unclean, dripping with moisture, the prisoners resolutely hunger struck. At the end of five days one of the women was reduced to such a condition that the Home Secretary ordered her released. The next day several more were released, and before the end of the week the last of the fourteen had gained their liberty. . . .

After this each succeeding batch of Suffragette prisoners, unless otherwise directed, followed the example of these heroic rebels. The prison officials, seeing their authority vanish, were panic stricken. Holloway and other women's prisons throughout the Kingdom became perfect dens of violence and brutality. Hear the account given by Lucy Burns of her experience:

"We remained quite still when ordered to undress, and when they told us to proceed to our cells we linked arms and stood with our backs to the wall. The Governor blew his whistle and a great crowd of wardresses appeared, falling upon us, forcing us apart and dragging us towards the cells. I think I had twelve wardresses for my share, and among them they managed to trip me so that I fell helplessly to the floor. One of the wardresses grasped me by my hair, wound the long braid around her wrist and literally dragged me along the ground. In the cell they fairly ripped the clothing from my back, forcing on me one coarse cotton garment and throwing the others on the bed for me to put on myself. Left alone exhausted by the dreadful experience I lay for some time gasping and shivering on the floor. By and by a wardress came to the door and threw me a blanket. This I wrapped around me, for I was chilled to the bone by this time. The single cotton garment and the rough blanket were all the clothes I wore during my stay in prison. Most of the prisoners refused everything but the blanket. According to agreement we all broke our windows and were immediately dragged off to the punishment cells. There we hunger struck, and after enduring great misery for nearly a week, we were one by one released."

How simply they tell it. "After enduring great misery—" But no one who has not gone through the awful experience of the hunger strike can have any idea of how great that misery is. . . .

Several days later we were horrified to read in the newspapers that these prisoners were being forcibly fed by means of a rubber tube thrust into the stomach. . . .

. . . As for the testimony of the victims, it makes a volume of most revolting sort. Mrs. Leigh, the first victim, is a woman of sturdy constitution, else she could scarcely have survived the experience. . . . She refused to touch the food that was brought to her, and three days after her arrival she was taken to the doctor's room. What she saw was enough to terrify the bravest. In the centre of the room was a stout chair on a cotton sheet. Against the wall, as if ready for action stood four wardresses. The junior doctor was also on hand. The senior doctor spoke, saying: "Listen carefully to what I have to say. I have orders from my superior officers that you are not to be released even on medical grounds. If you still refrain from food I must take other measures to compel you to take it." Mrs. Leigh replied that she did still refuse, and she said further that she knew that she could not legally be forcibly fed because an operation could not be performed without the consent of the patient if sane. The doctor repeated that he had his orders and would carry them out. A number of wardresses then fell upon Mrs. Leigh, held her down and tilted her chair backward. She was so taken by surprise that she could not resist successfully that time. They managed to make her swallow a little food from a feeding cup. Later two doctors and the wardresses appeared in her cell, forced Mrs. Leigh down to the bed and held her there. To her horror the doctors produced a rubber tube, two yards in length, and this he began to stuff up her nostril. The pain was so dreadful that she shrieked again and again. Three of the wardresses burst into tears and the junior doctor begged the other to desist. Having his orders from the government, the doctor persisted and the tube was pushed down into the stomach. One of the doctors, standing on a chair and holding the tube high poured liquid food through a funnel almost suffocating the poor victim. "The drums of my ears," she said afterwards, "seemed to be bursting. I could feel the pain to the end of the breast bone. When at last the tube was withdrawn it felt as if the back of my nose and throat were torn out with it."

. . . The ordeal was renewed day after day. The other prisoners suffered similar experiences. . . .

What does all this mean? Why is it that men's blood-shedding militancy is applauded and women's symbolic militancy punished with a prison cell and the forcible feeding horror? It means simply this, that men's double standard of sex morals, whereby the victims of their lust are counted as outcasts, while the men themselves escape all social censure, really applies to morals in all departments of life. Men make the moral code and they expect women to accept it. They have decided that it is entirely right and proper for men to fight for their liberties and their rights, but that it is not right and proper for women to fight for theirs.

They have decided that for men to remain silently quiescent while tyrannical rulers impose bonds of slavery upon them is cowardly and dishonourable, but that for women to do that same thing is not cowardly and dishonourable, but merely respectable. Well, the Suffragettes absolutely repudiate that double standard of morals. If it is right for men to fight for their freedom . . . then it is right for women to fight for their freedom and the freedom of the children they bear. On this declaration of faith the militant women of England rest their case. . . .

Katherine Roberts, *Pages from the Diary of a Militant Suffragette* (Letchworth and London: Garden City Press Limited, Printers, 1910), pp. 54, 57-59, 61.

Mrs. Roberts' diary describes the experiences of an ardent member of the Pankhursts' Women's Social and Political Union. Originally indifferent to the suffragette cause, she became in a very short time an active participant in the Union's public demonstrations. Although she was terrified at the thought of being sent to jail, she nevertheless deliberately exposed herself to arrest and imprisonment. The diary furnishes an interesting insight into the strategy and tactics employed against the Liberal government by Mrs. Pankhurst and her militant supporters.

June 28th [1909].

. . . I can hardly realise that to-morrow I shall take part in a raid on the House of Commons and the following day shall be in prison. . . .

June 29th.

I am almost ashamed to admit the fact, even to my diary, but I am feeling horribly frightened. I positively dread the prospect of this deputation to-night. I am sorry to be so cowardly and unworthy of the splendid women who will be my companions in the fight; but when I think of the London crowd and the mounted police I feel cold and a little sick with apprehension. . . .

I arrived at St. Pancras in time to drive here, have a short talk with my hostess, and go off to a meeting held by Mrs. Pankhurst for members of the deputation only. . . .

When I reached the place . . . I was much struck by the splendid organisation. Although there were at least 140 of us, each one received typewritten instructions explaining most clearly exactly what we were to do. I will not try to describe Mrs. Pankhurst's speech, beyond saying that I shall remember it always, and the strange impressiveness of the scene. She told us that a new stage in the women's agitation had now been reached. Hitherto, the Suffragettes had quietly submitted to being treated as common criminals for political offences (if, indeed, they could be called offences at all). Now, however, we were to make a protest against this, for the sake of political prisoners in the future. The opportunity was a good one, for there would probably be over 100 of us in Holloway to-morrow, and unity is strength.

She told us exactly what she wanted us to do. We were to refuse to wear prison clothes or to scrub out our cells, and as a protest against insufficient air in the cells we were to wait till a bell rang at 1 p.m. the first day, and then each of us must carefully, with the heel of a shoe, break a pane of glass in her window. She explained that, on our arrival at Holloway, we must stand together and refuse to go to our cells until we had seen the governor. If we were forcibly taken to the cells, we much refuse to be medically examined or to wear the prison clothes. If undressed by force and our own clothes removed, we must undress and get to bed. She made it very clear that we were to be polite always to the wardresses and everyone with whom we came in contact, that having always been our policy, that our strongest weapon was passive resistance and endurance, whatever the cost to ourselves.

Each detail was thought out and carefully explained. I could not help being struck by the fact that though everyone knew it would be very much easier to quietly submit, . . . yet all were ready to do as she wished.

"We shall be given solitary confinement," said Mrs. Pankhurst; "we shall be put in punishment cells, probably in different prisons. As for me, I don't know where I shall be put, but wherever we are, whatever happens, in spirit we shall be together."

. . . I talked to several of the women while waiting for my instructions. They all seemed quite prepared for the fact that they may be killed to-night, quite happy just to be helping the Cause, and cheerfully ready for the extra ordeal of the revolt in prison. . . .

[*Editors' note: The deputation to the Prime Minister, of which Mrs. Roberts was to have been a member, was postponed, for tactical reasons, past the date when she left England to go abroad, and she was consequently denied the opportunity—which she had so earnestly sought—to go to prison for the Cause.*]

CHAPTER IX

The Opposition

The opposition to the emancipation of women was truly formidable. That was to be expected, since most of the positions taken by feminists seemed a deliberate rejection of all that polite Victorian society held dear, if not sacred. The vocal opponents of the woman's movement were predominantly of the upper and middle classes and included in their ranks a number of highly articulate women whose vehemence, dialectical skill, and hostility almost equalled those of the male foes of emancipation. One of the most prominent of these ladies was Mrs. E. Lynn Linton, who for a span of more than twenty years, wrote dozens of articles critical of the "shrieking sisterhood" and the "wild women".

It was Mrs. Linton and the other opponents, male and female, of the woman's movement, who made the term "New Woman" a label for a creature who was a grotesque parody of a man. According to the stereotype developed by her critics, the New Woman, having failed to win a husband, attempted to compensate for her rejection by adopting mannish traits. Doggedly aggressive, deliberately offensive, frequently homely, she was a travesty of all that the term womanly implied. In fact, to such an extent was she alleged to have lost or betrayed her femininity, that some of her critics scornfully referred to her as "androgynous", a synonym for hermaphroditic, with its overtones of freakishness. [1]

Criticism of the woman's movement took several forms. Some opponents argued, for example, that women's rights constituted a violation of the laws of nature and of God. Those laws prescribed that woman be "womanly" and man, "manly". It was generally accepted that God had endowed woman with peculiarly feminine characteristics: tenderness, compassion, submissiveness, intuitiveness, selflessness, delicacy, and modesty. All things ugly, gross, or coarse were foreign to her God-given nature. She was the embodiment of everything pure and holy. As for

---

[1] As the anonymous author of an article in the *Saturday Review* asserted, "We do not want our women to be androgynous". See "Queen Bees or Working Bees?" *Satuday Review*, November 12, 1859, p. 576. Ten years later, that same notion was expressed thus: "The one thing men do not like is the man-woman, and they will never believe the College, or University, woman is not of that type". Montagu Burrows, "Female Education", *Quarterly Review*, CXXVI (1869), 465.

man, his unique qualities were assertiveness, ambition, pride, masterfulness, strength, and protectiveness. The woman who attempted to relinquish her divinely endowed feminine attributes by aping the purely masculine traits of the opposite sex was, according to the proponents of this view, literally flouting the will of the Almighty. She was not a New Woman; she was an old abomination: a creature embodying the worst qualities of Jezebel and Mary Wollstonecraft; in short, a woman who refused to accept the role that God had ordained for her.

In addition to transgressing the laws of God, the feminist program, especially when it received socialist support (as it did in the 1830's and 40's), was regarded as a threat to the entire structure of Victorian society. The institution of marriage and the property arrangements connected with it seemed particularly menaced. A society based on capitalist economics and male supremacy was bound to react harshly to any group which seemed to challenge those fundamental principles. It seemed to the anti-feminists that they were threatened by a brazen combination of diabolical radicals and reckless females, bent on attacking private property, undermining the Church, destroying the family, and promoting "flagrant immorality". It was a spectacle bound to appall the godly and infuriate the conventional.

Emancipated women, it was further maintained by the defenders of the *status quo*, would obviously feel under no obligation to marry, and would therefore weaken the sacred institution of the family. Since childbearing was obviously woman's natural function, and since marriage and a career were deemed incompatible, a woman opting for a profession was shutting herself off from a normal existence. Not only would there be a decline in the number of new marriages; already existing unions would be infected by the noxious doctrine of equality. There would be a conflict of ideas and possibly of interests. Marital harmony would be replaced by rivalry between husband and wife, which would develop into a sordid struggle for power.

Furthermore, it was not merely that both individuals in a marriage would be affected; the nation would suffer. Women who rejected their traditional role and sought work outside their homes would inevitably neglect their duties as wives and mothers, and society would have to bear the consequences of this dereliction. Woman must find fulfillment in living for others; her role was "to cheer others on";[1] not to compete with them. Her contribution must be supportive, her existence vicarious, and her joys derivative. It had to be so. Who would instruct her children in the lessons of Christian morality if she was employed in the busy marts of trade, or presiding over a schoolroom, or working in a surgery? The whole fabric of society would be frayed, and standards of public and

---

[1] E. Lynn Linton, *The Girl of the Period and other Social Essays*, 2 vols. (London: Richard Bentley & Son, 1883), I, 25.

private conduct would inevitably decline, if women were to abdicate their moral responsibility. The entire concept of the Angel in the House, or the Stainless Sceptre of Womanhood, was endangered by the unprincipled, immoral, unnatural New Woman.

Not only was the emancipated woman a threat to society; she was a danger to herself. The quest for education and employment placed her under a physical strain too great for the limited resources of the female anatomy: "Mind and health would almost invariably break down under the task".[1] In addition, the excessive brain activity required for intellectual pursuits, it was alleged, would result in the depletion of the vital force required for child-bearing, which was, after all, woman's unique and essential function — in a very literal sense, her *raison d'être*. Some alarmists maintained that women perverted by notions of equality would undergo physiological changes that would adversely affect their capacity to bear children. Furthermore, said Mrs. Linton, "the number of women who cannot nurse their own children is yearly increasing in the educated and well-conditioned classes, and coincident with this special failure is the increase in uterine disease".[2] Even if educated women were lucky enough to escape uterine disease, they ran the risk of developing larger foreheads ("a necessary consequence of the increase of brain power"),[3] which would detract from their appearance and make it even less likely they would become wives and mothers — a truly vicious circle.

In the eyes of the opposition, the refusal of women to accept their traditional role was sufficiently widespread to be termed a revolt. And, as in most revolts, the consequences of this one would be dire: ruined marriages, broken homes, blasted careers, sickly females, alienated husbands, and puny children. The medical profession, then as now on the side of the vested interests, contributed "scientific" evidence to support the view that woman's physical endowments did not permit her to engage in conventional masculine activities without exposing her, those she held dear, and society at large to grave risks.[4]

What the popular writers feared, and the medical profession predicted, the social Darwinists confirmed. Emancipation, they declared, was

---

[1] W. R. Greg, "Why are Women Redundant?" in *Literary and Social Judgments*, p. 301. Occasionally opponents even argued that suffrage for women must be denied on the grounds that either they were too weak to make it to the polls, or the natural excitability of women — if they were given the right to vote — would drive them mad. See W. A. Hale, "The Emancipation of Women", *Westminster Review*, CII (1874), 145.

[2] Cited in "Higher Education of Women", *Westminster Review*, CXXIX (1888), 153.

[3] *Ibid.*, p. 154.

[4] It is perhaps more than a coincidence that medicine was the first field to which educated women sought admission. Certain it is that doctors, particularly gynecologists and obstetricians, saw their monopoly threatened by this attempted invasion. See the remarks of James Stansfeld, cited in Stanton (ed.), *The Woman Question in Europe*, p. 84. Also note: "In 1880, Dr. Allen Sturge, now of Nice, was refused a hospital appointment, for which he was admittedly the most fitting candidate, and for which he had worked for years, at a hospital *founded by a woman*, because the committee could not get over the difficulty that he was married to a lady-doctor". *Ibid.*, p. 88.

incompatible with the married state. The educated classes were most susceptible to the case for women's rights, with the result that women of those classes would remain celibate while women of the inferior classes would continue to breed.[1] The reduction in the number of the biological elite and the survival of the unfittest would have grave social, economic, and political consequences: rule by the aristocracy and middle classes would give way to rule by the mob, and England would be condemned to inevitable decline. Ergo, accomplishing the feminist program was tantamount to committing national suicide. It is understandable then, that the woman's movement was denounced as "improper", "abnormal", "ridiculous", "repulsive", "impractical", "absurd", "monstrous", "dangerous", "abhorrent", "disastrous", and "fatal".

To all these terms could have been added "unnecessary", because, as the opposition correctly maintained, most women, whether because of contentment, inertia, fear, or ignorance, did not want to be emancipated. Even Caroline Norton, whose experience might reasonably have been expected to transform her into a militant feminist, repudiated the concept of sexual equality.

> The wild and stupid theories advanced by a few women, of "equal rights" and "equal intelligence" are not the opinions of their sex. I, for one (I, with millions more), believe in the natural superiority of man, as I do in the existence of a God. . . .
> The natural position of woman is inferiority to man. Amen! That is a thing of God's appointing, not of man's devising. I believe it sincerely, as a part of my religion. I never pretended to the wild and ridiculous doctrine of equality.[2]

It would require decades of persuasion, polemics, and propaganda to create a majority of women in favor of equal rights.

"Custody of Infants Bill, Postscript", *British and Foreign Review*, VII (1838), 394-411.

In May 1838 the *Metropolitan Magazine* published a widely read article, "An Outline of the Grievances of Women", whose otherwise unidentified female author called upon her readers to organize for the purpose of obtaining political power and an improved system of education for women.

In July the *British and Foreign Review* printed an attack on the Infant Custody Bill, followed by a Postscript in which the *Metropolitan Magazine* article was subjected to savage criticism by an anonymous reviewer (almost certainly John Mitchell Kemble, the editor of the *British and Foreign Review*), who obviously considered Caroline Norton to be its author.

---

[1] See the argument of C. W. Saleeby in *Woman and Womanhood* (New York and London: Mitchell Kennerley, 1911) for a eugenic approach to the problem.

[2] Perkins, *The Life of the Honourable Mrs. Norton*, pp. 149-50. Cf. Beatrice Webb, the eminent Fabian Socialist: "I have never met a man, however inferior, whom I do not consider to be my superior!" The impact of this remark is somewhat diluted by her explanation that it was provoked by irritation at being subjected, during an American suffragists' luncheon, to "the perpetual reiteration of the rights of women". *My Apprenticeship* (New York: Longmans Green & Co., 1926), p. 342.

"Towards her he [used] the most virulent language, and the cruellest innuendos, to be justified only by the worst possible interpretation of her words".[1]

Kemble's hatred of Mrs. Norton was based on both her support of the Infant Custody Bill, which he regarded as an invasion of the sacred rights of fathers, and her presumed advocacy of female political militancy and a university for women. In his attack on "An Outline of the Grievances of Women", (see pp. 59-63), one of the earliest statements of feminist principles, he was reduced to verbal abuse and name-calling: women who believed in the equality of the sexes were "she-devils" or "she-beasts"; they were disgusting and immoral beings who wished to brutalize society and "raise a feud of eternal discord and hatred throughout the whole moral world" (p. 405). In addition to those grounds for dislike, the activities of these termagants touched another nerve: Kemble's abhorrence of socialism. His vitriolic denunciation of Mrs. Norton, Harriet Martineau, and other "agitatrices" was based in part on their putative connection with Saint-Simonians and Owenites.[2]

> . . . If there be any one fact in the world which is invariable, which *is* of divine origin, which has been made and done by God himself, it is the constitution of the sexes, and the subordination of the female to the male. Elevate or depress the condition of them both as much as you will . . . you will never be able to get rid of the relative position of each. Neither in practice nor in theory can you get rid of this great law of the sexual relation. We ask this writer to show us one single instance of any country . . . in which females have ever been admitted to a perfect equality of rights and powers with men. We affirm . . . that such powers, if granted to them, would lead directly to a state of perpetual anarchy. . . . We affirm, likewise, that women do *not* possess any such inherent rights, and that these powers, therefore, *ought not* be granted. . . .
>
> . . . Cannot this writer understand, that if the law has in certain cases given powers to men which it has not given to women, . . . it is only because it has laid on men responsibilities which it has not laid on women? Does this imperious claimant, who wishes to invest her sex with all the male privileges of citizenship, wish them to undertake all the male duties of citizenship? . . . The first duty of every citizen of a state, —*the condition sine qua non of citizenship*, —is, that he shall undertake to bear arms at any moment when the state calls upon him to do so for its defence. Does any lady, any woman of common sense and delicacy, wish to see enrolled regiments of she-dragoons, or brigades of police-women?
>
> But to proceed [citing the author of "The Grievances of Women"]: "Did women constitute a portion of the senate, would not the unjust laws respecting property be abolished; would they continue after *marriage* in a state of tutelage?" Open your eyes and ears, good easy husbands! Here it seems lies the gist of the whole matter; no marital tutelage! That abomination of abominations to be utterly abolished! Marriage henceforth to be a state of perfect liberty for women to do whatever they please! . . .
>
> If any one can read the above insane rhapsody [on the need for women to agitate for

---

[1] John Killham, *Tennyson and* The Princess: *Reflections of an Age* (London: University of London, Athlone Press, 1958), p. 155, and p. 167n.

[2] *Ibid.*, pp. 152-53.

equal privileges] without a feeling of abhorrence and disgust, we pity him. The idea of setting the two sexes in organized hostility against each other, and the avowed intention of this she-fire-brand, if she can, to do it, is so disgustingly atrocious, that we can find no words strong enough to express our contempt and abhorrence. Were a sufficient number of women only so far demoralized by the counsels of such a leader as to endeavor to put them into execution, the world would be a thorough hell; all order, peace, virtue and decency would be at once banished from society; all the domestic relations and dearest charities of life would be destroyed. The *family,* the fountain of all society, would be at once and completely destroyed. . . . To propose to raise a feud of eternal discord and hatred throughout the whole moral world, . . . to set "one-half of the population" against the other, — to teach wives, mothers, sisters and daughters to hate their own husbands, sons, brothers and fathers, as so many *tyrants* who hold them in bondage, — "to allow no opportunities to pass unheeded," — to band themselves together to throw off the yoke, after the example of *religious Partisans!* — this is such a diabolical blasphemy and rebellion against the Providence of God, and all that is good and holy in the world, that it is impossible that any words can be found black enough to damn it, in its own true colours, to everlasting infamy. Who this human being — this person — this woman — this lady — may be, who has thus deliberately proposed to propagate such an infernal doctrine, we know not — nor have we any wish to know her. But what her name *ought* to be we know right well: she-*misanthrope,* — manhatress! for certainly no one has ever come forward with more disgusting bravado of indecency and offensiveness to stir up hatred against men! . . .

. . . The inflated lies, coolly *argued* out with the cold-blooded ratiocination of calculating selfishness, by this talented, celebrated, appreciated, writer, can excite no feeling within us but one of unmitigated disgust! Good God! can this woman be either a wife or a mother? Impossible! Such a woman can neither be married, nor is fit to be married. . . . How is it possible that any honest woman could ever consent to go before God's altar, and pledge her vow, to love, and honour, and obey a being, whom all the while she must hate as her *tyrant and master;* and whose yoke she has secretly resolved, in her inmost soul, to throw off "at the first opportunity?" Such a perjury as that none but a *she-devil* could do! Or how again is it possible that, without any feelings of real love . . . she should still submit willingly to his embraces? Such an act as that none but a *she-beast* could do! for certainly, if man *in genere* be a disgusting tyrant . . . it is certain that every individual of the same kind must be so too; and, therefore, the woman who could willingly engage to live with such an one, as his wife, must necessarily be a still more disgusting slave! We repeat it, any woman who holds the doctrines of this writer cannot have the slightest idea of what is the Divine sacredness and honour of marriage, — nor is fit to engage in it! . . .

. . . We think that it has become high time no longer to let pass *sub silentio* . . . the *falsehood* and *immorality* . . . of these so generally received and believed sentiments and doctrines! . . .

When all else has failed to reform them, people must be made to see and smell the foulness and stinkingness of the well-draped lie which is the poisonous source of disease at the bottom of all their vices; and if that does not disgust them, and make them wake up and turn away from it with abhorrence, . . . nothing but hell will.

E. Lynn Linton, "Womanliness", *The Girl of the Period and Other Social Essays,* 2 vols. (London: Richard Bentley & Son, 1883), II, 109-18.

In 1868, the *Saturday Review,* a staunch opponent of women's rights, published an article, "The Girl of the Period", in which the anonymous author (who subsequently identified herself as E. Lynn Linton) lamented the disappearance of the "fair young English girl" of the past, and the emergence of "the Girl of the Period", defined as "a creature who dyes her hair and paints her face, . . . whose sole idea of life is fun; whose sole aim is unbounded luxury; and whose dress is the chief object of such thought and intellect as she possesses" (I, 2-3).   This article was followed by a succession of others, dedicated "to all good girls and true women", in which Mrs. Linton continued to praise the old-fashioned virtuous woman and excoriate the modern "advanced" one.   Mrs. Linton had originally favored the movement for emancipation and, even as she denounced the "new woman", she still approved, at least in principle, of equal opportunities in education and legal protection for wives.   But she reacted harshly to what she considered the extravagance, superficiality, frivolity, and bad manners of the "emancipated" ladies of the day.   Her novels were populated by repulsive specimens of the "new woman", who were unattractive, made offensive comments on the relations between the sexes, and in general, served as horrible examples of what a lady should not be.   An excerpt from "Womanliness", one of Mrs. Linton's controversial and (in their day) sensational essays, is given below.

There are certain words, suggestive rather than descriptive, the value of which lies in their very vagueness and elasticity of interpretation, by which each mind can write its own commentary, each imagination sketch out its own illustration.   And one of these is Womanliness. . . .

We call it womanliness when a lady of refinement and culture overcomes the natural shrinking of sense, and voluntarily enters into the circumstances of sickness and poverty, that she may help the suffering in their hour of need; when she can bravely go through some of the most shocking experiences of humanity for the sake of the higher law of charity; and we call it womanliness when she removes from herself every suspicion of grossness, coarseness, or ugliness, and makes her life as dainty as a picture, as lovely as a poem.   She is womanly when she asserts her own dignity; womanly when her highest pride is the sweetest humility, the tenderest self-suppression; womanly when she protects the weaker; womanly when she submits to the stronger. . . .   We used to think we knew to a shade what was womanly and what was unwomanly. . . .   But if this exactness of interpretation belonged to past times, the utmost confusion prevails at present; and one of the points on which society is now at issue in all directions is just this very question—What is essentially unwomanly? and, what are the only rightful functions of true womanliness?   Men and tradition say one thing, certain women say another. . . .

There are certain old—superstitions must we call them?—in our ideas of women, with which we should be loth to part.   For instance, the infinite importance of a mother's influence over her children, and the joy that she herself took in their companionship—

the pleasure that it was to her to hold a baby in her arms — her delight and maternal pride in the beauty, the innocence, the quaint ways, the odd remarks, the half-embarrassing questions, the first faint dawnings of reason and individuality, of the little creatures to whom she had given life and who were part or her very being — that pleasure and maternal pride were among the characteristics we used to ascribe to womanliness; as was also the mother's power of forgetting herself for her children, of merging herself in them as they grew older, and finding her own best happiness in theirs. But among the advanced women who despise the tame teachings of what was once meant by womanliness, maternity is considered a bore rather than a blessing; the children are shunted to the side when they come; and ignorant undisciplined nurses are supposed to do well for wages what mothers will not do for love. . . .

It was also an old notion that rest and quiet and peace were natural characteristics of womanliness; and that life had been not unfairly apportioned between the sexes, each having its own distinctive duties as well as virtues, its own burdens as well as its own pleasures. Man wás to go out and do battle with many enemies; he was to fight with many powers; to struggle for place, for existence, for natural rights; to give and take hard blows; to lose perhaps this good impulse or that noble quality in the fray — the battle-field of life not being that wherein the highest virtues take root and grow. But he had always a home where was one whose sweeter nature brought him back to his better self; a place whence the din of battle was shut out; where he had time for rest and spiritual reparation; where a woman's love and gentleness and tender thought and unselfish care helped and refreshed him, and made him feel that the prize was worth the struggle, that the home was worth the fight to keep it. And surely it was not asking too much of women that they should be beautiful and tender to the men whose whole life out of doors was one of work for them — of vigorous toil that they might be kept in safety and luxury. But to the advanced woman it seems so; consequently the home as a place of rest for the man is becoming daily more rare. Soon, it seems to us, there will be no such thing as the old-fashioned home left in England. Women are swarming out at all doors; running hither and thither among the men; clamouring for arms that they may enter into the fray with them; anxious to lay aside their tenderness, their modesty, their womanliness, that they may become hard and fierce and self-asserting like them; thinking it a far higher thing to leave the home and the family to take care of themselves, or under the care of some incompetent hireling, while they enter on the manly professions and make themselves the rivals of their husbands and brothers.

Once it was considered an essential of womanliness that a woman should be a good house-mistress, a judicious dispenser of the income, a careful guide to her servants, a clever manager generally. Now practical housekeeping is a degradation. . . .

Once women thought it no ill compliment that they should be considered the depositaries of the highest moral sentiments. If they were not held the wiser nor the more logical of the two sections of the human race, they were held the more religious, the more angelic, the better taught of God, and the nearer to the way of grace. Now they repudiate the assumption as an insult, and call that the sign of their humiliation which was once their distinguishing glory. They do not want to be patient, self-sacrifice is only a euphemism for slavish submission to manly tyranny; the quiet peace of home is miserable monotony. . . .

A womanly woman . . . knows that she was designed by the needs of the race and the law of nature to be a mother; sent into the world for that purpose mainly; and she knows that rational maternity means more than simply giving life and then leaving it to others to preserve it. She has no newfangled notions about the animal character of motherhood, nor about the degrading character of housekeeping. On the contrary, she thinks a populous and happy nursery one of the greatest blessings of her state; and she puts her pride in the perfect ordering, the exquisite arrangements, the comfort, thoughtfulness and beauty of her house. She is not above her *métier* as a woman; and she does not want to ape the manliness she can never possess. . . .

In a word, the womanly woman whom we all once loved and in whom we have still a kind of traditional belief, is she who regards the wishes of men as of some weight in female action; who holds to love rather than opposition, to reverence, not defiance; who takes more pride in the husband's fame than in her own; who glories in the protection of his name, and in her state as wife; who feels the honour given to her as wife and matron far dearer than any she may earn herself by personal prowess; and who believes in her consecration as a helpmeet for man, not in a rivalry which a few generations will ripen into a coarse and bitter enmity.

Anne Mozeley, "Mr. Mill on the Subjection of Women", *Blackwood's Magazine*, CVI (1869), 309-21.

Beginning in the 1860's and continuing through the end of the century, the *Saturday Review* and *Blackwood's Magazine* provided a forum for the views of those who opposed the emancipation of women. Mrs. Lynn Linton, as we have seen, was a frequent contributor to both those journals, as was Anne Mozeley. A literary figure of some renown, Miss Mozeley edited the two-volume collection of Cardinal Newman's letters. She was also the author of a two-volume collection of essays which had originally appeared in the *Saturday Review* and subsequently went through four editions. After her death in 1891, a similar collection of her essays from *Blackwood's Magazine* was published in book form.

Immediately after the publication of John Stuart Mill's *The Subjection of Women* in 1869, a large number of articles in newspapers and journals appeared which attacked Mill's notions of sexual equality, although none of their comments was as devastating as Freud's subsequent contemptuous judgment that "one simply cannot find him human".[1] Among these polemics was one by Anne Mozeley, an excerpt from which is given below, that is typical of the criticisms leveled at Mill after the publication of *The Subjection of Women*.

After a careful perusal of Mr. Mill's essay *On the Subjection of Women*, we find some few points to stand out from the rest in such distinct prominence that it may be well to state them at starting, as the readiest way of conveying a general impression. The foremost of these is the scarcely-veiled assertion of himself as the sole advocate among men with fairness and perception enough to plead woman's cause, to discern what she is capable of, and to indicate her real work in the world. . . . He exactly corresponds to the lunatic who proved logically that all the rest of the world was insane.

[1] Ernest Jones, *The Life and Work of Sigmund Freud*, 3 vols. (New York: Basic Books, Inc., 1953-57), I, 176.

It is nothing to him that mankind from the beginning has seen the matter in another light. Custom, he calmly tells us, however universal, affords no presumption, and ought not to create any prejudice, in favour of woman's subjection to man. Neither men nor women have hitherto had an idea of woman's true vocation. . . . All that Mr. Mill allows is, that certain tendencies and aptitudes are characteristics of women, as woman has hitherto been. "I do not say," he cautiously adds, "as they will continue to be, for I consider it presumptuous in any one to decide what women are and are not, can or can not be, by natural constitution."

. . . It never has been denied in any age of the world that there are women of genius and of extraordinary administrative power, nor has mankind ever been unwilling to recognise this power and genius when it has declared itself. Only men and women of the old traditional way of thinking see . . . that these are exceptional cases which must not alter the existing relation between the sexes. . . . It is this common-sense view which irritates Mr. Mill against his countrywomen. . . . Taking experience and observation as against his theory, they are disposed to laugh at his cry for liberty on their behalf. When he tells them that society makes the whole life of a woman in the easy classes a continual self-sacrifice . . . they will not see it. . . . The idea of dependence upon men does not weigh unpleasantly upon women in the abstract; rather they have their own notion of liberty only to be attained through men, which is precisely his notion of bitter bondage. . . .

When we view Mr. Mill as the head of a movement, it is important to enforce that he aims at changing the very nature of woman. His object is to make her something radically different from what we know her. He sneers at the natural fear of change in this vital social question, and assures his readers that . . . what is contrary to woman's nature to do, they never will be made to do by simply giving their nature free play. But a country's institutions are not only moulded by the national character—they also mould it; and no one can pretend to say that the reticence and contented domesticity which Mr. Mill complains of in his countrywomen, and which men in general respect as an especial feminine virtue, will undergo no change under the call to publicity and rivalry with men which he would force upon them. Not that all women would respond to his appeal; there would be under his *régime* public women and private women—a recognised division from which we can imagine many inconveniences. . . .

Nor can we imagine the stronger division of the sex such intellectual gainers as he supposes, by being urged into a new arena. . . . We will go so far as to suspect that the most masculine-minded woman is conscious of a strain in continuous intercourse with men of vigorous thought. . . . In the contemplated rivalry in the same field of work, women aiming at posts and professions now filled by men would have a credit to keep up, a constant sex assertion to maintain, which might issue in eccentricities of tone, manner, habit, and costume not pleasant to think of. . . .

. . . Mr. Mill sneers at man's notion that the natural vocation of a woman is that of a wife and mother, and at his educating her accordingly. . . . Few men are educated for remote contingencies, as he would have all women to be. It is true that one woman in a million, may have the organisation, physical and mental, which would qualify her for a Chancellor of the Exchequer, or to shine in debate in the British Parliament, or to perform a difficult operation, or to construct a railway, or to build a cathedral, or to conduct an intricate lawsuit, or to sway a fierce democracy; but the chances are too infinitesimal to found a system upon. People must be educated for probabilities, and make their way to possibilities by themselves. . . .

. . . Mr. Mill shows a perfect indifference to the enormous risk of his proposed changes. . . . To place women on the standing he claims for them, the relation of marriage must cease to bind as it does now. . . . The truth is, his whole line is for exceptional women, either in power of mind, or in circumstances, or in temper, aims, and ambition. The vast body of women, we cannot doubt, know themselves to be better off now than they would be if thrown upon their own hands for support. As the American fine lady said to Mr. Hepworth Dixon, to account for her not joining the "woman's rights movement," "You see I like to be taken care of." It will be a bad time, we believe, for woman whenever it is announced to her as her privilege through the length and breadth of her ranks that henceforth she must take care of herself. . . .

Letters of Queen Victoria, May 6, 1870 and May 29, 1870, reprinted in Philip Guedalla, *The Queen and Mr. Gladstone* (Garden City, New York: Doubleday, Doran & Co., Inc., 1934), p. 271; and Sir Theodore Martin, *Queen Victoria as I Knew Her* (Edinburgh and London: William Blackwood & Sons, 1908), pp. 69-70.

In February 1870 William Gladstone, then in his first ministry, sent Queen Victoria a pamphlet, written by a critic of women's rights, which had won Gladstone's approval. Victoria responded in a similar manner, for, as she explained, she had "the strongest aversion for the *so called &* *most erroneous 'Rights of Woman'* ".[1] A few months later, when Parliament was considering a bill that would provide suffrage for women, Queen Victoria took the opportunity to spell out her views in more detail. In keeping with traditional notions of what constituted Perfect Womanhood, Victoria was determined, she said, to secure "the *salvation* of the *young women*" of England and effect "their *rescue* from *immorality*".[2] The Queen apparently did not find it inconsistent that she was competent to discharge the duties of the highest office in the land, while other women were disqualified, simply by reason of their sex, from filling positions at the lowest rank of the national civil service.

The excerpt from the first of the two letters which follows shows clearly the abhorrence which Victoria felt, particularly as she contemplated the entrance of women into the field of medicine. The excerpt from the second letter (written only a few weeks later) is notable for its inclusion of the pejorative language used so frequently by the opponents of emancipation. Women who chose to pursue their own destinies, pontificated the Queen, were "hateful, heartless, and disgusting", and succeeded only in unsexing themselves. Victoria, incidentally, in her assertion that God's will demanded subordination for women, fell back on a familiar argument, dear to the heart of the opposition.

---

[1] Letter from Queen Victoria to Mr. Gladstone, Feb. 10, 1870, reprinted in Philip Guedalla, *The Queen and Mr. Gladstone* (Garden City, New York: Doubleday, Doran & Company, Inc., 1934), p. 266.
[2] Letter from Queen Victoria to Mr. Gladstone, May 8, 1870; *ibid.*, p. 272.

Queen Victoria to Mr. Gladstone

OSBORNE. *May 6. 1870.*

. . . The circumstances respecting the Bill to give women the same position as men with respect to Parliamentary franchise gives her an opportunity to observe that she had for some time past wished to call Mr. Gladstone's attention to the mad & utterly demoralizing movement of the present day to place women in the same position as to professions—as *men;*—& amongst others, in the *Medical Line.* . . .

She is *most* anxious that it sh^ld be known how she not only disapproves but *abhors* the attempts to destroy all propriety & womanly feeling w^h will inevitably be the result of what has been proposed. The Queen is a woman herself — & knows what an anomaly her *own* position is: — but that can be reconciled with reason & propriety tho' it is a terribly difficult & trying one. But to tear away all the barriers w^h surround a woman, & to propose that they sh^ld study with *men*—things w^h d^d not be named before them — certainly not *in a mixed* audience — w^ld be to introduce a total disregard of what must be considered as belonging to the rules & principles of morality.

The Queen feels so strongly upon this dangerous & unchristian & unnatural *cry* & movement of "woman's rights," — in w^h she knows Mr. Gladstone *agrees,* (as he sent her that excellent Pamphlet by a Lady) that she is most anxious that Mr. Gladstone & others sh^ld take some steps to check this alarming danger & to make whatever use they can of her name. . . .

Let woman be what God intended; a helpmate for a man — but with totally different duties & vocations.

Queen Victoria to Mr. Martin

[May 29, 1870]

. . . The Queen is most anxious to enlist every one who can speak or write to join in checking this mad, wicked folly of "Woman's Rights," with all its attendant horrors, on which her poor feeble sex is bent, forgetting every sense of womanly feeling and propriety. Lady [Amberley] ought to get a *good whipping.*[1]

It is a subject which makes the Queen so furious that she cannot contain herself. God created men and women different — then let them remain each in their own position . . . Woman would become the most hateful, heartless, and disgusting of human beings were she allowed to unsex herself; and where would be the protection which man was intended to give the weaker sex? . . .

Margaret Oliphant, "The Laws Concerning Women", *Blackwood's Magazine*, LXXIX (1856), 379-87.

The following article, written by the well-known novelist and historical writer, Margaret Oliphant, was a direct response to Barbara Leigh Smith's

---

[1] The daughter-in-law of Lord John Russell, the Whig Prime Minister, and the sister of Lord Stanley, who in 1870 supported the bill which would have enfranchised women, Lady Amberley was an outspoken advocate of women's rights. After Parliament's rejection of a women's suffrage bill, those ladies prominent in the effort to secure the vote decided to form local suffrage societies in every parliamentary constituency; subsequently, speakers went into the countryside to champion their cause. In May 1870 Lady Amberley spoke at the Mechanics' Institute in Stroud. Her well-publicized efforts were, of course, ridiculed by the press, but she nevertheless was successful — twelve people volunteered to form a local women's franchise committee.

A Brief Summary in Plain Language of the Most Important Laws Concerning Women. When, in 1856 and 1857, Parliament was considering the legal position of wives, most of the popular journals of the day carried articles on this topic. Mrs. Oliphant's opinion—that wives were not victims of the law, and therefore, no legal changes were necessary—probably warmed the hearts of the editors of the traditionally conservative *Blackwood's Magazine.* Indeed, Mrs. Oliphant insisted that neither justice nor equity should be the guiding principle of those laws concerning husbands and wives: both Nature and Divine Providence demanded that a woman must "identify herself entirely with her husband", an argument employed frequently by the opponents of women's rights.

. . . At the first glance, it is reasonable to suppose that the masculine lawmaker has made use of his advantages for the enslavement of his feebler companion. . . .

. . . [But] this idea, that the two portions of humankind are natural antagonists to each other, is, to our thinking, at the very outset, a monstrous and unnatural idea. . . . There is no man in existence so utterly separated from one-half of his fellow-creatures as to be able to legislate against them in the interests of his own sex. . . . It is possible that the poor may legislate against the rich, or the rich against the poor, but to make such an antagonism between men and women is against all reason and all nature. . . .

If this antagonism is not true of man and woman in the abstract, how much less true is it of the particular relationship of man and wife. It is no fallacy of the law to say that these two are one person; it is a mere truism of nature. . . .

. . . Every man and every woman knows, with the most absolute certainty, that a household divided against itself cannot stand. It is the very first principle of domestic existence. In all this great world, with all its myriads of creatures, it is vain to think of forming a single home unless it is built upon this foundation. One interest and one fortune is an indispensable necessity. . . . The man is the natural representative of his wife in one set of duties—the wife is the natural representative of the husband in another, and if any one will tell us that the nursery is less important than the Exchange, or that it is a more dignified business to vote for a county member than to regulate a Christian household, we will grant that the woman has an inferior range of duty. Otherwise, there is a perfect balance between the two members of this one person. In this view—and we defy the most visionary champion of abstract female rights to disprove that this is the ordinary rule of common society—it is a mere trick of words to say that the woman loses her existence, and is absorbed in her husband. . . .

. . . The law compels no one, either man or woman, to enter into this perilous estate of marriage; but, being once within it, it is the law's first duty to hedge this important territory round with its strongest and highest barriers. The justice which means an equal division of rights has no place between those two persons whom natural policy as well as Divine institution teach us to consider as one. It seems a harsh saying, but it is a true one—Justice cannot be done between them; their rights are not to be divided; they are beyond the reach of all ordinary principles of equity. . . .

. . . To tell the truth, women are the only born legislators, let them complain of their position as they will. Only a few hundred of us at the best can have a hand, though of the smallest, in affairs of State; but to every woman of them all, Paul himself, though not much given to compliment, gives the right and the injunction—Rule the house.

Yes; the merest girl, eighteen years old, who, half in love and half in fun, dares to don the fatal orange-blossom—there she is, a child half-an-hour ago, now a lawmaker, supreme and absolute; and yet, most despotic and unconstitutional of monarchs, you hear them weeping over infringed rights and powers denied. Oh, inconsistent humanity!—as if those powers and rights were not seated, innate and indestructible, far away out of the reach of any secondary law!

"Girls, Wives, and Mothers: A Word to the Middle Classes", *Chambers's Journal*, LXXIII (1884), 33-35.

The diehard opponents of improved educational facilities for women continued their opposition even after it had become obvious that theirs was a lost cause. The anonymous author of the following selection, for example, was a critic of the new and more intellectually demanding education to which, by the 1880's, young ladies of the middle class were increasingly exposed. In this excerpt he pleads for the application of the principle of utility to education, in order that woman might function effectively in her true sphere—the nursery and the kitchen, and he warns of the dire consequences if the present trend is allowed to continue.

. . . Female education ought to . . . mentally and physically fit our women for the battle of life. . . . Every one of them . . . ought to be trained in conformity with the supreme law of her being, to prove a real helpmate to the man that takes her to wife. . . .

In the training of our boys, utility in after-life is seldom lost sight of. Why should it be too often the reverse in the education of our girls, whose great vocation in life, as wives and mothers, is a birthright they cannot renounce, which no lord of creation can deprive them of, and which no sticklers for what they are pleased to call the rights of women can logically disown? . . .

The woman not over- but mis-educated is becoming an alarmingly fruitful cause of the downward tendencies of much of our middle-class society. . . .

. . . She cannot sew to any purpose. If she deign to use a needle at all, it is to embroider a smoking-cap for a lover or a pair of slippers for papa. To sew on a button, or cut out and unite the plainest piece of male or female clothing, is not always within her powers, or at least her inclinations. . . .

She cannot knit. . . . To darn the hole that so soon appears in the loosely knitted fabric, would be a servile, reproachful task, quite staggering to the sentimental aspirations of our engaged Angelina. Yet darning and the divine art of mending will one day be to her a veritable philosopher's stone, whose magic influences will shed beams of happiness over her household, and fortunate will she be if she have not to seek it with tears.

By the sick-bed, where she ought to be supreme, she is often worse than useless. The pillows that harden on the couch of convalescence, too rarely know her softening touch. She may be all kindness and attention—for the natural currents of her being are full to repletion of sweetness and sympathy—yet as incapable of really skilled service as an artist's lay-figure. . . .

. . . No philosophy, no tinkering of the constitution, no success in the misnamed higher walks of life and knowledge, will atone for the failure of the mother. Let her shine a social star of the first magnitude, let her be supreme in every intellectual circle, and then marry, as she is ever prone to do, in spite of all theories; and if she fail as a mother, she fails as a woman and as a human being. She becomes a mere rag, a tatter of nature's cast-off clothing, spiritless, aimless, a failure in this great world of work.

As her family increases, the household shadows deepen, where all should be purity, sweetness, and light. The domestic ship may even founder through the downright, culpable incapacity of her that takes the helm. Her children never have the air of comfort and cleanliness. In their clothes, the stitch is never in time. The wilful neglect, and consequent waste, in this one matter of half-worn clothing is almost incredible. A slatternly atmosphere pervades her entire home. With the lapse of time our young wife becomes gradually untidy, dishevelled, and even dirty, in her own person; and at last sits down for good, disconsolate and overwhelmed by her unseen foe. Her husband can find no pleasure in . . . his home; there is no brightness in it to cheer his hours of rest. He returns from his daily labours to a chaos, which he shuns by going elsewhere; and so the sequel of misery and neglect takes form.

. . . Let us regard women's education, like that of men, as a means to a lifelong end. . . . Middle-class women will be the better educated, in every sense, the more skilled they are in the functions of the mother and the duties of the wife. . . . Give us a woman, then, natural in her studies, her training, her vocations, and her dress, and in the words of the wisest of men, who certainly had a varied experience of womankind, we shall have something "far more precious than rubies. She will not be afraid of the snow for her household; strength and honour will be her clothing; her husband shall have no need of spoil; he shall be known in the gates, when he sitteth among the elders; he shall praise her; and her children shall call her blessed."

Alexander Keiller, M.D., F.R.S.E., ex-President of the Royal College of Physicians, Edinburgh, "What may be the Dangers of Educational Overwork for both Sexes, with special Reference to the Higher Class of Girls' Schools, and the effects of Competitive Examinations?" *National Association for the Promotion of Social Science, Transactions* (1880), pp. 420-39.

Whereas the author of the preceding article had argued that the education, or "mis-education" of young women would cause the deterioration of the nation's moral fiber, many members of the medical profession, including Henry Maudsley, Professor of Medical Jurisprudence, University College, London; Robert Lawson Tait, sometime president of the British Gynaecological Society; and William Withers Moore, sometime president of the British Medical Association, believed that a rigorous education for females entailed physiological suicide. One spokesman for this school was Dr. Alexander Keiller, whose impressive credentials could only have served to fortify the opponents of women's education.

. . . I have already spoken of . . . the necessity for . . . the educational safety of and attention to the general health; and now what shall I say regarding the more special question . . . [of] the probable dangers of school overwork to girls? In dealing with this part of my subject I find it difficult to suppress the full expression of my convictions. . . . I know that I speak strongly, but do so by no means unadvisedly, for I have long been impressed by the wide-spread dangers of a system so totally and so cruelly unphysiological as that of demanding so much continued strain from those on whose after-school years the important question of health so very materially rests. . . .

It may truly enough be said that the female mind is sometimes found to be even more than a match for that of the male; and in the matter of education it has often been observed that the aptitude of girls in the learning of lessons is greater than that of boys, not only in the so-called superficial or ornamental, but even in the deeper and more solid branches of study.

The explanation of this is not far to seek, for in the so-called "weaker vessel" there is not only the strength of ready perception, but the keenness to excel and the determination to shine — qualifications and resolutions which the rougher sex takes more time to think about, seeing that they fancy they need not hurry. The singular and successful facility in this respect is well observed from session to session at the examinations in girls' schools, where prizes and bursaries of value are too keenly competed for. . . .

. . . Towards the end of June last I was urgently requested by their parents to visit at their school two young ladies about fourteen years of age, who had been for some time suffering from sleeplessness and loss of appetite. I did so, and had no difficulty in making out two real cases in point, cases of young heads and the reverse of robust bodies, requiring little medical knowledge but that of common sense and experience to treat, viz.: — Stop the obvious cause of the symptoms, and the symptoms will obviously cease; or, in other words, give up striving beyond the natural strength to gain prizes which are utterly valueless when compared with the priceless prize of bodily and mental health. My simple and altogether non-medical (that is at least non-physical) prescription was quite approved of by the talented teacher . . . with whom I then had . . . an interesting conversation on the subject of lessons in and out of school, and especially on the importance of noticing, and timeously preventing the influences of undue educational brain-toil in the young. . . . Young females, and especially those naturally delicate, assuredly ought not to be crammed and trotted out, as they often are on examination days, to compete for prizes at high pressure beyond the point of their safe endurance; and much more attention ought to be paid to their physical health than is generally done during their school attendance: and if I might venture to say more at present on this point, . . . females' education should be greatly left under the direction of those whose experiences and knowledge of the educational and social requirements of the sex are admitted to be extensive and sound [i.e., the medical profession].

. . . The object of female education and upbringing is not, or ought not to be, that of the manufacture of "blue-stockings," nor the perversion of woman's naturally intended powers, to which unduly forced education often proves injurious. . . .

The question given me to answer is not What are the Advantages or Disadvantages, but What are the Dangers connected with Education in our schools? . . . My principal aim . . . has been . . . to show, what medical observation and fact can abundantly establish, that the premature and too rapid forcing of mental power necessitates undue interference with the natural evolution of brain force, which, instead of proving a benefit to individuals or to society, is, on the contrary, a prolific source of weakness, and by no means infrequently the cause of disease and death. . . .

. . . There are [those] (and I know the best of them are of these opinions in this matter) . . . whose duty it is to see that facts are ascertained and wisely and prudently met in regard to those who are brought under their special commissional strutiny. The . . . Commissioners in Lunacy, and Lunatic Asylum Superintendents, are entirely with us in the views now expressed; they do not hesitate to report against the maddening influence of undue educational efforts, especially in regard to the transmission of hereditarily acquired, or more immediately aroused mental disturbance. It is indeed not too much to say . . . that it is the crying evil of the age, for, if it be the case, which many with no small reason aver, that its very insanity has much to do with the filling of our asylums with useless brains (and if so, need I say, with worse than useless bodies); . . . if education, which ought, and is, usually intended to encourage mental force, and thereby increase intellectual power; if it either directly or indirectly, hereditarily or otherwise, be found to obscure the light of reason, and to stamp out even its feeblest tracings; if this can be proved to be a not very uncommon result of extreme educational pressure—then it is more than high time that such a cause of a grave consequence be boldly met and speedily overthrown. . . .

"Queen Bees or Working Bees?" *Saturday Review*, Nov. 12, 1859, pp. 575-76.

The anonymous author of the review article excerpted below rejected the idea, advanced by Bessie Rayner Parkes, that all women should be educated to be self-supporting. Arguing from a presumed analogy between the position of a bankrupt businessman and that of a resourceless widow, he asserted that their plight, while unfortunate, was the natural outcome of conditions against which society could not and should not take preventive measures, such as educating women to support themselves. On the contrary, he maintained, it was in the interest of all concerned, that women not be trained in an occupation or profession.

. . . [Miss Parkes] argues thus:—If every woman could marry, it might perhaps be best to leave the bread-winning department to the man. . . . But, as things are, there are a vast number of women who never get husbands, or who lose them without jointures or life insurances; and what is to be done for them? Miss Parkes' answer is— Educate every woman on the assumption that she will never get a husband. Now, it would be quite enough to dispose of the whole question by reducing it to this very elementary conception. Our answer is summary, therefore—that, as the chances are very much in favour of every woman getting a husband, there is really no call upon us even to entertain the other hypothesis. But we say much more than this. We say that the greatest of social and political duties is to encourage marriage. The interest of a State is to get as many of its citizens married as possible. The equality of the sexes demonstrates this to be a law of nature. And we add that man, in European communities, has deliberately adopted the view that, as much as possible, women should be relieved from the necessity of self-support. The measure of civilization is the maximum at which this end is attained in any given community or nation. Women labourers are a proof of a barbarous and imperfect civilization. We should be retrograding in the art and science of civilization were more women encouraged to be self-supporters. And the reason of this is plain enough. Wherever women are self-supporters, marriage is, *ipso facto*, discouraged. . . . The prevailing theory is, let as many women as possible be dependent on marriage. Let woman be trained to this as the end of her being. And though it is not seldom more roughly expressed, there is the highest social wisdom in it. Distressed governesses and distressed workwomen are social anomalies, but the social fabric is for the greatest happiness of the greatest number. And this is attained by making marriage the rule. . . . Men do not like, and would not seek, to mate with an independent factor, who at any time could quit—or who at all times would be tempted to neglect—the tedious duties of training and bringing up children, and keeping the tradesmen's bills, and mending the linen, for the more lucrative returns of the desk or counter. It is not the interest of States, and it is not therefore true social policy, to encourage the existence, as a rule, of women who are other than entirely dependent on man as well for subsistence as for protection and love. . . .

. . . Miss Parkes not only argues as though every woman were a possible old maid and a contingent widow, but contends that her education is to be framed to meet this, which is only an accident of life. Married life is woman's profession; and to this life her training—that of dependence—is modelled. Of course by not getting a husband, or losing him, she may find that she is without resources. All that can be said of her is, she has failed in business; and no social reform can prevent such failures. The mischance of the distressed governess and the unprovided widow, is that of every insolvent tradesman. He is to be pitied; but all the Social Congresses in the world will not prevent the possibility of a mischance in the shape of broken-down tradesmen, old maids, or widows. Each and all are frequently left without resources; and each and all always will be left without resources; but it would be just as reasonable to demand that every boy should be taught two or three professions because he may fail in one, as it is to argue that all our social habits should be changed because one woman in fifty—or whatever the stastistics are—is a spinster or widow without any resources. We fear we are driven, in spite of Miss Parkes, . . . to the old-fashioned view, that it is better for all parties—men and women, for the State and for society—that women should not, as a rule, be taught some useful art, and so be rendered independent of the chances of life. We do not want our women to be androgynous. . . .

[W. E. Aytoun], "The Rights of Woman", *Blackwood's Magazine*, XCII (1862), 183-201.

William E. Aytoun, a Scottish barrister, popular poet, and professor of rhetoric at the University of Edinburgh, contributed about 150 articles and reviews on political and literary topics to *Blackwood's Magazine*. Writing in opposition to what had become the *sine qua non* of the movement for emancipation—the expansion of employment opportunities— the anonymous author of "Queen Bees or Working Bees?" in 1859 had deprecated any sort of vocational or professional instruction for women. Aytoun, in 1862, was somewhat more selective. Employing a prose style that seems to owe a good deal to Dickens, he attempted to demonstrate that training women for careers in the law or medicine was not only practically impossible and morally undesirable, but that it ran counter to certain basic instincts which—in the case of medicine particularly— constituted a permanent barrier to the realization of woman's aspirations. Writing with remarkable assurance (considering that his position was based on a number of dubious assumptions), Aytoun proceeded to advise women (p. 195) that they "must at once and for ever dismiss [their] visions of the bar!" while he regarded as "purely spasmodic, and not likely to lead to any practical results", the efforts of some ladies to invade the field of medicine (p. 198).

On the basis of these pronouncements, Aytoun can hardly be ranked as one of Victorian England's more perspicaceous prophets. But there is no doubt that arguments such as his (persuasively and entertainingly set forth, it must be admitted), made it difficult to win widespread support for women's entry into the professions.

. . . What is all this cackling which we hear about the abstract rights of woman, her wrongs, her privileges, and her place? The world is wellnigh six thousand years old, dating from the creation of the human race, and yet it would appear, if we are to pay attention to certain shrill protests, that, during all that while, the true mission of woman has been most woefully misunderstood, and her position shamefully degraded. . . .

The chief aim of the female reformers, as we understand their pleadings, is to enlarge the sphere of female employments, and to acquire the right of admission into what are called the learned professions. . . .

Know then, O fascinating candidate for the honours of the bar — in the volubility of whose speech we have perfect faith and reliance — that a great deal more than mere power of talk is expected from the able pleader. We shall not descant upon the long period of close and unremitting study, whereby alone he can master the intricacies of the legal science, because you would naturally reply, and very justly too, that there is no such limitation of the intellectual faculties of woman as to render such a task impracticable. But, perhaps, you are not aware of the actual position of the lawyer in regard to his client. In the first place, he must be the most absolute custodier of his secrets. Whatever is intrusted to his knowledge comes under the seal of the strictest secrecy, and the trust is so sacred that no merely trivial breach of it can be committed — the slightest divulgence is an act of the most culpable perfidy. Do not imagine that in saying this we intend, even covertly, to insinuate that the popular notion touching the incapacity of women to keep secrets is of universal application. We harbour no such ungenerous thought, being thoroughly convinced, from experience and observation, that a secret is quite as safe with a woman as with a man. . . . We simply wish to point out the fact that there cannot, righteously at least, be entire confidence between the married female lawyer and her husband. . . . Perhaps you esteem that a very slight objection. Well then, let us proceed further. Supposing a female lawyer to be only moderately good-looking, what about private consultations at the chambers of other counsel? Unless the bar is to be exclusively feminine, an event which it is impossible to contemplate, blooming pleaders must accept the necessities of their situation, and submit to be frequently closeted with smart and sometimes not unprepossessing seniors. . . . It is all very well to talk of professional honour; but we swear by the Knave of Clubs that if we found the wife of our bosom, whatever kind of gown she might be wearing, closeted with a rascally lawyer, we should force open the door with a poker, hit Mr. Sergeant Doublefee a pitiless pelt upon the numskull, and fetch madam home to expiate her offences by a week's solitary confinement on the antiphlogistic dietary of wholesome bread and water. . . .

. . . Let us suppose a female barrister in large and lucrative practice, specially retained to lead in a case of the utmost magnitude upon circuit. The day arrives — the Judge takes his seat — the list of jurors is called over. How is this? The hour of trial is past, and yet there is no appearance of our learned sister. In her place arises a stuttering animal of a junior—a fellow whom you could hardly trust to drive the wasps from a gooseberry bush—and the purport of his announcement is that he has received a letter from a gentleman in the obstetric line, stating, upon soul and conscience, that the fair pleader is in such a situation that she cannot possibly appear in Court for at least six weeks to come. In short, instead of delivering herself of a speech, she is about to be delivered of a baby! . . .

But you say that those objections, which you admit to be weighty ones, apply only to married persons. . . . We shall at once proceed to ascertain how the spinsters would fare if permitted to practise in the Courts. . . .

Have you ever reflected upon the probable consequences of turning loose some thirty or forty fascinating damsels, tricked out like Portia in the "Merchant of Venice," among a swarm of young barristers. . . . Can there be the slightest doubt that before the first fortnight was over, there would be open and shameless galopading in Westminster Hall, and the Parliament House of Edinburgh. Then what bolting in and out of libraries and robing-rooms—what infinite giggling in corridors—what skylarking in the box of the reporters! . . . No, our dear madam!—absolutely it will not do! You must at once and for ever dismiss your visions of the bar! . . .

. . . We are bound in candour to admit that specious reasons can be urged for a relaxation of the rule which has hitherto prevented women from attaining to a medical degree. . . . It does assuredly appear both natural and decorous that female complaints should be treated by female practitioners of skill; and notwithstanding usage to the contrary, we believe that a large number of married men, and even a considerable number of the unmarried, do secretly lean to that opinion. . . . Yet . . . there does arise a grave and serious difficulty. So wonderfully complicated is the human frame, that functional treatment is never safe, unless the operator is thoroughly versed in the whole science of anatomy. . . .

. . . It would be monstrous to grant medical degrees to women, and allow them to practise generally, unless they had undergone an examination quite as stringent as that which is presently required in the schools. Here there arises a difficulty, owing to the want of provision for the education of female students, as it is quite evident that their teaching must be conducted separately from that of the men. That difficulty, however, is only a pecuniary one, and as it possibly might be overcome, it would be unfair to insist upon it. But then occurs a wide question of expediency, which we must not so summarily dismiss.

In the study of medicine, if there is much to interest, there is also a great deal that we may unequivocally term repulsive. The details of practical anatomy, until custom has blunted the finer feeling, affect the generality of mankind with a sensation almost akin to loathing. It is, and is felt to be, an invasion of the prerogative of the grave. Yet accurate scientific knowledge, which can only be attained by means of practical anatomy—in plain words, through frequent and careful dissection—is so indispensibly necessary for the welfare and relief of the living, that the young student has no alternative but to conquer, as he best can, the antipathy and repugnance which beset him at the very outset of his career. Usage has extraordinary power. We firmly believe that there is no imaginable occupation, however horrible some may appear, to which a man cannot be reconciled through custom. . . . Still there are natural instincts . . . which . . . are universal and unconquerable; and not the least powerful of these is the thrill of horror which comes over us when we hear of women with pretensions to refinement engaging in work from which even the uneducated and ill-nurtured of their sex would recoil. . . . Now this instinct . . . cannot be overcome. No lapse of time will lessen it; no multiplication of instances remove it. . . . Are instincts, then, to be preferred to the dicta of dispassionate reason? We answer, Yes! An instinct which is universal is part of our common nature, and cannot be outraged with impunity. . . . We reverence and bless the nurse who applies an emollient — very different, indeed, would be our feelings if we saw a bare-armed fury striding into our chamber with a bistoury in her hand to perform a surgical operation.

There are even greater objections to the practice than to the study of medicine. A married female M.D. must of course be prepared to sally forth at any hour of the night, if summoned by a patient. What husband would submit to such a gross infringement of the connubial contract? Nay, it may be questioned whether he would feel gratified by the information that his wife had been selected by some notorious debauchee as his confidential medical adviser. If a maiden, the case is even worse. No daughter of Esculapius would be safe for a moment if, under professional pretexts, she might be decoyed into any den of infamy. Nor would the public sympathy be largely lavished upon the victim of such an outrage. . . .

For the reasons which we have just stated, and others which we care not to advance, because they will naturally occur to all who bestow due consideration on the subject, we must protest against the institution of the female doctorate. . . .

On the whole, we regard this movement on the part of the ladies as one purely spasmodic, and not likely to lead to any practical result. Their plea seems to us to be grounded on the notion of the equality of the sexes. Once admit that, and every sort of restriction becomes a palpable injustice. If women may be lawyers and physicians, why may they not also be lawgivers and members of the Cabinet? Why not have a female Chancellor as keeper of her Majesty's conscience — a lady Speaker of the House of Commons — or a Home Secretary in petticoats? Would it be fair to restrict the career of women to the Bar, and deny them promotion to the Bench? Why are peeresses in their own right prevented from sitting and voting in the House of Lords? Is it impossible to find a Dowager who might be Archbishop of Canterbury or a female representative of Jenny Geddes to officiate as Moderator of the General Assembly of the Church of Scotland? These become very serious questions, if entire equality be conceded; if it is denied, where is the line of demarcation to be drawn? We apprehend the real solution to be this, — that society, which is now very ancient, has from experience formed a code of laws for its own regulation, from which it would be highly inexpedient to deviate; — that by the common consent of mankind in all ages, certain vocations have been assigned to each of the sexes, as their proper and legitimate sphere of action and utility — and that any attempted readjustment of these could lead to nothing save hopeless error and confusion. . . .

. . . The true happiness and wellbeing of women is to be found in their performance of domestic duties. Whatever tends to that is wise, meritorious, and good. But to make women wholly independent, which is the real object of the recent agitation, implies an inversion of the laws of nature, which is simply impossible and absurd.

Grant Allen, "Plain Words on the Woman Question", *Fortnightly Review,* LII (1889), 448-58.

To Grant Allen, a novelist and frequent contributor to newspapers and journals, the emancipation, education, and employment of women were inextricably linked. In effect, Allen maintained that the ideal form of education for women was one that emancipated them from any "unwomanly" preoccupation and allowed them to concentrate on the highest form of employment appropriate to their sex: motherhood. In short, since woman's highest function was the maternal one, "a scheme of female education ought to be mainly a scheme for the education of wives and mothers" (p. 456). Women should not aspire to be self-supporting—that was an abnormal and deplorable state; true emancipation meant freedom from everything which might detract from their proper occupation—childbearing. Although Allen maintained that his program for women was "not one whit less emancipatory than the doctrine laid down by the most emancipated women" (p. 452), it was in effect a complete rejection of any idea of sexual equality.

If any species or race desires a continued existence, then above all things it is necessary that that species or race should go on reproducing itself. . . .

If every woman married, and every woman had four children, population would remain just stationary. . . . If less than all the adult men and women married, or if the marriages proved fertile on the average to a less degree than four children apiece, then that community would grow small and smaller. In order that the community may keep up to its normal level, therefore, either all adults must marry and produce to this extent, or else, fewer marrying, those few must have families exceeding on the average four children, in exact proportion to the rate of abstention. And if the community is to increase . . . then either all adults must marry and produce more than four children apiece, or else, fewer marrying, those few must produce as many more as will compensate for the abstention of the remainder and form a small surplus in each generation. . . .

. . . It will be abundantly apparent from these simple considerations that in every community . . . the vast majority of the women must become wives and mothers, and must bear at least four children apiece. . . . In our existing state six are the very fewest that our country can do with. . . .

Now, I have the greatest sympathy with the modern woman's demand for emancipation. . . . Only, her emancipation must not be of a sort that interferes in any way with this prime natural necessity. To the end of all time, it is mathematically demonstrable that most women must become the mothers of at least four children, or else the race must cease to exist. Any supposed solution of the woman-problem, therefore, which fails to look this fact straight in the face, is a false solution. . . . It withdraws the attention of thinking women from the true problem of their sex to fix it on side-issues of comparative unimportance. . . .

For what is the ideal that most of these modern women agitators set before them? Is it not clearly the ideal of an unsexed woman? Are they not always talking to us as though it were not the fact that most women must be wives and mothers? Do they not treat any reference to that fact as something ungenerous, ungentlemanly, and almost brutal? . . . Nay, have we not even, many times lately, heard those women who insist upon the essential womanliness of women described as "traitors to the cause of their sex"? . . . A woman ought to be ashamed to say she has no desire to become a wife and mother. . . . Instead of boasting of their sexlessness as a matter of pride, they

ought to keep it dark, and to be ashamed of it—as ashamed as a man in a like predica-
ment would be of his impotence. They ought to feel they have fallen short of the healthy
instincts of their kind, instead of posing as in some sense the cream of the universe, on
the strength of what is really a functional aberration.

Unfortunately . . . a considerable number of the ablest women have been misled
into taking this unfeminine side, and becoming real "traitors to their sex" in so far as
they endeavor to assimilate women to men in everything, and to put upon their shoulders,
as a glory and privilege, the burden of their own support. . . .

. . . Almost all the Woman's Rights women have constantly spoken, thought, and
written as though it were possible and desirable for the mass of women to support
themselves, and to remain unmarried for ever. The point of view they all tacitly take
is the point of view of the self-supporting spinster. Now, the self-supporting spinster is
undoubtedly a fact—a deplorable accident of the passing moment. . . . But we ought
at the same time fully to realise that she is an abnormality, not the woman of the future.
We ought not to erect into an ideal what is in reality a painful necessity of the present
transitional age. We ought always clearly to bear in mind—men and women alike—
that to all time the vast majority of women must be wives and mothers; that on those
women who become wives and mothers depends the future of the race; and that if
either class must be sacrificed to the other, it is the spinsters whose type perishes with
them that should be sacrificed to the matrons who carry on the life and qualities of the
species. . . .

. . . The Woman Movement . . . gives precedence to the wrong element in the
problem. What is essential and eternal it neglects in favour of what is accidental and
temporary. What is feminine in women it neglects in favour of what is masculine. It
attempts to override the natural distinction of the sexes, and to make women men—in
all but virility. . . .

Goldwin Smith, "Female Suffrage", *Macmillan's Magazine*, XXX (1874), 139-50.

The position of the brilliant polemicist Goldwin Smith on most public
questions was impeccably liberal. He was opposed to militarism, imperial-
ism, and clericalism; subscribed to the doctrines of the Manchester School;
was a "little Englander"; favored the Union in the American Civil War;
admired Gladstone; and detested Disraeli (who reciprocated the sentiment). But, although out of consideration for John Stuart Mill, Smith
signed the first petition to the House of Commons on behalf of votes for
women, he subsequently became an outspoken opponent of woman's
suffrage. In the following excerpt he argues that enfranchising women
must inevitably lead to the destruction of civilized society.

. . . The question whether female suffrage on an extended scale is good for the whole
community is probably identical, practically speaking, with the question whether it is
good for us to have free institutions or not. Absolute monarchy is founded on personal
loyalty. Free institutions are founded on the love of liberty, or, to speak more properly,
on the preference of legal to personal government. But the love of liberty and the
desire of being governed by law alone appear to be characteristically male. The female
need of protection, of which, so long as women remain physically weak, and so long as

they are mothers, it will be impossible to get rid, is apparently accompanied by a preference for personal government, which finds its proper satisfaction in the family, but which gives an almost uniform bias to the political sentiments of women. The account commonly accepted of the reactionary tendency which all admit to be generally characteristic of the sex, is that they are priest-ridden. No doubt many of them are priest-ridden, and female suffrage would give a vast increase of power to the clergy. But the cause is probably deeper and more permanent, being, in fact, the sentiment inherent in the female temperament, which again is formed by the normal functions and circumstances of the sex. And if this is the case, to give women the franchise is simply to give them the power of putting an end, actually and virtually, to all franchises together. It may not be easy to say beforehand exactly what course the demolition of free institutions by female suffrage would take. . . . But there can be little doubt that in all cases, if power were put into the hands of the women, free government, and with it liberty of opinion, would fall.

In France, it is morally certain that at the present moment [1874], if votes were given to the women, the first result would be the restoration to power of the Bourbons, with their reactionary priesthood, and the destruction of all that has been gained by the national agonies of the last century. The next result would be a religious crusade against German Protestantism and Italian freedom. . . .

. . . That women would be likely to vote for one set of aspirants to political office rather than for the opposite set, would be a very bad reason for withholding from them the suffrage even for a day; but that they would probably overturn the institutions on which the hopes of the world rest, is as good a reason as there can be for withholding anything from anybody. When free institutions are firmly established in Europe, the question of Female Suffrage may perhaps be raised with less peril, so far as political interests are concerned; but to take a female vote on their fate at present, would be as suicidal as it would have been to take a female vote on the issues between Charles the First and the Parliament in the middle of the Civil War. . . .

It is alleged that female influence would mitigate the violence of party politics. But what ground have we, in reason or experience, for believing that women, if introduced into the political arena, would be less violent than men? . . . Being more excitable, and having, with more warmth and generosity of temperament, less power of self-control, women would when once engaged in party struggles, be not less but more violent than men. All our experience, in fact, points this way. In the Reign of Terror, and in the revolt of the Commune, the women notoriously rivalled the men in fury and atrocity. . . . That party politics require mitigation, and perhaps something more, may be readily admitted; but we are not likely to make the caldron boil less fiercely by flinging into it female character and Home.

That Home would escape disturbance it is surely difficult to believe. . . . A man and his wife taking opposite sides in politics would be brought into direct and public collision, especially if they happened to be active politicians, about a subject of the most exciting kind. Would the harmony of most households bear the strain? Would not a husband who cared for his own happiness be apt to say that if his wife wanted it she might have the vote, but that there should be only one vote between them?

Men are not good housekeepers, and there need not be anything disparaging in saying that women, as a rule, are not likely to be good politicians. . . .

Without pressing the argument against "Premiers in the family way" too far, it may safely be said that the women who would best represent their sex, and whose opinions would be worth most, would be generally excluded from public life by conjugal and maternal duty. Success with popular constituencies would probably fall to the lot, not of . . . grave matrons and spinsters, . . . but of dashing adventuresses, whose methods of captivating their constituents would often be by no means identical with legislative wisdom, or calculated to increase our veneration for their sex. . . .

That there are women eminently capable of understanding and discussing political questions nobody will deny. . . . But it by no means follows that it is expedient to put political power into the hands of the whole sex; much less that it is expedient to do so at a moment when it is morally certain that they would use their power to cancel a good deal of what has been done in their interest, as well as in that of their partners, by the efforts of the last two hundred years. . . .

"An Appeal Against Female Suffrage", *Nineteenth Century*, CXLVIII (1889), 781-88.

It is undeniable that the proponents of votes for women in the late nineteenth century were in a distinct minority; most English women were either indifferent to getting the vote or opposed to it. Claiming to speak for this silent majority, more than a hundred prominent ladies in 1889 signed "An Appeal Against Female Suffrage", published in a popular journal, the *Nineteenth Century*. Many of the signers had earlier supported the educational aspirations of women; moreover, they acknowledged the importance of woman's social role, particularly in the care of the sick, the insane, and the poor, but that women should claim the vote seemed, to them, dangerous — politically, socially, and morally. One of the signers, Mrs. Humphry Ward, was to become (in 1908) the leader of the National Anti-Suffrage League. The publication of "An Appeal Against Female Suffrage", marks the appearance of the first organized opposition to woman's suffrage, although, of course, isolated voices had, for the preceding twenty years or so, protested the erosion of masculine authority.

Among the supporters of female suffrage, "An Appeal" caused consternation. Emily Davies correctly observed that, in general, the signers themselves were not particularly distinguished, but merely the "wives of distinguished men".[1] Nevertheless, the publicity given to this manifesto undoubtedly strengthened the opposition's contention that women indeed did not want the vote.

We, the undersigned, wish to appeal to the common sense and the educated thought of the men and women of England against the proposed extension of the Parliamentary suffrage to women.

1. While desiring the fullest possible development of the powers, energies, and education of women, we believe that their work for the State, and their responsibilities towards it, must always differ essentially from those of men, and that therefore their share in the working of the State machinery should be different from that assigned to

---

[1] Stephen, *Emily Davies and Girton College*, p. 348.

men. Certain large departments of the national life are of necessity worked exclusively by men. . . . In all these spheres women's direct participation is made impossible either by the disabilities of sex, or by strong formations of custom and habit resting ultimately upon physical difference, against which it is useless to contend. . . . Therefore it is not just to give to women direct power of deciding questions of Parliamentary policy, of war, of foreign or colonial affairs, of commerce and finance equal to that possessed by men. We hold that they already possess an influence on political matters fully proportioned to the possible share of women in the political activities of England.

At the same time we are heartily in sympathy with all the recent efforts which have been made to give women a more important part in those affairs of the community where their interests and those of men are equally concerned. . . . But we believe that the emancipating process has now reached the limits fixed by the physical constitution of women, and by the fundamental difference which must always exist between their main occupations and those of men. . . .

2. If we turn from the *right* of women to the suffrage—a right which on the grounds just given we deny—to the effect which the possession of the suffrage may be expected to have on their character and position and on family life, we find ourselves no less in doubt. It is urged that the influence of women in politics would tell upon the side of morality. We believe that it does so tell already, and will do so with greater force as women by improved education fit themselves to exert it more widely and efficiently. But it may be asked, On what does this moral influence depend? We believe that it depends largely on qualities which the natural position and functions of women as they are at present tend to develop, and which might be seriously impaired by their admission to the turmoil of active political life. These qualities are, above all, sympathy and disinterestedness. Any disposition of things which threatens to lessen the national reserve of such forces as these we hold to be a misfortune. It is notoriously difficult to maintain them in the presence of party necessities and in the heat of party struggle. Were women admitted to this struggle, their natural eagerness and quickness of temper would probably make them hotter partisans than men; . . . the whole nation would suffer in consequence. . . .

3. . . . If votes be given to unmarried women on the same terms as they are given to men, large numbers of women leading immoral lives will be enfranchised on the one hand, while married women, who, as a rule, have passed through more of the practical experiences of life than the unmarried, will be excluded. To remedy part of this difficulty it is proposed . . . to admit married women with the requisite property qualification. This proposal . . . introduces changes in family life, and in the English conception of the household, of enormous importance. . . .

4. A survey of the manner in which this proposal has won its way into practical politics leads us to think that it is by no means ripe for legislative solution. A social change of momentous gravity has been proposed; the mass of those immediately concerned in it are notoriously indifferent; there has been no serious and general demand for it, as is always the case if a grievance is real and reform necessary; the amount of information collected is quite inadequate to the importance of the issue; and the public has gone through no sufficient discipline of discussion on the subject. Meanwhile pledges to support female suffrage have been hastily given in the hopes of strengthening existing political parties by the female vote. No doubt there are many conscientious supporters of female suffrage amongst members of Parliament; but it is hard to deny

that the present prominence of the question is due to party considerations of a temporary nature. . . .

   5. It is often urged that certain injustices of the law towards women would be easily
and quickly remedied were the political power of the vote conceded to them; and that
there are many wants, especially among working women, which are now neglected,
but which the suffrage would enable them to press on public attention. We reply
that during the past half century all the principal injustices of the law towards women
have been amended by means of the existing constitutional machinery; and with regard
to those that remain, we see no signs of any unwillingness on the part of Parliament to
deal with them. On the contrary, we remark a growing sensitiveness to the claims of
women, and the rise of a new spirit of justice and sympathy among men. . . .

   In conclusion: nothing can be further from our minds than to seek to depreciate the
position or the importance of women. It is because we are keenly alive to the enormous
value of their special contribution to the community, that we oppose what seems to us
likely to endanger that contribution. We are convinced that the pursuit of a mere outward equality with men is for women not only vain but demoralising. It leads to a
total misconception of woman's true dignity and special mission. It tends to personal
struggle and rivalry, where the only effort of both the great divisions of the human
family should be to contribute the characteristic labour and the best gifts of each to
the common stock.

*[Editors' note: Among the names appended to the "Appeal" were: Dowager Lady
Stanley of Alderly, Lady Frederick Cavendish, Lady Randolph Churchill, The Duchess
of St. Albans, Mrs. Goschen, Viscountess Halifax, The Countess of Wharncliff, Mrs.
Mundella, The Countess of Morley, Mrs. Henry Broadhurst, Lady Constance Shaw
Lefevre, Mrs. T. H. Green, Mrs. Leslie Stephen, Mrs. Humphry Ward, Miss Beatrice
Potter, Mrs. J. R. Green, Mrs. Frederic Harrison, Mrs. Huxley, Mrs. Henry Hobhouse,
Mrs. Lynn Linton, Mrs. Kegan Paul, Mrs. W. Bagehot, Mrs. H. H. Asquith, Mrs.
Spencer Walpole, Mrs. Alma-Tadema, Miss F. H. Chenevix Trench, Mrs. W. E. Forster,
Mrs. Matthew Arnold, Mrs. Arnold Toynbee, Mrs. Buckle].*

Almroth E. Wright, M.D., F.R.S., *The Unexpurgated Case Against
Woman Suffrage* (London: Constable & Company Limited, 1913),
pp. 77-83, 85-86.

   Sir Almroth Wright, a prominent physician who perfected the anti-
typhoid vaccine, was the teacher and colleague of Sir Alexander Fleming,
and a friend of George Bernard Shaw, who used him as a model for one
of the main characters in *The Doctor's Dilemma*. He had strong ideas
on the Woman Question, and although he was ostensibly attacking suffragists in the highly polemical work quoted below, it seems clear that
he regarded women in general with only slightly disguised contempt.
Whether he was referring to the "not very unusual type of spinster" who
was in "a condition of retarded development" because of her "unsatisfied
sexuality" (p. 38); or contrasting the "wider and public morality" of the
male with the "narrow and domestic . . . —I had almost called it
animal—morality" of the female (p. 46); or suggesting that in matters
of public policy "one would not be very far from the truth if one alleged

that there are no good women, but only women who have lived under the influence of good men" (p. 47); Dr. Wright made clear his conviction that giving the vote to women would result in disaster. His views were so extreme that even anti-suffragists found his opinions offensive; one of them, Mrs. Humphry Ward, in a letter to *The Times,* repudiated his views. The excerpts below are from Dr. Wright's letter to the editor of *The Times,* which appeared on March 28, 1912, and was published in 1913, with some minor changes, as an appendix to the book cited above.

SIR, — For man the physiological psychology of woman is full of difficulties.

He is not a little mystified when he encounters in her periodically recurring phases of hypersensitiveness, unreasonableness, and loss of the sense of proportion.

He is frankly perplexed when confronted with a complete alteration of character in a woman who is child-bearing.

When he is a witness of the "tendency of woman to morally warp when nervously ill", and of the terrible physical havoc which the pangs of a disappointed love may work, he is appalled.

And it leaves on his mind an eerie feeling when he sees serious and long-continued mental disorders developing in connexion with the approaching extinction of a woman's reproductive faculty.

No man can close his eyes to these things; but he does not feel at liberty to speak of them. . . .

As for woman herself, she makes very light of any of these mental upsettings.

She perhaps smiles a little at them. . . . [*Editors' note: Dr. Wright says in a foot-note: "In the interests of those who feel that female dignity is compromised by it, I have here omitted a woman's flippant overestimate of the number of women in London society who suffer from nervous disorders at the climacteric." The "overestimate" to which he refers appears in the letter to* The Times: "*The woman of the world will even gaily assure you that 'of course half the women in London have to be shut up when they come to the change of life.'* "]

None the less, these upsettings of her mental equilibrium are the things that a woman has most cause to fear; and no doctor can ever lose sight of the fact that the mind of woman is always threatened with danger from the reverberations of her physiological emergencies.

It is with such thoughts that the doctor lets his eyes rest upon the militant suffragist. He cannot shut them to the fact that there is mixed up with the woman's movement much mental disorder; and he cannot conceal from himself the physiological emergencies which lie behind.

The recruiting field for the militant suffragists is the million of our excess female population — that million which had better long ago have gone out to mate with its complement of men beyond the sea.

Among them there are the following different types of women: —

(a) First . . . come a class of women who hold, with minds otherwise unwarped, that they may, whenever it is to their advantage, lawfully resort to physical violence. . . .

(b) There file past next a class of women who have all their life-long been strangers to joy, women in whom instincts long suppressed have in the end broken into flame. These are the sexually embittered women in whom everything has turned into gall and bitterness of heart, and hatred of men. . . .

(c) Next there file past the incomplete. One side of their nature has undergone atrophy, with the result that they have lost touch with their living fellow men and women.

Their programme is to convert the whole world into . . . an epicene institution in which man and woman shall everywhere work side by side at the selfsame tasks and for the selfsame pay. . . .

(d) Inextricably mixed up with the types which we have been discussing is the type of woman . . . who is poisoned by her misplaced self-esteem; and who flies out at every man who does not pay homage to her intellect.

She is the woman who is affronted when a man avers that *for him* the glory of woman lies in her power of attraction, in her capacity for motherhood, and in unswerving allegiance to the ethics which are special to her sex. . . .

The programme of this type of woman is, as a preliminary, to compel man to admit her claim to be his intellectual equal; and, that done, to compel him to divide up everything with her to the last farthing, and so make her also his financial equal. . . .

(e) Following in the wake of these embittered human beings come troops of girls, just grown up.

All these will assure you, these young girls — and what is seething in their minds is stirring also in the minds in the girls in the colleges and schools which are staffed by unmarried suffragists — that woman has suffered all manner of indignity and injustice at the hands of man.

And these young girls have been told about the intellectual, and moral, and financial value of woman — such tales as it never entered into the heart of man to conceive.

The programme of these young women is to be married upon their own terms. . . .

To obey *a man* would be to commit the unpardonable sin. . . .

It will have been observed that there is in these programmes, in addition to the element of mental disorder and to the element of the fatuous, which have been animadverted upon, also a very ugly element of dishonesty. In reality the very kernel of the militant suffrage movement is the element of immorality. . . .

Up to the present in the whole civilised world there has ruled a truce of God as between man and woman. That truce is based upon the solemn covenant that within the frontiers of civilisation . . . the weapon of physical force may not be applied by man against woman; nor by woman against man. . . .

And it is this solemn covenant, the covenant so faithfully kept by man, which has been violated by the militant suffragist in the interest of her morbid, stupid, ugly, and dishonest programmes.

Is it wonder if men feel that they have had enough of the militant suffragist, and that the State would be well rid of her if she were crushed under the soldiers' shields like the traitor woman at the Tarpeian rock? . . .

If woman suffrage comes in here, it will have come as a surrender to a very violent feminist agitation — an agitation which we have traced back to our excess female population and the associated abnormal physiological conditions.

If ever Parliament concedes the vote to woman in England, it will be accepted by the militant suffragist . . . as a victory which she will value only for the better carrying on of her fight *à outrance* against the oppression and injustice of man.

A conciliation with hysterical revolt is neither an act of peace; nor will it bring peace. . . .

Peace will come again. It will come when woman ceases to believe and to teach all manner of evil of man despitefully. It will come when she ceases to impute to him as a crime her own natural disabilities, when she ceases to resent the fact that man cannot and does not wish to work side by side with her. And peace will return when every woman for whom there is no room in England seeks "rest" beyond the sea, "each one in the house of her husband," and when the woman who remains in England comes to recognise that she can, without sacrifice of dignity, give a willing subordination to the husband or father, who, when all is said and done, earns and lays up money for her.

CHAPTER X

Counter-Thrust

Feminist ladies were, of course, not inclined to yield to either their male or female critics. Calmly, with impeccable logic, they methodically demolished the increasingly frenzied arguments of the opposition. The contrast in tone was so striking as to cause an observer to remark that in this debate the feminine champions of emancipation and their masculine opponents seemed to have exchanged roles. It was the men who argued heatedly, irrationally, and emotionally; the women who responded coolly, rationally, and logically.[1]

To their critics' assertion that woman's role was to be a molder of men, and that it was therefore unnecessary for her to seek an education, feminists retorted that it was inconsistent to leave the shaping of the spiritual, moral, and ethical development of the rulers of the British Empire in the hands of ignorant and uneducated females.

In addition, feminists claimed that educated women would be unlikely to become the victims of the ennui, apathy, and lack of purpose which cursed the lives of those whose intellectual gifts were allowed no opportunity to develop. Giving them that opportunity would provide an antidote to the meaningless existence led by so many single women, with its inevitable by-products of frustration and invalidism.

Rebutting the masculine charge that emancipated women would flee their homes, causing the institutions of marriage and motherhood to suffer irremediable harm, middle-class feminists insisted that they were not opposed to either marriage or motherhood. They conceded that wives and mothers had to discharge their responsibilities, and that the family and home were the backbone of civilization. What these feminists actually wanted were alternative avenues to fulfillment for those single women who could not hope to achieve marriage and motherhood, or for those married women and widows who no longer had family responsibilities. Furthermore, according to proponents of women's rights, since it could not be predicted which women would marry, training and edu-

---

[1] Hale, "The Emancipation of Women", p. 141.

266

cation were necessary to prevent the unmarried from becoming burdens to their families or public charges. It was not the intention of middle-class feminists to destroy the institution of marriage; some of them, in fact, maintained that emancipation would buttress the institution of marriage by changing it from a dominant-submissive relationship to a harmonious and joyful union between two rational human beings who were different but equal or, at least, equivalent.[1]

The opposition, as we have seen, asserted that the laws of Nature had prescribed different roles for men and women and, consequently, it was almost blasphemous to suggest that their functions be merged. Most feminists agreed that Nature might indeed have so decreed; it was their intention, however, not to usurp man's role but to fulfill the one designed for women. The special talents and endowments of women should be employed for the benefit of society as a whole, not merely for that of their immediate families. What was generally conceded to be woman's genius for organization need not be limited by the walls of her home; she could translate her experience into a wider sphere — in effect, "house-keeping on a national scale". The victims of England's vast social problems — poverty, crime, disease, immorality — stood in need of the compassion, tenderness, and godliness which women were uniquely qualified to provide. Thus, to the charge that the effect on society of women's emancipation was bound to be destructive, the feminists replied that, on the contrary, the emancipation of women was a prerequisite for the purification of society. Emancipation, however, meant liberty, not license. Frances Power Cobbe's heartfelt exhortation — "For God's sake, my young friends, beware of such women!"[2] — expresses the revulsion felt by serious feminists to the superficial females whose "emancipation" consisted merely of flouting the canons of Victorian morality.

Feminists asserted that emancipation represented not a step backward for civilization but an advance, leading toward the full development of the potential of half the human race, and that goal, they maintained, could not possibly be harmful to society. Liberating the energies of England's women was simply a stage in freeing men and women alike from the shackles of custom and prejudice. The lives of Louisa Twining, Mary Carpenter, Frances Power Cobbe, Emily Davies, Elizabeth Garrett Anderson, and Millicent Garrett Fawcett afforded a persuasive demonstration of the salutary effects of emancipation. With these pioneers serving as the model of what all women might be, the static cult of the Angel in the House was bound to give way to a dynamic ideal: that of the "free and ennobled" woman who, by ridding herself of the artificial restraints imposed on her by a male-dominated society, would lead England to a superior level of culture and civilization.

[1] Cobbe, *The Duties of Women*, pp. 15, 134-36.
[2] *Ibid.*, p. 139.

Elizabeth Garrett Anderson, "Sex in Mind and Education: A Reply",
Fortnightly Review, XXI (1874), 582-94.

In 1874 the *Fortnightly Review* published an article, "Sex in Mind
and Education", by Dr. Henry Maudsley, Professor of Medical Jurisprudence, University College, London, and an eminent psychiatrist.
Dr. Maudsley's ideas were essentially those of Edward H. Clarke, a professor at Harvard and author of *Sex in Education*, a book which had
catalogued the "dangers" that resulted from women's pursuit of higher
education in America. Maudsley, who shared Clarke's fears, alleged
that there was "sex in mind as distinctly as . . . sex in body",[1] and he
therefore warned the women of England to eschew educational or professional careers which would drive them beyond their physiological
limitations.

The publication of this article was, of course, a direct threat to the
continued progress of women's education, and activists like Miss Davies,
Miss Buss, and Miss Beale recognized it as such. In the light of Dr.
Maudsley's grave predictions of exhaustion, brain fatigue, and mental
disease, feminists feared that parents might question the wisdom of permitting their daughters to continue their education on the secondary or
college level. Consequently, Elizabeth Garrett Anderson was called
upon to respond to Maudsley's argument on a professional level, having
finally established herself as a practicing physician, after a struggle so
distasteful that she refused to be called Dr. Anderson, although she had
gained the M.D.[2]

Mrs. (following her usage) Anderson was well suited to offer a rebuttal
to Maudsley, since her own career effectively refuted his allegation that
women were not equipped, mentally or physically, to cope with the drain
on their resources that would result from their undertaking to acquire
an education similar to that of men. With the encouragement of her
father, Newson Garrett (who was at first opposed to the idea), and her
lifelong friend, Emily Davies, Elizabeth Garrett, after some misgivings,
had decided to emulate the first woman M.D., Elizabeth Blackwell. The
obstacles placed in her path were formidable, although, unlike Sophia
Jex-Blake and her companions, she was not subjected to mob violence
(see p. 156). She accepted a position as a nurse in Middlesex Hospital in
order to gain experience, and was forced to leave because of pressure
from the male students, whose resentment at her presence came to a
head when she gave the correct answer (which none of them could supply)
to an instructor. In 1865 she qualified for a license from the Society of
Apothecaries, with the result that her name was placed on the Medical
Register the next year. Since a woman could still not obtain the M.D. in
England, she took her examinations at the University of Paris in 1870.

[1] Henry Maudsley, "Sex in Mind and Education", *Fortnightly Review*, XXI (1874), 468.
[2] Stephen, *Emily Davies and Girton College*, p. 80.

Returning to London, she established a dispensary which developed into the New Hospital for Women. Mrs. Anderson was also one of the founders of the London School of Medicine for Women, and served as its dean from 1883 to 1903. Her career was marked by the establishment of two precedents: she was the first woman to be elected to the London School Board and, after her retirement, became the mayor of Aldeburgh, in Suffolk—the first of her sex in England to achieve such an office. She was not only a successful physician and administrator, but a happy and well-adjusted wife and mother.

In effect, Mrs. Anderson's life and career were living proof that Dr. Maudsley's dire warnings could be safely ignored.

. . . The position Dr. Maudsley has undertaken to defend is this, . . . that women's health is likely to be seriously injured if they are allowed or encouraged to pursue a system of education, laid down on the same lines, following the same method, and having the same ends in view, as a system of education for men.

He bases his opinion on the fact that just at the age when the real educational strain begins, girls are going through an important phase of physiological development, and that much of the health of their after-life depends upon the changes proper to this age being effected without check and in a normal and healthy manner. Moreover, the periodical recurrence of the function thus started, is attended, Dr. Maudsley thinks, with so great a withdrawal of nervous and physical force, that all through life it is useless for women to attempt, with these physiological drawbacks, to pursue careers side by side with men. . . .

. . . Is it true, or is it a great exaggeration, to say that the physiological difference between men and women seriously interferes with the chances of success a woman would otherwise possess? We believe it to be very far indeed from the truth. When we are told that in the labour of life women cannot disregard their special physiological functions without danger to health, it is difficult to understand what is meant, considering that in adult life healthy women do as a rule disregard them almost completely. . . . Among poor women, where all the available strength is spent upon manual labour, the daily work goes on without intermission, and, as a rule, without ill effects. For example, do domestic servants, either as young girls or in mature life, show by experience that a marked change in the amount of work expected from them must be made at these times unless their health is to be injured? It is well known that they do not.

With regard to mental work it is within the experience of many women that that which Dr. Maudsley speaks of as an occasion of weakness, if not of temporary prostration, is either not felt to be such or is even recognised as an aid, the nervous and mental power being in many cases greater at those times than at any other. This is confirmed by what is observed when this function is prematurely checked, or comes naturally to an end. In either case its absence usually gives rise to a condition of nervous weakness unknown while the regularity of the function was maintained. It is surely unreasonable to assume that the same function in persons of good health can be a cause of weakness when present, and also when absent. . . .

As to the exact amount of care needed at the time when this function is active and regular, individual women no doubt vary very much, but experience justifies a confident opinion that the cases in which it seriously interferes with active work of mind or body are exceedingly rare; and that in the case of most women of good health, the natural recurrence of this function is not recognised as causing anything more than very temporary *malaise*, and frequently not even that. . . .

. . . The assertion that, as a rule, girls are unable to go on with an ordinary amount of quiet exercise or mental work during these periods, seems to us to be entirely contradicted by experience. Exceptional cases require special care, and under the arrangements of school life in England, whatever may be the case in America, they get it. But does it follow from this, that there is any ground for suspecting or fearing that the demands made by the special functions of womanhood during the time of development are really more in danger of being overlooked, or inadequately considered, under the new system of education than they were under the old? Dr. Maudsley seems to think there is, but he brings no evidence in support of his opinion. He is apparently not aware that most important improvements in physical training are being introduced alongside with other reforms. The time given to education is being prolonged, and the pressure in the early years of womanhood, when continuous work is less likely to be well borne, is being lightened; girls are no longer kept standing an hour or more at a time, or sitting without support for their backs; school hours and school terms are shortened; and, above all, physical exercise is no longer limited to the daily monotonous walk which was thought all-sufficient in old-fashioned schools and homes. In spite of these undeniable facts, Dr. Maudsley charges the reformers with having neglected the physical requirements of girls, in order to stimulate their mental activity. . . . To those in a position to know the facts, such a charge as this seems peculiarly misplaced and unjust. . . . The schoolmistresses who asked that girls might share in the Oxford and Cambridge Local Examinations, were the first also to introduce gymnastics, active games, daily baths, and many other hygienic reforms sorely needed in girls' schools. . . .

But it may still be urged, that admitting the advantage to girls of assimilating their play-ground hours to those of boys, of substituting outdoor games for worsted work or crouching over the fire with a storybook, yet that when it comes to school work the case is different, and that to make girls work as hard as boys do, and especially to allow them to work for the same examinations, would be to press unfairly upon their powers. In answer to this, we must take note of some facts about boys.

It must not be overlooked, that the difficulties which attend the period of rapid functional development are not confined to women, though they are expressed differently in the two sexes. Analogous changes take place in the constitution and organization of young men, and the period of immature manhood is frequently one of weakness, and one during which any severe strain upon the mental and nervous powers is productive of more mischief than it is in later life. . . . All that we wish to show is that the difficulties which attend development are not entirely confined to women. . . .

The cases that Dr. Clarke brings forward in support of his opinion against continuous mental work during the period of development could be outnumbered many times over even in our own limited experience, by those in which the break-down of nervous and physical health seems at any rate to be distinctly traceable to want of adequate mental interest and occupation in the years immediately succeeding school life. Thousands of young women, strong and blooming at eighteen, become gradually languid and feeble under the depressing influence of dulness, not only in the special functions of womanhood, but in the entire cycle of the processes of nutrition and innervation, till in a few years they are morbid and self-absorbed, or even hysterical. If they had had upon leaving school some solid intellectual work which demanded real thought and excited genuine interest, and if this interest had been helped by the stimulus of an examination, in which distinction would have been a legitimate source of pride, the number of such cases would probably be infinitely smaller than it is now. . . .

But Dr. Maudsley supports his argument by references to American experience. He says in effect, "That which the English educational reformers advocate has been tried in America and has failed; the women there go through the same educational course as the men, and the result is that they are nervous, specially prone to the various ailments peculiar to their sex, not good at bearing children, and unable to nurse them." These are grave charges, and we can scarcely wonder at Dr. Maudsley's thinking "it is right to call attention to them." But it is also right to see if they are true. . . . Granting that the facts are stated correctly, the doubtful point is, what causes this condition of things? Dr. Clarke says that, among other causes, it is due to an education which is at once too continuous, too exciting, too much pressed, and which is taken at too early an age. But against this we have to notice the testimony of many independent witnesses to the effect that the evils complained of are seen to a much greater extent among the fashionable and idle American women — those guiltless of ever having passed an examination — than they are among those who have gone through the course of study complained of. Then, again, it is notorious that the American type in both sexes is "nervous." The men show it as distinctly, if not even more distinctly than the women; and not those men only who have any claim to be considered above the average in intellect or culture. If Dr. Clarke's explanation of the existence of this type in women is correct, what is its explanation in men? . . .

But the truth is, that the system against which Dr. Clarke protests, and to which his arguments are directed, is . . . essentially different from that which is now being gradually introduced in England. Dr. Maudsley has, with what we must call some unfairness, applied what was written against one plan, to another which is unlike it in almost every important point. Whether the system in America deserves all that Dr. Clarke says against it, Americans must determine. . . . But we can speak of the conditions under which English girls work, and we are able to say distinctly that on many vital points they are just those which Dr. Clarke and the other American doctors urge as desirable. . . .

. . . To those who share Dr. Maudsley's fears, we may say that though under any system there will be some failures, physiological and moral, neither of which will be confined to one sex, yet that experience shows that no system will live from which failure in either of these directions as a rule results. Nature in the long run protects herself from our mistakes; and when we are in doubt, we may be guided by the general principles of equity and common sense, while waiting for the light of a larger experience.

Dorothea Beale, "University Examinations for Women", *National Association for the Promotion of Social Science, Transactions*, 1874, pp. 478-90.

In replying to Dr. Maudsley, Elizabeth Garrett Anderson had challenged, as unfair, his attempt to discredit higher education for women in England on the basis of Dr. Clarke's criticism of American practices. The same year, in a paper presented to the Social Science Association, the well-known educator, Dorothea Beale, principal of the Cheltenham Ladies' College, carried the argument further by actually citing the

American experience to disprove the contention that women were not equal to the physical demands of a degree program, and that admission to the professions (for which a university degree was a prerequisite) would unsex them.

. . . The question of the admission of women to degrees has for the last dozen years been before the University of London. . . .

This year [1874] Convocation voted that degrees ought to be granted to women, but the Senate, the governing body, refused. The objections urged may be ranged under two heads.

1. It is said the strain necessary for passing the examination would be injurious to health. The law forbids suicide—to allow, to encourage women to compete for degrees, is to invite them to self-destruction.

To this first argument it may be answered (a) That rational beings must be trusted to decide what is most for their good, and that people generally know their own interests best. . . . (b) That if the taking degrees is beyond their strength, it is not the province of a University to establish precautions for the maintenance of women's health, but to test intellectual ability and acquirements. That to prevent women from injuring their health by over-study would be like shutting the park gates to keep out the crows; in fact, one might use nearly all the arguments of the Areopagitica. (c) It may be urged that study on the whole promotes health; and if a few women, fired by ambition, should injure themselves by over-study, they are not alone in this, nor indeed more prone to such a crime than men; that if study slays its tens, idleness and frivolity slay thousands; that an uncultivated mind is especially liable to become the prey of unchecked emotions, and emotions exhaust the system more than intellectual work. Worry and anxiety, too, wear out the frame, and many women have broken down whilst making ineffectual efforts to support themselves and others. . . . University certificates have raised the value of women's work in teaching; and if degrees were granted, they would be still further raised above the cares and privations which undermine health far more than study does. . . . It can be shown that where the granting of degrees upon a large scale has been tried, the health of the graduates, and the average duration of life, has been above the average. There are now forty-six colleges in America, where the education of the students, men and women, is carried on together. . . . Taking the average of death-rate of graduates for thirty years in seven large colleges for men, and comparing it with one of the largest female colleges, Holyoke—a college which has graduated nearly fifteen hundred students—we find . . . the life of the women graduates is longer than that of the men graduates from six out of seven of these colleges. The attendance list shows, too, that the absence from lectures of the women students in most colleges differs only by a fraction from that of the men. . . . We read of the diminution of nervous headaches, the almost total disappearance of hysterics. "These," writes an experienced teacher, "are born of silly mothers and fashionable follies, and I find them easily cured by equal doses of ridicule and arithmetic."

We can, of course, give no direct testimony as yet to the health of graduates in England; but I remember the outcry raised when it was proposed to open the local examinations to girls. The deed was done, and none of the evils predicted have yet fallen on us. More than fifty of our students have passed University examinations, and not one, as far as I know, has suffered at all in health. . . .

2. It is said, Admit women to professions, and they will enter into competition

with men, and render life still harder for them. And in the fierce struggle of life, all gentle and womanly qualities will be destroyed; the foundations of social and family happiness will be undermined; women, instead of being content to be [helpmeets] for man, will force their way into public life.

First, we answer, that if good work is done, the community as a whole must be thereby gainers; and, secondly, that though women may diminish the earnings of some men, they may relieve others of heavy burdens. Many a father toils early and late to provide for the present and future of grown-up daughters, and scarcely sees the suburban villa to which he returns late and worn-out to find his daughters worn-out too — but with idleness and ennui. Many a brother has been taxed to provide for a sister. Take from men the burdens they need not bear, and the strain, now so unequal, will be diminished. Unmarried women without property must live, and the question is, Shall they do so by their own work, or by that of others? . . .

Lastly, is it good that, at least in our modern society, unmarried women should be dependent upon the earnings of others? Is it good for a girl to feel, as she often does, that she is a burden of which her family would gladly be rid? In the interest of morality, of domestic happiness, it is not good.

As regards the idea of a similar education and examinations turning women into men, and depriving them of all grace and gentleness, this has no basis either in reason or in fact. . . . "It is not true," says Mr. Fitch [a respected educator and one of the Taunton Commissioners], "that the studies, which are supposed to elevate and refine men, have an opposite effect on the other sex; but though grossly untrue many believe it. The finest manners I ever saw among young people, the most perfect modesty and freedom from affectation, were in a class of girls brought to me to demonstrate a proposition in Euclid."

Lastly, if there be in this movement anything contrary to the laws of God as revealed in woman's mental constitution, "it will come to nought." Those who are now so anxious to climb the highest peaks will faint [in the early stages of the ascent] and descend into the valley with a truer idea of their own powers. There is nothing like a wholesome dose of experience for making fools wise — let them have it! . . .

Helen McKerlie, "The Lower Education of Women", *Contemporary Review*, LI (1887), 112-19.

In the following article a feminist replies to Mrs. Lynn Linton, whose support of the old-fashioned virtues of English womanhood, the author maintains, actually promotes "the lower education of women", and reduces the female sex "to one dead level of unintellectual pursuit" (p. 119). By contrast, this feminist critic demands that women be given an education that will rescue them from the sterility of the intellectual desert to which Mrs. Linton airily condemned them.

We have all read an admirable treatise from the hand of a gifted penwoman [E. Lynn Linton], slashing at all our hopes, and attempting to destroy the very fabric of the movement for the Higher Education of Women. And wherefore? Because — we gather from her argument — it means loss of money, time, and, above all things, strength. A highly educated woman, we are told, is incapacitated for her natural functions. She is a woman destroyed, a man not made. All her finer and more valuable attributes are blurred. She is unsatisfying as a companion, worthless as a wife, incapable as a mother. A girl's physical strength can never carry her bravely through the arduous struggle for honours, degrees, and professorships, and land her safely at the other side. Mental success must be obtained at the loss of physical powers. A girl is weaker, physically, mentally, morally, than a man; therefore she must take the lowest seat.

. . . We are told a woman's highest aim is to be a good animal. Undoubtedly to be a good animal is one of the requisites of successful living. But is it life altogether? Without infringing on man's royal prerogative, have women not a right to live—to live as beings answerable for their all? Our opponent says, and others have said before her, "There is one sphere for woman's thought and work and action." But when we come to inquire what it is, it appears that the one sphere is that of wife, mother, and household drudge. Perhaps these Professors of the Lower System of Education know of some sphere for women's souls. If so, their discreet silence is to be commended. We might have supposed that the domestic sphere did not include all the thought of which even a woman is capable. But no; there is a sharp line drawn; so far can they advance, but here they must stop. . . . We ask: is this compatible with human nature? Is there any point at which humanity can stand still, intellectually, socially, mentally, morally? No; we progress or retrograde. Towards what shall we move? is the only question.

Now the progress of the Lower System of Education does not seem to tend towards improvement. The aim seems to be to teach women to suit themselves to others' requirements, because their well-being depends on others' approval. A woman's laudable ambition, say this school of philosophers, is first to become a wife, forgetting that the desire to become a wife does not necessarily include the desire to become a good wife. The direct road to become a wife is not by the development of the intellect, but by the development of certain feminine qualities, bad and good. A girl is to cultivate her love of dress, her taste for frivolities, her desire to please. Her life must embody soft pleasure, that she may be the embodiment of it to a sterner companion. What does a feminine life imply in these people's mouths? Vanity, ease, luxury, dissipation to the prescribed amount; lack of method, disrespect of time, carelessness of everything. Little failings incidental to those of the weaker sex are to be condoned, and little weaknesses made greater; for by their weakness they shall rule. Haphazard, aimless, helpless, women's lives must be; for their help comes from without. They are not strong enough, poor things, to fight life's battle. They must find some one to fight it for them. But does their taste for amusement and frivolities always stop when they have gained the husband? Is the desire for admiration, sometimes grown into a craving, always satisfied in the humdrum domestic career for which the Professors of the Lower System are so anxious that girls should be carefully prepared? Have these women any serious thoughts and worthy studies to fall back upon when they are once "settled?" They know nothing of all that. They were only taught to win men's admiration, to gratify their own desires. Why should marriage change them? There is no terminus in the education of human character; there are only stations. . . .

. . . Let us consider the dicta laid down for us by the advocates of the Lower System. "Women are made and meant to be, not men, but mothers of men." "A noble wife, a noble mother, &c." True, most true; but what are the means to the end? Should we set out with the object of making a good wife or a good mother before we have considered how to make a good woman? How do we get good human character? Is it not by the cultivation of all higher attributes, and the suppression of all lower? . . . We want good characters. Will good characters ever be formed by helpless, dependent lives? Do great individuals spring from a cowed and conquered people? . . . Look at the inmates of the workhouse, the paupers who cringe and fawn. What effect has that dependence on character? Yet the noble wife is to spring from a training not very different. All her life long she has never tasted the bread of independence. She waits whiningly for others to provide all that she requires, and hangs her whole weight upon some one man, from necessity, not choice. Why does a man's opinion immediately suggest a broad, well-balanced view, while the term "feminine" implies in most cases something weak and contemptible? Does it mean that man's vices are noble, and woman's virtues, faults? No, it means that a man has been trained and educated by the struggle of life. Each generation of men starts at a higher stage of development than the last; while women, so far as their minds and characters go, have been left uncultured, and in the general affairs of life they have made no progress worth speaking of. . . .

. . . "Women," say they, "do not desire emancipation." It is true. They have never been slaves. What they do desire is education; education that will enable them to find happiness within themselves; that will give them glad hours, bright dreams, and noble ambitions, under whatever roof they may call their home. They desire intellectual preparation for intellectual intercourse—if needs be, stimulated by competition. But they do not intend because of this to give up all claim to the happy life ordained for them as companions to men. On the contrary, they wish to become better fitted for that life than they are at present. They wish to enable themselves to enter into all men's views and thoughts. They wish to live with them as rational beings, as classmates in the school of life, though one may perhaps be on the higher, the other on the lower, form. . . . It is better for a woman to look on all good men as her friends—one dearest and best of all—than to look on all men as foes, to be battled with according to the rules of the lists. . . . And men and women can never work side by side unless the ground, whether for battle or for production, is the same; nor can they be either worthy allies or useful fellow-labourers, unless they have together prepared a plan of campaign, and together considered the work that needs doing and the means that are ready to hand. . . .

. . . The advocates of the Lower System, through Mrs. Lynn Linton, . . . admit that there is a difficulty as to women's employment. How do they meet it? The scheme is simple; they condemn women to manual labour. They may be tinkers, tailors, port-manteau-makers, or anything of that kind. We gather that they may cover toys with poisonous paint at 2s. a week, and yet our philosophers would not exclude them from the highest society. Nothing is degrading to women so long as it is not intellectual. Our "noble wives and mothers" are not strong enough for quiet study or intellectual excite-ment in a well-aired lecture-room; but they may stand for twelve hours at a stretch behind a counter in a draughty and ill-ventilated shop. They may strain eyes and injure weary backs over sewing. There is no danger, apparently, of destroying fair young faces, of blunting fine feelings, of decreasing vital force, by such a profession as that of the theatre. Women may be the hangers-on of fashion, and may minister, without danger to themselves, to its shifting whims in every department. . . . Women may do all this, and verily they would have their reward. But there is one thing a woman may not do. She may not be independent. She may depend upon a husband, or upon a fashion in flowers or jackets, but she must not be mistress of her own destiny; above all, she must not think. . . .

. . . Is man, who devotes his life to art, thought, or scientific discovery, to be satisfied with a wife who is either a frivolous society doll, or a sweet and patient drudge, or a woman with the ideas of the shopman with whom he would find no pleasure in associating? Are the great men who are to be born in the future, if only women will refrain from study, to be guided by the remembrance of their mother's face, as she appeared in powder and paint in some stupid vaudeville before a cheering theatre; are they to gaze admiringly on the trade gesticulation, or to listen lovingly to tales of sharp bargains and skilful adulteration?

Women whose characters have been formed by mechanical labour, unmitigated by higher education, are, according to these thinkers, to be the mothers of the Bacons and Goethes of the future. They object to over-pressure. So do we; but we object to it in any direction, and if in one direction more than another it would be in the direction from which comes least general profit, that of the mechanical and the material. Our fiery leveller would abolish all grades of rank and breeding and reduce women to one dead level of unintellectual pursuit. Men would alone be in possession of thought and knowledge, and would form an aristocracy of culture. This is rank anarchy and demoralization. How under such a system could a philosopher of the Lower System obtain a hearing even for criticism of her own sex? We maintain, on the contrary, that the effort for higher education is simply an effort to secure in the case of women what has always been the case with men. Women's ideals should be formed, as men's have been, by those who have lived out of the roar of traffic, out of the glare of politics, far from the influence of mobs, away from the contamination of commerce and the drudgery of manual labour. The women we want to form women's ideal of education are women with calm, well-balanced minds and hallowed hearts, equal to men in ideas and mental prowess, if inferior to them in mental, because in physical, endurance, and perhaps making up in spiritual insight for their lack of physical strength. This is the goal towards which we invite all women to strive whose position is fortunate enough to enable them to do so. Happily, in spite of the Lower plan of Education for women, the road is plain and the gates are already open; and it requires no gift of prophecy to foresee the time when highly educated women may be taught to study some stranded philosopher of the Lower System, long reduced to a fossilized condition, as we now study the extinct creatures of the mud period of the earth's history.

Emily Pfeiffer, *Women and Work* (London: Trübner & Co., 1888), pp. 163-72.

The following essay is a response to those scientists who "proved" that the subordinate status of women was inevitable, a natural outcome of woman's physiological deficiencies. Those who held that view, Mrs. Pfeiffer argued, were unable to distinguish cause from effect. It was not that woman's "inferior" brain condemned her to a non-intellectual existence; the conditions of that existence—a kind of mental strait jacket, made it impossible for her brain to develop to its natural capacity.

. . . Since the earlier portions of this essay were written, the article of Professor Romanes on the leading characters which mentally differentiate men and women, has appeared in the *Nineteenth Century*.

. . . I venture to question some of those conclusions in regard to the female brain, wherein Professor Romanes, in so knightly a fashion, with so many kindly, even flattering admissions, so softly but so surely lets us down.

The fact that the average weight of women's brains is said . . . to be about five ounces less than that of men, would seem at once, if not for ever, to settle the point in disfavour of equality of intellect, if size and weight were alone adequate to give the full measure of functional efficiency. That such is not the case, that, on the contrary, a small brain with more and deeper convolutions will present a larger surface to stimulating impressions than a larger brain less highly organised, will be acknowledged by no one more readily than by Professor Romanes himself. It is not an unlikely assumption that the facts in regard to the brains of women, have been gathered mostly from the outside, and that a more extended and intimate knowledge of their interior composition might lead to discoveries which would cause the feats occasionally accomplished with so disprized an instrument, to appear less unaccountable. . . .

From the showing that in the savage state the disparity of size between the brains of men and women, is less than when both have been subject to civilising influences, the deduction is made by Professor Romanes that woman is by nature less progressive than man. It would be possible, I think, to give another reading to this fact.

In concluding that if woman has not equally progressed, it is that she is not equally progressive, I believe that too little value is assigned to the relatively less intellectually stimulating nature of her work and condition in civilised society, and also to that deadweight of custom and opinion—the stunting nature of the ideals which have borne upon her. The sole work adapted to develop her full powers in any given direction has been that deriving from the high and onerous charge laid upon her by Nature; the rest may be said chiefly to have consisted of men's "leavings". . . . That women should have submitted to such a state of things may be taken by some as in itself a proof of inferiority. It is not so. Their submission is primarily the consequence of the burthen and labour of maternity; . . . and secondarily, because owing to the more refined and spiritual character of the force which the woman can bring to bear upon circumstances, a state of high social advance is needed before her characteristic influence can become fully effective. . . .

. . . Professor Romanes [maintains] that "it is in original work that the disparity" contended for "is most conspicuous." "It is," he tells us, "matter of ordinary comment, that in no one department of creative thought can women be said to have at all approached men, save in fiction." To this one saving clause he does not perhaps accord sufficient importance. For three such names, in our own country alone as those of Jane Austin, Charlotte Brontë, and George Eliot to appear upon the list in the course of less than fifty years, is no light thing when it is remembered that against them in the same time, from among all the manly host, we can only bring those of Sir Walter Scott, Thackeray, and Dickens as of equal or superior weight. . . .

When we come to compare the sexes, as Professor Romanes has done, in power of judgment, it can hardly be taken to imply innate defect if we find the female deficient in a matter so avowedly dependent on wealth of knowledge and training. As it is, there are questions of deep significance, on which the views of the average woman might, judged from a high standpoint, be held to be in advance of those of the average man. She is less given to "spend her life for that which is not bread, and her labour for that which profiteth not." In other words, the "love" which gives our spiritual measure, is apt in the woman to be higher pitched. When reason is overthrown from emotional causes, the loss or ruin of the home affections is the most potent agent with women: the loss of money with men.

I think we must, many of us, both men and women, have felt some surprise that the claim for superior self-control should have been made for the former. . . . Is it believed that beings in whom the sense perceptions are specially acute, bear pain with silent endurance as liking it? The tears of the woman are more ready because she is quicker to feel. . . . Of hysterics among women I am persuaded that a great deal more is heard than seen, and that the disease is unknown among those who have found work fitted to their powers; but the language is sadly in want of some term which would imply the same phase of emotional outbreak in the other sex. In view of the derivation of the word "hysteria," the proprieties of speech forbid us to call the utter loss of mental balance which is seen in the half-childish, half-animal rage of men, often provoked by the merest trifles, by that name. . . .

[My] remarks . . . are the expression of no vain desire to claim for women a present equality with men in force of intellect, or, in some respects, of character; their object is to vindicate, as at least an open question, the inherent capacity of the retarded sex for illimitable progress upon its own lines. . . .

Emily Davies, "Letters Addressed to a Daily Paper at Newcastle-Upon-Tyne, 1860", reprinted in *Thoughts on Some Questions Relating to Women* (Cambridge: Bowes & Bowes, 1910), pp. 13-18.

Emily Davies, whose efforts on behalf of higher education and votes for women have been cited elsewhere in this volume (see pp. 123-9), was also concerned with providing jobs for them, and had founded a branch of the Society for the Employment of Women shortly after meeting Madame Bodichon in 1858. In the excerpt that follows, Miss Davies argues that employment is the answer to the problem of "redundant women" and counters the objections of hostile critics who contend that the large-scale entry of women into the labor market is fraught with danger for them and society at large.

The arguments brought forward against the employment of women in fields of labour hitherto closed against them, are so various, and in some instances, so confused and mutually contradictory, that it is somewhat difficult to state them fairly. I believe, however, that almost all the current objections are based upon one or other of these two assumptions: either, that the proposed changes are undesirable in an economical point of view; or, that they are objectionable on moral and social grounds. To begin with the first class. It is said that the labour market is already amply supplied, and that by the introduction of more workers, the rate of wages would be lowered, by which the whole community would suffer. If this were so, it would at least be fair that all should suffer alike, and not that, as now, the heaviest share of the burden should be borne by the weaker sex. But is not the whole argument based upon a fallacy? It seems to be forgotten that whether women work or not, they must exist, and if they are not allowed to labour . . . , they must be burdensome to society. Nothing is saved by keeping them inactive and the produce of their labour is lost. No man in his senses would keep two or three of his sons doing nothing, in order to give the rest a better chance of getting on; yet this would be as reasonable as to refuse work to women lest there should not be enough left for men. If the labour market should become over-stocked, it would be necessary to seek fresh outlets; and it seems likely that the colonies will supply openings for both men and women during many years to come. I do not think, however, that the admission of women into certain trades and professions, from which they are now excluded, would perceptibly affect the general rate of wages. It should be borne in mind that female workers would be continually drafted off by marriage, and that consequently the number of additional competitors would not be very formidable.

This brings me to another argument, which is so reasonable that I am anxious to give it full consideration. It is urged that as, in the great majority of cases, women would give up their business on entering upon that other business of marriage, it is not worth while to throw away upon them an expensive preparation for anything else. I reply, that the training of clerks is not expensive. They learn by experience, for which they do not pay in money. Capital is no doubt required to set up in trade, but even that expenditure could scarcely be looked upon as thrown away, as it is generally easy to dispose of a business, supposing there is no other member of the family to succeed to it. The money spent in preparing for the medical profession is sunk, but a few years of practice would probably repay the actual cost, and to the mother of a family it would, to a great extent, be made up by saving the expense of a family doctor. The Rev. Charles Simeon is reported to have said to a friend, "If you have a thousand pounds to give your son, put it in his head rather than in his pocket." The advice is equally applicable to the case of daughters. Give them an education which in case of need they can turn to some profitable account, rather than invest the savings destined for their use in the Funds, or in joint-stock banks, those attractive but dangerous concerns, whose downfall from time to time brings ruin on hundreds of helpless women.

The objectors to an extension of the sphere of women, on moral and social grounds, take a different line of argument. It is contended by some that a certain degree of helplessness in women is not only becoming but useful, as a stimulus to exertion in men. This is scarcely a fair argument, unless it could be proved that it is also good for women to sit with folded hands admiring the activity of men. I believe, however, that it is in itself without foundation. Single men do not feel stimulated by the vague knowledge that there are a good many women in the world requiring to be supported, and married men would in any case have their families to provide for. A fear has indeed been expressed that, if women had anything else to do, they would be unwilling to marry, and a diminution in the number of marriages (justly regarded as a serious evil), would ensue. But those who entertain such an apprehension must surely look upon matrimony as a very unhappy estate. If women can only be driven into it by *ennui*, or as a means of earning a livelihood, how is it that men are willing to marry? Are the advantages all on their side? The experience of happy wives and mothers forbids such a supposition. It is likely, on the contrary, that, by making women more capable, the number of marriages would be increased, as many men would be glad to marry, who are now deterred from doing so by prudential considerations.

There remains one more objection, which, I believe, lies at the root of all. It is averred that "public life" is injurious to women; that they are meant for the domestic circle; and that, though we are bound to sympathise with, and relieve to the extent of our ability, cases of individual suffering, we must on no account interfere with the law of nature, which has made home, and home only, woman's sphere. It is most true that no advantages, real or apparent, to be gained in public life would compensate for the loss of the domestic virtues; but does it necessarily follow that, if women took a more active part in the business of the world, they would therefore cease to care for home?

Let us look at this bugbear—this *bête-noire* called "public life"—fairly in the face. What is it we mean by it? Is there any woman living who does not go more or less into public; and what is it that makes the difference between justifiable and unjustifiable publicity? Probably no woman in the three kingdoms leads a more public life than the Queen, yet it may be questioned whether a more admirable wife and mother is to be found among her subjects. . . . The fact is, that "to us, the fools of habit," what is new is dangerous; what we have long been accustomed to, is proper and becoming. Fathers who would shake their heads at the idea of taking their daughters into their own counting-houses, allow them to stand behind a stall at a bazaar, or to lead off at a charity ball—far more public scenes, and where, indeed, publicity is essential to success. And if we really hold the doctrine that it is improper for a woman to follow any calling which cannot be pursued at her own fireside, how is it that we flock to hear public singers? It is idle to say that we would not allow our own daughters or sisters to perform in public. We have no right to sanction by our presence, and to derive enjoyment from the exercise of, a profession which in theory we condemn as unfeminine and, if so, of a demoralising tendency.

In conclusion, I may be permitted to say a few words to those liberal-minded persons who are favourable to the movement now in progress, but who content themselves with standing aside and wishing it God-speed, under the impression that that is all they can do. You can—nay, you must—either help this movement forward, or, in a greater or less degree, retard it. . . . Whoever and whatever you are, you can testify against the notion that indolence is feminine and refined; and that if a lady may, in certain cases, be permitted to work, her labour must at any rate be unpaid. You can assist in breaking down those false notions of propriety by which women are hampered in so many directions. And so you may help them to exchange a condition of labour without profit, and leisure without ease, for a life of wholesome activity, and the repose that comes with fruitful toil.

[Emily Faithfull], "A Clerical View of Woman's Sphere", *Victoria Magazine,* XVII (1871), 355-58.

To Emily Faithfull and the other founders of the Society for Promoting the Employment of Women, printing seemed one of the occupations in which the male monopoly could be successfully challenged. In 1859 they established the Victoria Press, which for several years printed the yearly *Transactions* of the Social Science Association, and in 1862 Miss Faithfull was named Printer and Publisher in ordinary to the Queen. The next year she and Emily Davies collaborated in establishing the monthly *Victoria Magazine,* which Miss Davies edited the first year and Miss Faithfull thereafter, until its demise in 1880. The magazine had some distinguished contributors and, although it published a number of articles dealing with female emancipation, was directed mainly to the general reader.

Herself the daughter of a clergyman, Miss Faithfull was critical of those churchmen who asserted that sexual equality was counter to the word of God. In 1870, at a crowded meeting of the Victoria Discussion Society, she insisted that the woman's movement was completely consistent "with the highest Christian rule".[1]

In the following selection she answers the charge that feminists were subverting the sacred relationship of the sexes, which had been sanctified by the Bible as well as by centuries of Christian teaching and practice. (The Mr. Burgon referred to is the same whose sermon of 1884 is quoted on pages 48-51 above.)

A sermon recently preached at St. Mary's Vincent Square, Westminster, gives another melancholy proof of the inability of the ordinary type of clergyman to follow even at a humble distance in the footsteps of the Great Master. A little while since Mr. Burgon avowed in an Oxford pulpit that he "loathed" womanly benevolence, enterprise and usefulness, that he was "shocked" at letters sent to newspapers signed with a woman's own name, . . . and now we have the Rev. Charles Dunbar seeking notoriety by the same means. He summons his congregation to warn them that "there is a movement on foot to overturn the whole fabric of society, by dragging women down from their high position and their previous seclusion, to make them strive and fight upon equal terms with fierce-passioned and grasping men, in a heartless, cold, hard, and calculating world."

. . . Mr. Dunbar talks with a simplicity which would be amusing were it not cruel, of a movement on foot for "dragging women down." Does he only credit "dames of high degree" with womanly virtues and instincts? Or is he ignorant of the rough and demoralizing work to which women have been subjected since the days when the sale of a wife in England was a legal transaction, to the generation of which Corbett [*sic*] said, "it is a common thing to see women working like beasts, chained to carts, upon the common roads of England."

"The movement on foot" began by protesting against the employment of women in coal shafts, as pinmakers at Warrington, where they worked from twelve to sixteen hours a day and when tired were struck with straps and sticks in spite of the "delicacy of the sex". . . . "Whatever tends to destroy the meekness, the retiring modesty—I will not shrink from saying it—the submission and obedience of women, tends to destroy the Bible ideal of her true honour and dignity," says the Rev. Charles Dunbar. Why, then, has he not lifted up his voice against the work in which women have been engaged to the destruction of their souls and bodies, entailing scenes which Lord Shaftsbury said, not a fortnight since, he could not venture to describe in his place in the House of Lords; instead of reserving his indignation for a few women who ask for representation in Parliament to make known the unfit employments which have long degraded them and who seek political equality with their fellow workers in order to obtain an equal wage and social consideration.

"In advocating this movement for 'the equality and the rights of women,' few people will deny that they are acting in defiance of the revelation from God given to them through St. Peter and St. Paul." We unhesitatingly reply that if we could not reconcile "this movement" with the highest Christian rule we would never advocate it more. But men like Mr. Dunbar and Mr. Burgon need to be reminded that "the letter killeth, but the spirit giveth life." God's government of the world is one of progress, and the only wonder is that the subjection and slavery to which St. Paul recommended submission lasted so long. . . .

[1] "A Protest Against Woman's Demand for the Privileges of Both Sexes", p. 354.

On the very day we read Mr. Dunbar's announcement that the SCHOOL BOARD was not a favourable place for the cultivation of a "meek and quiet spirit," the report of the latest discussion of the London School Board reached us. We found from it that hours had been occupied in debating on the propriety of mixed schools, and in considering whether washing, cooking, and elementary drawing should be taught in girls' schools. What is Mr. Dunbar thinking of? Has he no female relatives who have taught him that a woman's decision in matters of this nature is not only valuable but imperative? Is he able to set at naught God's announcement that "it was not good for man to live alone," which was surely not narrowed to a mere physical basis?

But to the "law and to the testimony" cry such divines as the Pharisees of old, deliberately shutting their eyes to the fact that each act of Christ proclaimed the principle of the perfect equality of all human beings, men and women, as the basis of all social philosophy and religious life. . . .

. . . The exercise of the franchise is doubtless the bugbear before which Mr. Dunbar trembles and despairs. We must remind him, however, that the science of politics considered in its widest sense is the science of humanity, and effects [*sic*] women as much as men and as long as women can complain of . . . difficulties which no one has attempted to confute, women will have cause to regard their representation in Parliament as inefficient, and in spite of the vials of clerical wrath which are poured upon them from the pulpits of clergymen of the Burgon and Dunbar stamp they must endeavour to reach the ear and the heart of those who can and ought to interfere on their behalf, even if they use the terrible means of writing to newspapers and "sign their own names," when they request the help and confidence of those who can alone enable them to rescue their fellow women — on whom such tender epithets are lavished — from degradation and despair. Really, we feel tempted to exclaim in the words of the inspired Book, from which these preachers vainly imagine they have drawn arguments which demolish all who differ from them, — "Eyes have they, and see not, they have ears, and hear not", and, for their own sakes, we devoutly wish we could also add, while this is the case, "neither speak they through their throats."

W. A. Hale, "The Emancipation of Women", *Westminster Review,* CII (1874), 137-55.

The following excerpt deals, point by point, with the various objections raised by the opponents of votes for women. In a cogent, lucid, well-reasoned, and temperate analysis, Hale refutes, for example, the argument that women are congenitally unfit to vote; that they are too excitable to be trusted with a role in the electoral process; that they are virtually represented by their husbands; and that, because most women are indifferent to the franchise, all of them should be denied it.

. . . The chief objections that have been raised to the emancipation of women [are] objections mostly of detail, raised by those who, unable to grasp a large general idea, instinctively fix their eyes successively on the supposed difficulties in carrying it out. Some of these objections — most of them, in fact — serve to display the curious ingenuity of the human mind in imagining hindrances to any alteration of an established order of things, the first feeling being always, not, how can we see our way to grant this? but, how shall we discover a sufficient number of objections to justify our refusal? . . .

Here, however, is the first, perhaps only, objection which really deserves attention, that the majority of women do not desire the suffrage.

We answer, that the minority which does desire it is a constantly increasing one (not adequately represented even by the increasing number of signatures to petitions). We must further point out that a large portion of the majority, which does not desire it, has simply not been educated to think about it, and has passed a great part of life without the subject having been brought before it at all; whilst the minority, that does desire it, includes very many women of the highest intellect and cultivation, who have thought deeply on the subject, and many who, feeling for themselves and their neighbours the need of better protection than masculine legislation has hitherto allowed them, gladly welcome the faintest hope of emancipation. Next, as to those who desire the suffrage without signing petitions for it, few men can realize, without some effort of the imagination, the pressure put upon women in all cases where their views differ from those of the masculine public. . . . Next, we must take into account that intense shrinking from masculine sarcasm and mockery which has been so carefully fostered in women that they have justly been said to "live under a gospel of ridicule". . . . Few can realize . . . how much silent revolt goes on in subjected classes before they openly rebel. In men this silent revolt is generally held to be dangerous, and worth inquiring into; in women, for obvious reasons, it is not. And with women it will be longest maintained, and with more corroding bitterness in proportion, in spite of the persuasions, half contemptuous, half flattering, which now, more frequently than before, alternate with sneers. . . .

We are ready to allow that there are women — and doubtless even some thinking and cultivated ones amongst them . . . who deprecate female suffrage altogether; many more who are absolutely indifferent, and all of these are apt to conceive that their own individual dislike or indifference is argument enough against extending the suffrage to those who do desire it. . . . We hold, nevertheless, that even these, the indifferent — all in fact — would be directly or indirectly benefited in time by the change. Those who do not want the franchise need not exercise it — that is their own affair, as it is of men, who in like manner may decline to vote, though we hold that the choice ought to be given to them nevertheless. We doubt, however, whether these very female dissentients will not be glad, when the time comes, to use their own votes, after seeing how easily and quietly other women have used theirs before them. And what is more, we suspect the masculine objectors will be equally glad to profit by these votes.

Finally, the argument that women do not want the franchise and would be better without it, is in spirit the same as that by which slaveholders have always justified slavery. We do not hold that the negro's ignorance of the moral evils of his position was an argument for keeping him in it. . . .

. . . It is said that women are unfit for the vote, because they are women. It is true that the training enforced upon women, directly and indirectly, for ages, by men, whereby their characters and minds are in some sort the artificial creation of men, has seemingly had for its object to make them unfit for the powers men exercise. Women have, in consequence, for ages made no combined effort for emancipation; but exactly as they become aware of the real nature of this traditional training, does this supposed unfitness lessen, and the best way at this moment completely to fit them to exercise those powers is to grant them.

What mental or moral "fitness" is sought for as a qualification for the masculine voter, except by that rough sort of classification which does not exclude the drunkard, the wife-beater, the illiterate, the liberated convict, and the semi-idiot? And when you place beside these Harriet Martineau, Florence Nightingale, George Eliot, and many more whose names we all know, as well as the numbers of women who show every kind of practical fitness in common life—to say that *these* are unfit because they are women, and *those* are fit because they are men, is very like begging the question.

But there are special unfitnesses urged against women. We cannot condescend to dwell on the argument that they are incapable of giving their vote for want of physical strength, or that [their] chronic state of "blushing and fear" . . . would make it improper and impossible for even a middle-aged woman to face the bustle of polling-places. . . . But we will mention one other (we think the only special) unfitness alleged against them. . . . This special unfitness resides in their greater "impulsiveness," "excitability," and "sympathy," which are supposed to include and imply "unreasonableness" and "injustice." Till, however, it is argued that Ireland, for example, is naturally disqualified for the suffrage because the Celt is more "excitable," "impulsive," and "sympathetic" than the Saxon—or indeed till, as we must repeat, moral or intellectual qualifications are made a *sine qua non* in any class of masculine voters whatever, this objection can hardly stand. . . .

Next, it has been alleged that already too many *men* have the suffrage, as a reason for withholding it from women. Even granting the fact, it is not just to say that, because A has had too much given him of a good thing, therefore B shall have none at all, especially when B even requires it as a protection against A. . . .

Here, naturally, comes the assertion, that "women are virtually represented by men." Indeed, on every proposed extension of political rights, it has been usual for the classes who thought their interests opposed to it to urge that *they* virtually represented the others. This assertion is disproved by the whole course of class legislation in all ages and everywhere; and the harshness of masculine legislation for women certainly forms no exception to the rule.

If we are reminded that some classes of men are still unrepresented, we answer (putting aside the probably near approach of household suffrage), that *all* women of *all* classes are unrepresented, are all declared to labour under an irremediable birth-disqualification. Individual *men* of the unenfranchised classes can rise to acquire a vote: a woman never can. And women only ask for the vote on the same conditions as those on which it is conferred upon men.

Let us consider here the confessed difficulty of protecting wives in certain classes against the violence of their husbands, as bearing on the plea of "virtual representation". . . . Compare the penalties inflicted in these cases with those in which a wife has assaulted a husband, or one man another man. *Here* there is no difficulty in carrying out the full severity of the law. We do not assert that those who administer it do not *wish* to enforce it in behalf of women, though judges and juries do sometimes give us cause to suspect them of considering an assault by the inferior on the superior, by the weaker on the stronger, as more heinous than one with the conditions reversed.

The wife is, in these classes, so helplessly in her husband's power, so trained to feel the violence of her master as a part of his conjugal superiority, that she very often dares not, perhaps actually does not, resent his brutality. It seems to us that at least one approach towards remedying this state of things would be to surround her social status with every equal right and dignity the law can give her. Law should not aim at rendering her *more* helpless, *more* dependent than inferior strength would naturally make her. . . . That almost superstitious, dog-like patience and loyalty which lead a wife to submit to a beating without a complaint, and which some men tenderly praise as the *ne plus ultra* of wife-like excellence, might, we think, be exchanged for a nobler form of devotion by making her her husband's legal and social equal; and one indirect step towards this will be giving women some share in making the laws which concern themselves.

A favorite objection is, that the exercise of the suffrage will interfere with women's duties. It cannot be seriously meant by this that the taking up of a few hours every few years in delivering a vote will hinder a woman — even the most hard-working — in her daily duties more than it would a hard-working man. Indeed, in the present case, it is only asked for unmarried women and widows, many of them possessed of ample leisure and sufficient means. . . .

Further, these objectors will add that if you grant the suffrage to the single having the proper qualification, wives will by-and-by demand it as well, either by a change in the qualification for a vote, or in the marriage law. We answer, let that question be discussed when the time comes. It is neither just nor generous to refuse a rightful concession for fear other concessions may be asked for. Meanwhile the supposed moral difficulty of granting the suffrage to wives still rests mainly on the old assumption that women only wait the opportunity to discard their natural duties and affections; that men can be safely trusted with absolute authority over their families, but women not even with the exercise of an independent opinion; that wives at present neither have, not in fact ought to have, any difference of opinion from their husbands (except on trivial points), but certainly would, if they were once permitted to act on their opinions; and that they will necessarily seize the vote as an occasion for quarrel; also on the assumption that it is the business of the State to provide against these little domestic difficulties in married life (but only, of course, by laying restrictions on the wife). We can scarcely suppose, however, that any man blessed with an affectionate wife seriously anticipates that, once possessed of a vote, she would make it her business to thwart and oppose him. If his wife is not an affectionate one, we fear the legislature cannot help him, and we are very sure it is not its business to do so. . . .

There is also the contradictory assumption that the wife's vote will be merely a double of her husband's, thus giving him two votes instead of one. Between these last two assumptions of perverse opposition on the one hand, and undue submission on the other, we may fairly strike a balance, and hope the State will fare none the worse in the end for the female married vote, should it be granted. . . .

Lastly, there is the objection — the most formidable of all to some minds — that all female aspirants to the suffrage are "strong-minded women," and that "strong-minded women are very disagreeable". . . . We daresay that the agitators for the abolition of slavery made themselves very disagreeable. . . . People engaged in a great struggle will not always pause to consult the conventional rules of good taste, yet the cause may be a good one nevertheless. . . .

And now come two more serious reproaches addressed to women. "They have done so much mischief." "They are agitating from a love of power."

The accusation of "doing mischief" means, we imagine, only that women are not infallible in their judgment, any more than men (why is a human liability to mistake *more* disqualifying to women than to men?), or that there are points on which the objectors differ from some women, or that there always will be points on which some men will differ from some women, it being assumed, of course, that women will always be in the wrong. . . . No past experience can be appealed to as decisive, since women have never been placed in the position supposed; although the absolute denial of all direct legitimate exercise of power sometimes drives intense and ardent natures into exercising it by methods less wholesome than a recognised responsibility would employ. But even granting this—alas! have men never done mischief, terrible mischief, during the long ages of masculine domination? Take, as one instance, the legislation for Ireland up to this century, and more recent times still; could any female legislation be more blind, unjust, inhuman, and—mischievous?

Is the world, as governed by men, a thing even now to congratulate ourselves upon? and may not women think that even a slight co-operation of their own with the other sex in the councils of the nation—we are not now speaking of admission to Parliament—might have prevented, might still prevent, some of this mischief?

The reproach that "women are agitating from love of power," does not come with quite a good grace from that sex which has hitherto monopolized all power, exercised, as we think, with such grievous injustice to the other. But, in fact, the reproach is undeserved. Those who make it show such a misunderstanding of the deeply conscientious feelings and convictions on which this new movement is founded, as almost disqualifies them from discussing this question with us at all. Power to protect themselves from injustice women may be allowed to desire. But a still stronger motive is the belief that the welfare of society requires a different position for their whole sex. . . .

The men of the past did what seemed the best in those days; the men of the present are not to blame for the altered conditions which have made it the worst. But they will be to blame if they persist in upholding it and in regarding attempted reforms as attempts to "remove the landmarks of society;" if, in a word, they endeavour to force the life of successive generations of women into the old Chinese shoe of subjection and restraint fancying that if they just make it a little easier, all will be right. The shoe must be made to fit perfectly, and women themselves must decide whether it does so. . . .

Millicent Garrett Fawcett, "The Appeal Against Female Suffrage: A Reply", *Nineteenth Century*, XXVI (1889), 86-96.

Millicent Garrett Fawcett, the younger sister of Elizabeth Garrett Anderson, was, as we have seen, concerned with improving the quality of female education, but it was as a champion of woman's suffrage that she became most active and prominent. "A brilliant conversationalist and extremely witty",[1] well-matched intellectually with her husband, the noted Henry Fawcett, professor of political economy at Cambridge and an M.P. with very liberal views, she was also an accomplished public speaker and a successful author, having published biographies of several prominent Victorian women and a history of the suffrage movement. From 1897 to 1919 she was president of the National Union of Women's Suffrage Societies which, unlike the Pankhurst-dominated, authoritarian, and militant Women's Social and Political Union, was organized on democratic lines, and strove to obtain the vote through constitutional and non-violent means.

[1] Harry Furniss, *Some Victorian Women, Good, Bad, and Indifferent* (London: John Lane, The Bodley Head Limited, 1932), p. 116.

The *Nineteenth Century,* in its issue of July 1889, published a two-part reply, by Millicent Garrett Fawcett and M. M. Dilke, to "An Appeal Against Female Suffrage", which had appeared in the same journal the previous month (see pp. 260-2). In the following excerpt from her part of the reply, Mrs. Fawcett, using her pen like a scalpel, deflates the pretensions of the ladies who had signed the "Appeal" and exposes the fallacies of their arguments.

. . . The ladies who sign the *Nineteenth Century* Protest against the enfranchisement of women . . . do not wish it to be supposed that they are opposed to the recent improvements that have taken place in the education of women, or to their increased activity in various kinds of public work. . . .

. . . But, on reading the names appended to the Protest, the most striking fact about them is that hardly any out of the hundred and four ladies who now rejoice in these changes have helped them while their issue was in any way doubtful. . . . The women to whose initiative we owe the improvements which the hundred and four rejoice in, are not to be found in the *Nineteenth Century* list. . . . The names of the women to whose unselfish and untiring labours we owe what has been done for women during the last twenty-five years in education, in social and philanthropic work, in proprietary rights, in some approach towards justice as regards the guardianship of children, in opening the means of medical education, are conspicuous by their absence, and for an excellent reason: they support the extension of the suffrage to duly qualified women. . . .

A further consideration of the *Nineteenth Century* list of names shows that it contains a very large preponderance of ladies to whom the lines of life have fallen in pleasant places. There are very few among them of the women who have had to face the battle of life alone, to earn their living by daily hard work. . . .

A large part of the Protest is directed against women taking an active part in the turmoil of political life. This has nothing to do with voting or not voting. For instance, women vote in school board elections; but they can please themselves about taking part in the turmoil of a school board contest. Thousands of women vote who keep completely clear of meetings, canvassing, committees, and all the rest of the electioneering machinery. On the other hand, women do not vote in Parliamentary elections, but they are invited and pressed by all parties to take an active part in the turmoil of political life. Among other inconsistencies of the protesting ladies, it should not be forgotten that many of them, as presidents and vice-presidents of women's political associations, encourage the admission of women to the ordinary machinery of political life, although they say in this Protest that this admission would be dangerous to the best interests of society. If women are fit to advise, convince, and persuade voters how to vote, they are surely also fit to vote themselves. On the other hand, if it is true, as the *Nineteenth Century* ladies state, that women on the whole "are without the materials for forming a sound judgment" on matters of constitutional change, why are we invited by these same ladies to form our unsound judgments, and do all in our power to induce others to share them? If we have no materials, or insufficient materials, for forming a sound judgment in politics, we should not be invited to enrol ourselves in Primrose Leagues, or in the Women's Liberal Federation, or in the Women's Liberal Unionist Association. To say simultaneously to women, "The materials for forming a sound judgment are not open to you," and "We beg you to influence electors to whom is entrusted the fate of the empire," is to run with the hare and hunt with the hounds.

One position or the other must be abandoned, unless these ladies have cultivated with unusual skill the art of believing two contradictory things at the same time.

The Protest against women's suffrage has no doubt been called forth by the rapid progress made by the women's suffrage movement to an important place as a practical question of politics. The hundred and four ladies attribute this almost entirely "to party considerations of a temporary character". . . .

. . . If the ladies who sign this Protest were rather more intimately acquainted with the history of the women's suffrage movement, they would know that it has lost as much as it has gained by mere party feeling. . . .

The "party, nothing but party" politician in England, as well as in America, looks with distrust on women's suffrage. Women would be an unknown quantity, less amenable to party discipline, less expectant of party loaves and fishes, and consequently less obedient to the party whip than the present electorate. They might take the bit in their mouth and insist on voting in a way inconvenient to their party on temperance, and on matters of religion and morals. . . . If women's suffrage should tend to strengthen the group, which exists in every constituency, of the voters whose political views are not dictated to them from a central office in Parliament Street or Victoria Street, but are the result of independent thought, study of facts, and conscientious obedience to moral considerations, it is a matter of very small importance which party will gain or lose by the female vote; all parties will be the better for it.

. . . Up to the present, "the party" whether Liberal, Conservative, or Radical, has given women's suffrage more kicks than halfpence; but we have received invaluable help from the best and most independent men of all parties. . . . It should not be forgotten that many of the men who have had the most formative influence on the current of thought, political and otherwise, in England during the last twenty-five years, have supported the political enfranchisement of women. A cause that has been supported by Mr. J. S. Mill, Mr. Walter Bagehot, Sir Henry Maine, the Rev. F. D. Maurice, and Mr. Charles Darwin, stands on something stronger than "the passing needs of party organisations."

It was natural that the subscribers to the Protest should make the most of a subject on which the supporters of women's suffrage are not at one: viz. the admission or the exclusion of married women. . . . Both the Bills for women's suffrage that were introduced this session . . . would have enfranchised those women who have already received the municipal, county council, and school board suffrages; *i.e.* single women and widows who are householders, property owners, and otherwise fulfil the conditions imposed by law on male electors.

The *Nineteenth Century* ladies think that these Bills would "enfranchise large numbers of women leading immoral lives," and on the other hand, by excluding wives, would shut out those women "who as a rule, have passed through more of the practical experiences of life than the unmarried". . . . By the words "large numbers of women leading immoral lives," it may be presumed that the ladies refer to some women who might become qualified to vote under the lodger franchise. Among "the materials for forming a sound judgment" in this matter are the following facts, which are not beyond the grasp of the female intellect: Two consecutive years' residence in the same apartments, and also personal application to be placed upon the Parliamentary register are required of any one claiming the lodger franchise. These conditions have, as regards the male sex, made this franchise almost a dead letter: for example, in the borough of Blackburn, with 13,000 electors, only fifteen men vote under the lodger franchise. In most constituencies the lodgers are an absolutely insignificant fraction of the whole body of electors. The conditions which prevent men lodgers from becoming electors would be even more effective in preventing women lodgers, of the unhappy class referred to, from getting upon the register. On the other hand, the large class of most respectable and worthy women who live in lodgings, such as teachers and others engaged in education, would have no difficulty in fulfilling the conditions demanded, and would form a valuable addition to the electorate.

Foreigners often talk of English hypocrisy; and this bugbear about women's suffrage rendering it possible for an immoral woman to vote for a member of Parliament, appears an excellent example of it. How long has a stainless moral character been one of the conditions for exercising the Parliamentary suffrage? When it is remembered that no moral iniquity disqualifies a man from voting, that men of known bad character not only vote but are voted for, it is hardly possible to accept as genuine the objection to women's suffrage based on the possibility of an immoral woman voting. . . . Who can say, if women's suffrage were carried, that the new electors would not be of a character calculated to raise, rather than depress, the moral level of the constituencies to which they belong?

The next objection of the hundred and four is that, if wives are excluded, those who would be shut out are women "who have, as a rule, passed through more of the practical experiences of life than the unmarried;" whilst if they are included, "changes of enormous importance, which have never been adequately considered, would be introduced into home life." The editor [of the *Nineteenth Century*] echoes, and in echoing magnifies, the fear here implied, for he "submits" that ladies should "for once" come forward and signify publicly their "condemnation of the scheme now threatened," "in order to save the quiet of home life from total disappearance." He must be very unhappy if he feels that the quiet of home life depends for its existence on an Act of Parliament.[1] The quiet of home life, for those who are blessed with what deserves to be called a home, is one of those things that "looks on tempests and is never shaken". . . . I think he will survive women's suffrage. . . . The case for the enfranchisement of women who are standing alone and bearing the burden of citizenship as ratepayers and taxpayers, seems unanswerable. If we have household suffrage, let the head of the house vote, whether that head be a man or a woman. The enfranchisement of wives is an altogether different question. The enfranchisement of single women and widows gives electoral power to a class who are in a position of social and financial independence. To give these women votes would be a change in their political condition, bringing it into harmony with their social, industrial, and pecuniary position. This would not be the case with wives. If they were enfranchised, the effect, in ninety-nine cases out of a hundred, would be to give two votes to the husband. . . .

In conclusion, the ladies of the *Nineteenth Century* Protest may be reminded that the friends of women's suffrage value the womanliness of women as much as themselves. True womanliness grows and thrives on whatever strengthens the spontaneity and

---

[1] At this point, the editor of the *Nineteenth Century* retorts in a footnote that he "does *not* feel that the existing quiet of home life depends upon any Act of Parliament; but he does feel that such an act as Mrs. Fawcett and her friends desire would fatally injure it. For it would give a colourable pretext to the wire-pullers and agitators of all political factions to intrude wherever there was a vote to be struggled and wrangled after, and into countless homes now happily free from them and their squabbles". The hostility of editor James T. Knowles toward extending the franchise to women was already known to the readers of the *Nineteenth Century*. Appended to the list of signatures to "An Appeal Against Female Suffrage" (June 1889) was Knowles's personal plea calling on other women to add their names to the protest.

independence of the character of women. Women, for instance, are more womanly
in England, where Florence Nightingale and Mary Carpenter have taught them how
women's work ought to be done, than they are in Spain, where they accept the masculine standard in matters of amusement and go in crowds to see a bull-fight. . . . We
do not want women to be bad imitations of men, we neither deny nor minimise the
differences between men and women. The claim of women to representation depends
to a large extent on those differences. Women bring something to the service of the
state different from that which can be brought by men. Let this fact be frankly recognised and let due weight be given to it in the representative system of the country.

Millicent Garrett Fawcett, "The Future of Englishwomen: A Reply",
Nineteenth Century, IV (1878), 347-57.

More than a decade before the appearance of Millicent Garrett Fawcett's
reply (cited above) to "An Appeal Against Female Suffrage", the *Nineteenth Century* had published an anti-feminist article, "The Future of
English Women", by Mrs. Sutherland Orr, to which Mrs. Fawcett also
responded. Mrs. Orr maintained that there was an implicit danger in
the drive for emancipation: if the movement continued to advance, it
would inevitably lead to disastrous consequences; nothing less, in fact,
than the "decomposition" of society. Therefore, she concluded, it was
essential to call a halt immediately.[1]

Mrs. Fawcett's reply was not confined to the suffrage question, but
was in effect a clear statement of the hopes and aspirations embodied in
the middle-class feminist program. In rejecting Mrs. Orr's plea for a
cessation of feminist activity, Mrs. Fawcett defined what might well be
called the ultimate goal of feminism: "to hasten the time when every
woman shall have the opportunity of becoming the best that her natural
faculties make her capable of "(p. 357).

Because she can be considered a spokeswoman for middle-class Victorian
feminism, and since this article contains her views on such matters as
marriage, careers, and the role of single women in society, an excerpt
from it is included here (although it is not in strict chronological order)
as a kind of summary of the whole feminist position.

. . . Mrs. Orr says that . . . if it [the woman's movement] continues to advance
and runs its course unchecked, dire and terrible evils are to be expected from it. If
female emancipation reaches its full and final attainment, "not only the power of love
in women, but for either sex its possibility, will have passed away." The miserable
man of the future will vainly seek the woman's love he can no longer find, and then in
prophetic vision Mrs. Orr imagines that she sees "Nature, outraged and no longer to
be eluded, avenging herself." The women of the future will probably refuse to bear
children; or if they are mothers, their qualifications to become truly motherly mothers
will be of the feeblest, and their children may be expected to be puny and miserable,
alike in body, intellect, and soul. . . .

[1] A. Orr, "The Future of English Women", *Nineteenth Century*, III (1878), 1010-28.

What every one who reads Mrs. Orr's article with attention will ask is, "Where does she find the slightest foundation in actual facts for her gloomy predictions as to the effect of freedom upon Englishwomen?" There has been already much experience on which an opinion may be formed. I do not now refer to the handful of women in the upper and middle ranks of life who have made professional careers for themselves, although the fact that many of them have married and have become loving wives and tender mothers weighs for something against Mrs. Orr's argument. But they, perhaps it may be said, are exceptional. Still it is worth something to know that the power of emotion and sympathy has not been dried up in them, that it has been rather intensified and strengthened. Much more useful experience . . . may be found if we consider the circumstances of the women from whom the class of domestic servants are drawn. . . . They have been free to choose their own employments, to take one situation or quit another; they are generally removed from parental control. . . . They are entirely self-supporting and independent, with a career and, in a humble way, a competency of their own. Yet we do not see in them any symptom of the disappearance of the capacity of the kind of love which leads to marriage; we do not see any weakening of the family affections generally. I have often personally been struck by the considerable sacrifices servants have been ready to make for their parents, and with their motherliness to a little group of motherless brothers and sisters. In those cases in which my own servants have spoken to me about their approaching marriage, I have detected none of that harsh, unlovely drying up of the emotions, which Mrs. Orr expects to see in women of her own rank if independent professional careers are thrown open to them. . . . Nothing, it seems to me is so truly contrary to the emotional ideal in marriage as the social tone which condemns for women every career but marriage. Mrs. Orr is mistaken in saying that the "women's rights party," with Mr. Mill at their head, agree in regarding marriage simply as a legal contract in which the emotional element forms no important part. . . . I believe I represent the vast majority of women who have worked in this movement when I say that I believe that the emotional element in the marriage contract is of overwhelming importance; and that anything which puts forward the commercial view of marriage and sinks the spiritual or emotional view is degrading both to men and women. . . . Mrs. Orr is herself what I must call a sinner against marriage, in the slighting way in which she speaks of single women: they are, in her language, "superfluous," "supernumerary;" they have a "mutilated existence;" if they pass through life without wishing to marry, they are "devoid of sentiment;" the whole woman's rights movement would come to an end, she says, if half a million or so of marrying men could be imported and told off in some Utopian fashion to marry all the adult single women who are asking for education, votes, and other masculine luxuries. They are clamouring, she says in effect, for their "rights;" but, whether they know it or not, they would be satisfied with husbands. As I came to these adjectives "supernumerary" and "superfluous," there arose in my mind visions of some of the noblest and best of women, whose lives are filled to the brim with useful work, well and conscientiously done, who have been free to devote themselves to this absorbing work because they have been unmarried. Are Florence Nightingale, . . . Octavia Hill, and many others, to be cast aside, as it were, with the contemptuous adjective "superfluous," as if in marriage alone women could find an honourable career? It seems to me that a woman is or is not "superfluous" in proportion as she finds and performs useful work which the world, or some little bit of the world, wants done. "There was the work wanting to be done, and I wanting to do it," says Miss Martineau in her autobiography.

Whoever can honestly say that, is not superfluous, even if she be an old maid of the most old-maidish type. Whoever cannot say it, is superfluous, even though she may have had as many husbands as the woman of Samaria. . . .

The real difference of opinion between myself and Mrs. Orr seems to be this—that she believes that no man or woman can be at his or her best unmarried, whereas I am a humble follower of St. Paul and believe that it is best for some people to pass through life unmarried. In any case . . . as long as there are half a million more English women than men, and as long as polygamy is illegal and conventual institutions have only a limited popularity, so long there must necessarily be a considerable number of single women at large in our country. Starting from these undeniable facts, the question arises, is it not for the benefit of society that the women who have the greatest natural fitness for marriage should marry, whilst those who have fewer natural qualifications for the endurance and enjoyment of the special pains and pleasures of married life, should find other honourable and useful careers open to them? . . . Free-traders urge that all artificial restrictions upon commerce should be removed, because that is the only way of insuring that each country and each locality will occupy itself with that industry for which it has the greatest natural advantages, or the least natural disadvantages. In like manner, we say, remove the artificial restrictions which debar women from higher education and from remunerative employments (they are already free to perform, if they choose, many kinds of important unpaid work); and the play of natural forces will drive them into those occupations for which they have some natural advantage as individuals, or at least into those for which their natural disadvantages are the least overwhelming. . . . On the whole, there is no more reason for fearing that women will as a body beset those professions for which they are manifestly and physically unfit, than that free trade would cause Lancashire agriculturists to cultivate the vine, or Scottish farmers to plant the olive instead of the larch. There is one mistake which Mrs. Orr will pardon me for pointing out. She speaks in one or two places as if women had claimed to have men turned out forcibly from some employments which they are supposed to consider the exclusive field for women's labour. This is an entire error. There have been and are many demands for excluding women from various kinds of work. I never heard any woman express the slightest wish that men should be turned out of any sort of employment or occupation. The one thing that has been asked, and the one thing that is in process of being granted, is a fair field and no favour. . . .

Mrs. Orr expresses the opinion that instead of striving to gain entrance to educational privileges and learned professions which have hitherto been the exclusive field of masculine enterprise, "it would be a wiser ambition on the part of women to reconquer their own sphere," and apply themselves vigorously to the better performance of household work. . . .

When Mrs. Orr says "Let women reconquer their own sphere," and implies that they should devote themselves to housekeeping, and let doctoring and other masculine occupations alone, I think she does not sufficiently consider the individual cases of the women who want remunerative work. Take as an example the case of a family consisting of a father and mother and half-a-dozen daughters. The father is a professional man, two-thirds of whose income cease at his death; the mother is an active woman, and, at the time when the youngest of her daughters reaches the age of eighteen, still a vigorous housekeeper. Three of the daughters marry; one remains at home to help her mother in the management of the household. What are the others to do? How does Mrs. Orr's suggestion of "reconquering their own sphere" help them? Their own home is orderly and well governed. . . . What generally happens . . . is that all three unmarried daughters stay at home with practically no real or sufficient occupation; they spend their time making their dresses, and endeavouring, by snipping and altering and turning, always to be in the latest fashion, and to make the 30l. a-year or so which they have for dress and pocket-money go as far as 35l. or 40l. This, it appears to me, is an unhealthy and unnatural existence; why should the labour of three fine, strong, active young women produce such an insignificant result? Further, they are apt to present, as time goes on, the unlovely spectacle of middle-aged spinsters aping the appearance and manners of girls of eighteen. They are eagerly and perhaps vainly hoping for marriage, which would give them a reasonable occupation and work worth doing. They are not prepared, as the *Saturday Review* says, "to judge calmly of an offer when it comes." This state of things is surely not at all conducive to the realisation of a high ideal of marriage. Let us now suppose what would have happened if these two young women had had an ambition to find some career for themselves more satisfactory than that of a third-rate dressmaker. One goes to Girton or Newnham, and thus, by getting a university training, prepares herself for the profession of teaching, and in a few years she may be earning 200l., 300l., or 400l. a-year. The other goes to the school of medicine for women; and after the proper course has been gone through and the examinations passed, she begins practice: if she has anything like a real faculty for her profession, her income will very speedily outstrip her sister's; and, moreover, she too will have found a work worthy of a rational human being — a work that calls out some of the best and noblest qualities. If either of these sisters marries after she is established in her profession, it will not be for the sake of escaping from the *ennui* of perpetual young-ladyhood. It will not be because in no other way could she find useful work to do in the world: the chances of the marriage being happy will be improved by the fact that it was a real choice, and not a Hobson's choice, such as marriage is when other careers of usefulness are closed.

So far as present experience goes, look where one will for it, there is no evidence in support of Mrs. Orr's assertion that such careers as those I have sketched will tend to dry up the capacity of love either in men or women. . . . The constitution of the human character, with its mysterious affections and aspirations, is planted on too firm a foundation to be "decomposed" or turned over by the granting of more liberty to women, who after all are only a little behind their brothers in asking for it. Those who write and speak against the extension of liberty of action and conscience to men or women have always said that the change they deprecate will undermine or decompose the foundations of society. A few years pass by, the change is accomplished, and it turns out that society is not undermined or decomposed at all, but is all the healthier and more vigorous, through being possessed of a larger proportion of free citizens. The "foundations of society" are really stronger than the enemies of progress suppose; if they were not, the undermining and decomposing would have been effected long ago. It is rather irreverent perhaps, but I always feel when I hear that society will be undermined by the ballot or by household suffrage, or in France by the establishment of a Republic, that if society is in such a very delicate state, the sooner it is undermined and something stronger put in its place the better it will be. . . .

. . . I have written as I have done because I felt it right, as a hearty sympathiser with every effort now being made to obtain a larger and freer life for women, to show, if I could, that the way we are going is not the road to ruin that Mrs. Orr thinks it — that the whole of our aim is to hasten the time when every woman shall have the opportunity of becoming the best that her natural faculties make her capable of. In one of Oliver Cromwell's letters, he says: "It will be found an unjust and unwise jealousy to deprive a man of his natural liberty upon the supposition that he might abuse it. When he doth abuse it, judge." So I would ask that women should be judged by their use of the liberty they at present enjoy, and not by imaginary abuses of liberty of which at present the world has had no experience.

Bibliography

This bibliography lists those primary sources which were found to be most useful in the preparation of this volume, and those secondary works which seemed most directly related to the materials that were chosen for inclusion in the text.

There are several valuable bibliographical essays dealing with Victorian women. O. R. McGregor's scholarly and provocative article, "The Social Position of Women in England, 1850-1914: A Bibliography", *British Journal of Sociology*, VI (1955), 48-60, is still useful, as much for its insights as its information. More recently, S. Barbara Kanner has published a two-part select bibliography, "The Women of England in a Century of Social Change, 1815-1914", Part One of which appears in *Suffer and Be Still* (Bloomington: Indiana University Press, 1972), and Part Two in *A Widening Sphere* (Bloomington: Indiana University Press, 1977), both edited by Martha Vicinus.[1] The first part is in large measure devoted to the traditional concerns of Victorian feminists—education, employment, political activity, legal position, etc.—while the second concentrates on women's personal concerns—e.g., marriage, the family, the home, and sickness and health care. Kanner is an extremely helpful guide to the vast amount of periodical literature on The Woman Question. Students might also wish to consult Jill Roe's thoughtful article, "Modernisation and Sexism: Recent Writings on Victorian Women", *Victorian Studies*, XX (1977), 179-92, for a discussion of relevant works published since 1973. Finally, there is, of course, *Poole's Index to Periodical Literature* (particularly the unabridged edition), valuable for its comprehensive listings of articles dealing with the Woman Question.

General Works

In general, the student who seeks an understanding of woman's place in Victorian society will look in vain in the standard texts on the nineteenth century where, for the most part, the position of women is simply ignored. An honorable exception that shows a grasp of the nature of the problem is Henry Hamilton's *A History of the Homeland* (New York: W. W. Norton & Co., Inc., 1948). Hamilton has a particularly valuable chapter entitled "The Place of Women in Society", that, among other things, provides a good general survey of the working life of women in pre-industrial England. It is refreshing to find in an economic history, S. G. Checkland's *The Rise of Industrial Society in England, 1815-1885* (New York: St. Martin's Press, 1964), an understanding of woman's role during the period of England's transformation into the workshop of the world; see especially the section entitled The Integrity of the Family. Walter E.

---

[1] *Because of the frequency with which these books are cited in this bibliography, publication data will henceforth be omitted.*

Houghton's deservedly esteemed *The Victorian Frame of Mind* (New Haven: Yale University Press, 1957) is excellent for an understanding of the intellectual background of the period, and his discussions of, for example, home, love, and sex are essential reading. Richard D. Altick's *Victorian People and Ideas* (New York: W. W. Norton & Co., Inc., 1973), although written primarily to provide background for the literature of the nineteenth century, has some useful comments about the position of women. Three volumes of Esmé Wingfield-Stratford, *The Victorian Tragedy* (London: George Routledge & Sons, Ltd., 1930); *The Victorian Sunset* (New York: William Morrow & Co., Inc., 1932); and *The Victorian Aftermath* (New York: William Morrow & Co., Inc., 1933) provide lively commentaries on various aspects of nineteenth-century society, including the role of women. G. M. Young's *Victorian England: Portrait of An Age* (London: Oxford University Press, 1936) is a somewhat difficult but rewarding book which has the merit of recognizing the uniqueness of woman's place in the history of the time.

There are several literary studies which cast light on various aspects of the Victorian woman. Among them are Robert P. Utter and Gwendolyn B. Needham, *Pamela's Daughters* (New York: The Macmillan Company, 1936); Patricia Thomson, *The Victorian Heroine: A Changing Ideal, 1837-1873* (London: Oxford University Press, 1956); Françoise Basch, *Relative Creatures: Victorian Women in Society and the Novel* (New York: Schocken Books, 1974); and Katherine West, *Chapter of Governesses: A Study of the Governess in English Fiction, 1800-1849* (London: Cohen & West, Ltd., 1949). Amy Cruse, *The Victorians and Their Reading* (Boston: Houghton Mifflin Company, 1935) contains an interesting chapter entitled "The New Woman", which covers traditional attitudes towards woman's role as well as the emergence of emancipated views.

Woman's Role: Traditional Views

Numerous writers in the Victorian era echoed and amplified the thoughts of the eighteenth-century physician John Gregory, who, in *A Father's Legacy to His Daughters* (London: W. Strahan, T. Cadell, 1774), counseled, in effect, the submission of women. The following works have this in common: whatever the philosophy or the viewpoint of the writers, their object was to provide some sort of argument justifying the traditional position of women. See, for example, T. H. Lister, "Rights and Condition of Women", *Edinburgh Review*, LXXIII (1841), 189-209; J. G. Phillimore, "Women's Rights and Duties", *Blackwood's Magazine*, LIV (1843), 373-97; T. H. Rearden, "Mission of Woman", *Westminster Review*, LII (1849-50), 352-67; Margaret Oliphant, "The Laws Concerning Women", *Blackwood's Magazine*, LXXIX (1856), 379-87; Margaret Oliphant, "The Condition of Women", *Blackwood's Magazine*, LXXXIII (1858), 139-54; Margaret Oliphant, "Mill's Subjection of Women", *Edinburgh Review*, CXXX (1869), 572-602; "Queen Bees or Working Bees?" *Saturday Review*, November 12, 1859, pp. 575-76; [W. E. Aytoun], "The Rights of Woman", *Blackwood's Magazine*, XCII (1862), 183-201; John Ruskin, *Sesame and Lilies* (London: Smith Elder & Co., 1865, and many subsequent editions); Anne Mozeley, "Mr. Mill on the Subjection of Women", *Blackwood's Magazine*, CVI (1869), 309-21; Mrs. [Sarah Ann] Sewell, *Woman and the Times We Live In* (London: n.p., 1869); E. Lynn Linton, *The Girl of the Period and Other Social Essays*, 2 vols. (London: Richard Bentley & Son, 1883), and a number of other articles by Mrs. Linton including "The Partisans of the Wild Women", *Nineteenth Century*, XXXI (1892), 455-64; "Girls, Wives, and Mothers: A Word to the Middle Classes", *Chambers's Journal*, LXXIII (1884), 33-35; John William

Burgon, *A Sermon Preached Before the University of Oxford, June 8, 1884* (Oxford and London: Parker & Co., 1884); Grant Allen, "Plain Words on the Woman Question", *Fortnightly Review,* LII (1889), 448-59.

A starting point for understanding the code of socially approved behavior laid down for upper- and middle-class ladies might be the popular manuals of Sarah Stickney Ellis, including *The Women of England: Their Social Duties and Domestic Habits* (1838); *The Mothers of England, Their Influence and Responsibility* (1843); *The Wives of England, Their Relative Duties, Domestic Influence and Social Obligations* (1843); and *The Daughters of England, Their Position in Society, Character and Responsibilities* (1845). These four works were later conveniently incorporated in a single volume entitled *The Daily Monitor and Domestic Guide* (New York: Edward Walker, 1850). See also [Isabella Beeton], *The Book of Household Management* (London: S. O. Beeton, 1861, and many reprints), the most widely used of books of this genre. In a modern work, J. A. Banks and Olive Banks, *Feminism and Family Planning* (New York: Schocken Books, 1964) may be found valuable chapters (entitled "The Perfect Wife" and "The Spread of Gentility") that describe the lifestyle, aspirations, and obligations of the middle-class family. This book, incidentally, is more useful to those interested in the Woman Question than its title suggests. Also interesting on customs and mores is C. Willett Cunnington's *Feminine Attitudes in the Nineteenth Century* (New York: Haskell House Publishers Ltd., 1935). For a criticism of the "perfect lady" sterotype, see Patricia Branca, *Silent Sisterhood: Middle Class Women in the Victorian Home* (Pittsburgh: Carnegie-Mellon University Press, 1975).

Among the approaches to the Woman Question was the "scientific" one, particularly popular in the Age of Darwin. The men quoted, although their work was done in different fields, nevertheless concurred in the notion that woman's physical and intellectual limitations doomed her to a role different from that of man, and inferior to it. Well-known physicians made prominent contributions to this literature. See, for example, William Acton, *The Functions and Disorders of the Reproductive Organs,* 3rd ed. (London: John Churchill, 1862); Edward H. Clarke, *Sex in Education* (Boston: James R. Osgood & Co., 1873); T. S. Clouston, "Female Education from a Medical Point of View", *Popular Science Monthly,* XXIV (1883), 214-28; Henry Maudsley, "Sex in Mind and Education", *Fortnightly Review,* XXI (1874), 446-83; Alexander Keiller, "What May Be the Dangers of Educational Overwork?" *National Association for the Promotion of Social Science, Transactions,* 1880, pp. 420-39; John Thorburn, *Female Education from a Physiological Point of View* (Manchester: Owens College, 1884). Two of England's pioneering women doctors replied to the arguments. See Elizabeth Garret Anderson's answer to Dr. Maudsley, "Sex in Mind and Education: A Reply", *Fortnightly Review,* XXI (1874), 582-94; and Dr. Edith Pechey's response to Dr. Keiller, in *National Association for the Promotion of Social Science, Transactions,* 1880, pp. 439-54. Among the works by biologists, anthropologists, sociologists, and other members of the scientific community who proclaimed that woman's role in society was dictated by the evolutionary process were the following: George J. Romanes, "Mental Differences Between Men and Women", *Nineteenth Century,* XXI (1887), 654-72; Patrick Geddes and J. Arthur Thomson, *The Evolution of Sex,* rev. ed. (London: The Walter Scott Publishing Co., Ltd., 1914); G. Ferrero, "The Problem of Woman, from a Bio-Sociological Point of View", *The Monist,* IV (1893-94), 261-74; C. Lombroso, "The Physical Insensibility of Woman", *Fortnightly Review,* LVII (1892), 354-57; W. L. Distant, "On the Mental Differences Between the Sexes", *Royal*

Anthropological Institute of Great Britain and Ireland, Journal, IV (1874), 78-87; and several works by Herbert Spencer: *Education: Intellectual, Moral, and Physical* (London: n.p., 1861); *The Study of Sociology,* Part V of the International Scientific Series (London: Kegan Paul & Co., 1872); and *The Principles of Sociology,* 3 vols. (London: Williams & Norgate, 1876); see in particular vol. I, section 340, "Domestic Institutions".

An excellent survey of attempts to analyze the feminine character according to the doctrines of various scientific and humanistic disciplines may be found in Viola Klein, *The Feminine Character: History of an Ideology* (New York: International Universities Press, 1949). Chapter II of this work, incidentally, provides an overview of woman's role in historical perspective which is all the more valuable since it is not confined to the British experience. Several good articles pursue the role of scientists in perpetuating traditional attitudes. See Jill Conway, "Stereotypes of Femininity in a Theory of Sexual Evolution", in *Suffer and Be Still*, pp. 140-54; Elizabeth Fee, "The Sexual Politics of Victorian Social Anthropology", *Feminist Studies*, I (1973) 23-39; Joan N. Burstyn, "Education and Sex: The Medical Case Against Higher Education for Women in England, 1870 to 1900", *Proceedings of the American Philosophical Society*, CXVII (1973), 79-89.

Woman's Role: Feminist Views

Three books which can properly be called classical statements of the feminist position are Mary Wollstonecraft's *A Vindication of the Rights of Woman* (Dublin: James Moore, 1793), and many subsequent editions); William Thompson, *Appeal of One Half of the Human Race, Women, Against the Pretensions of the Other Half, Men* (London: Longman, Hurst, Rees, Orme, Brown & Green, 1825; reprint edition, New York: Burt Franklin, 1970); John Stuart Mill, *The Subjection of Women* (London: Longmans, Green, Reader & Dyer, 1869, and many subsequent editions). Of the three, Thompson's is the least known, and the most radical.

Among the writers who may be considered precursors of the feminist spokesmen of the mid-Victorian period is Priscilla Wakefield, *Reflections on the Present Conditions of the Female Sex, with Suggestions for its Improvement* (London: n.p., 1798). W. J. Fox, the radical Unitarian minister and subsequently a member of the House of Commons, expressed his militant views on the role of women in "A Political and Social Anomaly", *Monthly Repository*, VI (1832), 637-42. The prolific writer on artistic subjects, Anna Jameson, for whom the coterie of Langham Place ladies felt a deep respect and a warm regard, wrote in 1832 *Characteristics of Women*, 2 vols. (London: Saunders and Otley, 1832) which provided keen insights into the nature of Shakespeare's heroines, and by extension, into the feminine character as a whole. Another prominent harbinger of "advanced" views was the redoubtable Harriet Martineau who, in her voluminous writings, presented arguments for the feminist cause; see, for example, her three-volume *Society in America* (London: Saunders & Otley, 1837), and "Criticism of Women", *Westminster Review*, XXXII (1838-39), 454-75. The *Metropolitan Magazine* in 1838 carried a bold statement of feminist principles in its article entitled "An Outline of the Grievances of Women", XXII (1838), 16-27. There was also *A Plea For Women* (Edinburgh: W. Tait, 1843) by Mrs. Hugo Reid, which called for the equality of the sexes and championed the education of women.

Socialists, in their commitment to rearrange the economic and social order, were naturally concerned with the position of women, who were, in their eyes, simply another exploited class. Whatever the doctrinal differences that separated the various schools might have been, they were all convinced that woman could not be emancipated within the framework of a capitalist society. Robert Owen's *Book of the New Moral World,* Part 6 (London: E. Wilson, 1836, and many reprints), spells out the role that women would play in the new era. Marx's collaborator, Friedrich Engels, in *The Origin of the Family, Private Property, and the State* (Chicago: C. H. Kerr & Co., 1902; London: Marxist-Leninist Library, 1943), sets forth the Marxist analysis of the origin of the basic institutions of capitalist society, including the position of women. August Bebel in *Woman in the Past, Present, and Future* (London: Modern Press, 1885), sees the contemporary relationship between the sexes as the most glaring example of a society in the process of decay. An excellent article which both attempts to explain Bebel's views to the English public and presents their own analysis of the Woman Question is Eleanor Marx Aveling and Edward Aveling, "The Woman Question: From a Socialist Point of View", *Westminster Review,* CXXV (1886), 207-22. *The Economic Foundations of the Woman's Movement,* by M. A. [Mabel Atkinson], Fabian Tract No. 175 (London: Fabian Society, 1914) presents a non-Marxist socialist analysis of the historical factors in the evolution of the position of woman in English society.

Critics of the new and revolutionary socialist doctrines roundly condemned the views of Owen and Saint Simon on a number of grounds; but, since any change in sex relationships was seen as a direct threat to the perpetuation of existing institutions (marriage and the home, for example), the socialist advocacy of feminine equality was singled out for particularly virulent denunciation. See, for example, "Custody of Infants Bill, Postscript", *British and Foreign Review,* VII (1838), 394-411; and "Woman and the Social System", *Fraser's Magazine,* XXI (1840), 689-702.

Secondary sources that are helpful in understanding the socialist commitment to women's rights (as well as society's outraged reaction to that commitment) include M. Ostrogorski, "The St. Simonians and Woman's Role", Appendix I of *The Rights of Women* (London: Swan Sonnenschein & Co., 1893); and John Killham, *Tennyson and* The Princess: *Reflections of An Age* (London: University of London, Athlone Press, 1958). Richard K. P. Pankhurst has written several extremely valuable books and articles which shed light on the socialist case for women's rights: *William Thompson, 1775-1833: Britain's Pioneer Socialist, Feminist and Co-operator* (London: Watts & Co., 1954); *The Saint Simonians: Mill and Carlyle* (London: Sidgwick & Jackson [1957]); "Anna Wheeler: A Pioneer Socialist and Feminist", *Political Quarterly,* XXV (1954), 132-43; "Saint-Simonism in England", *Twentieth Century,* CIIL (1952), 499-512; CIL (1953), 47-58 (a two-part article).

The literature on women's participation in the Chartist movement is limited. The *English Chartist Circular,* a newspaper published from 1841 to 1844, attempted to rally the support of women to the Chartist cause, as indicated by the following titles: "Address to the Women of England!" by John Watkins, Chartist, April 12, 1841; "Address from London Delegates Council to Male and Female Chartists", August 15, 1841; and "To the Females of the Metropolis and its Vicinity", September 15, 1842. William Lovett, who drew up the People's Charter and was one of the prominent figures in the movement, was a member of the minority who favored woman suffrage; see *The Life and Struggles of William Lovett,* 2 vols. (London: Trübner & Co., 1876). The activities of members of various radical groups, including the Chartists, can be traced in E. P. Thompson, *The Making of the English Working Class* (New York: Random House, 1963).

Much of the mid-Victorian discussion of woman's role arose out of the need for a solution to the problem of the "redundant woman". General concern with the surplus female population was the theme of numerous articles from the 1860's on. See, for example, the review article entitled "Our Single Women", *North British Review*, XXXVI (1862), 62-87; "Social Reform in England", *Westminster Review*, LXXXVII (1866), 350-72; and the tongue-in-cheek approach in "A Tête-à-Tête Social Science Discussion", *Cornhill Magazine*, X (1864), 569-82; J. B. Mayor, "The Cry of the Women", *Contemporary Review*, XI (1869), 196-215; and "Excess of Widows over Widowers", *Westminster Review*, CXXXI (1889), 501-05. Adna Ferrin Weber's *The Growth of Cities in the Nineteenth Century* (New York: The Macmillan Company, 1899) discusses the problem of "surplus women" in a European framework. The traditional answer to the question, "what shall we do with our old maids?" was "marry them off or ship them out". One of the most widely read and extensively cited articles on this subject was W. R. Greg's "Why are Women Redundant?" (1862), reprinted in *Literary and Social Judgments* (Boston: James R. Osgood & Co., 1873).

To persons living in the heart of a great empire, it seemed logical to use the colonies as reservoirs for that part of the population which could not be accommodated at home. Emigration, whether of middle- or working-class women, was a live issue in the Victorian era. The following articles give evidence of that interest: "Mr. Sidney Herbert's Emigration Scheme", *The Economist*, December 29, 1849, p. 1445; M.S.R., "On Assisted Emigration", *English Woman's Journal*, V (1860), 235-40; S.C., "Emigration for Educated Women", *English Woman's Journal*, VII (1861), 1-9; Maria Rye, "Female Middle Class Emigration," *English Woman's Journal*, X (1862), 20-30; Jane Lewin, "Female Middle Class Emigration", *English Woman's Journal*, XII (1864), 313-17; and Adelaide Ross, "Emigration for Women", *Macmillan's Magazine*, VL (1882), 312-17. A brief survey of the emigration movement by Mrs. Stuart Wortley is included in *Woman's Mission*, edited by the Baroness [Angela] Burdett-Coutts (London: Sampson Low, Marston & Co., 1893), pp. 87-91. A recent article helpful in understanding the feminist response to emigration is A. James Hammerton, "Feminism and Female Emigration, 1861-1886", in *A Widening Sphere*, pp. 52-71.

Feminists, in general, rejected the idea that a woman had to be married, and that, if she did not find a mate at home, she should go to the outer bounds of the Empire, if necessary, to get one. Frances Power Cobbe in "What Shall We Do With Our Old Maids?" *Fraser's Magazine*, LXVI (1862), 594-610, rejects Greg's recommendation that surplus women emigrate. Jessie Boucherett, on the other hand, in "How To Provide for Superfluous Women", (in *Woman's Work and Woman's Culture*, edited by Josephine E. Butler [London: Macmillan & Co., 1869], pp. 27-48), suggested that the problem of redundant women might be solved by the large scale emigration of *men*.

But most feminists, such as Cobbe and Boucherett, were skeptical of emigration as a panacea for the plight of the single woman, and placed greater reliance on making women functioning and independent members of society, as Frances Power Cobbe explains in "The Final Cause of Woman" (*ibid.*, pp. 1-26). Other explicit statements of the middle-class feminist view of woman's place in the universe include "Redundant Women", *Victoria Magazine*, XV (1870), 97-108; Millicent Garrett Fawcett, "The Future of Englishwomen: A Reply", *Nineteenth Century*, IV (1878), 347-57; and Maria G. Grey, "Men and Women", *Fortnightly Review*, XXXII (1879), 672-85. Perceptive comments on the emergence of a feminist ethos can be found in E. Ethelmer, "Feminism", *Westminster Review*, CIL (1898) 50-62; and in Victor Gollancz, ed., *The Making of Women: Oxford Essays in Feminism* (London: George Allen & Unwin,

Ltd., 1917). For a general overview of the activities of the "ladies of Langham Place", see the excellent radio talk by Margaret Maison, "Insignificant Objects of Desire", *The Listener,* LXXXVI, (July 22, 1971), 105-07.

Social Reform

A field into which women were able to penetrate early was that of social reform. But even in this realm women encountered some opposition and had to win society's acceptance. Anna Jameson's *Sisters of Charity* (London: Longman, Brown, Green & Longmans, 1855); Bessie Rayner Parkes's "Charity as a Portion of the Public Vocation of Woman", *English Woman's Journal,* III (1859), 193-96; and Frances Power Cobbe's "Social Science Congresses, and Women's Part in Them", *Macmillan's Magazine,* V (1861), 81-94, are three pioneering statements calling for women to apply their uniquely feminine gifts to the social evils that beset the nation.

Women enthusiastically entered into a variety of social activities. A few years after its inception, the *English Woman's Journal* published "Official Employment of Women in Works of Charity", IX (1862), 361-64. One of the fields in which women vigorously participated was that of public health. See Mary Anne Baines's "The Ladies National Association for the Diffusion of Sanitary Knowledge," *National Association for the Promotion of Social Science, Transactions,* 1858, pp. 531-32; Bessie Rayner Parkes's, "Ladies Sanitary Association", *English Woman's Journal,* III (1859), 73-85; and "The Details of Woman's Work in Sanitary Reform", *English Woman's Journal,* III (1859), 217-27, 316-24.

The name most prominently associated with workhouse reform is that of Louisa Twining. See her *Workhouses and Women's Work* (London: n.p., 1858); "On the Training and Supervision of Workhouse Girls", *National Association for the Promotion of Social Science, Transactions,* 1859, pp. 696-703; and her autobiography, *Recollections of Life and Work* (London: E. Arnold, 1893). Frances Power Cobbe gives a vivid illustration of conditions in the workhouse, particularly the intermingling of the incurably sick with the healthy members of the workhouse population in "Workhouse Sketches", *Macmillan's Magazine,* III (1861), 448-61.

Mary Carpenter, one of the great philanthropists of the nineteenth century, wrote extensively about the rescue of poor, delinquent, and criminal children. Her books and articles include *Reformatory Schools for the Children of the Perishing and Dangerous Classes, and for Juvenile Offenders* (London: C. Gilpin, 1851); *Juvenile Delinquents, their Condition and Treatment* (London: W. & F. G. Cash, 1853); "Reformatories for Convicted Girls", *National Association for the Promotion of Social Science, Transactions,* 1857, pp. 338-46; "On the Disposal of Girls from Reformatory Schools", *ibid.,* 1858, pp. 413-19; "Treatment of Female Convicts", *ibid.,* 1864, pp. 415-22. Two years after her death, her biography, written by her nephew Joseph Estlin Carpenter, was published; see *The Life and Work of Mary Carpenter* (London: Macmillan & Company, 1879). Frances Power Cobbe, Miss Carpenter's sometime co-worker, pays tribute to her in *The Life of Frances Power Cobbe as Told by Herself,* 2 vols. (Boston and New York: Houghton, Mifflin & Company, 1894); also see "A Group of Female Philanthropists", *London Quarterly Review,* LVII (1881), 49-81. Millicent Garrett Fawcett includes a sketch of Miss Carpenter in *Some Eminent Women of Our Time* (London: Macmillan & Company, 1889), as does Edwin A. Pratt in *Pioneer Women in Victoria's Reign* (London: George Newnes, Limited, 1897).

One of the nineteenth century's most imaginative, innovative, and successful practitioners of enlightened paternalism was Octavia Hill. Her efforts are described in

"Organized Work Among the Poor", *Macmillan's Magazine,* XX (1869), 219-26; in *Employment or Alms-Giving: Being an account of the plan of relief now adopted in a district of Marylebone* (London: n.p., 1871); and in *Letters to Fellow Workers, 1864-1911,* edited by Elinor Southwood Ouvry (London: The Adelphi Book Shop, 1933). See also *Life of Octavia Hill, as Told in Her Letters,* edited by C. Edmund Maurice (London: Macmillan & Co., Limited, 1914). A comprehensive survey of the variety of social reform activities in which Victorian women participated can be found in *Woman's Mission,* edited by the Baroness [Angela] Burdett-Coutts (London: Sampson Low, Marston & Company, 1893), which includes articles by such noted women as Louisa Twining and Florence Nightingale.

A first-rate article which inquires into the motives of nineteenth-century philanthropists is that of Brian Harrison, "Philanthropy and the Victorians", *Victorian Studies,* IX (1966), 353-74. Useful information on the activities of social reformers is available in Kathleen Heasman, *Evangelicals in Action: An Appraisal of Their Social Work in the Victorian Era* (London: Geoffrey Bles, 1962); and David Owen, *English Philanthropy, 1660-1960* (Cambridge, Mass.: Harvard University Press, 1964). An excellent recent study of Mary Carpenter is Harriet Warm Schupf's "Single Women and Social Reform in Mid-Nineteenth Century England: The Case of Mary Carpenter", *Victorian Studies,* XVII (1974), 301-17.

It seemed to some middle-class ladies that the most effective way to diminish human misery and to relieve social tension was by improving education for the poor. Examples of this idea put into action were the Ragged School movement and attempts to educate pauper girls in workhouse schools. See A. A. Cooper, "The Ragged Schools", *Quarterly Review,* LXXIX (1846), 127-41; three articles by Mary Carpenter: "Relation of Ragged Schools to the Educational Movement", *National Association for the Promotion of Social Science, Transactions,* 1857, pp. 226-32; "The Application of the Principles of Education to Schools for the Lower Classes of Society", *ibid.,* 1861, pp. 344-51; and "The Education of Pauper Girls", *ibid.,* 1862, pp. 286-93; Ellice Hopkins, "The Industrial Training of Pauper and Neglected Girls", *Contemporary Review,* XLII (1882), 140-54; M. B. Smedley, "Workhouse Schools for Girls", *Macmillan's Magazine,* XXXI (1874), 27-36; Jessie Boucherett, "Mrs. Nassau Senior's Report on the Education of Pauper Girls", *Englishwoman's Review,* 1875, pp. 49-54.

Nor was the reformers' concern limited to workhouse girls. An effort was made to raise the horizons and to improve the quality of life of factory girls who, although they were technically not paupers, nevertheless were intellectually pauperized. One such attempt was the creation of mechanics' institutes and "colleges" for working women. See Fanny Hertz, "Mechanics' Institutes for Working Women", *National Association for the Promotion of Social Science, Transactions,* 1859, pp. 347-54; J. G. Fitch, *Working Women's College: An Address Delivered to the Students of the College Session* (London: n.p. [1872]); Frances Martin, "A College for Working Women", *Macmillan's Magazine,* XL (1879), 483-88.

Education

It was generally agreed for most of the nineteenth century that the education provided for middle-class girls was shockingly bad. The incompetence of the teachers and the intellectual destitution of the pupils are described in "An Inquiry into the State of Girls' Fashionable Schools", *Fraser's Magazine,* XXXI (1845), 703-12; "Why Boys Are Cleverer Than Girls", *English Woman's Journal,* II (1858), 116-19; W. B. Hodgson, "The General Education of Woman", *English Woman's Journal,* V (1860), 73-85;

Harriet Martineau, "Middle Class Education: Girls", *Cornhill Magazine*, X (1864), 549-68; Millicent Garrett Fawcett, "The Medical and General Education of Women", *Fortnightly Review*, X (1868), 554-71; Millicent Garrett Fawcett, "The Education of Women of the Middle and Upper Classes", *Macmillan's Magazine*, XVII (1868), 511-17; Helen McKerlie, "The Lower Education of Women", *Contemporary Review*, LI (1887), 112-19. The most comprehensive examination of the shortcomings of schools for girls is found in D. Beale, ed., *Reports Issued by the Schools' Inquiry Commission on the Education of Girls* (London: David Nutt, 1869).

The case for reform of education was stated by, among others, F. D. Maurice, in *Lectures to Ladies on Practical Subjects* (Cambridge, Eng.: Macmillan & Co., 1855); and in "The Education of Girls", *National Association for the Promotion of Social Science, Transactions*, 1865, pp. 268-90; [Bessie Rayner Parkes], *Remarks on the Education of Girls* (London: John Clapman, 1854); Emily Shirreff, *Intellectual Education and its Influence on the Character and Happiness of Women* (London: J. W. Parker, 1858); "Female Education in the Middle Classes", *English Woman's Journal*, I (1858), 217-27; Mary Carpenter, *et al.*, "Female Education", *National Association for the Promotion of Social Science, Transactions*, 1869, pp. 351-64; "The Girl of the Future", *Victoria Magazine*, XV (1870), 440-57, 491-502; Emily Shirreff, "The Schools of the Future", *Contemporary Review*, XVII (1871), 443-60; Mrs. William [Maria G.] Grey, *On the Special Requirements for Improving the Education of Girls* (London: William Ridgway, 1872); Millicent Garrett Fawcett, "Old and New Ideals of Education for Women", *Good Words*, XIX (1878), 853-60.

From the 1860's on, the question of the desirability of higher education for women was vigorously debated. See "The University of Cambridge and the Education of Women", *English Woman's Journal*, XII (1863), 276-79; Emily Davies, *The Higher Education of Women* (London and New York: Alexander Strahan, 1866); George Butler, *The Higher Education of Women* (Liverpool: Thomas Brakell, 1867); M. Burrows, "Female Education", *Quarterly Review*, CXXVI (1869), 448-79; Emily Shirreff, "College Education for Women", *Contemporary Review*, XV (1870), 55-66; "The Education of Women: Admission to Universities", *Westminster Review*, CIX (1878), 56-90; "The Higher Education of Women", *Westminster Review*, CXXIX (1888), 152-62; J. G. Fitch, "Women and the Universities", *Contemporary Review*, LVIII (1890), 240-55; Thomas Case, "Against Degrees for Women at Oxford", *Fortnightly Review*, LXIV (1895), 95-100; Millicent Garrett Fawcett, "Degrees for Women at Oxford", *Contemporary Review*, LXIX (1896), 347-56; Percy Gardner, "The Women at Oxford and Cambridge", *Quarterly Review*, CLXXXVI (1897), 529-51; J. R. Tanner, "Degrees for Women at Cambridge", *Fortnightly Review*, CXVII (1897), 716-27. Several of Emily Davies' essays in *Thoughts on Some Questions Relating to Women, 1860-1908* (Cambridge: Bowes & Bowes, 1910; reprint edition, New York: AMS Press, 1973) are concerned with the higher education of women: "University Degrees and the Education of Women", 1863; "Some Account of a Proposed New College for Women", 1868; "Home and the Higher Education", 1878; and "Women in the Universities of England and Scotland", 1896. Rita McWilliams-Tulberg, in a recent article, "Women and Degrees at Cambridge University, 1862-1897" (in *A Widening Sphere*, pp. 117-45), traces the movement to secure a Cambridge education for women.

An excellent article which analyzes the religious opposition to higher education is Joan N. Burstyn's "Religious Arguments Against Higher Education for Women in England, 1840-1890", *Women's Studies*, I (1972), 111-31. For the medical opposition to higher education, see the writings of physicians listed under the heading Woman's Role: Traditional Views, p. 297. Also note Dorothea Beale's reply in "University Examinations for Women", *National Association for the Promotion of Social Science, Transactions,* 1874, pp. 478-90.

The efforts to improve secondary education are described in Emily Davies, "Secondary Instruction as Relating to Girls", and "On the Influence Upon Girls' Schools of External Examinations" reprinted in *Thoughts on Some Questions Relating to Women* (Cambridge: Bowes & Bowes, 1910; reprint edition, New York: AMS Press, 1973); Emily Shirreff, *The Work of the National Union* (London: W. Ridgway, 1872); Sara A. Burstall, *English High Schools for Girls* (London: Longmans & Co., 1907); *Public Schools for Girls: A Series of Papers on Their History, Aims, and Schemes of Study,* edited by Sara A. Burstall and M. A. Douglas (London: Longmans & Co., 1911); Laurie Magnus, *The Jubilee Book of the Girls' Public Day School Trust, 1873-1923* (Cambridge: University Press, 1923). A recent study that sheds light on secondary education in Victorian England is J. S. Pedersen's "Schoolmistresses and Headmistresses: Elites and Education in Nineteenth-Century England", *Journal of British Studies,* XV (1975), 135-62.

Two excellent short summaries of the progress made in the field of female education by women who themselves were active in that cause are Maria G. Grey's "The Women's Educational Movement", in *The Woman Question in Europe,* edited by Theodore Stanton (London: Sampson Low & Co., 1884);[1] and H. M. Stanley's "Personal Recollections of Women's Education", *Nineteenth Century,* VI (1879), 308-21. General histories of women's education include Christina S. Bremner, *The Education of Girls and Women in Great Britain* (London: Swan Sonnenschein, 1897); Alice Zimmern, *The Renaissance of Girls' Education in England: A Record of Fifty Years Progress* (London: A. D. Innes & Co., 1898); Sara A. Burstall, *Retrospect and Prospect: Sixty Years of Women's Education* (London: Longmans & Co., 1933); Josephine Kamm, *Hope Deferred: Girls' Education in English History* (London: Methuen & Co., Ltd., 1965).

The biographies listed below describe the activities of that dedicated band of women whose self-appointed mission was the improvement of education: Blanche A. Clough, *A Memoir of Anne Jemima Clough* (London: E. Arnold, 1897); Elizabeth Raikes, *Dorothea Beale of Cheltenham* (London: Archibald Constable & Co., 1908); Josephine Kamm, *How Different from Us: A Biography of Miss Buss and Miss Beale* (London: The Bodley Head, John Lane Ltd., 1958); Annie E. Ridley, *Frances Mary Buss and Her Work for Education* (London: Longmans & Co., 1895); and Sara A. Burstall, *Frances Mary Buss, An Educational Pioneer* (London: Society for the Propagation of Christian Knowledge, 1938).

Histories of individual schools and colleges include Muriel Byrne and Catherine Mansfield, *Somerville College, 1879-1921* (Oxford: University Press, 1922); Barbara Stephen, *Girton College, 1869-1932* (Cambridge: University Press, 1933); Mary Agnes Hamilton, *Newnham, An Informal Biography* (London: Faber & Faber, Ltd., 1936); Margaret Tuke, *A History of Bedford College for Women, 1849-1937* (London: Oxford University Press, 1939); R. Glynn Grylls, *Queen's College, 1848-1948* (London: George Routledge & Sons, 1948); Amy Key Clarke, *A History of Cheltenham Ladies College, 1853-1953* (London: Faber & Faber, Ltd., 1953). For the feminine experience at

---

[1] *Because of the frequency with which this book is cited in our bibliography, publication data will henceforth be omitted.*

Oxford, see Vera Brittain, *The Women at Oxford: A Fragment of History* (New York: The Macmillan Company, 1960). Barbara Stephen's *Emily Davies and Girton College* (London: Constable & Co., Ltd., 1927; reprint edition, Westport, Conn.: Hyperion Press, Inc., 1976) is a first-rate book that has a greater range than its title indicates.

Employment

The occupations in which women were mainly engaged before the movement to expand their opportunities for employment are dealt with in W. R. Greg, "Juvenile and Female Labour", *Edinburgh Review*, LXXIX (1849), 402-35; Clara Balfour, *Working Women of the Last Half Century* (London: W. & F. G. Cash, 1854); [John Duguid Milne], *Industrial and Social Position of Women in the Middle and Lower Ranks* (London: n.p., 1857); Harriet Martineau, "Female Industry", *Edinburgh Review*, CIX (1859), 293-336; G. W. Hastings, *et al.*, "The Industrial Employment of Women", *National Association for the Promotion of Social Science, Transactions*, 1857, pp. 531-48. Ivy Pinchbeck's *Women Workers and the Industrial Revolution, 1750-1850* (London: Frank Cass & Company, Limited, 1930; reprint edition, New York: Augustus M. Kelley, 1969) is a comprehensive study of the employment of women in agriculture, industry, and trade. An analysis of working women which includes chapters on the textile worker, the non-textile worker, the dressmaker, and the governess in the years 1832-1850 is found in Wanda Fraiken Neff, *Victorian Working Women* (New York: AMS Press, 1966). See also Margaret Hewitt's *Wives and Mothers in Victorian Industry* (London: Rockliff Publishing Corp., 1958).

The attempt to challenge the social attitudes which either confined a woman to a parasitical existence in her home, or limited her to a few overcrowded and underpaid occupations outside it, is the subject of Anna Jameson, *The Communion of Labour* (London: Longman, Brown, Green, Longmans & Roberts, 1856); Barbara Leigh Smith Bodichon, *Women and Work* (New York: C. S. Francis & Co., 1859); Emily Davies, "Letters Addressed to a Daily Paper at Newcastle-upon-Tyne, 1860", reprinted in *Thoughts on Some Questions Relating to Women* (Cambridge: Bowes & Bowes, 1910; reprint edition, New York: AMS Press, 1973), pp. 1-18; Bessie Rayner Parkes, *Essays on Women's Work*, 2nd ed. (London: Alexander Strahan, 1865); W. B. Hodgson, *The Education of Girls, and the Employment of Women of the Upper Classes Educationally Considered*, 2nd ed. (London: Trübner & Co., 1869); Emily Faithfull, *Woman's Work, with Special Reference to Industrial Employment* (London: The Victoria Press, 1871).

The work of the Society for Promoting the Employment of Women and its first practical venture, the Victoria Press, are discussed in: "Association for Promoting the Employment of Women", *English Woman's Journal*, IV (1859), 54-59; "Report of the Society for the Employment of Women", *National Association for the Promotion of Social Science, Transactions*, 1860, pp. xviii-xx; Bessie Rayner Parkes, "A Year's Experience in Woman's Work", *ibid.*, pp. 811-19; Emily Faithfull, "The Victoria Press", *ibid.*, pp. 819-21; "A Ramble with Mrs. Grundy", *English Woman's Journal*, V (1860), 269-72; Edwin A. Pratt, *Pioneer Women in Victoria's Reign* (London: George Newnes, Limited, 1897).

A large portion of the *English Woman's Journal* and, subsequently, the *Englishwoman's Review* was devoted to the problem of employment. The following articles are from the *English Woman's Journal*: "On the Adoption of Professional Life by Women", II (1858), 1-19; "What Can Educated Women Do?" IV (1859), 217-27; Jessie Boucherett, "On the Obstacles to the Employment of Women", IV (1860), 361-75;

"Statistics on the Employment of Women", V (1860), 1-6; Jessie Boucherett, "On the Education of Girls, With Reference to Their Future Position", VI (1860), 217-24; Jessie Boucherett, "On the Choice of a Business", X (1862), 145-53; Jessie Boucherett, "Remunerative Work for Gentlewomen", X (1862), 183-89. The following articles were published in the *Englishwoman's Review:* Jessie Boucherett, "Occupations of Women", 1874, pp. 85-90; Helen Blackburn, "The Pursuits of Women", 1874, pp. 237-46; E. P. R. Laye, "Women and Careers", 1878, pp. 193-201.

The conditions that made the governesses the most abject of middle-class women are described in "Modern Governess System", *Fraser's Magazine*, XXX (1844), 571-83; Lady Eastlake, *"Vanity Fair, Jane Eyre,* and the Governesses' Benevolent Institution", *Quarterly Review*, LXXXIV (1848), 153-85; "Social Position of Governesses", *Fraser's Magazine*, XXXVII (1848), 411-14; Bessie Rayner Parkes, "The Profession of the Teacher", *English Woman's Journal*, I (1858), 1-13; "The Market for Educated Female Labour", *English Woman's Journal*, IV (1859), 145-52.

Specific proposals for making the position of the governess more bearable were advanced in J. G. Fitch, "The Professional Training of Teachers", *National Association for the Promotion of Social Science, Transactions*, 1859, pp. 411-17; and M. Calverley, "Who Teaches Our Little Ones?" *Good Words*, XIX (1878), 390-93. A good recent article on the position of the governess is that of M. Jeanne Peterson, "The Victorian Governess: Status Incongruence in Family and Society", *Victorian Studies*, XIV (1970), 7-26.

Medicine seemed an especially appropriate and attractive field to middle-class women who were seeking professional careers. See, for example, Elizabeth Blackwell and Emily Blackwell, "Medicine as a Profession for Women", *English Woman's Journal*, V (1860), 145-61; Emily Davies, "Female Physicians" (1861) and "Medicine as a Profession for Women" (1862), reprinted in *Thoughts on Some Questions Relating to Women* (Cambridge: Bowes & Bowes, 1910; reprint edition, New York: AMS Press, 1973); S. Gregory, "Female Physicians", *English Woman's Journal*, IX (1862), 1-11.

The persistent attempts of a handful of pioneering women to obtain admission to medical school, and the equally determined resistance of the embattled males who saw their monopoly threatened, are chronicled in Lawson Tait, F.R.C.S., "The Medical Education of Women", *Birmingham Medical Review*, III (1874), 81-94; James Stansfeld, "Medical Women", *Nineteenth Century*, I (1877), 888-901; Frances Elizabeth Hoggan, M.D., "Women in Medicine", in *The Woman Question in Europe*, pp. 63-89; Robert Wilson, "AESCULAPIUS VICTRIX", *Fortnightly Review*, XXXIX (1886), 18-33; Sophia Jex-Blake, *Medical Women: A Thesis and a History*, 2nd ed., rev. (Edinburgh: Oliphant, Anderson & Ferrier, 1886); Elizabeth Blackwell, *Pioneer Work in Opening the Medical Profession to Women* (London and New York: Longmans, Green & Co., 1895; reprint edition, New York: Source Book Press, 1970); Louisa Garrett Anderson, *Elizabeth Garrett Anderson, 1836-1917* (London: Faber & Faber, Ltd., 1939); Jo Manton, *Elizabeth Garrett Anderson* (New York: E. P. Dutton & Co., Inc., 1965); Dorothy Clarke Wilson, *Lone Woman: The Story of Elizabeth Blackwell* (Boston and Toronto: Little, Brown & Company, 1970); Edythe Lutzker, *Edith Pechey-Phipson, M.D.* (New York: Exposition Press, Inc., 1973); Margaret Todd, *The Life of Sophia Jex-Blake* (London: MacMillan & Company, 1918); Louisa Martindale, *The Woman Doctor and Her Future* (London: Mills & Boon, Ltd., 1922); E. Moberly Bell, *Storming the Citadel: The Rise of the Woman Doctor* (London: Constable & Co., Ltd., 1953).

Among other areas where it was suggested that women might increasingly be employed as either clerks or supervisors were insurance companies, libraries, newspapers, elementary school management, the civil service, hospital administration, and telegraph offices: See "Life Assurance Agency as an Employment for Females", *English Woman's Journal*, III (1859), 120-23; "Female Engravers from the Sixteenth to the Nineteenth Century", *ibid.*, pp. 259-70; "Ladies as Clerks", *Fortnightly Review*, XII (1875), 335-40; "Female Clerks", *Englishwoman's Review*, 1875, pp. 367-68; "Women in the Civil Service", *Victoria Magazine*, XII (1868-69), 438-46; J. Manners, "Employment of Women in the Public Service", *Quarterly Review*, CLI (1881), 181-200; "Women in the Civil Service", *Englishwoman's Review*, 1875, pp. 197-202; M. E. Harkness, "Women as Civil Servants", *Nineteenth Century*, X (1881), 369-81; Mrs. Jellicoe, "Women's Supervision of Women's Industry", *English Woman's Journal*, X (1862), 114-19; A. Trollope, "The Young Women at the Telegraph Office", *Good Words*, XVIII (1877), 377-84; "Women in Libraries", *Englishwoman's Review*, 1899, pp. 240-44; E. Crawford, "Women in Journalism", *Contemporary Review*, LXIV (1893), 362-71; J. Pendleton, "Newspaper Woman", *Good Words*, XLIII (1902), 57-60; "Ladies and Hospital Nursing", *Contemporary Review*, XXXIV (1879), 490-503; "The Duties of Women as Managers of Elementary Schools", *National Association for the Promotion of Social Science, Transactions*, 1878, pp. 439-42.

Secondary works that deal with the activities of Victorian women in a number of new fields include: James Ramsay MacDonald, ed., *Women in the Printing Trades* (London: P. S. King & Sons, 1904); Edith J. Morley, ed., *Working Women in Seven Professions* (London: George Routledge & Sons, 1914); Lucy R. Seymer, *A General History of Nursing* (London: Faber & Faber, Ltd., 1932); Dorothy Evans, *Women and the Civil Service* (London: Sir I. Pitman & Sons, Ltd., 1934); Hilda Martindale, *Women Servants of the State, 1870-1938* (London: George Allen & Unwin, Ltd., 1938). An excellent recent book, Lee Holcombe's *Victorian Ladies at Work* (Hamden, Conn.: The Shoe String Press, Inc., 1973), has chapters on the teaching and nursing professions, as well as on women in the distributive trades, clerical occupations, and civil service.

Efforts to improve the economic position of working-class women through trade union organization are dealt with in: E. Williams, "The Protective and Provident Movement Among Women", *National Association for the Promotion of Social Science, Transactions*, 1876, pp. 729-33; Helen Blackburn, "Trade Unions for Women", *Englishwoman's Review*, 1874, pp. 281-82; "Women's Protective and Provident League", *ibid.*, 1875, pp. 84-85; Emilia F. S. Dilke, "Benefit Societies and Trade Unions for Women", *Fortnightly Review*, LI (1889), 852-56; C. Black, "Organization of Working Women", *ibid.*, LII (1889), 695-704; Emily Pfeiffer, *Women and Work* (London: Trübner & Co., 1888); H. M. Browne, "A New Union for Women", *Westminster Review*, CXXXVIII (1892), 528-35; E. March-Phillips, "Progress in Trades Unions for Women", *Fortnightly Review*, LX (1893), 92-104; Emilia F. S. Dilke, "Industrial Position of Women", *ibid.*, pp. 499-508; E. Holyoake, "Capacity of Women for Industrial Union", *Westminster Review*, CXXXIX (1893), 164-68; Emilia F. S. Dilke, *Benefit Societies and Trade Unions for Women* (London: Chapman & Hall [1893]). A good account of labor organization for women is Barbara Drake's *Women in Trade Unions* (London: G. Allen & Unwin, Ltd., 1920). See also the recent biography by Harold Goldman, *Emma Paterson: She Led Women into a Man's World* (London: Lawrence & Wishart, Ltd., 1974).

From the following works can be gauged the extent to which women came to participate in new areas of employment: "The Twentieth Anniversary of the Society for the Employment of Women", *Englishwoman's Review*, 1879, pp. 289-97; Jessie Boucherett, "The Industrial Movement", in *The Woman Question in Europe*, pp. 90-107; B. L. Hutchins, "A Note on the Distribution of Women in Occupations", *Journal of the Royal Statistical Society*, LXVII (1904), 479-90.

Law

Any discussion of the legal position of women in the nineteenth century must begin with William Blackstone's *Commentaries on the Laws of England* (Oxford: The Clarendon Press, 1765-69, and many subsequent editions); see, in particular, Volume I, Chapter 15, "Of Husband and Wife".

The legal injustices under which English women suffered are described in Barbara Leigh Smith's *A Brief Summary in Plain Language of the Most Important Laws Concerning Women* (London: n.p., 1854), and Caroline Norton's *English Laws for Women in the Nineteenth Century* (London: n.p., 1854). Two articles published in the 1860's stand as the quintessential feminist critique of the mid-nineteenth-century legal system: "The Legal Position of Women and its Moral Effects", *Meliora*, VIII (1865), 93-102; and Frances Power Cobbe's "Criminals, Idiots, Women, and Minors", *Fraser's Magazine*, LXXVIII (1868), 777-94.

The thorny problem of married women's property rights (or lack of them) is dealt with in "Property of Married Women", *Westminster Review*, LXVI (1856), 331-47; T. E. Perry, "Rights and Liabilities of Husband and Wife", CV (1857), 181-205; "Property of Married Women", *English Woman's Journal*, I (1858), 58-59; Arthur Hobhouse, "Is it Desirable to Amend the Present Law, Which Gives the Personal Property and Earnings of a Wife to Her Husband?" *National Association for the Promotion of Social Science, Transactions*, 1868, pp. 238-48, 275-80; "History of the Married Women's Property Bill", *Englishwoman's Review*, 1873, pp. 177-84; W. A. Holdsworth, *Married Women's Property Act* (London and New York: G. Routledge & Sons, Ltd., 1882); R. Thicknesse, "The New Legal Position of Married Women", *Blackwood's Magazine*, CXXXIII (1883), 207-20.

J. W. Kaye's "The Marriage and Divorce Bill", *North British Review*, XXVII (1857), 162-93, approves, with some reservations, the controversial bill which the following works treat critically: "The New Law of Divorce", *English Woman's Journal*, I (1858), 186-89; A. Waddilove, "The Law of Marriage and Divorce as at Present Existing in England, Ireland and Scotland", *National Association for the Promotion of Social Science, Transactions*, 1861, pp. 191-99; W. O. Morris, "On the Marriage Question", *ibid.*, pp. 199-212; "Laws of Marriage and Divorce", *Westminster Review*, LXXXII 1864), 442-54. An excellent modern study, O. R. McGregor's *Divorce in England* (London: William Heinemann, Ltd., 1957), focuses on divorce in both its historical and sociological setting.

The works by Caroline Norton listed below illustrate the difficulties faced by nineteenth-century Englishwomen separated from their husbands, in attempting to obtain the custody of their children and the right to dispose of their own property: Pearce Stevenson [Caroline Norton], *A Plain Letter to the Lord Chancellor on the Infant Custody Bill* (London: James Ridgway, 1839); and *A Letter to the Queen on Lord Chancellor Cranworth's Marriage and Divorce Bill* (London: Longman, Brown, Green & Longmans, 1855). Janet E. Courtney's *The Adventurous Thirties: A Chapter in the Women's Movement* (London: Oxford University Press, 1933; reprint edition,

Freeport, New York: Books for Libraries Press, Inc., 1967) includes a section on Mrs. Norton, and useful insights are provided by two full-length biographies, Jane Grey Perkins' *The Life of the Honourable Mrs. Norton* (New York: Henry Holt & Company, 1909); and Alice Acland's *Caroline Norton* (London: Constable & Co., Ltd., 1948).

The literature dealing with the effort to repeal the Contagious Diseases Acts is truly voluminous; more than 500 pamphlets, addresses, and tracts were issued by those who sought to repeal the Acts, 40 or so written by the leader of the crusade, Josephine Butler. One of the most famous of these is Mrs. Butler's *Social Purity* (London: Morgan & Scott, 1879). For understanding her motives in undertaking this work, see her *Recollections of George Butler*, 2nd ed. (Bristol: Arrowsmith, n.d.). *Personal Reminiscences of a Great Crusade* (London: Horace Marshall & Son, 1898) is, of course, essential reading. Benjamin Scott's *A State Iniquity: Its Rise, Extension and Overthrow* (London: Kegan Paul, Trench, Trübner & Co., Ltd., 1890) covers some of the same ground and, because of Scott's personal involvement, is fascinating reading.

Several biographies of Mrs. Butler have been published, including one by her grandson, A. S. G. Butler, *Portrait of Josephine Butler* (London: Faber & Faber, Ltd., 1954). See also E. Moberley Bell's *Josephine Butler, Flame of Fire* (London: Constable & Co., Ltd., 1963). Glen Petrie has written *A Singular Iniquity: The Campaigns of Josephine Butler* (New York: Viking Press, 1971). J. L. and B. Hammond's *James Stansfeld: A Victorian Champion of Sex Equality* (New York: Longmans, Green & Company, 1932) is valuable both for its information on Stansfeld and its discussion of the Contagious Diseases Acts.

Recent analyses of the Contagious Diseases Acts can be found in E. M. Sigsworth and T. J. Wyke, "A Study of Victorian Prostitution and Venereal Disease", in *Suffer and Be Still*, pp. 77-99; and F. B. Smith, "Ethics and Disease in the Later Nineteenth Century: The Contagious Diseases Acts", *Historical Studies*, XIV (1971), 118-35. Two studies which focus on the local application of the Acts are those by Judith R. Walkowitz and Daniel J. Walkowitz, " 'We are not beasts of the field': Prostitution and the Poor in Plymouth and Southampton Under the Contagious Diseases Act", *Feminist Studies*, I (1973), 73-106; and Judith Walkowitz, "The Making of an Outcast Group: Prostitutes and Working Women in Nineteenth-Century Plymouth and Southampton", in *A Widening Sphere*, pp. 72-93.

Even after the passage of the Married Women's Property Act of 1882, the Custody of Infants Act of 1886, and the Maintenance in case of Desertion Act of the latter year, reformers contended that this legislation, although an improvement on the whole, still discriminated against the women who were supposedly its beneficiaries. It is indicative of the *Westminster Review's* advanced position on the Woman Question that four of the following critical essays appeared in its pages: Frances E. Hoggan, *The Position of the Mother in the Family in its Legal and Scientific Aspects* (Manchester: A. Ireland & Co., 1884); "Law in Relation to Women", *Westminster Review*, CXXVIII (1887), 698-710; Matilda M. Blake, "Women and the Law", *ibid.*, CXXXVII (1892), 364-70; "Judicial Sex-Bias", *ibid.*, CIL (1898), 147-60; IGNOTA, "Present Legal Position of Women in the United Kingdom", *ibid.*, CLVIII (1905), 513-39; Augustine Birrell, "Women Under English Law", *Edinburgh Review*, CLXXXIV (1896), 322-40.

The following books provide convenient summaries of the legal position of the Victorian woman: Thomas Barrett-Lennard, *The Position in Law of Women* (London: Waterlow, 1883); Arthur Rackham Cleveland, *Women Under English Law* (London:

Hurst & Blackett, Ltd., 1896); A. Beatrice Wallis Chapman and Mary Wallis Chapman, *The Status of Women Under the English Law* (London: G. Routledge & Sons, Ltd., 1909); Ralph Thicknesse, *The Rights and Wrongs of Women: A Digest* (London: Woman Citizen Publishing Society [1909]); Eugene A. Hecker, *A Short History of Women's Rights* (New York and London: G. P. Putnam's Sons, 1910); Wilfred Hooper, *Englishwoman's Legal Guide: A Popular Handbook* (London: David Nutt, 1913); Maud Crofts, *Women Under English Law* (London: National Council of Women of Great Britain, 1925); Erna Reiss, *Rights and Duties of Englishwomen: A Study in Law and Public Opinion* (Manchester: Sheratt & Hughes, 1934); R. H. Graveson and F. R. Crane, eds., *A Century of Family Law, 1857-1957* (London: Sweet & Maxwell, Ltd., 1957).

Recent articles illustrating a number of aspects of women's legal position in the Victorian period include: Leonore Davidoff, "Mastered for Life: Servant and Wife in Victorian and Edwardian England", *Journal of Social History,* VII (1974), 406-28; 446-59; and Lee Holcombe, "Victorian Wives and Property: Reform of the Married Women's Property Law, 1857-1882", in *A Widening Sphere,* pp. 3-28.

Female Suffrage

William Thompson's previously cited *Appeal of One Half the Human Race, Women, Against the Pretensions of the Other Half, Men,* published in 1825, is the earliest explicit argument for female suffrage. Over the next quarter century, a few scattered tracts and letters to newspapers advocated female suffrage, as did Harriet Taylor's anonymously published article, "The Enfranchisement of Women" (in the *Westminster Review,* LV [1851], 289-301). The campaign for the vote did not enter a more active phase, however, until the 1860's, when there was a small but vocal minority pleading for the enfranchisement of women in pamphlets, periodicals, letters to editors, and addresses to the House of Commons: Mrs. [Barbara Leigh Smith] Bodichon, *Reasons for the Enfranchisement of Women* (London: The Social Science Association, 1866); John Stuart Mill, *The Admission of Women to the Electoral Franchise* (London: Trübner & Co., 1867); Charles Kingsley, "Women and Politics", *Macmillan's Magazine,* XX (1869), 552-61; Frances Power Cobbe, *Why Women Desire the Franchise* (London: The London National Society for Women's Suffrage, 1869); Arthur Arnold, "The Political Enfranchisement of Women", *Fortnightly Review,* XVII (1872), 204-14; and two articles by Emily Pfeiffer, Woman's Claim", *Contemporary Review,* XXIX (1881), 265-77; and "The Suffrage for Women", *Contemporary Review,* XXXXVII (1885), 418-35.

Lydia E. Becker was a dedicated and tireless propagandist on behalf of female suffrage, addressing meetings, taking part in debates, and publishing the following pamphlets and papers in support of the cause: "Female Suffrage", *Contemporary Review,* IV (1867), 307-16; *Liberty, Equality, Fraternity: A Reply to Mr. Fitzjames Stephen's Strictures on Mr. J. S. Mill's Subjection of Women* (Manchester: A. Ireland & Co., 1874); and "On the Women's Suffrage Question", *National Association for the Promotion of Social Science, Transactions,* 1877, pp. 701-04; Miss Becker also edited the *Woman's Suffrage Journal,* which was published from 1870 to 1890.

The following articles on female suffrage from the *Westminster Review* reflect the fact that, as has already been observed in connection with the divorce, property, and child custody laws, in any matter pertaining to women's causes, that journal consistently held an enlightened view: "The Claims of Women to the Franchise", *Westminster Review,* LXXXVII (1867), 63-79; "The Political Disabilities of Women", *ibid.,* XCVII

(1872), 50-60; W. A. Hale, "The Emancipation of Women", *ibid.*, XCIX (1874), 137-55; "Emancipation for Women", *ibid.*, CII (1877), 137-74; "Women Ratepayers' Right to Vote", *ibid.*, CXXII (1884), 375-81; W. S. B. McLaren, "The Emancipation of Women", *ibid.*, CXXVIII (1887), 165-73; IGNOTA, "Women's Suffrage", *ibid.*, CXLVIII (1897), 357-72; IGNOTA, "Woman's Lost Citizenship", *ibid.*, CLIX (1903), 512-22.

Two attempts to justify women's suffrage on a legal (or, in Pankhurst's article, a quasi-legal) basis are R. M. Pankhurst's "The Right of Women to Vote Under the Reform Act, 1867", *Fortnightly Review*, X (1868), 250-54, and Charlotte C. Stopes's *The Constitutional Basis of Women's Suffrage* (Edinburgh: The Darien Press, 1908). Millicent Garrett Fawcett gives a lucid summary of the pre-Pankhurst suffragist movement in two works, "The Women's Suffrage Movement", in *The Woman Question in Europe*, pp. 1-29; and in *Women's Suffrage: A Short History of a Great Movement* (London and Edinburgh: T. C. & E. C. Jack, 1912; reprint edition, New York: Source Book Press, 1970). Helen Blackburn's *Women's Suffrage: A Record of the Women's Suffrage Movement in the British Isles* (London: Williams & Norgate, 1902) is a more thorough treatment of the same period and has a comprehensive bibliography.

James Keir Hardie's *The Citizenship of Women: A Plea for Women's Suffrage* (London: Women's Freedom League, 1905) is a statement of the case by the socialist M.P., one of the founders of the Independent Labor Party, who championed the Pankhursts' cause in the House of Commons and on the public platform.

Among the reminiscences, memoirs, and autobiographical works of those who participated in the militant phase of the suffrage movement, are the following: E. Sylvia Pankhurst, *The Suffragette: The History of the Woman's Suffrage Movement, 1905-1910* (New York: Sturgis & Walton Co., 1911; reprint edition, New York: Source Book Press, 1970); Katherine Roberts, *Pages from the Diary of a Militant Suffragette* (Letchworth and London: Garden City Press Limited, Printers, 1910); F. W. Pethick-Laurence, *Women's Fight for the Vote* (London: The Women's Press, 1910), and *Fate Has Been Kind* (London and New York: Hutchinson & Co., Ltd., 1943); Emmeline Pankhurst, *My Own Story* (London: Eveleigh Nash, 1914; reprint edition, New York: Source Book Press, 1970); Constance Lytton, *Prisons and Prisoners: Some Personal Experience* (London: William Heinemann, Ltd., 1914); Annie Kenney, *Memories of a Militant* (New York: Longmans, Green & Co., 1924); E. Sylvia Pankhurst, *The Suffragette Movement* (London and New York: Longmans, Green & Co., 1931); Emmeline Pethick-Laurence, *My Part in a Changing World* (London: V. Gollancz, Ltd., 1938); Christabel Pankhurst, *Unshackled* (London: Hutchinson & Co., Ltd., 1959); Hannah Mitchell, *The Hard Way Up: The Autobiography of Hannah Mitchell, Suffragette and Rebel* (London: Faber & Faber, Ltd., 1967).

The constitutionalist (non-militant) point of view is represented by the books of Millicent Garrett Fawcett, *The Women's Victory—and After: Personal Reminiscences, 1911-18* (London: Sidgwick & Jackson, Ltd., 1920); and *What I Remember* (London: T. F. Unwin, Ltd., 1925). Much of Ray Strachey's *"The Cause:" A Short History of the Women's Movement in Great Britain* (Port Washington, New York: Kennikat Press, 1928) is devoted to the suffrage movement.

Biographies of leading figures in the history of the women's suffrage movement include: Ray Strachey, *Millicent Garrett Fawcett* (London: John Murray Publishers, Ltd., 1931); E. Sylvia Pankhurst, *The Life of Emmeline Pankhurst* (London: T. W. Laurie, Ltd., 1935); and Josephine Kamm, *The Story of Emmeline Pankhurst* (Des

Moines and New York: Meredith Press, 1968). A thoughtful biographical essay on
Emmeline Pankhurst by Rebecca West appears in *The Post Victorians* (London: Ivor
Nicholson & Watson, Ltd., 1933).

The views of the opponents of female suffrage range in tone from sweet reasonable-
ness to unbridled vehemence. Among the former are J. McGrigor Allan, "A Protest
Against Women's Demand for the Privileges of Both Sexes", *Victoria Magazine,* XV
(1870), 318-56; and in the latter category are E. Belfort Bax, *The Legal Subjection of
Men: Reply to the Suffragettes* (London: The New Age Press, 1908); the same author's
The Fraud of Feminism (London: Grant Richards, Ltd., 1913); and Almroth E.
Wright, *The Unexpurgated Case Against Women's Suffrage* (London: Constable &
Co. Ltd., 1913). Somewhat more restrained are A. V. Dicey, *Letters to a Friend on
Votes for Women* (London: John Murray, 1912), and Goldwin Smith, "Female Suf-
frage", *Macmillan's Magazine,* XXX (1874), 130-50. "An Appeal Against Female
Suffrage", *Nineteenth Century,* XXV (1889), 781-88, presents the point of view of
more than a hundred socially prominent ladies who were opposed to female suffrage.
It was effectively rebutted by Millicent Garrett Fawcett and M. M. Dilke in "The Appeal
Against Female Suffrage: A Reply", *ibid.,* XXVI (1889), 86-103. William Ewart
Gladstone's *Female Suffrage: A Letter . . . to Samuel Smith, M.P.* (London: John
Murray, 1892) places him squarely in the ranks of the anti-suffragettes. R. B.
Haldane's "Economic Aspects of Women's Suffrage", *Contemporary Review,* LVIII
(1890), 830-38, is a penetrating analysis of the motivation of those opposed to female
suffrage; and a good insight into the mentality of the opposition is also provided by the
suffragist IGNOTA, in "Privilege v. Justice to Women", *Westminster Review,* CLII
(1899), 128-41.

Secondary works dealing with various aspects of the Pankhurst phase of the suffrage
movement include: George Dangerfield, *The Strange Death of Liberal England*
(New York: Random House, Inc., 1935); Barbara Bliss, "Militancy: The Insurrection
that Failed", *Contemporary Review,* CCI (1962), 306-09; Roger Fulford, *Votes for
Women: The Story of a Struggle* (London: Faber & Faber, Ltd., 1957); David
Mitchell, *The Fighting Pankhursts: A Study in Tenacity* (London: Jonathan Cape,
Ltd., 1967); Marian Ramelson, *The Petticoat Rebellion: A Century of Struggle for
Women's Rights* (London: Lawrence & Wishart, Ltd., 1967); Constance Rover, *Women's
Suffrage and Party Politics in Britain, 1866-1914* (London: Routledge & Kegan Paul,
Ltd., 1967); Andrew Rosen, *Rise Up, Women! The Militant Campaign of the Women's
Social and Political Union, 1903-1914* (London and Boston: Routledge & Kegan Paul,
Ltd., 1974); David Morgan, *Suffragists and Liberals: The Politics of Woman Suf-
frage in England* (Totowa, N.J.: Rowman & Littlefield, 1975).

Index